The Anthem Dictionary of Literary Terms and Theory

Foreword

In the introduction to his influential study *Keywords* (1976), Raymond Williams recalled how, returning to Cambridge University in 1945 after several years in the army, he felt that he no longer had much in common with the students he had left behind. 'The fact is', he complained, 'they just don't speak the same language'.

It is a common phrase. It is often used between successive generations, and even between parents and children. I had used it myself, just six years earlier, when I had come to Cambridge from a working-class family in Wales. In many of the fields in which language is used it is of course not true. Within our common language, in a particular country, we can be conscious of social differences, or of differences of age, but in the main we use the same words for most everyday things and activities, though with obvious variations of rhythm and accent and tone... When we come to say 'we just don't speak the same language' we mean something more general: that we have different immediate values or different kinds of valuation, or that we are aware, often intangibly, of different formations and distributions of energy and interest.

Keeping this in mind, *Keywords* reveals that often it is the words we pass over without too much thought – 'culture', 'tradition', 'art' and so on – whose meanings have been contested most fiercely. Modified by some speakers, broken apart and put back together by others, such words baffle simple dictionary definitions. Across the centuries they have developed into lively sites of agreement and quarrel, solidarity and conflict. Put another way, Williams's study shows how a shared language is also the medium in which all sorts of historical or social differences can be asserted and tested; the flexibility of words that at first glance might seem flatly neutral – 'nature', 'popular', 'common' – reminds us that linguistically, as in so many other ways, there are many private worlds within our shared human world.

One common experience of readers coming to literary criticism for the first time is that critics, too, 'just don't speak the same language' as everyone else. No doubt part of this can be attributed to the private inflections which some critics give to everyday words (witness the philosophical contortions of 'absence' and 'presence' as they appear in the writings of Jacques Derrida, or the contradictory set of ideas that have clustered around a word like 'history'), so that reading a new critic can also mean learning to tune into the unique qualities of his or her voice – its modulations of thought, its nuances of vocabulary – in the same way that one might turn the dial on an old-fashioned radio to remove the hiss and crackle of other stations. But to a new student the most confusing, intimidating and sometimes downright irritating aspect of literary criticism tends to be the amount of specialised vocabulary used. Why do so many critics seem unable to say what they mean, the standard complaint runs, without disguising it in fancy or obfuscating terminology? Of course, critics are not alone in being tempted to dress up ordinary ideas in extraordinary language: witness the fondness in some parts of the world for referring to cups as 'beverage containers' or oranges sold as 'nutritious citrus snacks'. But literary criticism is especially vulnerable to such accusations, not least because unlike critics of the other arts (ballet or painting, for example), the critic of literature must work in the same medium as his or her subject, and there is often a noticeable gap between the clear-eyed precision of a literary work and the critic's far murkier efforts to explain it.

Take this example, from Homi Bhabha's study *The Location of Culture* (1994):

> If, for a while, the ruse of desire is calculable for the uses of discipline, soon the repetition of guilt, justification, pseudo-scientific theories, superstition, spurious authorities and classification can be seen as the desperate effort to 'normalise' normally the disturbance of a discourse of splitting that violates the rational enlightened claims of its enunciatory ability.

That sentence won second prize in the annual Bad Writing Contest promoted by the journal *Philosophy and Literature*. (Just imagine how bad the first prize-winner was.) Of course, Bhabha might claim that such rhetoric is necessary if his argument – roughly, that 'normal' ways of thinking about the world are an illusion that needs to be disrupted – is to be true to itself; in refusing to allow readers to take its words for granted, this is a piece of criticism that does what it says. Even so, there are times in reading some criticism when students might be forgiven for wondering whether the rhetoric is designed simply to put them off or keep them out. (It is worth noting that the verb 'to gloss', the root of 'glossary', can mean to cover up as well as to explain, as one might add a coat of gloss paint to make a surface shiny and hard enough to prevent it from being penetrated.) In these circumstances, critical terms can start to look less like keywords than passwords: little verbal passports to that strange parallel world where reading is a professional activity rather than a private pleasure.

Indeed, it is the professionalisation of literary criticism that has often been blamed for this movement of critical language away from ordinary speech. Before the rise of 'English' as a University discipline in the twentieth century, the story goes, critics and readers were far closer in approach, both in terms of the ideas they had and the words they used; it is only since the subject has needed to justify itself as the intellectual equal of subjects such as law or the sciences, that critics have felt the need to invent a more specialised vocabulary. Like most forms of nostalgia, this says rather more about present anxieties than it does about the past. The idea that literary criticism only became wordily opaque with the rise of University English certainly doesn't square with the evidence of Renaissance criticism, much of which is almost impenetrable to anyone without a handbook of classical rhetoric or a Latin dictionary to hand. As C. S. Lewis once remarked, this was 'a world of "prettie *epanorthosis*", *paronomasia*, *isocolon*, and *similiter cadentia*', and such terms tripped off a Renaissance critic's tongue just as easily as *metafiction* or *carnivalesque* would later rise to the lips of their twentieth-century heirs. Some critical terms, such as *metaphor*, are common to both periods, and to use them is to recognise that the history of literary criticism, like literature itself, involves continuity as well as change.

Even if the range of critical vocabulary has increased over the years, this is not necessarily to be regretted. There is some truth in the argument that critics are like other professionals – plumbers, for example – in needing a specialised vocabulary in order to talk to each other without spending all their time wondering 'now what on earth did s/he mean by *that*?' Plumbers can do their job much more efficiently if one says to another 'the ball valve is broken: turn off the stopcock', rather than 'the round thingie in that tank of water above the toilet isn't working: turn that little metal wheel under the sink round until the water stops gushing out' – by which time the odds on your house flooding will have risen sharply. Similarly, critics can do their job much more efficiently if one says to another 'this sonnet is complicated by feminine line-endings', rather than 'this 14-line poem is given an unexpected twist by employing 11-syllable lines each of which ends with an unstressed syllable.' A crude analogy, perhaps, given how unlike plumbers critics are in most other respects (they are certainly less well-paid), but the general principle still holds: critical terms are an important part of a professional tool-kit. Whether rooted in classical rhetoric, or generated by more recent academic debates, all of which are generously represented in this Anthem Dictionary, employing them alongside a less specialised language can save time and prevent confusion. Nor is this process limited to the body of writing traditionally thought of as literature. One of the most important features of this book is that it shows how often 'literary terms' emerge from, or bleed into, many other areas of culture, such as music and film. If these terms offer helpful keyholes into the workings of individual literary texts, they also open up our views of literature as a whole; indeed, they show how learning to think more precisely about literature might also encourage us to look at the rest of the world with the same sort of care we usually restrict to the parts of it contained within the covers of a book.

One note of caution: although this Anthem Dictionary provides a critical tool-kit, it cannot substitute for practice in using these tools. It is never enough merely to learn a professional vocabulary without knowing how to apply it, any more than it would be to read a book about soccer skills and then turn up for a trial with Manchester United. Moreover, although Peter Auger supplies an unusually rich range of definitions, packed with helpful examples and inter-connections, these are offered as critical rules-of-thumb rather than rigid truths. Terms such as *tragedy* or *gothic* bring together a historical patchwork of beliefs and conventions which are joined as much by their differences as by their similarities. Nudged in a new direction by each original work, these terms are always on the move. Indeed, one might reasonably claim that all successful pieces of writing are exceptions to the rules they have helped to shape. When William Empson, aged 70, was asked to write a piece in honour of the 80-year-old I. A. Richards, his teacher at Cambridge, he observed that the trouble with getting old is that everyone becomes the same age. Similarly, the trouble with knowing what a *sonnet* should look like, and then spotting a few, can be that they all become the same poem, whereas a good piece of writing is more likely to attend to conventions without itself being conventional. The same it true of good criticism. Knowing how to spot an *iambic pentameter* is

The Anthem Dictionary of Literary Terms and Theory

Peter Auger

Anthem Press
An imprint of Wimbledon Publishing Company
www.anthempress.com

This edition first published in UK and USA 2010
by ANTHEM PRESS
75–76 Blackfriars Road, London SE1 8HA, UK
or PO Box 9779, London SW19 7ZG, UK
and
244 Madison Ave. #116, New York, NY 10016, USA

British Library Cataloguing in Publication Data
A catalogue record for this book is available from the British Library.

Library of Congress Cataloging in Publication Data
A catalog record for this book has been requested.

ISBN-13: 978 1 84331 871 2 (Pbk)
ISBN-10: 1 84331 871 7 (Pbk)

ISBN-13: 978 0 85728 981 0 (eBook)
ISBN-10: 0 85728 981 0 (eBook)

Contents

no substitute for reading enough verse to train one's ear to recognise *how* metre is being used to control the movement of a line of thought. After all, learning to read is not just something we do as children and can then take for granted, like learning to ride a bicycle. It is something we continue to do.

For anyone wishing to read more carefully and more confidently, there are few better places to start than this Anthem Dictionary. With over 1000 definitions of terms ranging from *abbreviation* to *zeugma*, all of them explained in a lively and reader-friendly style, plus an index of main themes, a timeline of cited works, and an extensive checklist of further resources, it provides a map and a phrasebook for readers who want to get their bearings in an often bewildering world.

Robert Douglas-Fairhurst
Magdalen College
Oxford

Preface

My aim has been to write a no-nonsense introduction to the different ways that people read English literature. It is intended to help readers develop critical reading skills and make up their minds about what literature is. While researching the material for this book, I also looked at the different ways people have written literary dictionaries: I have had particular reference to the works by Chris Baldick, M.H. Abrams, J.A. Cuddon and Ross Murfin and Supriya M. Ray. My final authority on nitty-gritty poetic, rhetorical and spelling/etymological matters has been *The Princeton Encyclopedia of Poetry and Poetics*, edited by Alex Preminger and T.V.F. Brogan, *A Handlist of Rhetorical Terms* by Richard A. Lanham and the *Oxford English Dictionary*.

I've been fortunate to write this book in the supportive surrounds of two Oxbridge colleges: Pembroke College, Cambridge and Merton College, Oxford. In particular, I'd like to thank the English fellows at Pembroke who helped shape the opinions given in this book, as well as furnishing me with a few of the examples here. I've written this book while receiving financial support from the Arts and Humanities Research Council (AHRC), for which I'm very grateful. My parents have provided accommodation, financial support and much else besides for a far longer period, and I dedicate this work to them as a small token of gratitude. Finally, I want to mention someone who was notably absent during the writing of this work: Zen Cho. She was the ideal reader I had in mind while writing, and was often in my thoughts otherwise.

Peter Auger
Oxford, May 2010

A

abbreviation A shortened form of a word or phrase. There are numerous abbreviations commonly used in written English, many of which are formed from Latin phrases and can be confusing for the Latin-less reader. As with all literary terms, abbreviations are only helpful if the audience is familiar with them. This book uses a few abbreviations that direct the reader quickly to further information: 'e.g.' (*exempla gratis*, 'for example'), 'i.e.' (*id est*, 'that is'), CF. (*confer*, compare), C. (*circa*, around), p./pp. (page/s) and l./ll. (line/s). There are short entries on several others (see p. 349 for a list). In general, using other abbreviations is frowned upon in formal writing, particularly if they involve SLANG or COLLOQUIALISMS. An exception is the use of ACRONYMS (a word formed from the initial letters of several others).

abjection An act of expulsion that occurs when something is considered repellent or unworthy. In CULTURAL STUDIES, the term is associated with Julia Kristeva and fits into PSYCHOANALYTIC thinking: the thing 'abjected' exists on the boundaries of our notion of EGO (i.e. what we consider part of ourselves). We assert our self-identity by establishing a distance between ourselves and the thing that horrifies us. This describes the process by which minority groups are marginalised, and so is potentially relevant to such diverse fields as FEMINIST CRITICISM, QUEER THEORY and DISABILITY STUDIES. These ideas have been applied to specific literary texts and GENRES, such as the GOTHIC NOVEL and HORROR STORY.

abridgement The shortening of a work, often without the AUTHOR'S consent. The two main reasons this is done are to remove CONTENT considered inappropriate (i.e. BOWDLERIZE it), and to make the work suitable for another MEDIUM, such as a film ADAPTATION or modernized EDITION. Abridgements are useful if they make a text more accessible; however, the process risks distorting the original, and so are to be treated with caution. Full-length versions are usually preferable when available. For an example of a comic abridgement, see the entry for HAIKU.

absence/presence In DECONSTRUCTION it refers to the crucial difference between something that is there, and so possesses meaning and authority, and something that has no fixed existence or significance. Speech is often assumed to be based on a speaker who is present, and guarantees meaning (i.e. you said it, therefore it has a single meaning). However, DECONSTRUCTION argues that this doesn't count as 'presence', since different interpretations are still available. The reason given is that Western language, both in spoken and written forms, is LOGOCENTRIC: it is based upon the MYTH of a ever-present LOGOS (the Word) that gives everything meaning.

abstract language A form of expression suggesting a quality, action or state of being, such as 'delicious', 'delivery' and 'deceit'. Abstract language describes general concepts that have no physical existence; by contrast, CONCRETE LANGUAGE describes particular objects that can be sensed. 'Wet paint' is concrete, but 'wet' by itself is abstract. This distinction isn't relevant to ABSTRACT and CONCRETE POEMS. By itself, 'abstract' also means a summary of a long written argument (in a book, article or ESSAY).

The idea of abstract language has attracted plenty of philosophical speculation. Some philosophers would dispute that 'wet', for example, exists as an abstract concept, on the grounds that a conception of 'wet' requires us to imagine a wet object. This contradicts PLATONIC philosophy, which describes a 'theory of forms' in which abstract concepts (i.e. forms) have a separate existence to the shadowy, concrete realm that we experience. This theory led Plato to dismiss poetry on the grounds that it is an IMITATION of sensory experiences in our lower world, which makes it twice removed from actual truth. And it's true that poetry is generally more CONCRETE than abstract in its DICTION: i.e. FIGURATIVE LANGUAGE and IMAGERY hint at abstract concepts through CONCRETE language. Literary writers have been responding to this objection ever since. Philip Sidney, with Plato's objection in mind, argued that poetry combines the best elements of philosophy and history: it describes abstract philosophical truth using examples taken from history. ALLEGORY is a fine example of this. The take-home message from this discussion is that poetic 'truth' involves a combination of abstract and CONCRETE ideas: it appeals to both thought and feeling.

abstract poem A term devised by Edith Sitwell to describe poetry in which words are chosen primarily for their sound rather than their meaning. These 'patterns of sounds' evoke strong emotions, even though in some cases they sound similar to NONSENSE VERSE.

academic drama (school drama) Plays performed at British schools and universities in the sixteenth century. They were based on Roman DRAMA (the comedies of Plautus and Terence, and Senecan tragedy), and were mostly performed in Latin, though sometimes in the VERNACULAR. The earliest surviving COMEDY in English was written by a schoolmaster called Nicholas Udall, and was probably performed by pupils of Westminster school. It's called *Ralph Roister Doister* (1552), and is written in DOGGEREL VERSE.

acatalectic (eh-cat-a-**lek**-tik; Greek 'not coming to a sudden end') A line of VERSE that has the expected number of SYLLABLES. It neither lacks the final syllable (is CATALECTIC), nor has an extra syllable (HYPERMETRICAL).

accent The EMPHASIS placed on a spoken SYLLABLE. It is similar in meaning to STRESS ('Oh *yes*'), though accent can also refer to EMPHASIS created by changes in pitch ('"oh yes!", he squealed') or lengthening ('oh yesssss!'). It is the basis of ACCENTUAL VERSE. More generally, accent refers to a variation in how a language is spoken (e.g. American accent), where the changes don't create a DIALECT.

There are broadly three kinds of syllable accent. A word accent is the natural EMPHASIS placed on a word when spoken; e.g. '*si*lent' or 're*mem*ber'. A sense accent draws attention to one part of a phrase, and can change a sentence's meaning: if I say 'Remember *me*, when *I* am gone away', then I am asking you to remember me, rather than my friends, family or anyone else, whereas if I say '*Remember* me, when I am gone away', then I am asking not to be chased, forgotten or mourned, but remembered. Finally, a metrical accent (the term 'STRESS' is sometimes used for this type) is a stressed BEAT created by the metrical pattern. The first two lines of Christina Rossetti's sonnet 'Remember' have an IAMBIC pattern: Re*mem*ber *me*, when *I* am *gone* a*way* | Gone *far* a*way* in*to* the *si*lent *land*.' As this example shows, poetry subtly combines different types of accent, and often creates effects that influence meaning: e.g. the stresses on 'mem', 'me' and 'I' are metrical stresses that match the word accents. This draws attention to the repeated 'me' and emphasises the speaker's presence ('me'). Accents sometimes clash as well; in particular, a WRENCHED ACCENT occurs when the metrical accent does not match the word accent.

accentual verse METRICAL writing in which only the number of STRESSES per line is fixed. There is therefore no limit on the number of unstressed SYLLABLES per line or the total LINE length. Most English VERSE is ACCENTUAL-SYLLABIC; i.e. it has a set number of stressed and unstressed SYLLABLES. Nonetheless, accentual verse has a secure place in English literary history: most OLD ENGLISH verse is accentual, as is MEDIEVAL poetry in ALLITERATIVE METRE. Gerald Manley Hopkins revived the tradition when developing what he called SPRUNG RHYTHM. Here is an example from *Gawain and the*

Green Knight (ll.1952–53). The first LINE contains four stressed SYLLABLES (in italics) and nine unstressed, and the second LINE four STRESSED and seven unstressed:

> With *mer*þe and *myn*stralsye, wyth *me*tez
> at hir *wy*lle,
> þay *ma*den as *me*ry as any *men mo*ȝten
>
> [With amusements and minstrelsy, with dishes
> to their pleasing,
> They enjoyed themselves, as any man might]

accentual-syllabic verse METRICAL writing which contains a fixed number of STRESSED and unstressed SYLLABLES per line. The VERSE falls into a regular pattern that can be classified according to the repeated units of stressed and unstressed syllables (called FEET), and the number of syllables per line (i.e. how many FEET it contains). The majority of English VERSE uses this system. For example: a LINE contains eighteen syllables, six of them stressed. The repeated unit has one stressed syllable and two unstressed, so can be identified as DACTYL (– o o). It takes six dactyls to fill the line, and therefore can be called a DACTYLIC HEXAMETER. Variations from the basic METRE create poetic effects, and so does the combination of different ACCENTS and stresses. It is important to know how accentual-syllabic verse works in order to hear and describe AURAL and RHYTHMIC poetic effects.

acephalous (adj.; eh-**sef**-a-lus; Greek, 'headless') A VERSE LINE that lacks the first SYLLABLE expected by the METRE. The most common acephalous lines are IAMBS that have lost their first unstressed syllable. An acephalous line is HYPOMETRICAL. It is generally found less frequently than its opposite, CATALECTIC lines (missing syllables at the end). It can be contrasted with ANACRUSIS, which is the addition of an extra syllable(s) at the beginning of a line.

acronym A word formed from the initial letters of several others, as in U.S.A. (United States of America) and A.I.D.S. (Acquired Immune Deficiency Syndrome). It is a form of ABBREVIATION used in both formal and informal DISCOURSES. When writing LITERARY ESSAYS, however, acronyms of literary works (*KL* for *King Lear*) are often considered inelegant: e.g. *Two Gentlemen* is preferable to *TGV* for *The Two Gentlemen of Verona*.

acrostic poem (Greek, 'top of the line') A poem in which the initial letters of each line spell out a word. The term also applies when words are spelt from the middle or final letters of each line, or in a diagonal pattern.

Acrostic poems have been used for intimate or secret communication: e.g. in early Christian worship, and lovers writing to their beloved. They are occasionally found in LITERATURE, such as in the introductory 'Argument' to Ben Jonson's *The Alchemist* (1612). As this book's author knows from experience, some school-children's first verse composition is an acrostic poem based on their name.

act A section within a PLAY, usually beginning and ending with all the ACTORS off-stage. Acts are normally composed of individual SCENES, each involving different characters onstage. There is no agreed number of acts in plays: three and five are common, but many plays are simply divided into scenes. When quoting from plays, using act, scene and LINE numbers is preferable because this allows people with different EDITIONS to use the same references.

In modern THEATRE, drawing theatre curtains or using music normally makes the cues in the script obvious. In Greek DRAMA CHORAL speeches marked a change in scene, and the five-act division was initiated in Roman theatre (i.e. in SENECAN TRAGEDY). This was picked up by ELIZABETHAN and JACOBEAN dramatists, but was not established until the seventeenth century. Many EARLY MODERN plays have act-divisions that were added by later editors, William Shakespeare among them. Amidst this potential confusion, the safest CRITERION for an act-division is that everyone leaves the stage, because a dramatist always does this deliberately to create a lull in the action.

actor (actress) An individual who performs a ROLE in a play. Careful critics are always precise about the difference between the individual performer and the CHARACTER being brought to life. All Hamlets will speak the words 'To be or not to be' (unless using the first QUARTO text, which doesn't have this speech), but it is up to each actor to breathe emotion into the CHARACTER'S words during a performance.

adage (add-idge) A SAYING or PROVERB that has been around for centuries. Desiderius Erasmus published numerous volumes containing thousands of adages in the early sixteenth century, beginning with *Adagiorum collectanea* (1500). These were crucial publications for the development of HUMANISM, because they exemplified the process of mining CLASSICAL texts for quotations that could be reused.

adaptation The reworking of a text into a different MEDIUM; e.g. DRAMATIZED version, TV adaptation, novelization, ABRIDGEMENT or BOWDLERIZED EDITION. In terms of pure literary merit, adaptations will not necessarily contribute much to an understanding of the TEXT, particularly when the new work is 'inspired by', 'based on' or 'a new version of' the original. Yet there's no grounds to be sniffy about adaptations outright, since some are serious engagements with the original, and have the power to bring a work to a new audience. Many adaptations succeed on their own merits, regardless of their fidelity to the original: e.g. the film version of Ian McEwan's *Atonement* (2007) was warmly received—winning one Academy Award and being nominated for numerous others—but this says nothing about how faithful or otherwise it was to the book. British KITCHEN SINK DRAMAS offer several more examples of successful film adaptations, partly because they are REALIST works that translate well to film.

Adaptation is a form of TRANSLATION. It offers an insight into how different cultures and media understand a work. For example, Nahum Tate rewrote William Shakespeare's *King Lear* with a happy ending. This may seem a strange thing to do now, but it reflects how people were reacting to the play in the late seventeenth century. A more respected adaptation is Grigori Kozinstev's film *Korol Lir* (1971), which grapples with Shakespeare's portrayal of human fragility whilst drawing connections with the plight of Russian peasants. Arguments could be had about whether these adaptations are still truly Shakespearean, but then you could ask what being 'faithful' really is, and whether that is even desirable. Adaptations offer the chance to explore how people have reacted to texts over time, and this makes them potentially fascinating.

adjective (comparative; superlative; adverb) A word that describes a NOUN: e.g. 'silver', 'scintillating' and 'sympathetic'. An **adverb** describes a VERB, and usually ends in '-ly': e.g. 'patiently' and 'stubbornly'. A **comparative** adjective shows that something possesses a quality in a different degree from something else: e.g. 'smarter' and 'more delicate'. A **superlative** adjective shows that something possesses a quality in the greatest degree among others: 'the best', 'most marvellous'. If the original adjective has one or two syllables '-er'/ '-est' is added; if three or more then 'more'/'most' is used.

adynaton (Greek, 'feeble') A FIGURE involving exaggeration that exceeds the bounds of possibility. It is a FORM of HYPERBOLE that consciously reaches the limits of what language can express. As such, it is related to APORIA (when the speaker cannot find the right words) and gestures to the SUBLIME. An example from Andrew Marvell's 'To his Coy Mistress' (ll. 13–18):

An hundred years should go to praise
Thine eyes, and on thy forehead gaze.

Two hundred to adore each breast;
But thirty thousand to the rest.
An age at least to every part,
And the last age should show your heart.

aesthetic (n. and adj.; aesthetics; Greek, 'able to be perceived by the senses') As an adjective, it means concerned with beauty and/or perception of beauty. As a noun, it means the principles or theory upon which an idea or expression of beauty is based. It's possible to speak of a writer's aesthetic (e.g. 'Hemingway's aesthetic involves the use of simple DICTION'). **Aesthetics** is the branch of philosophy that thinks hard about beauty.

Many thinkers about aesthetics mull over the relation between beauty, goodness and truth: i.e. whether beauty indicates moral virtue, and/or SUBLIME truth. To put it simpy, the debate is whether beauty really is only in the eye of the beholder. Some POST-STRUCTURALIST and MARXIST CRITICS argue that it definitely is, and claim that the idea of higher beauty is an IDEOLOGICAL belief that has no basis in reality.

aesthetic distance The relation between a LITERARY work and its audience. Aesthetic distance provides the necessary detachment that allows an audience to have a shared response to a TEXT, regardless of personal reaction or thoughts. Aesthetic distance means that the audience treats the work as an artistic FICTION (ripe for AESTHETIC experience), and not a version of reality. Aristotle's notion of *CATHARSIS* results from aesthetic distance. The notion of aesthetic distance has been challenged by MARXIST, FEMINIST, POSTCOLONIAL and NEW HISTORICIST critics amongst others, who argue that aesthetic reaction is not detached from personal experience, but is determined by CONTEXTUAL factors, such as the audience's class or GENDER.

aestheticism (aesthete) An intellectual current in the nineteenth century that held that art should be enjoyed for its sheer beauty. Moral, DIDACTIC and social considerations were accordingly considered irrelevant. Aestheticism has roots in the earlier ROMANTIC idea that art should move the individual. It has philosophical origins in Immanuel Kant's claim that artistic merit rests on an ability to detach oneself from society, whilst remaining part of it. This notion of critical DISINTERESTEDNESS justified the social self-exclusion of the **aesthete** (as those who followed aestheticism were known). It also connected aestheticism with a social élite. Art is appreciated for its own intrinsic worth, not for its possible practical value: this is art for art's sake (*'l'art pour l'art'*). Aestheticism is associated with numerous VICTORIAN figures. The PRE-RAPHAELITES were major players: its leading POETS were Christina Rossetti and Charles Swinburne. Walter Pater was the movement's unofficial philosopher. Oscar Wilde is SYNONYMOUS with aestheticism too. Literary DECADENCE is a French relative of the movement.

affective Relating to the emotions. It describes how someone responds to a work with feeling. This isn't be confused with 'EFFECTIVE', which means something that does its job (and is a bit vague as a critical term). Readers are affected by literary works, though some critics would argue this is no basis for an interpretation—see the next entry.

affective fallacy The error of basing an interpretation on the reader's SUBJECTIVE impressions, rather than a work's OBJECTIVE properties. While not denying that literature 'affects' reader in diverse imaginative and emotional ways, affective fallacy suggests that this provides a superficial basis on which to study a work. W.K. Wimsatt and M.C. Beardsley devised this term, along with its counterpart, INTENTIONAL FALLACY. They were setting out the grounds for analysing a text as an AUTOTELIC (self-contained) AESTHETIC object. This cornerstone of NEW CRITICISM has been challenged by READER-RESPONSE CRITICISM, which focuses precisely on individual reactions to a text.

affective memory The ability to remember past emotions and feelings. METHOD ACTING requires ACTORS to use such memories when presenting similar emotions and frames of mind onstage. The actor's INTERPRETATION is based on personal experience. It has always been a controversial idea.

after-piece A short one-act COMEDY performed after the main PLAY. The earliest after-pieces in English theatres were JIGS, and they made a comeback in the eighteenth century as an innovation that made it easier for theatre owners to charge an entry fees for latecomers.

agitprop drama An ABBREVIATION for 'agitation propaganda' that refers specifically to Soviet DRAMA intended to promote revolutionary ideas to the masses. Like SOCIALIST REALISM, it was written to be DIDACTIC, inspirational and in tune with the common people. FOLK and AVANT-GARDE LITERATURE influenced its development. Later it came to describe any play with strong IDEOLOGICAL CONTENT, including DOCUMENTARY THEATRE. Agitprop drama has affinities to Bertolt Brecht's EPIC THEATRE, though the two shouldn't be confused.

agon (ah-**gone**; Greek, 'contest') A verbal contest, especially in Greek DRAMA. An agon takes place between a PROTAGONIST and ANTAGONIST, as those names suggest; indeed, most plays revolve around a central DRAMATIC CONFLICT (see also 'tension'). STICHOMYTHIA is a rapid, often competitive exchange of LINES. 'Agony' derives from 'agon'.

alba An alternative term for AUBADE; i.e. a poem featuring lovers at dawn who are about to part.

alexandrine In English PROSODY, another term for a six-stress, twelve SYLLABLE line; i.e. an IAMBIC HEXAMETER. Its name is taken from the French alexandrine, which is a crucial element in French PROSODY. Its English equivalent is much less significant, and there are few examples. The final line of the SPENSERIAN STANZA is an alexandrine, and it was used occasionally by the seventeenth-century poet Michael Drayton, among others.

allegory (Greek, 'speaking otherwise') An extended METAPHOR: any work in which the NARRATIVE contains some secondary, NON-FICTIONAL meaning. The allegory's LITERAL sense is a VEHICLE for deeper ABSTRACT or political/historical ideas. The IMAGES make it easier to comprehend complex meaning. John Bunyan's *Pilgrim's Progress* is one of the best known allegorical works: the adventures of the main CHARACTER, Christian, are intended to be read as an exposition of Christian theology. PERSONIFICATION is often a give-away that allegorical meaning is present: Bunyan, for example, gives characters names like Mr Worldly Wiseman, Faithful, and Hopeful to encourage allegorical READING. Allegories do not contain SYMBOLS: the difference here is that allegorical IMAGES only make sense within their immediate FICTIONAL CONTEXT, and do not have existence outside of the STORY, as SYMBOLS do. Allegory contains clues for its INTERPRETATION within itself, unlike PARABLES, FABLES, and EXEMPLA, where INTERPRETATION can only begin once the story has ended.

Allegorical writing has been used in many different ways in Western literature. The Bible is strongly allegorical, particularly in the way that the Old Testament anticipates the New (the suffering servant in Isaiah, for example, is routinely read as a 'TYPE' or 'figure' identified with Israel by Jewish interpreters, and with Jesus by Christians). Most CLASSICAL MYTHS can be (and have been) given an allegorical interpretation. Allegory was a popular FORM in MIDDLE ENGLISH, William Langland's *Piers Plowman* being a major example. DREAM VISIONS (e.g. Chaucer's *Book of the Duchess*) use allegory to establish a safe distance between the AUTHOR and the political meanings suggested by the POEM. Other notable allegories in English include Edmund Spenser's *The Faerie Queene* (1590, 96), Jonathan Swift's *Gulliver's Travels* (1726), George Orwell's *Animal Farm* (1945), and also Richard Adams's *Watership Down* (1972).

'Allegory' not only describes a FORM of writing, but also refers to a STYLE of READING (see also 'Four Levels of Meaning'). An allegorical reader must anticipate how the parts of the allegory fit into a larger STRUCTURAL whole, before having read the entire WORK: this creates an INTERPRETATIVE dilemma known as the HERMENEUTIC CIRCLE. This thought makes INTERPRETATION seem like a game that the writer has set up, with the reader hunting for a 'correct' READING that doesn't necessarily exist. There is a awkward POSTMODERN suggestion that all INTERPRETATIONS are actually allegorical READINGS: readers always find different meanings from what is literally written, if indeed the TEXT has a meaning. In a recent cinema advert, for example, the speaker claims that the film *The Wizard of Oz* is actually all about teenagers and their loss of respect for the elderly. This is a neat allegorical reading, but few would agree that Dorothy really is a public nuisance in the film. The postmodern view is that all interpretations are flawed, so this eccentric INTERPRETATION is ultimately as acceptable as any other: any critical view is a SUBJECTIVE opinion.

In this way allegory provokes deep questions about READING, such as whether the reader has to read a book as the AUTHOR intended, what a 'correct' INTERPRETATION would look like, and whether NON-FICTIONAL meaning should be given priority over FICTIONAL. This sort of question shows how allegory is connected to fundamental issues about how LITERATURE binds together meaning and expression, CONTENT and FORM (see also 'metaphor').

alienation effect (A-**Effect**; German, *Verfremdungseffekt* or *V-Effekt*) A key strategy in Bertolt Brecht's EPIC THEATRE that forced the audience to be aware that it was watching a FICTIONAL DRAMA. Brecht didn't want his audiences to become immersed in the FICTIONAL reality of the PLAY, but to be detached (or alienated) from it. This could be achieved in various ways, such as by making ACTORS just speak the script rather than transform themselves into the CHARACTERS they represent (cf. METHOD ACTING), and by having CHARACTERS/ACTORS comment on the action. This turns the PLAY into a sort of PARABLE that encourages audiences to use the lessons of the PLAY in their own lives. Brecht was totally against Aristotle's idea of CATHARSIS, which used the DRAMATIC illusion to guide the audience's reaction, and so drain all emotions that could be dangerous to society. Alienation, by contrast, rouses revolutionary energy and tells the audience to go out and change the world. The theoretical prose works *A Short Organum for the Theatre* (1949) and *The Messingkauf Dialogues* (published 1963) explain these ideas in more detail. The alienation effect is partly derived from the RUSSIAN FORMALIST idea of poetic DEFAMILIARIZATION. Marxism and MARXIST CRITICISM are important CONTEXTS too.

The ALIENATION EFFECT is exemplified in Brecht's major plays from the 1920s onwards. *The Threepenny Opera* (*Die Dreigroschenoper*, 1928) and *The Good Person of Szechwan* (*Die gute Mensch von Sezuan*, 1943) are CLASSIC works of EPIC THEATRE. Both plays use the *DEUS EX MACHINA* DEVICE (a sudden and unlikely PLOT intervention) to create an alienation effect. *The Threepenny Opera*'s ending, which sees Macheath miraculously pardoned, is so out-of-the-blue that the audience cannot help but recall that this wouldn't have happened in real life. *The Good Person of Szechwan* PARODIES the *DEUS EX MACHINA*: the Three Gods arrive on stage towards the ending, but pointedly decide not to intervene.

alliteration A FIGURE involving the REPETITION of the same letter(s) at the beginning of nearby words: e.g. 'Wiry and white-fiery and whirlwind-swivellèd snow' (Gerald Manley Hopkins, 'The Wreck of the Deutschland', l.103). The DEVICE is sometimes used to give POETRY STRUCTURE and RHYTHM; this is known as ALLITERATIVE METRE, which is found in *Beowulf* and medieval poems of the alliterative revival. Its usage in post-fourteenth-century British LITERATURE is largely decorative, and not restricted to POETRY. SIBILANCE is alliteration based on 's' sounds.

Alliteration is a form of CONSONANCE and ASSONANCE (most writers don't restrict alliteration's definition to repeated consonants). Like those techniques, alliteration occurs when language is shaped to create artificial effects beyond everyday usages. Many tongue-twisters are phrases so dense with alliteration that they become tricky to pronounce: e.g. 'Three thrushes threw themselves through the thicket.' In LITERATURE, it can (amongst other uses) be EMPHATIC or ONOMATOPOEIC, or lend a musical quality to phrases. Although it can be spotted without difficulty on the page, it is worth considering what AURAL effects it has when heard: the Hopkins quotation above, for example, uses alliteration in a much subtler way than simply clustering 'w's together on the page.

alliterative metre A form of ACCENTUAL VERSE (based on the number of STRESSES per line), as found in OLD ENGLISH and some MIDDLE ENGLISH VERSE. Each LINE is divided two half-lines (or HEMISTICHS) with two stresses each. In general, ALLITERATION (repetition of consonants/vowels) connects together the two (sometimes one) STRESSES in the first half with at least one of the

STRESSES in the second half. It is used in the Old English EPIC POEM *Beowulf*, and was still a standard PROSODIC FORM during the late fourteenth-century 'Alliterative Revival', which is associated with William Langland and the *Gawain*-poet. However, as alliterative metre developed, the number of unstressed SYLLABLES became more flexible. As English LITERATURE followed Chaucer's example by introducing RHYMED PENTAMETER lines, ALLITERATION became a decorative DEVICE independent of METRE. In poems like *Piers Plowman*, however, it still provided the METRICAL backbone:

> Wolleward and weetshoed wente I forth after
> As a recchelees renk that of no wo reccheth,
> And yede forth like a lorel al my lif tyme,
> Til I weex wery of the world and wilned eft
>   to slepe,
> And lened me to a Lenten—and longe tyme
>   I slepte (XVIII.1–5)
>
> [Without shirt or shoes I went on, like a reckless man who doesn't care about suffering, and went on like an idler all my life, until I grew weary of the world and often desired to sleep again, and I lazed around until Lent—I slept a long time]

altar poetry A kind of PATTERN POETRY in which the poem's LINEATION resembles an altar. The poem's CONTENT complements its shape. It is closely associated with seventeenth-century poets in English, such as George Herbert, Francis Quarles, and George Wither, though Dylan Thomas has also contributed to the tradition.

ambiguity A word or phrase with a vague or double meaning. 'The food wasn't that bad' is ambiguous on the page, since it could mean the food was fairly good, or that it was pretty awful. In this, as in most everyday examples, TONE of VOICE and EMPHASIS would make the intended meaning apparent. PUNS and *DOUBLE ENTENDRES* are other everyday occurrences of ambiguity. True ambiguity is a hindrance to communication in everyday language, but in LITERATURE, and POETRY in particular, it is normally a virtue. This is because it allows a writer to drive towards secondary meaning beneath the surface of a WORD. Ambiguity appears most often as PARADOX, IRONY and other TROPES. Certainly it is one of the easiest ways to introduce complexity, and potentially OBSCURITY, into a LITERARY WORK. Ambiguity puts a burden on the reader to decide on meaning: poetic truth is shown, not stated.

It has been a prominent literary term ever since William Empson's *Seven Types of Ambiguity* (1930). Empson extended the meaning of ambiguity to cover other ways in which a poem's meaning is unsettled, and relies on CONNOTATIONS and ALLUSIONS. INTERPRETATIONS of ambiguity are potentially ingenious but far removed from the original TEXT, unless regulated by the specific CONTEXT from which it comes. Ambiguity within poetic texts is a major interest of NEW CRITICISM, and is attractive in so far as it encourages readers to pick at the hidden riches and tensions within a WORK. DECONSTRUCTION-influenced critics (sometimes using the word POLYSEMY instead of ambiguity) pushed the concept of ambiguity further, to suggest that language is inherently unstable. According to this argument, ambiguity is not just basic to literature—it is present in all forms of communication.

amoebean verse (ah-me-**be**-an; Greek, 'interchanging') A style of POETIC writing based on rapid exchanges between two parties, which developed from CLASSICAL PASTORAL POETRY. It typically involves a competition, and is similar to a FLYTING and STICHOMYTHIA. 'August' in Edmund Spenser's *Shepheardes Calender* (1579) is a shining example in English:

Perigot. I saw the bouncing Bellibone, [pretty girl]
Willye. Hey ho Bonibell,
Per. Tripping ouer the dale alone,
Wil. She can trip it very well:
Per. Well decked in a frock of gray, [dressed]
Wil. hey ho gray is greete,
Per. And in a Kirtle of greene saye,
[skirt; quality cloth]
Wil. the greene is for maydens meete:
(ll. 62–68)

amphibrach (Greek, 'both ends short') A METRICAL FOOT consisting of a STRESSED SYLLABLE with an unstressed one either side (o – o). Rare in English VERSIFICATION, though words like 'alarming' and 'excitement' are single-word examples.

amphimacer (cretic) A METRICAL FOOT consisting of an unstressed SYLLABLE with an stressed one either side (– o –). Rare in English.

amplification A vague term that describes expansion upon an idea. It covers accumulation of material, comparison, HYPERBOLE, PERIPHRASIS and use of rhetorical FIGURES to develop a point. According to RHETORICAL THEORY, COPIA (copiousness) was a skill possessed only by the finest minds. Although literary writers sometimes strive to keep it brief (if writing EPIGRAMS, for example), most forms of literary writing involve amplification of some type (see 'periphrasis'). The term is too general to be of much use in critical writing.

anachronism (Greek, 'backwards-timing') An event, object or person that has been placed in a time period where it doesn't belong. Anachronism disrupts the WILLING SUSPENSION OF BELIEF; i.e. it is a reminder that the work is FICTIONAL. Many movie mistakes are unintentional anachronisms: the Internet Movie Database (imdb.com) notes that the film *Gladiator* (2000), for example, shows numerous items on screen (sunglasses, a gas cylinder, lycra shorts etc.) that did not exist in CLASSICAL Rome. This kind of anachronism is found in literature as well: William Shakespeare's *Julius Caesar* makes reference to a clock ('The clock hath stricken three.' (2.1.191)) that hadn't been invented by the CLASSICAL period. Anachronism isn't necessarily bad, though, just as historical accuracy isn't the only CRITERION for worthwhile literature. It is used deliberately, for example, in modern-dress productions of Shakespeare's plays. The 2005 production of *Richard II* starring Kevin Spacey, for instance, had the ACTORS wearing suits and used projector-screens to show news reports. By doing this, the production kept the play fresh, stressed that the work is in some sense timeless, and encouraged the audience to draw connections between politics in the seventeenth and twenty-first centuries.

anacoluthon (ana-co-**loo**-thon, Greek, 'inconsistent') A FIGURE involving a sudden shift in a sentence that leaves the beginning incomplete. It is sometimes used to suggest that a speaker is overcome with emotion: 'I saw his face for the first time and—oh, he was so beautiful!'. It is sometimes purely persuasive: 'I was going to offer you…but I'm sure you wouldn't be interested' is intended to make the listener interested. In the following uncollected Marianne Moore poem, 'All of It, as Recorded', the pointed anacoluthon becomes obvious in the second stanza:

> Down the village street, a lame boy
> And the women leaned on
> The half-open doors and said nothing.
> Down the village street, a lame old man

And the women leaned on
The half-open doors and said nothing.

Down the village street, a bier
And the children saw it as the actor
Sees the letter which he writes
In the second act of the play.

anacrusis (Greek, 'striking up [a tune]') The placing of an additional (EXTRAMETRICAL) SYLLABLE(s) at the start of a VERSE LINE. The extra SYLLABLE is usually unstressed. It rarely occurs in English PROSODY, in part because IAMBIC metres (the most common variety) already begin with an unstressed syllable. In contrast, ACEPHALOUS describes lines that have lost syllable(s).

anadiplosis (Greek, 'duplication') A FIGURE involving REPETITION of the end of one phrase at the beginning of the next. It chains together phrases, often leading to a CLIMAX. As a structural feature in POETRY it is known as a CORONA, the best known example being John Donne's 'La Corona'. It is similar to EPANALEPSIS, which is repetition at the beginning and end of the same line. Wallace Stevens uses fluid anadiplosis in 'The Load of Sugar-Cane' (1923):

The going of the glade-boat
Is like water flowing;

Like water flowing
Through the green saw-grass,
Under the rainbows;

Under the rainbows
That are like birds,
Turning, bedizened, [dressed up]

While the wind still whistles
As kildeer do, [a bird-species]

When they rise
At the red turban
Of the boatman.

anagnorisis (Greek, 'recognition') Aristotle's term for the moment in a TRAGIC PLOT when the HERO gains crucial knowledge that leads him/her out of ignorance (*HAMARTIA*) and causes a reversal in fortune (*PERIPETEIA*).

This CLIMAX arouses pity or fear at the hero's FATE. It is an essential concept in Aristotle's writing on tragedy; more generally, recognition or discovery forms the heart of many plots, either in a sudden twist or the final DÉNOUEMENT.

analogy (analogue; adj. analogous; Greek, 'proportion') An extended comparison (or SIMILE) that places together two images or ideas sharing something in common. Analogies are often used in arguments to explain a point more clearly. **Analogous** is similar to 'similar', but suggests that two items are similar in one aspect only: a fish's bone structure may be analogous to a human one (since both have backbones), but that doesn't mean they are similar. An **analogue** is a story that is a parallel version of another with a different origin. For example, no direct source is known for Geoffrey Chaucer's 'The Miller's Tale', but various other tales, including French FABLIAUX, are spoken of as analogues.

analysis (adj. analytical; Greek, 'breaking down') The breaking down of something into its parts, with the aim of finding out more about the whole. Its opposite is SYNTHESIS, which means joining two things together. The term's first recorded use is in the 'generall argument' of Edmund Spenser's *Shepheardes Calendar* (1579, though the word is written in Greek there). The semi-scientific study of texts was championed by FORMALIST and NEW CRITICS, since both deemed analytical study crucial in discovering how a text functions. This assumption of AUTOTELIC, organic unity in a TEXT was fiercely contested by structuralist and other critics, who maintained that a TEXT belongs within a DISCOURSE, and that INTERTEXTUAL relations produce and affect individual TEXTS; in other words, pure analysis is flawed, because meaning is not produced from the text in isolation. A possible compromise is to conclude that analysis is a useful tool, whilst being sensitive to aspects of literature that work only within larger READING CONTEXTS, and cannot be dissected.

anapaest (adj. anapaestic) A METRICAL FOOT consisting of two unstressed SYLLABLES followed by a STRESSED one. 'Supersede', 'Middle-Earth' and 'anapaest' are anapaests. Along with DACTYLS it forms the basis of TERNARY METRES, though it can be hard to divide up a sequence of three-beat FEET into anapaests and DACTYLS. An anapaestic METRE creates a RISING RHYTHM. Anapaests sound humorous to many twenty-first-century ears, in part because they are the dominant FOOT in LIMERICKS: e.g. 'there was an old man from Nantucket'. However, it has been used in more serious poems, such as Lord Byron's 'The Destruction of Sennacharib'. Here is the second stanza, where you can sense that the metrical pattern controls Byron's writing:

> Like the leaves of the forest when summer is green,
> That host at the sunset with their banners were seen: [army]
> Like the leaves of the forest when autumn hath blown,
> That host on the morrow lay withered and strown.

anaphora (Greek, 'carrying back') A FIGURE involving REPETITION of a word or phrase at the beginning of successive CLAUSES. It often builds to a CLIMAX, is EMPHATIC, or is used to create a list. It has been widely used in English literature from Geoffrey Chaucer (e.g. *Troilus and Cressida*) to T.S. Eliot ('The Waste Land'). Elizabeth Bishop wrote a poem called 'Anaphora' (1946), the closing words of which can be read as encapsulating anaphora's ability to convey relentless beauty: 'the fiery event of every day in endless | endless array.' Anaphora was frequently used to stirring, quasi-biblical effect by Walt Whitman in 'Leaves of Grass' (note also the use of EPISTROPHE at line-ends):

> The law of the past cannot be eluded,
> The law of the present and future cannot be
> eluded,
> The law of the living cannot be eluded, it is
> eternal,
> The law of promotion and transformation
> cannot be eluded,
> The law of heroes and good-doers cannot be
> eluded,
> The law of drunkards, informers, mean persons,
> not one iota thereof can be eluded.

anastrophe (Greek, 'turning back') A FIGURE involving unusual word-order, for poetic effect or to fit the METRICAL pattern. In CLASSICAL RHETORIC it referred to the inversion of two words, but its use tends now to be broader. It is closely related to HYPERBATON, and similar to HYSTERON PROTERON. Anastrophe is found in the opening lines of Richard Crashaw's 'An Epitaph upon Husband and Wife who Died and were Buried Together':

> To these, whom death again did wed,
> This grave's the second marriage-bed.
> For though the hand of Fate could force,
> 'Twixt soul and body a divorce,

It could not sever man and wife,
Because they both lived but one life.

'To these' is placed first to stress the poem's subject. 'Divorce' is delayed to create a rhyme with 'force', but it also complements the sense: it weakens 'divorce' by pushing it to the end, and so stresses the inseverable union between 'man and wife' in the following COUPLET (which has regular word-order). Anastrophe makes 'divorce' sound unnatural.

anecdote A short, amusing story that appeals more for its CONTENT than how it's told. They are usually small DIGRESSIONS within a larger NARRATIVE, such as a BIOGRAPHY. Anecdotes can be a form of gossip, and this made them particularly popular in the eighteenth and nineteenth centuries.

Angry Young Men (c.1950s) A group of British playwrights and novelists who protested against the marginalisation of working-class values in society and culture. John Osborne's *Look Back in Anger* (1956) is the key work that launched a trend for other KITCHEN-SINK DRAMAS. The term is too broad to be that useful, and was rejected by some of those it described.

anonymous (Greek, 'no name') A work with no identified AUTHOR. 'Anonymous', 'anon' and 'A.N. Other' have a great many works attributed to them. Geoffrey Chaucer (c.1340–1400) was the first English writer to advertise himself through his works; before then, AUTHORS did not put their name to their works, and CONVENTION has us speak of the '*Gawain*-poet' or '*Beowulf*-poet' as major medieval AUTHORS. Medieval anonymity is connected to religion: it would have been inconsistent for the religious individual who wrote *The Cloud of Unknowing* (c.1350–1400) to have put his or her name to the work. Anonymous works written from the EARLY MODERN period onwards (particularly DRAMA and POETRY) have tended to be neglected, which is not necessarily connected to the quality of the work. See 'death of the author' for critical assaults on the author-figure's prominence in the literary CANON. John Mullan's *Anonymity: A Secret History of Literature* (2008) explores at greater length why AUTHORS across literary history chose anonymity.

antagonist An opponent or rival in a literary work who is set against the main CHARACTER or PROTAGONIST. The word 'AGON' (contest) in the word's middle is a reminder that the 'antagonist' is the second person in a CONFLICT that the work will resolve. The antagonist is the ANTITHESIS of the protagonist. Antagonists are not necessarily 'evil' VILLAINS, though in many CONVENTIONAL STORIES the antagonist presents a challenge or temptation that the good CHARACTER must resist. The antagonist is neither a HERO/ HEROINE nor an ANTIHERO (i.e. someone who doesn't live up to the expectations of a HERO).

anthem A song that asserts an identity or shared values: e.g. a national anthem. Wilfred Owen's 'Anthem for Doomed Youth' uses the word with bitter IRONY.

anthology (Greek, *anthos-logia,* 'flower-collection') A published collection of literary extracts. The Ancient Greeks produced anthologies, and there are numerous EARLY MODERN English anthologies: the first was Richard Tottel's *Songes and Sonettes*, better known as *Tottel's Miscellany* (1557). Some early anthologies relished the comparison of literary works with flowers, since RHETORICAL FIGURES were described using botanical METAPHORS (see p. 386 for the Silva Rhetoricae—the rhetorical wood). Modern anthologies (see p. 385) provide one of the best ways to encounter new material There is a tendency to judge anthologised AUTHORS by how much of their material is included, but it's worth paying attention to quality over quantity.

anthropomorphism (Greek, 'becoming human') The process of attributing human characteristics to something non-human, in particular the gods/God. A popular anthropomorphic image of the Christian God is the old man with a white beard who lives in the clouds surrounded by angels. The term also describes animals that are given human personalities, as in BEAST FABLES. PATHETIC FALLACY is something different: it describes the error of giving human attributes to nature.

anticlimax An unexpected slide from noble, grand feelings to the trivial, especially during a passage of mounting intensity (CLIMAX). It undercuts what has gone before, often with IRONY: e.g. 'He's extremely handsome…at least he says he is.' It is a rhetorical FIGURE consciously used by the speaker or writer, unlike BATHOS, which is often unintended, and is identified by the audience. Anticlimax is usually used for COMIC or SATIRIC effect, and is particularly found in MOCK-HEROIC literature.

antihero (antiheroine) A leading CHARACTER in a NARRATIVE or DRAMATIC work who fails to meet CONVENTIONAL 'heroic' expectations: e.g. courage, nobility, high achievement. It is often confused with 'ANTAGONIST' (a CHARACTER who rivals another), and with VILLAIN (someone willing to perpetrate wicked or criminal acts). Antiheros are failures who do not live up either the audience's or their own hopes. Willy Loman in *Death of a Salesman* is a CLASSIC antihero: he is an unsuccessful salesman nearing the end of his career who daydreams and ends up killing himself. In this case, the antihero is also a TRAGIC HERO, and Loman is arguably more representative and EFFECTIVE as a tragic CHARACTER precisely because he is an ordinary person (whereas in earlier TRAGEDY heroes belonged to a social élite (see 'STYLE')).

antimasque A brief COMEDY or FARCE performed before a main MASQUE. It is a BURLESQUE of the main performance: a GROTESQUE, chaotic and crude PLAY that reverses the refinement, order and elegance of the MASQUE. The earliest example of an antimasque is found in Ben Jonson's *The Masque of Queens* (1609).

antimetabole (anti-meh-**tab**-oh-ly, Greek, 'turning about') A FIGURE in which two words are repeated in reverse order: 'all for one and one for all'. Like CHIASMUS (*abba* pattern), it can sharpen the sense or highlight ANTITHESIS. Antimetabole only involves word-switching, whereas chiasmus is more sophisticated because it inverts whole ideas and structures. This difference is apparent from the first COUPLET of William Shakespeare's Sonnet 147, which contrasts 'fever/disease' and 'longing/longer'. The repetition is not just a matter of elegance, as is normally the case with antimetabole: it is a CHIASMUS that expresses a subtle causal relationship between the opposites:

> My love is as a fever, longing still
> For that which longer nurseth the disease.

antipathy (Greek, 'against-feeling') Hostility towards other beings or things. It is an ANTONYM for SYMPATHY, and is an important way of creating reaction in an audience; for example, by feeling loathing for the bad guy/ ANTAGONIST.

antiphon (**antiphonal;** Greek, 'sounding in turn') A VERSE composition or HYMN in which two sets of voices alternate, or which takes the form of call and response. It is particularly associated with devotional works. STICHOMYTHIA and AMOEBEAN verse are related forms.

antiphrasis (an-**tif**-rah-sis, Greek, 'expression through opposites') Single-word IRONY; for example, 'quiz' for 'exam' and 'the pond' for 'the Atlantic Ocean'. It is often combined with LITOTES (understatement) in contemporary English.

antistrophe (an-**ti**-strow-fee, Greek, 'turning about') A FIGURE of REPETITION that refers either to repetition at the end of consecutive phrases (also known as EPISTROPHE), or with inversion (compare with CHIASMUS). Given this vagueness, it is preferable to use more specific terms. Antistrophe is also the second section of a Greek choral ode (as found particularly in tragedies), which responds to a STROPHE using the same METRICAL pattern, and is followed by an EPODE (which has its own pattern).

antithesis (pl. antitheses; Greek, 'opposition') A FIGURE in which contrasting ideas are placed together. It creates a sense of balance and symmetry (particularly if combined with ANTIMETABOLE or CHIASMUS). It can clarify dilemmas and suggest a solution; alternatively, it can lead to PARADOX. In this way, this RHETORICAL FIGURE is linked to its other, philosophical meaning: in DIALECTICAL reasoning, antitheses are a challenge to a THESIS that leads to the discovery of a SYNTHESIS (resolution). Antithesis is found especially regularly in AUGUSTAN POETRY and throughout William Shakespeare's works. Here are the antithetical first six lines of sonnet 116:

> Let me not to the marriage of true minds
> Admit impediments; love is not love
> Which alters when it alteration finds,
> Or bends with the remover to remove,
> O no, it is an ever-fixed mark
> That looks on tempests and is never shaken.

antonym A word which is opposite in meaning to another. 'Good' is an antonym of 'bad', 'tall' is an antonym of 'short' and 'SYNONYM' is an antonym of 'antonym'.

anxiety of influence A term coined by the American critic Harold Bloom to describe the fear (supposedly suffered by writers after John Milton) that there is no longer anything new to write about. In a 1973 book of the same name, Bloom argued that the writer is afraid of copying the work of previous writers, and can only generate new work by through a creative misreading (or misprison) of other works. This was a bold reinterpretation of the role of ORIGINALITY, IMITATION and TRADITION in literature. These concepts tie in with PSYCHOANALYTIC CRITICISM and the OEDIPUS COMPLEX, the major symptom of which is a son who wants to gain self-identity by destroying his father. 'Anxiety of influence' presents literary writing as a defensive act that attempts to protect the AUTHOR'S sense of uniqueness. Bloom also described an 'ANTITHETICAL criticism' that explored these relations between writers further. Bloom's writing on the anxiety of influence is fairly male-centred, but has been expanded by some FEMINIST CRITICS.

aphorism (apophthegm) A general truth expressed within a few words. SENTENTIA (or sentence) is a slightly posher, more literary SYNONYM. Oscar

Wilde is particularly known for his aphorisms: e.g. 'The only thing worse than being talked about is not being talked about'. ADAGES, PROVERBS, EPIGRAMS and maxims can all be aphorisms, but don't have to be. An **apophthegm** (a-pe-thim) is a concise prose saying.

apocrypha (adj. apocryphal; Greek, 'hidden way') Works of doubtful authenticity. The term originally referred to biblical writings that were not included in the Old or New Testament. It is often applied to works that have been dubiously attributed to CANONICAL AUTHORS: e.g. *Arden of Faversham* and *Locrine* are among the Shakespeare apocrypha.

Apollonian/Dionysian Adjectives used to describe the main characteristics of the Greek gods Apollo and Dionysus. Apollo is the god of wisdom and prophecy, and is associated with rational thought, self-consciousness and RHETORIC. Dionysus (Bacchus in Roman mythology) is the god of wine: intoxicated, instinctive, ecstatic, UNCONSCIOUS. Related to this fundamental tension are other sweeping dichotomies, like CLASSICISM/ ROMANTICISM and HELLENISM/HEBRAISM. As with all such divisions, it's usually more helpful to think in terms of more/less than either/or. This opposition was taken up by Friedrich Nietzsche to explain the origins of tragedy (see 'chorus'). It has been probed by numerous others before and after: e.g. D.H. Lawrence was preoccupied with the THEME. It is central to Peter Schaffer's play *Equus* (1973), in which the leading CHARACTERS are a psychiatrist called Martin Dysart and Alan Strang, his patient. Dysart is made to question whether he, as an Apollonian figure, has any right to 'cure' Alan's full-blooded, Dionysian practices (which in the play involve doing strange things with horses).

apology In LITERARY CRITICISM 'apology' has a meaning that is the opposite of the everyday sense of 'apologise' or 'excuse oneself': it means a defence or justification of one's actions and beliefs. Plato's *Apology* (c.400 B.C.E.) is an account (largely fictionalized, probably) of the philosopher Socrates' defence speech in the trial that led to his execution, on the charge of not showing reverence to the gods. An apology of a different variety is Philip Sidney's *An Apologie for Poetrie* (1595) which sets out to defend the importance and relevance of poetry as an art.

aporia (Greek, 'doubt') A state of uncertainty. It has roots in Plato's and Aristotle's philosophy, but as a RHETORICAL term means a dilemma, for which Hamlet's 'To be or not to be' soliloquy is an extended and famous example. In this sense, the doubt can be either sincere or feigned. 'Aporia' overlaps with ADYNATON when it describes an inability to find the right words. It is often represented on the page with points ('...') or a dash ('—'). In DECONSTRUCTIONIST criticism 'aporia' refers to an irresolvable interpretative dilemma; in other words, a PARADOX that leaves meaning UNDECIDABLE. At this point intended meaning departs from the meaning understood, and *DIFFÉRANCE* is apparent.

aposiopesis (Greek, 'becoming silent') A FIGURE in which the speaker breaks off mid-sentence, either from overwhelming passion, or for rhetorical effect. e.g. 'why I oughta....'; 'I can scarce speak to thee; thou'lt not believe | With how deprav'd a quality—O Regan!' (*King Lear*, 2.4.136–37). It can expose language as insufficient, where it is related to APORIA and can result in ADYNATON (exaggeration containing an impossibility). Or it can leave the audience to complete the sentiment (its function in this case is like understatement, or LITOTES). It is usually marked on the page with points ('...') or a dash ('—').

apostrophe (Greek, 'turning away') A FIGURE in which the speaker breaks off to address a person (living or dead) or a PERSONIFIED idea as if it were living. The term's ETYMOLOGY probably refers to the ACTOR literally turning away from the stage to address the audience. It is an EFFECTIVE means of conveying deep-seated emotion or projecting feelings onto a scene (compare with PATHETIC FALLACY). An apostrophe is also a PUNCTUATION mark (') that indicates ELISION ('don't'; 'it's', meaning 'it is') or possession ('a child's rattle'). Here is a RHETORICAL apostrophe from John Milton's MASQUE-DRAMA *Comus*:

> O night and shades,
> How are ye joined with hell in triple knot
> Against the unarmed weakness of one virgin
> Alone, and helpless!
>
> (Second brother, ll.579–82)

apparatus The supporting materials included in an scholarly EDITION of a work. Textual apparatus can include any or all of the following: footnotes, bibliography, textual notes, appendices, GLOSSARY, introduction and so on.

arcadia (also **arcady**) An ideal rural landscape inhabited by shepherds living an honest, simple life away from the city. Arcadia originally referred only to a hilly region in Greece that provides the setting for Virgil's *Eclogues*. Later PASTORAL poetry adapted the idea of Arcadia, and Philip Sidney took it as the title for his immensely popular prose romance *Arcadia* (1590). In Virgil a tension exists between the harsh realities of a shepherd's life and a rosy portrayal of their lifestyle. By the Renaissance, however, Arcadia only connoted an idyllic landscape filled with abundant natural resources, pleasant pastimes and SONG, opposed to the miseries of city life. The phrase '*et in Arcadia ego*' is associated with the art of Nicholas Poussin; it means 'and I also in Arcadia' and is a reminder that death lurks everywhere.

arch rhyme A set of consecutive RHYMING words in the pattern *abba*: e.g. rust/old/mould/dust. It is a CHIASTIC pattern, which appears in QUATRAIN-FORM in PETRARCHAN SONNETS. It can also be formed from CROSSED RHYME.

archaism (archaic) The deliberate use of a word that sounds old-fashioned or is no longer in use. 'Thee' is an archaic FORM of the informal 'you'; 'perambulator' of 'pram'. It instinctively feels like a form of POETIC DICTION, since it reaches beyond the normal bounds of language, and recalls the past (like ANACHRONISM). It has been an established technique in English poetry for centuries, and underlines a writer's awareness of and contribution to existing TRADITION. It can be also used for PARODIC or SATIRICAL effect. Edmund Spenser made extensive use of Chaucerian DICTION (in what were strictly MEDIEVALISMS) to recall the past. Spenser's earliest readers would have recognised phrases like this one as archaic:

> Ah foolish old man, I scorne thy skill,
> That wouldest me, my springing youngth to spil.
> I deeme, thy braine emperished bee
> Through rusty elde, that hath rotted thee.
>
> ('Februarie', ll.51–54)

archetypal criticism A critical approach that seeks to identify and analyse universal THEMES, MOTIFS, TOPICS, SYMBOLS, IMAGES and other aspects of literature found across the globe. MYTHIC CRITICISM has similar interests, and both are inspired by Karl Jung's notion of the COLLECTIVE UNCONSCIOUS and literary STRUCTURALISM. POSTMODERN and POST-STRUCTURALIST criticism have both found that archetypal criticism lacks awareness of the historical and geographical uniqueness of works, which makes it impossible to pull out patterns that transcend historical periods and cultures.

archetype (Greek, 'first image') An original element found in MYTH and LITERATURE considered to represent a universal aspect of human experience. An archetype is a master MOTIF or TYPE. IMAGES (e.g. sun and moon), SYMBOLS (circles), ideas (love and death) and certain CHARACTERS have all been considered archetypes. The idea has been pursued by anthropologists, psychologists and literary critics alike, and has given rise to ARCHETYPAL and MYTHIC CRITICISM. A major charge against this approach is that it ignores cultural differences, seeking to find uniformity without being sensitive to the ultimate diversity of literary expression.

architectonics The logical STRUCTURE and design of a TEXT. The architectonics of Edmund Spenser's poetry has been a particular area of interest, for it has been shown that some of his poems have detailed numerical structures with SYMBOLIC significance. His *EPITHALAMION*, for example, contains 24 stanzas and 365 long lines to suggest that the wedding day belongs within a yearly cycle.

argument In a specifically literary CONTEXT, a summary (or ABSTRACT) found at the beginning of a long section of a work. Generally, it means a point made with reasoning and supporting evidence (see 'rhetoric'). Each CANTO in Edmund Spenser's *The Faerie Queene* (1590, 96) contains an argument QUATRAIN: e.g. 'The knight with that old Dragon fights | two dayes incessantly: | The third him ouerthrowes, and gayns | most glorious victory'(I.xi.Argument.1–4).

article A word placed before a noun to clarify whether something specific or unspecific is meant. 'A' or 'an' is the **indefinite** article; 'the' is the **definite** article.

arts Academic disciplines and cultural practices that are not banded under the heading 'science' or 'social science': e.g. theology, history, modern languages, literature, performing arts, film. The 'fine arts' refers specifically to artistic creation in 'high' culture, particularly in visual forms like painting and architecture. 'Arts' describes a wide area of culture. With regard to academic subjects, it is nearly SYNONYMOUS with 'HUMANITIES', which emphasises that the arts are concerned with SUBJECTIVE human experience and expression. It is important for those engaged in the arts to ask themselves at some point 'why do we need the arts?' and, to quote the title of a recent book by John Carey, *What Good Are the Arts?* (2005). That book argues that art is anything anyone has ever considered a work of art, and that the arts enlarge our sense of the world, making us more sensitive and attentive to it. The arts offer an alternative form of human accomplishment that affect us deeply in many different ways, and remind us that there is more to life than endless progress towards an undefined goal.

aside A brief speech spoken apart from other CHARACTERS onstage. By CONVENTION, the other characters are understood not to have heard what was said—if they really couldn't hear, then the audience wouldn't know what was said either. By contrast, a SOLILOQUY is spoken when a character is alone onstage or being overheard. Asides can be spoken to other characters or directly to the audience. Since it relies on stage CONVENTION, it is not found in truly NATURALISTIC DRAMA. COMIC asides often work well:

1. Lord Did you hear of a stranger that's
come to court [to-]night?
Cloten A stranger, and I know not on't?
2. Lord [*Aside*] He's a strange fellow himself,
and knows it not.
(William Shakespeare, *Cymbeline*, 1.6.32–36)

assonance The REPETITION of the same vowel(s) within nearby words where consonants differ. Although it can be spotted when reading, it is essentially an AURAL effect, even more so than CONSONANCE (consonant repetition): e.g. 'the rush of thunder', 'the gleaming screen'. Whereas RHYME involves matching vowels and consonants ('bat' and 'cat'), assonance only requires the same vowels ('bat', 'car'). It can create musical effects, as at the beginning of Keats's 'Ode on a Grecian Urn':

Thou still unravish'd bride of quietness,
Thou foster-child of Silence and slow Time.

Assonance at the beginning of words is usually called ALLITERATION. As with CONSONANCE, if you pick up on similar vowel sounds when reading, it is appropriate to describe it as assonance. Then it is worth considering whether the AUTHOR uses assonance for a particular reason here, and how it interacts with the sense. Assonance marks a point at which language becomes musical and/or literary, and depends on keen-eared readers to detect its subtle influence.

asyndeton (Greek, 'unconnected') A rhetorical FIGURE in which CONJUNCTIONS (or, less often, PRONOUNS) are omitted from consecutive CLAUSES. Perhaps the most famous example is Caesar's '*Veni, vidi, vici*' (I came, I saw, I conquered), where asyndeton adds pomp and distinctiveness to the phrase. POLYSYNDETON is the opposite. It is related to ELLIPSIS and PARATAXIS, since asyndeton is a means of compressing thoughts without directly indicating the connections between them. It has been used by various writers across literary history, including twentieth-century AUTHORS like John Berryman:

> Books drugs razor whisky shirts
> Henry lies ready for his Eastern tour,
> swollen ankles, one hand,
> air reservations, friends at the end of the hurts,
> a winter mind resigned: literature
> must spread, you understand.
>
> (*Dream Songs*, 169.1–6)

aubade (oh-**bahd**) A LYRIC POEM set at day-break involving two lovers who are about to be separated. Also called ALBA. It is a timeless literary situation, which has been described in English by such diverse writers as Geoffrey Chaucer (in *Troilus and Crisede*), John Donne in 'The Sunne Rising' and Philip Larkin, whose 'Aubade' (published in 2003) begins:

> I work all day, and get half drunk at night.
> Waking at four to soundless dark, I stare.
> In time the curtain edges will grow light.

Augustan poets (c.1700–50) The term originally referred to the major Latin poets writing during the reign of the Emperor Augustus: Horace, Ovid and Virgil. It was taken up to describe NEOCLASSICAL poets in eighteenth-century Britain who styled themselves after the Romans, with Alexander Pope as the most important figure, followed by writers like John Gay and John Philips.

author (**co-author; adj. authorial;** from Greek, 'increase, originate') A person who creates a work using his or her intellectual and imaginative abilities. A **co-author** is someone who shares creative responsibility for a work. 'Co-author' is also used as a verb, though 'author' seldom is. The term 'authoress' is not used much anymore.

The concept of the 'author' has been a major critical battle-ground. A naïve view of the literary author is that he or she communicates a set message to an audience through a literary work. Our task as readers is then to absorb the meaning that the author intended: all interpretation is controlled by what the author thinks, and anything the author would not have thought is irrelevant. This is known as the INTENTIONAL FALLACY. Related to this is the BIOGRAPHICAL FALLACY, which states a work largely reflects events that occurred in an author's life. The problem with both opinions is that they ignore the interpretative (HERMENEUTIC) difficulties of accessing an author's thoughts. There is an unbridgeable distance between author and reader.

When Roland Barthes announced the DEATH OF THE AUTHOR, he was arguing that authors do not control the meaning of their TEXTS. This threw emphasis onto the reader and the text itself, and made possible better appreciation of unstable, AMBIGUOUS meaning within a TEXT. On the one hand, NEW CRITICISM could be said to have anticipated this, because it had already identified the INTENTIONAL FALLACY, and stressed the work's existence as an independent, AUTOTELIC entity. Yet this approach supported an ultimate unity to a work, which linked it to authorial control (see 'implied author' for a possible solution). Michel Foucault undermined the relevance of the author further still and opened the way to NEW HISTORICISM. He argued that the 'author function' is an idea created by social, economic and cultural forces, and that works are created by accumulated information that passes into an author's mind, and onto the page. In short, it claims that 'authors' are controlled and created by society, which denies the relevance of SUBJECTIVE VIEWPOINT.

The 'author' is a concept that has changed dramatically over history, as has our notion of ORIGINALITY. The development of written over ORAL LITERATURE, and the introduction of printing both made the idea of the 'author' more prominent. Most English-speaking authors before Geoffrey Chaucer were ANONYMOUS. The name 'Shakespeare', for example, has an absurd number of CONNOTATIONS now, and it all began with the publication of the 1623 FOLIO. In the twenty-first century, the author's personality remains vital to how a book is marketed (see also 'pen-name'), and authors who avoid publicity (e.g. J.D. Salinger) are declared 'reclusive' by the media. TEXTUAL CRITICISM (and the concept of SOCIOLOGY OF TEXTS) uncovers the difficulty of establishing an 'authoritative' TEXT of a WORK.

Without doubt, these historical factors are hugely relevant to a consideration of authorship. Circumstances of composition cannot be completely ignored. This is not, however, the same as abandoning the author's influence altogether. De-centring the author opened up space for new areas of CRITICISM: READER-RESPONSE CRITICISM, which prioritises a work's impact on readers (see 'reception theory'); NEW HISTORICISM, which explores works as historical documents; POST-STRUCTURALISM, which explores problems with TEXTS and meaning, and many others. Equally, works like A.D. Nuttall's *Shakespeare the Thinker* (2007) seek to revive interest in the author as a unique individual who shapes a work. In the twenty-first century, authorship remains something that every critic and reader needs to consider, because it plays a key role in determining how people respond to texts.

autobiography A piece of writing about one's life. Autobiographical writing is never a purely factual record of someone's experience: it's always SUBJECTIVE in the selection and presentation of facts. AUTHORS variously practice self-CENSORSHIP, present a certain image of themselves, have memory lapses, and unconsciously shape recollections in a certain way. A *roman à clef* is an autobiographical account that contains a fictional CHARACTER representing the AUTHOR. This exception aside, it is even riskier to read literary works as being straightforward autobiography; see 'biographical' and 'intentional fallacy', 'persona', 'author', and 'death of the author' for some reasons. PSYCHOANALYTIC CRITICISM has tried to uncover autobiographical CONTENT in works from a psychological perspective, and more recently PSYCHOBIOGRAPHY has looked for evidence about an author's mental condition within works.

Autobiography appears in many forms. St. Augustine's *Confessions* (397) is considered the first Western BIOGRAPHY (see also 'confessional literature'), and the first surviving autobiography in English is *The Book of Margery Kempe* (c.1432–38), which tells of Kempe's mystical visions and consequent run-ins with the authorities. In the seventeenth century, more autobiographies and memoirs appeared as people kept diaries and journals of everyday incidents. Autobiography and literature continued to interact in numerous ways: e.g. William Wordsworth's recollections in *The Prelude* (1805, 50) and the thinly veiled autobiographical CONTENT in D.H. Lawrence's *Sons and Lovers* (1913) are two works that incorporate memories of growing up. More generally, many FIRST-PERSON NARRATORS speak as though telling their life-story. In the twentieth century, autobiography became dominated by the famous, particularly in terms of publishing: many leading figures in politics, entertainment, sport and other fields have written autobiographies (sometimes with the help of a GHOST-WRITER), and have made lots of money doing so.

autograph (Greek, 'self writing') Anything written in an AUTHOR'S hand-writing (not necessarily his or her signature). A HOLOGRAPH is a document written entirely in the author's hand-writing.

automatic writing Composition that excludes conscious thought; writing without thinking. It tries to tap directly into UNCONSCIOUS thought. Automatic writing is particularly associated with SURREALIST (and Dadaist) writers, and some MODERNISTS tried it too (e.g. W.B. Yeats). Many writers speak of a compulsion to write, but equally literary composition is usually considered something that requires insight, perceptiveness and technical skill, and not just a state of mind conducive to art (which could be recreated using drugs or alcohol).

autotelic (Greek, 'self-ending') An adjective describing a work whose ultimate end is itself, and so is self-contained. The principle is important to NEW CRITICISM, a movement which encouraged ANALYSIS based on TEXTS' internal coherence, without reference to outside CONTEXTS. It also belongs to a strict FORMALIST approach, in which STRUCTURE and technique create all meaning. An autotelic work exists for itself, and is neither DIDACTIC nor written for some external purpose. POST-STRUCTURALIST critics argue, by contrast, that all works are inseparable from the social and cultural DISCOURSES that create them: in other words, there is no such thing as a 'text', only 'INTERTEXTS'.

avant-garde (French, 'front-line') Art and literature that is experimental and on the fringes of mainstream culture. It is associated with such twentieth-century French cultural movements as SYMBOLISM and THEATRE OF THE ABSURD. The concept of an avant-garde reflects a historical change in the way artists are perceived; rather than be involved with political figures and centres of power through PATRONAGE, the avant-garde champion progress and ORIGINALITY at the social margins.

axiom (Greek, 'worthy') A statement that is generally accepted to be true, and needs no justification. It is like a MAXIM, but self-evidently true. An axiom that is so obviously true that it's bland is a 'truism'.

B

ballad A SONG that tells a story. Its other main features are: BALLAD METRE, plain LANGUAGE, fast-moving action, dialogue, impersonal NARRATOR, REFRAINS and other forms of REPETITION. It is a traditional form with origins in ORAL LITERATURE. In the sixteenth and seventeenth centuries, the TEXTS of popular ballads are available to buy as single sheets, and were called BROADSIDE ballads. ROMANTIC poets revived the ballad as a FORM, since it was well-suited to their taste for simple, everyday language. William Wordsworth and Samuel Taylor Coleridge's *Lyrical Ballads* (1798) uses 'ballad' in the title not to describe a STANZA form, so much as a literary style that could be familiar and accessible to everyone. Some later ballads written in BALLAD METRE are usually known as 'literary ballads' (see next entry for examples). Not to be confused with BALLADE.

ballad stanza (ballad metre) A verse FORM consisting of QUATRAINS with four (or three) stresses per line, and rhymed COUPLETS *abcb* or *abab*. It is similar to COMMON MEASURE. The ballad stanza has a light, dance-like movement that works well for telling stories. It is sometimes described as a HEPTAMETER form (i.e. seven pairs of stressed and unstressed syllables per line), but originally the form was fairly flexible. Ballad metre developed as a medieval ORAL tradition, and only later were ballads recorded on paper, particularly on printed single sheets (BROADSIDES) for the general public. The form later came to influence eighteenth- and nineteenth-century poets, who wrote the ballads most celebrated today: these include Samuel Taylor Coleridge's 'Rime of the Ancient Mariner' and John Keats' 'La Belle Dame Sans Merci'. Here are the first four stanzas of Keats' ballad:

I

O what can ail thee, knight-at-arms,
Alone and palely loitering?
The sedge has wither'd from the lake
And no birds sing.

II

O what can ail thee, knight-at-arms!
So haggard and so woe-begone?

The squirrel's granary is full,
  And the harvest's done.

III

I see a lily on thy brow
  With anguish moist and fever dew,
And on thy cheeks a fading rose
  Fast withereth too.

IV

I met a lady in the meads,
  Full beautiful a faery's child,
Her hair was long, her foot was light,
  And her eyes were wild.

ballade A FIXED FORM involving three eight-line STANZAS that rhyme *ababbcbc* and a final four-line ENVOI that rhymes *bcbc*. It shouldn't be confused with BALLAD STANZAS. Perhaps due to the complex rhyme scheme, it has seldom been used in English. A rare example is Geoffrey Chaucer's *The Monk's Tale*, which contains eight-line ballade stanzas and may have provided the basis for the SPENSERIAN STANZA (*ababbcbcc*). G.K. Chesterton's 'A Ballade of Suicide' (1915) is a piece of LIGHT VERSE that sees the rhyme scheme tip towards COMEDY. This is the first stanza:

The gallows in my garden, people say,
Is new and neat and adequately tall;
I tie the noose on in a knowing way
As one that knots his necktie for a ball;
But just as all the neighbours on the wall
Are drawing a long breath to shout "Hurray!"
The strangest whim has seized me. . . After all
I think I will not hang myself to-day.

bard A poet who performs verse, especially in celebration of a nation's achievements. It originally referred to a Celtic MINSTREL, but is now used more loosely—including as a high-flown EPITHET for William 'the Bard' Shakespeare (but see 'bardolatry' below).

bardolatry Uncritical adoration of William Shakespeare and his works. It is a PORTMANTEAU WORD created from 'BARD' and 'idolatry'. Hero worship of Shakespeare in criticism centres on the principle that 'it's by Shakespeare, therefore it must be good'.

baroque (from Portuguese, 'rough pearl') In literature, it means highly elaborate and ornate in STYLE. It primarily refers to a GENRE of visual art and music of the seventeenth and eighteenth centuries, and as a literary term its use is often restricted to a narrow set of works, such as Milton's *Paradise Lost* (1667), METAPHYSICAL POETRY and Thomas De Quincey's *Confessions of An Opium Eater* (1821). Like 'GROTESQUE', though, it is a useful literary term in its own right, and can be used separately from its art historical and musical CONTEXTS. It can refer broadly to any literature that is highly IMAGINATIVE, contains PURPLE PATCHES and makes generous use of FIGURATIVE LANGUAGE, ALLUSIONS, CONCEITS, METAPHORS and other IMAGERY.

bathos (**adj. bathetic; bay**-thoss, Greek, 'depth') An attempt to express grand and noble thoughts that becomes comically mundane. Instead of reaching SUBLIME heights, the passage's STYLE veers towards the ridiculous. PATHOS arouses genuine, discomfiting emotions, but bathos induces laughter. The spectator who finds the body-count at the end of *King Lear* (1604) so great that it becomes amusing has found it bathetic. Ever since Alexander Pope popularised the word in his 1728 ESSAY *Peri Bathous* it has largely been used as a derogatory term to mock AUTHORS; for example, to criticise ROMANTIC poets seeking to glorify the humble. However, authors can manipulate bathos for their own ends: James Joyce's *Ulysses* (1922), for example, consciously toys with bathos as it parallels Odysseus with Leopold Bloom, an unremarkable Dublin resident.

beast fable A tale in which animals talk and act like humans. Beast fables are ALLEGORICAL: they always make some DIDACTIC or SATIRICAL point about human traits and actions. Like FABLES or PARABLES in general, beast fables are an ancient form. *Aesop's Fables* is still the ARCHETYPAL collection of beast fables; it is said that Aesop lived around 600 B.C.E., but his fables weren't written down until the first century by a Latin writer, Phaedrus. Geoffrey Chaucer's *The Nun Priest's Tale* (1387) is an early example of a beast fable in English, and George Orwell's *Animal Farm* (1945) essentially works within the same tradition.

beat In poetry, EMPHASIS placed on a SYLLABLE, particularly as it forms part of a RHYTHM or METRE. STRESS, ACCENT and ICTUS are more precise literary terms.

Beat Generation (c.1950s) A group of American writers based around San Francisco in the 1950s with countercultural and anti-intellectual values. The name 'beat' originally implied tiredness, then took on associations of 'upbeat', 'beatific', and musical 'BEAT'; later they were characterized as 'beatniks', which was replaced by the term 'hippie' in the 1960s. The three defining works of the Beat Generation are *On the Road* by Jack Kerouac (1957), William Burroughs' *Naked Lunch* (1959) and Allen Ginsburg's *Howl* (1956). It is reminiscent of nineteenth-century DECADENCE, and its closest British equivalents were the apparently less chilled 'ANGRY YOUNG MEN'.

bias A weighted opinion that prevents someone from being neutral. PREJUDICE is a SYNONYM, and both terms come with negative CONNOTATIONS. A basic task of POSTCOLONIAL, FEMINIST, GENDER and DISABILITY-centred CRITICISM is to identify how literature perpetrates discrimination, and to correct the CANONICAL bias towards white male AUTHORS. In this light, bias is unsavoury and inhumane. Yet there are some who find that bias has a benign side as well. The philosopher Hans-Georg Gadamer (a key figure in HERMENEUTIC theory) argued that bias is inevitable (i.e. humans are never OBJECTIVE), and that it acts as a foundation for all understanding. He sought to revive bias and prejudice as descriptive terms that have no inherently negative implications. Bias, he claims, forms the basis of someone's unique vision, regardless of how much it is resisted by others. Other critics rightly point to the great suffering that bias has caused over history, but then bias may be an inevitable part of all forms of expression, literary or otherwise.

bibliography (also **bibliographic studies**; Latin, 'book writing') A list of writings about a subject, or a list of an AUTHOR'S works. It also refers to the area of literary studies concerned with the book as a physical object (or electronic entity). There are three strands: 'descriptive bibliography' is describing books; 'analytical bibliography' is the study of how books are produced and composed (e.g. printing); and 'textual bibliography' is applying knowledge about a physical book to reading a text. All three can directly inform how we read literary works. Many advances in the field have been made in Shakespeare studies, where the perplexing array of QUARTO and FOLIO EDITIONS creates juicy bibliographic problems. The idea of the SOCIOLOGY OF TEXTS is a current strand of bibliographic thinking that argues for historicised readings of individual EDITIONS. Though a relatively technical form of LITERARY CRITICISM, it is still more of an art than a science (as is editing). For the general reader, two areas in particular are worth consideration: how the physical condition of books affects your response, and where the text you are reading originally came from.

***Bildungsroman* (pl. –ane;** German, 'coming-of-age novel') A NOVEL that depicts the main CHARACTER'S development into adulthood. The PROTAGONIST comes to terms with the world and gains a sense of identity in the process. Many *Bildungsromane* are FIRST-PERSON NARRATIVES, but a THIRD-PERSON NARRATIVE is equally workable. The German term, alongside its near-synonym *Erziehungsroman* ('education novel'), originally described eighteenth-century German books, like Johann Wolfgang von Goethe's *Wilhelm Meisters Lehrjahre* (Wilhelm Meister's Apprenticeship, 1795). A *Künstlersroman* ('artist novel') is also related; it describes an individual's creative development. The terms are used more widely now, and examples of *Bildungsromane* can be found throughout the novel's history. Here are examples from each of the past three centuries: Henry Fielding's *Tom Jones* (1749), *Great Expectations* (1860) by Charles Dickens and J.D. Salinger's *Catcher in the Rye* (1951).

binary metre (duple metre) A RHYTHMIC pattern (a METRE) based on standard units (FEET) of two syllables. Binary metres are more common in English than TERNARY (TRIPLE) METRES are. IAMBS form the basis of most binary metres; TROCHEES are the main alternative, but are more often used within iambic metres for variation. It is almost impossible to have a SPONDAIC binary metre, because that would require every BEAT to be STRESSED. In general terms, binary metre involves an alternation of stressed and unstressed beats. In SCANSION, if two stressed or unstressed syllables come together, then you should ask why the pattern has been varied and how this affects the sense.

biographical fallacy The error (FALLACY) of reading a literary text to learn more about how an AUTHOR lived, and what he or she felt about life. This assumes that the actual author and NARRATIVE PERSONA are the same person, and it usually very difficult to justify this connection. This isn't to say that TEXTS shouldn't be interpreted in CONTEXT of when and where they were written, and where they belong in an author's OEUVRE. The INTENTIONAL FALLACY is slightly different: it concerns an attempt to read a text for what the author wanted to say.

biography Writing about a person's life. Biography and literature overlap in many places. Plutarch's *Parallel Lives* (c.100), which pairs major Greek and Roman figures, was one of the earliest biographies, and was being read in the Renaissance (William Shakespeare drew on Plutarch, particularly in his Roman plays). Medieval HAGIOGRAPHIES (saints' lives) are biographical accounts sprinkled with LEGENDARY tales and ANECDOTES. James Boswell's *Life of Johnson* (1791) is a massive and still-read account of Samuel Johnson's life, whose own *Lives of the English Poets* (1779–81) was a major development in British biography. Elizabeth Gaskell's *Life of Charlotte Brontë* (1857) is a major novelist's account of another major novelist. Like AUTOBIOGRAPHY, BIOGRAPHY became popular with general readers in the twentieth century, and biographies of literary FIGURES are common—though see 'biographical fallacy' for the danger of interpreting AUTHORS' works based on their life experiences.

black comedy A DRAMA that uses COMIC elements to offer a negative view of humanity and its achievements. It implies that humans are laughable and not to be taken seriously: life is a FARCE. In THEATRE OF THE ABSURD, this was combined with existentialist philosophy to offer a particularly grim outlook on life. It can be described as a type of TRAGICOMEDY.

Black Mountain poets (c. 1950s) A group of experimental American poets based around Black Mountain College in North Carolina, U.S.A.. Charles Olson was a central figure, and OPEN FORM was an important concept in the AVANT-GARDE, POSTMODERNIST poetry they were writing.

blank verse LINES of POETRY in unrhymed ('blank') IAMBIC PENTAMETER, i.e. with ten syllables and five stresses. It is at the heart of English literary tradition, having been brought into the language by Henry Howard, Earl of Surrey, and used throughout Shakespeare's plays, Milton's *Paradise Lost* (1667), Wordsworth's *The Prelude* (1805, 50) and many other works. Blank verse is traditionally thought of as coming closest to replicating the natural RHYTHMS of everyday English speech. Indeed, there is a danger of recognising blank verse in places where it isn't being used. Shakespeare has a deep understanding of the blank verse pattern, but he wasn't consciously writing 'blank verse' and often writes lines with added syllables (EXTRAMETRICAL) or fewer than ten (CATALECTIC), mixed with other verse FORMS and making skilful use of ENJAMBEMENT and END-STOPPED lines. Reading blank verse involves observing closely how the poet departs from the regular pattern. FREE VERSE is not the same as blank verse; in fact, it is almost its opposite. FREE VERSE has no set METRE, and developed in part as a reaction to the dominance of the IAMBIC pattern on English poetry. Here is an example of its earliest use, in Henry Howard, Earl of Surrey's *Aeneid* TRANSLATION (c.1537):

> Aeneas, with that vision stricken down,
> Well near bestraught, upstart his hair for dread,
> Amid his throat his voice likewise gan stick.
> For to depart by flight he longeth now,
> and the sweet land to leave, astonied sore
> With this advice and message of the gods.
>
> (4.359–64)

blazon (noun and verb) In LITERATURE, it refers to an itemised description of the physical features of a beautiful woman. It is a poetic CONVENTION associated with the SONNET, thanks to Petrarch, and is found in numerous ELIZABETHAN sonnet sequences, e.g. Philip Sidney's *Astrophel and Stella* (1591). Originally, a blazon was a shield with heraldic markings or other bright-coloured decorations.

Bloomsbury Group (c.1910s) An informal group of writers based in the Bloomsbury area of central London around the 1910s. The COTERIE was a mixture of middle-class artists, writers and thinkers, whose two major literary figures were Virginia Woolf and E.M. Forster.

bluestockings A group of intellectual communities of men and women active in the latter half of the eighteenth century. They were known for being informal and sociable, as well as taking a serious interest in learning; the name comes from a early member who came in his cheap blue stockings, rather than the richer white silk variety. Already in the eighteenth century the term 'bluestocking' specifically came to mean a group of women taking an active interest in intellectual pursuits, at a time when women were denied access to education. The term came to have a scoffing tone in the nineteenth-century Britain, which has faded given the great advances in equality since then.

bob and wheel A METRICAL structure that sometimes concludes verse paragraphs in ALLITERATIVE METRE. It consists of a short line with one STRESS (the bob) and up to four slightly longer, rhymed lines (the wheel). Most readers first come across the bob and wheel when reading *Sir Gawain and the Green Knight*.

bombast (also **fustian**) The use of aggressively pompous and elaborate language. HYPERBOLE is often involved. The most vivid examples in English literature are found in ELIZABETHAN DRAMA.

bowdlerize The deletion of sections from a work that are considered indecent. Thomas Bowdler's *Family Shakespeare* of 1818 was the original bowdlerized text. Though it seems the height of Victorian prudishness, this form of CENSORSHIP does make sense in the preparation of ABRIDGED versions or ADAPTATIONS for children. All the same, a bowdlerized work leaves an attentive reader distracted by the editor's intrusive private morals.

broadside A single sheet of paper printed on one side. Most broadsides printed over the past five hundred years have been lost, since they were intended to be sold and read quickly. Of particular interest to literary scholars are broadside BALLADS, which have survived thanks to the efforts of collectors at the time.

broken rhyme The creation of a RHYME by splitting up a word between a line-ending and the beginning of the next: e.g. 'I asked for him to be sent, | and so he came to the ent- | rance, not knowing where I went.' It is largely found in LIGHT VERSE, where such levels of POETIC LICENCE are most usual, though Gerard Manley Hopkins uses serious broken rhyme on occasion.

bucolic A synonym for PASTORAL; i.e. POETRY about the life and experiences of shepherds. Virgil's *Eclogues* are also known as his *Bucolica*.

burden (also **burthen**) A repeated element in a poem that emphasises the theme, and could be repeated aloud by the audience. It is an alternative term for REFRAIN or CHORUS, though it is sometimes reserved for a repeated phrase that begins (rather than ends) stanzas, such as in CAROLS. 'Burden' also means the main idea of a work.

burlesque (noun, verb and adj.; French, 'mockery') In LITERARY CRITICISM, a general term for any composition that ridicules a GENRE'S form and STYLE through IMITATION. Burlesques are written for COMIC or SATIRICAL effect, and usually have an IRONIC and FARCICAL TONE. 'High' burlesque describes a work that adopts an inappropriately lofty style for some lowly subject-matter (e.g. MOCK-HEROIC); 'low' burlesque describes a disrespectful treatment of something exalted (and is also known as TRAVESTY). Burlesque often involves PARODY, defined as the imitation of particular characteristics for comic ends. A LAMPOON is also different: it means an attack on someone's character through CARICATURING. 'Burlesque', 'parody' and 'TRAVESTY' are sometimes treated as SYNONYMS, but it's worth keeping 'burlesque' as the broader term for imitation designed to make an audience laugh. One of the earliest fully burlesque works in English is Francis Beaumont's play *The Knight of the Burning Pestle* (first performed in 1607), which mocks CHIVALRIC ROMANCES by having a grocer disrupt a performance of a play. ANTIMASQUES are another good example of burlesque, and date from a similar time. In everyday speech, burlesque can also refer to an erotic variety show; this is completely separate to the literary usage.

Burns stanza A six-line STANZA with a RHYME scheme *aaabab*. Lines four and six are DIMETERS, and the others TETRAMETERS. It was around long before Robert Burns used the form in the eighteenth century, but the general reader is most likely to encounter it when reading Burns.

by-play In DRAMA, action that takes place away from the main events and movements on-stage, usually silently.

C

c. (C.) century or centuries. It also means 'around', particularly when the 'c' is placed in italics. So 'around the twelfth century' could be 'c. 12th c.'

cacophony (**adj. cacophonous**; ka-**ko**-foh-nee; Greek, 'sounding badly') The intentional use of rough-sounding language (DISSONANCE). Like its opposite, EUPHONY, there are no objective criteria for cacophony: it needs to be heard by the individual reader. It tends to involve CONSONANCE or intrusive consonant sounds. As with all aural effects, it's important to be sensitive to how cacophony interacts with the sense.

cadence (from Italian, 'falling') The natural RHYTHMS of speech, particularly in PROSE and FREE VERSE. It applies to movements in the voice (e.g. RISING and FALLING RHYTHMS), distinct from the patterns determined by METRE. Each voice has its own cadences based on phrasing, pacing and delivery of words. Closer to its musical sense, cadence also refers to the shaping at the end of phrases. Many writers possess highly distinctive cadences; e.g. Thomas Browne's are particularly cherished:

> I beleeve that our estranged and divided ashes shall unite againe, that our separated dust after so many pilgrimages and transformations into the parts of mineralls, Plants, Animals, Elements, shall at the voyce of God returne into their primitive shapes; and joyne againe to make up their primary and predestinate formes. As at the Creation, there was a separation of that confused masse into its species, so at the destruction thereof there shall bee a separation into its distinct individuals.
>
> (from *Religio Medici*, first part (1642))

caesura (**pl. caesuras/ caesurae**; ses-**you**-rah; Greek, 'cutting') A pause in a line of VERSE that affects the METRE. It is a natural break in the sense, and follows speech RHYTHMS rather than metrical rules. They can occur towards the beginning of lines (known as initial caesuras), in the middle (medial) or towards the end (terminal). A line can have more than one caesura or none at all.

In English PROSODY, caesuras often come at the end of a sentence or CLAUSE, which always brings a GRAMMATICAL pause. In SCANSION (metrical ANALYSIS) a caesura is normally marked with a | |. So caesuras can often be spotted when reading from punctuation marks like full stops and commas. Whereas punctuation marks indicate a grammatical break, caesuras affect how a line sounds, and shape the rhythmic pattern. Pauses that the reader introduces (e.g. for breath or EMPHASIS) are not caesuras. Missing words do not create them either. A HIATUS is a sudden disruption in the metre, unlike the firm break of the caesura. Line-endings are not marked as caesuras, but have much the same effect. Caesuras were used in OLD ENGLISH and some MIDDLE ENGLISH poetry (particularly that written in ALLITERATIVE METRE) to divide a line into two half-lines. After that time, caesuras were used to vary EMPHASIS and delivery in forms like BLANK VERSE and IAMBIC PENTAMETER. Note that caesura has a different meaning in CLASSICAL PROSODY, where it refers to a pause within a FOOT (confusingly, the term DIAERESIS is closer to the sense in English).

camp (noun and adj.) Exaggerated, showy or THEATRICAL behaviour, associated with male homosexuals. It can be linked with literary AESTHETICISM (i.e. a love of art for its own sake) and in some cases BURLESQUE (a mocking IMITATION). QUEER THEORY has explored how camp behaviour subverts traditional gender roles, and shows them to be artificial.

campus novel A PROSE FICTION with a university setting. Kingsley Amis's *Lucky Jim* (1954) was among the earliest examples.

canon (adj. canonical) A group of authentic or representative works. It can refer to the complete works of a single AUTHOR, distinct to APOCRYPHAL items; e.g. 'the Shakespearean canon'. It also connotes the works most cherished and revered by a particular culture; e.g. the literary timeline in this book (p. 357 onwards) contains canonical works of English literature.

Literary canons are there to be challenged. They are not set in stone, and no individual or group has control over what is canonical and what isn't. Scholars have devoted attention to the many factors that affect the process of canon formation. To understand why Shakespeare is indisputably canonical today, for example, you could look at: the publication of the first FOLIO in 1623; his language, which remains (fairly) comprehensible to later readers; the thematic breadth of the plays; the interpretative puzzles they throw up; later readers' responses (e.g. ADAPTATIONS, PSYCHOANALYSIS); and the absence of copyright, which means the plays can be performed for free.

Whether there are common criteria for a canonical text is less certain ground. It is sometimes argued that canonical works present strong moral visions that can educate us or make us reassess our worldview, though this is disputable. Canonical works are those which a consensus of readers has found to be important, and which it is therefore likely future readers will also respond to well. Yet, even if ninety-nine out of hundred readers of Shakespeare will be entranced, individual readers still need to come to their own judgment, so that responses to CLASSIC texts stay fresh. While canonical status brings prestige and a wider readership to a work (particularly in schools and universities), eventually the weight of past interpretations becomes a burden when simply trying to read a text.

Another important issue is whether canons are truly representative, or simply perpetuate the values of a cultural élite, especially one in which white males have traditionally favoured white males. MARXIST, FEMINIST and POSTCOLONIAL critics have all tugged at the boundaries of literary canons, and with good reason. It is important for canons to be kept fluid, and to ensure that marginal writers are not brushed aside. Yet the canon remains a focal point for literary discussion, and contains all those works with the richest RECEPTION HISTORIES, and those which ask searching questions about aspects of the human condition. Canons occur naturally and are beneficial, providing that they are not revered without thinking (e.g. BARDOLATRY).

canto (Italian, 'song') A division in long poem, particularly an EPIC or NARRATIVE work. Edmund Spenser's *The Faerie Queene*, Alexander Pope's *Rape of the Lock* and Lord Byron's *Don Juan* are three works divided into cantos. Quotations from *The Faerie Queene*, for example, take the form book.canto.stanza.line. For example, a referenced quotation to Book 3, Canto 6, Stanza 6, lines1 and 2 would be: 'But wondrously they were begot, and bred | Through influence of th'heauens fruitfull ray' (III.vi.6.1–2).

caricature An exaggerated portrayal of an individual that centres on one distinguishing feature. Caricatures are often COMIC and well-intentioned, though often used for satirical effect too. A literary caricature is often obvious from the CHARACTER'S name. Caricatures, such Charles Dickens', can also offer insightful social commentary.

carnivalesque A form of writing that allows popular voices to be heard. The term is associated with Mikhail Bakhtin's work *Rabelais and his World* (1965), which focused on François Rabelais's NOVELS *Gargantua* and *Pantagruel* (1532–52). These novels, like a carnival, break the usual hierarchies of order and decency. Instead Rabelais and others allow voices of 'low' culture to be heard, with accompanying crude humour and concentration on the body, its functions, sex, death and the sensual (like a piece of FOLK LITERATURE). It is often described as GROTESQUE: a noisy, distorted, in-yer-face presentation of the world. Bakhtin was interested in the liberating, authority-defying humour of such works, which created HETEROGLOSSIA (the presence of many voices). This quality can be found in other GENRES too, such as MENIPPEAN SATIRE.

carol A dancing SONG, particularly one performed in the Middle Ages. Now it means a song of religious celebration, especially at Christmas. This doesn't just mean carols like 'Hark the Herald Angels Sing' and 'O Come All Ye Faithful': Robert Southwell's 'The Burning Babe' is a fine example of a literary carol. It begins like this:

As I in hoary winter's night
    Stood shivering in the snow,
Surprised I was with sudden heat,
    Which made my heart to glow.

And lifting up a fearful eye
    To view what fire was near,
A pretty Babe all burning bright
    Did in the air appear.

caroline (1625–49) Relating to the period during which King Charles I reigned in England. 'Caroline' comes from the Latin form of Charles, 'Carolus'. In this period, literature became increasingly political, as Britain drew closer to Civil War in 1642; however, this was also a period in which METAPHYSICAL POETRY was written and (finally) published. See page 365 for some important works from the period.

carpe diem (Latin, 'seize the day') A commonplace theme (TOPOS) that declares the importance of enjoying the present moment. '*Carpe diem*' is a quotation from Horace's *Odes* (1.xi), and the idea recurs across world literature: for example, it is present in the title of Saul Bellow's *Seize the Day* (1956) and is the subject of Robert Herrick's 'To the Virgins, To Make Much of Time' (1648). Many people know the first line Herrick's poem, but few have actually read how the *carpe diem* theme develops. Here's the whole poem:

Gather ye rosebuds while ye may,
    Old Time is still a flying;

And this same flower that smiles today,
  Tomorrow will be dying.

The glorious lamp of heaven, the sun,
  The higher he's a getting;
The sooner will his race be run,
  And nearer he's to setting.

That age is best which is the first,
  When youth and blood are warmer;
But being spent, the worse, and worst
  Times, still succeed the former.

Then be not coy, but use your time,
  And while ye may, go marry;
For having lost but once your prime,
  You may forever tarry.

case The FORM of a NOUN, which shows its relation to other words in a SENTENCE. **Nominative** case indicates the subject of a verb. **Accusative** case indicates the OBJECT of a verb. **Genitive** indicates possession, either with 'of' or ''s' (the Saxon genitive). **Dative** indicates the indirect object, i.e. the person affected by an action indirectly. In the sentence, 'Neil gave Georgina's apple to Doris': Neil is in the nominative (doing the giving), the apple is in the accusative (being given), Georgina is in the genitive (it's her apple), and Doris is in the dative (the object is given to her).

catachresis (Greek, 'misuse') A strained or improper word-usage, especially a far-fetched metaphor. The oft-cited literary examples are *Hamlet*, 3.1.60—'To take arms against a sea of troubles' (because it makes no sense to fight the sea)—and Milton's 'Lycidas' lines 119–20: 'Blind mouths! that scarce themselves know how to hold a sheep-hook' (because mouths can't hold sheep-hooks). It can create original and surprising thoughts. MIXED METAPHOR describes everyday instances of the same.

catalectic (**adj., noun catalexis**; cat-a-**lek**-tik; 'Greek 'coming to a sudden end) A line of VERSE that is missing the final SYLLABLE(s) expected, based on the METRE. In English PROSODY, it most frequently occurs in TROCHAIC verse (where the final unstressed SYLLABLE is not much missed), or in DACTYLIC or ANAPAESTIC verse (because ending with a FOOT of two SYLLABLES is EMPHATIC). Catalectic lines are HYPOMETRICAL. It is sometimes used to turn a LIGHT (FEMININE) ENDING into a HEAVY (MASCULINE) one. ACEPHALOUS is the opposite of CATALECTIC: it describes lines missing SYLLABLE(s) from the start.

catastrophe (Greek, 'downturn') A sudden, disastrous development towards the end a DRAMATIC work. A catastrophe provides clarity in the same way that a *DÉNOUEMENT* (unravelling) does, and the rest of the work assesses the impact of this event. In Greek tragedy, catastrophe takes the form of a sudden reversal of fortune (what Aristotle called *PERIPETEIA*).

catch-22 situation Not really a literary term, but one derived from literature that causes confusion and so is worth noting: it means a no-win situation, or a 'double-bind'. In Joseph Heller's 1961 novel of the name, Catch-22 is a Army Air Force regulation stating that only insane pilots cannot fly, and all pilots concerned for their safety are sane. So the pilot who says he is insane and doesn't want to fly on a dangerous mission is obviously concerned for his safety, and is therefore sane, so must fly. But if he declares himself sane, well, then he has to fly anyway.

catharsis (Greek, 'purgation') A Greek medical term referring to the washing away of unclean or dirty substances, which was used by Aristotle in the *Poetics* to describe how TRAGEDY affects its audience. Its precise meaning is still disputed, which is why there is no agreed English TRANSLATION. It could refer to the cleansing of a CHARACTER'S wickedness, and seems to match well the sensation of peacefulness, rather than trauma or distress, at the end of TRAGEDIES. In this sense, it may be a response to Plato's criticism of tragedy—that tragedy stirs dangerous passions in the audience—in its apparent claim that DRAMA acts as a safe outlet for violent emotions. As Aristotle suggests, a well-structured PLOT is necessary to guide the audience's reaction towards *catharsis*. Bertolt Brecht argued that this idea of *catharsis* is a form of social control, which disposes of an audience's energy, thus ensuring safe democratic consensus with no prospect of renewal through revolution. See 'alienation effect' and 'epic theatre' for Brecht's alternative.

cavalier drama/poets (c.1630s) A collective term for a group of poets and dramatists writing during King Charles I's reign (the Caroline period). 'Cavalier' refers to supporters of the king (royalists) in the English Civil War. Richard Lovelace, Robert Herrick and Edmund Waller are some of the better known cavalier poets. As a DRAMATIC form it was generally slow-moving, artificial, and affected by its sympathy for the values of a courtly élite. Sir John Suckling is the best-known of the cavalier dramatists, but this is because he also wrote poetry, and CAVALIER POETRY is more widely available. The term 'Sons of Ben' used to be used to indicate the influence of Ben Jonson on these writers, in contrast to the 'School of Donne' (i.e. METAPHYSICAL POETRY), and the 'School of Spenser' (writers thought to be harking back to Elizabeth's reign). Like Jonson, the cavalier poets were generally engaged in public life and wrote witty, graceful LYRIC POETRY.

Celtic Revival (c.1880–1940) A general movement in Irish literature to forge an independent Irish literary tradition by looking to the Celtic past. W.B. Yeats is the best-known figure of this movement, and made contributions in both theatre and poetry. However, the interest in Irish national culture had begun decades before, and symbolised a larger desire for political and cultural independence from Britain.

censorship The removal of aspects of a work deemed unsuitable on grounds of taste, morals or politics. Although relatively few writers in English have felt government pressure to produce PROPAGANDA, censorship remains a significant aspect of the historical CONTEXT that affects how works are produced. The advent of printing in the fifteenth century brought with it government interest over who could print, and what was printed. With DRAMA, for example, the Master of Revels vetted all new plays for performance from 1574. The need for plays to be approved continued with the 1737 Licensing Act, which was finally laid to rest in 1968. In addition to direct censorship, it also introduced self-censorship on the part of writers wishing to avoid trouble—though it's impossible to know how much of an effect this had. There have been a few celebrated cases, such as the charges of obscenity against *Lady Chatterley's Lover* on publication by Penguin in 1960, but otherwise censorship remains a shady undercurrent in English literary history.

cento (Latin, 'patchwork clothing') A composition that is created from quotations from to other works. It is a form of IMITATION that requires the AUTHOR to locate and arrange existing material in a skilful manner. It is similar to PASTICHE, only more diverse. It is particularly associated with EARLY MODERN writing that looked to CLASSICAL writers as exemplars, and is linked to the tradition of noting down memorable quotations in COMMONPLACE BOOKS.

cf. (*confer*, Latin) Compare. Also appears as 'cp.' In scholarly writing, it is not unknown for a critic to make use of a quiet 'cf.' in footnotes to pour scorn on another's work: e.g. 'cf. Mayhew's curious opinions on this subject'.

chapbook The name given (at a later time) to cheap books and pamphlets containing BALLADS, fairy stories, nonsense verse, illustrations and the like in the sixteenth to eighteenth centuries. Chapmen were the people travelling around to sell them to the general public.

character (**characterization**; from Greek, 'stamp, impression') In literature, a person depicted in a work. It often has the CONNOTATION of personality and values; e.g. 'of dubious character'. Less often, it means a PROSE description of someone's qualities. **Characterization** is the process of creating a character in a literary work. It is worth considering the earlier sense of character, i.e. 'stamp' or 'handwriting': character is the indelible part of an individual that takes a form recognisable to others.

Characterization is basic to most literary composition. Character and MOTIVATION, particularly that of the PROTAGONIST, are entwined with the PLOT. Aristotle writes in the *Poetics* that character (ETHOS) must be well integrated with plot (*muthos*), and both elements are certainly related. Aristotle places great importance on the plot, but many readers would argue that characters are more central to a work than plot is (e.g. Jane Austen's *Emma*). Some GENRES involve extended studies in character (e.g. *BILDUNGSROMAN*), and some readers approach or write about works through character studies. This is not an approach followed by many academic critics, because of the risk of treating FICTIONAL personages as real people. A.C. Bradley's classic study *Shakespearean Tragedy* (1904) went out of fashion for a time because it argued that characters (e.g. Hamlet and King Lear) were the essential element. L.C. Knights' equally classic ESSAY 'How Many Children had Lady Macbeth?' (1933) argued that it is pointless to try to establish background information about FICTIONAL characters.

There are certainly critical problems with treating fictional characters as fully rounded; and comparing a NON-FICTIONAL literary character with real-life ones isn't always much easier or more rewarding. In DRAMA, rather than speak of what, say, 'Hamlet' does on-stage, using the plural 'Hamlets' is one way of acknowledging the fact that a character is only created during a performance: e.g. 'Hamlets are generally dressed in dark colours onstage, but the one in this performance wasn't.' There is a difference between character (a fictional part), a role (what ACTORS play), and the ACTOR (who performs a role to realise a character). Although writers and performers are crucial in establishing character, in all literary genres the reader or audience is equally vital to the process.

Characterization has also inspired critical debate. Some writers, particularly in DRAMA, make use of TYPES and STOCK CHARACTERS such as the old miser. These characters, and many others, do not develop during a work and remain static; others are dynamic and progress over the work.

E.M. Forster made an influential, though disputable, distinction between FLAT AND ROUND CHARACTERS, i.e. that flat characters are basically CARICATURES, whereas round characters are more complex and complete creations. Yet Charles Dickens' 'flat characters' are insightful miniature studies of human traits that together provide a rich, true-to-life microcosm of society in novels like *Bleak House* (1852). By contrast, George Eliot's *Middlemarch* (1871) analyses the complex network of motivations and relations between characters, but is not necessarily more accurate or insightful for portraying more 'rounded' characters.

Character names bring to light another CRITERION by which characterization is judged: the difference between showing and telling an audience what a character is like. 'Showing' means allowing description, action, dialogue and sometimes narration to create an unobtrusive impression of an character. Since the twentieth century, 'showing' is generally preferred to 'telling', which involves direct introduction to characters, often with comments from the NARRATOR about their personality. In the twentieth century, for example in THEATRE OF THE ABSURD, writers tested the notion that characters need to be life-like at all. Readers still have ample scope to hold opinions about a character's personality, and how that character is being portrayed by the AUTHOR: in other words, character and characterization are inseparable.

cheville (French, 'plug') Any word or phrase that fills a gap in the metre, but contributes little to the sense. It's good to remember that poets do this, though the term is a little obscure. In this stanza from Andrew Marvell's 'The Definition of Love' (ll. 9–12), 'does' and 'and' are arguably chevilles:

> And yet I quickly might arrive
> Where my extended soul is fixed;
> But fate does iron wedges drive,
> And always crowds itself betwixt.

chiasmus (**adj. chiastic**; ky-**az**-muss; Greek, 'crossing' (from the letter chi, X)) A FIGURE involving the REPETITION of two words or ideas in reverse, creating an *abba* pattern. ANTIMETABOLE occurs when the same two words are repeated. It can be combined with ANTITHESIS, OXYMORON, and ANADIPLOSIS. In almost all cases, it creates an elegant and pithy summary. It was particularly popular in eighteenth-century verse for its symmetry.

Chicago critics A group of academics at the University of Chicago in the 1950s who followed what was known as 'neo-Aristotelianism'. The main figure is Ronald Crane, and the key text is *Critics and*

Criticism (1952). Its foundations are in thoughts about critical practice (METACRITICISM) and doubts about NEW CRITICISM, which the Chicago critics found narrowly SUBJECTIVE in its approach. So a properly OBJECTIVE critical style was encouraged, and the Chicago critics focused on the same elements that Aristotle was interested in: especially PLOT, CHARACTER and DICTION as elements that encouraged a response to the whole work (see also 'contextual criticism'). The distinction between FORM and STRUCTURE was important. It came at the beginning of the general movement in CRITICISM away from narrow FORMALIST readings to consideration of larger questions of history and RHETORIC, issues which these same critics addressed in later works.

children's literature Writing aimed at children or young adults. Though fairy stories and other traditional FORMS existed much earlier, children's literature only existed as a separate GENRE from around the middle of the eighteenth century, and led to ADAPTATIONS of CLASSIC works; e.g. Charles and Mary Lamb's *Tales from Shakespeare* (1807). There is a case that writing specifically directed at children should be read and thought about separately from other works of literature, but then it can often be difficult to draw the distinction in practice; e.g. whether J.K. Rowling's *Harry Potter* books are still children's literature, despite having been read by so many adults.

Chinese box An old-fashioned term referring to a story that contains other stories within it. 'Russian doll' will be a more familiar image to many. FRAME STORY is preferable as a technical term; it describes the larger story, rather than a system of interrelated, 'Chinese box' stories. Roald Dahl's 'The Wonderful Story of Henry Sugar' (1977), for example, contains numerous 'Chinese box' narratives enclosed within the larger story: the narrator describes Henry Sugar's experiences, and Henry reports the life-story of Imrat Khan, an Indian yogi, who in turn talks about his master, Banerjee. It is almost accidental in this case, but is often introduced as a structural DEVICE: e.g. in Emily Brontë's *Wuthering Heights* (1847), the NARRATIVE is the visitor's report of what the housekeeper knows about the Linton family. This is a literary strategy that distances the reader from the events described, and so would usually be called a 'FRAME STORY'.

chivalric romance A medieval NARRATIVE in poetry or prose that features questing knights and courtly values, such as courage, loyalty and courtesy. They are normally written in a high STYLE befitting upper-class PROTAGONISTS. It was a Europe-wide form of literature, and its subject-matter is similarly international. The four standard divisions are: Matter of Britain (ARTHURIAN); Matter of England (native HEROES); Matter of France (Charlemagne and co.) and Matter of Rome (Troy). Thomas Malory's *Morte d'Arthur* (1485) is the great example in English.

chorus A group of performers who react to and comment on the action, particularly in DRAMA. The chorus is an important element of Greek TRAGEDY, and often guides the audience's reaction. A tragic chorus is typically shocked and afraid at disaster and the gods' wrath, but quick to provide interpretation of events. The chorus does this by singing and dancing in masks on the stage, sometimes in choric ODES. In EARLY MODERN drama the chorus has become an individual who introduces the action, such as John Gower in William Shakespeare's *Pericles*. 'Chorus' is also an alternative term for REFRAIN (e.g. most pop songs have a chorus), and can refer to a large group of singers, normally divided into four voice parts.

The chorus is thought to have its origins in Ancient Greek religious rituals before becoming an element of tragedy. According to Nietzsche in *The Birth of Tragedy*, the chorus performed DIONYSIAN rituals in a precursor of drama: they took part in spontaneous and passionate events with each individual losing themselves in the group. As the PROTAGONIST emerged in TRAGEDY, and then the second and third ACTORS, this group dynamic was diluted as rational-thinking CHARACTERS became prominent. Theatre became more APOLLONIAN as the individual became more prominent, and Nietzsche blamed Euripides in particular for hastening the irreversible rise of RHETORIC and self-conscious performance. Nietzsche's account has factual flaws, but the concept remains worthy of attention.

chronicle A prose narrative of historical events, usually presented in chronological order. Medieval chronicles are important sources for our knowledge of the Middle Ages, and have been used as material for later literature too: Bede's *Ecclesiastical History* (c.730) and Geoffrey of Monmouth's *Historia Regum Britanniae* (c.1135) are crucial texts. Raphael Holinshed's *Chronicles* (1577) is a late example of the chronicle. See 'CHRONICLE PLAY' and 'HISTORY PLAY' for details of the influence of these works on dramatists. Into the seventeenth century chronicles were gradually replaced by BIOGRAPHY, TRAVEL WRITING and other forms of NON-FICTIONAL writing.

chronicle play An alternative term for an ELIZABETHAN HISTORY PLAY. The term is often used to describe any play with historical CONTENT; however, it is most appropriate to use 'chronicle' for sixteenth-century DRAMAS that use early chronicle histories (e.g. Bede's and Geoffrey of Monmouth's) and Raphael Holinshed's *Chronicles* (1577) as source materials. William Shakespeare frequently made use of Holinshed's work in his history plays. The chronicle play is a development of the MEDIEVAL MORALITY PLAY and PAGEANT into a popular secular form. Thomas Sackville and Thomas Norton's *Gorboduc* (1561) is based on British chronicle history (and is regarded as the earliest English TRAGEDY).

Ciceronian A style of ORATORY associated with Cicero, characterized by lengthy, weighted PERIODS with well-balanced subordinate CLAUSES. It was very influential on European Renaissance HUMANISTS, some of whom even strove to use only vocabulary that Cicero used (Erasmus ridiculed this form of IMITATION in *Ciceronianus* (1528)). It is an elaborate and refined form of composition, but can be very rigid. The Ciceronian style gradually lost favour as it was increasingly considered very conservative and pompous.

circumlocution (Latin, 'speaking around') An alternative term for PERIPHRASIS.

city comedy A COMIC DRAMA about and set in Jacobean (1603–25) London: e.g. Ben Jonson's *Bartholomew Fair* (1614).

classic An exceptional, exemplary and/or enduring work. A 'classic' is one or more of these things. The general sense is that a classic will be read for many decades after its initial composition, and will provide an example to later writers. If a work continues to be talked about and studied over time, then it will gradually be acknowledged as a classic. Mark Twain, however, was more sceptical: he defined 'classic' as 'a book which people praise and don't read'. All 'classic' works, whether or not people actually read them, are part of the literary CANON. An 'instant classic' is something thought certain to have this longevity as soon as it is made available. 'Classic' rarely refers to the cultures of Ancient Greece and Rome now: however, 'Classics' is the related subject, and 'classical' the usual adjective.

classicism (adj. classical) The principles and STYLE associated with Ancient Greece and Rome. NEOCLASSICISM is the intense interest in classical ideals that emerged in the eighteenth century, though classicism was already central to RENAISSANCE HUMANISM and the EARLY MODERN period in general. The term 'Middle Ages' shows the dominance of classical culture in the Western mindset: it describes a whole millennium (c.400–1400) as an in-between period in which classical ideas languished, before being taken up again around the fifteenth century across Europe.

Classicism is a broad term and difficult to define with absolute precision, especially when contrasted with ROMANTICISM. Major elements of classicism include: interest in classical languages and RHETORIC; classical forms, such as TRAGEDY and EPIC; proportion and balance; directness and simplicity; DECORUM, order and social stability; and an emphasis on rationalism over faith. Aristotle's *Poetics* and Horace's *De Arte Poetica* are the key texts that defined the classical STYLE in literature, though IMITATION of classical AUTHORS was by no means limited to these two texts. Virgil and Cicero (see 'Ciceronian') were highly influential, for example, on the development of VERNACULAR language. A typical EARLY MODERN, humanist education made children aspire to classical ideals and standards, and only in the late twentieth century has classical learning become a more exclusive and rarely studied discipline. ROMANTICISM, broadly defined, is a reaction to the principles of classicism: it brought out the vital importance of individual spontaneity and nature against the shared urban ideals of classicism. One line of thought is that classicism encourages social cohesion and stability, and was discarded once Western society was so affluent that communal survival was less urgent. Nature was no longer such a threat, but something to have idealistic thoughts and write poetry about.

clause A section of a SENTENCE which contains its own subject and verb. Clauses are usually separated by PUNCTUATION marks: commas (,), COLA (:) and SEMICOLA (;). The principle subject, verb and object are contained in the **main clause**, and all other clauses (usually joined together by a CONJUNCTION) are **subordinate**. In the sentence 'Michael missed the match, because he slipped away to Scotland', 'Michael [...] match' is the main clause, and 'slipped [...] Scotland' is the subordinate clause which adds detail to the main clause. In literary language it is sometimes difficult to untangle main and subordinate clauses, but it is essential to do so to grasp the meaning.

clerihew A piece of LIGHT VERSE, consisting of a QUATRAIN divided into two RHYMING COUPLETS.

cliché (adj. clichéd) A memorable phrase that has been used so often that it has lost the impact it originally had. Many clichés are dead METAPHORS: e.g. 'raining cats and dogs', 'every dog has its day', 'let sleeping dogs lie', 'dog-eat-dog' and 'tail wagging the dog'. Some clichés are specialist terms picked up by the media, like 'credit crunch'. In general, clichés show that language is always changing, and that words gradually take on new meanings as they are used. Because they are intrinsically unoriginal, clichés are effectively the opposite of literary language, and would only be found in PARODY or works replicating COLLOQUIAL speech.

climax The moment in a play or story to which all the previous action has been leading. It is often a moment of CRISIS, and can involve a dramatic plot twist, such as a reversal of fortune (*PERIPETEIA*), recognition (*ANAGNORISIS*), disaster (CATASTROPHE) and/or explanation (*DÉNOUEMENT*). An ANTICLIMAX is a moment that defeats the audience's expectations. 'Climax' is also a rhetorical term that refers to the increasing momentum of a speech, usually achieved through connected CLAUSES (see also 'incremental repetition').

closed couplet A pair of VERSE lines in which the sense, METRE and SYNTAX are completed at the end of the second line. The COUPLET is END-STOPPED, and is almost always emphasised by RHYME. It is used often in self-contained EPIGRAMS, as well as continuous verse (such as HEROIC COUPLETS). As in this example, a change in TONE or EMPHASIS often occurs at the break between lines. It is always worth exploring how a closed couplet relates to the lines around it, or to the title (if it has one). A complete poem by Robert Herrick called 'Her Legs':

> Fain would I kiss my Julia's dainty leg,
> Which is as white and hairless as an egg.

closet drama A play written to be read or recited, rather than performed. A closet drama will nonetheless have scene changes, settings, multiple CHARACTERS and dialogue; if these features are not prominent, then the play is more likely to be described as a DRAMATIC POEM (or DRAMATIC MONOLOGUE if one speaker). SENECAN TRAGEDIES are widely held to be closet dramas, while the two best-known British examples are probably John Milton's *Samson Agonistes* (1671) and Percy Bysshe Shelley's *Prometheus Unbound* (1820). The term is sometimes used in a general sense for any play that is no longer performed, and is only encountered by being read (by specialists).

coda (from Latin, 'tail') A short, concluding section at the end of a work, often pointing towards the wider consequences of what has gone before. A TAIL-RHYMED stanza provides opportunity for a FORMAL poetic coda, but a coda need not be formally marked. An EPILOGUE is very similar from a coda, but is separated to the rest of the TEXT.

codex (pl. codices; Latin, 'block of wood) A book of manuscripts. Much of the surviving Old English verse is held in four codices: *The Vercelli Book*, *The Exeter Book*, *The Nowell Codex* and the *Junius Manuscript*.

coinage The creation of a new word or phrase; also the expression created. NEOLOGISM is an alternative term.

collation (from Latin, 'compare') A twentieth-century editorial practice in which an editor gathers together different versions of a work to create an authoritative TEXT, the one that the AUTHOR 'would have wanted'. The notion of finding the ideal text has been discredited in BIBLIOGRAPHIC STUDIES. Most editors now prefer to consider the so-called SOCIOLOGY OF TEXTS, and appreciate the unique importance of each version of a work. Editors of *Hamlet*, for example, once tried to combine the three different versions that survive (first and second QUARTOS and FOLIO) into a definitive single version. Now they are more likely to select one version as a COPYTEXT and use the other EDITIONS to EMEND errors in that version.

collective unconscious A concept associated with the psychologist Karl Jung that describes the set of images and ideas shared by a whole community, which is manifested in MYTHS and ARCHETYPES. Jung criticised Sigmund Freud's brand of psychoanalysis for concentrating too much on the individual UNCONSCIOUS: Jungian PSYCHOANALYTIC CRITICISM looked for more universal patterns. For example, the OEDIPUS COMPLEX is said to reveal a truth about jealousy and desire in Western society's collective unconscious, but becomes ridiculous if applied to individual desire. MYTHIC(AL) and ARCHETYPAL CRITICISM both branched off from the idea of collective unconscious.

colloquialism (Latin, 'speaking together') A word or phrase used in everyday speech. Colloquialisms are informal, relaxed uses of language, but nonetheless follow CONVENTION. Most speakers of a language would understand a colloquialism; by contrast, SLANG is more innovative and restricted to a certain social group. In British English, 'dosh', 'dough' and 'bread' are colloquialisms for money, whereas 'moolah', 'cheese' and 'paper' are distinctly slangy. In literature, colloquialisms are used to convey VERNACULAR, DEMOTIC or DIALECT speech.

colon (pl. cola, colons) A PUNCTUATION mark (:) used to introduce quotations and lists, and to separate CLAUSES where the second one builds on the first (Clare is smart: she won first prize). In earlier usages, it marks a break within rhetorical PERIODS, with 'colon' providing the name for separate clauses in the PERIOD. These meanings have different plural forms: 'cola' for multiple clauses, 'colons' for multiple ':' signs.

comedy (adj. comic, comedic; Greek, *komos*, 'revel, village-singer') A DRAMA with a happy ending, written to make an audience smile or laugh. The adjective '**comic**' is a general term for something associated with 'comedy'. '**Comedic**' is the specific technical term for something containing elements of comedy, and 'comical' means something is funny: a silly moustache is part of a 'comedic' costume, and would hopefully be 'comical' to the audience.

Unlike TRAGEDY, there are no real theories of comedy. Rather than address great themes of life and death, comedy has always focused more on ordinary life and individual foibles. Comedy is created from pleasantly unexpected incidents. It generally has a sense of POETIC JUSTICE, and offers a reassuring celebration of life and love at some level. It presents an optimistic view of the world and society. These features are all blurred in FORMS like TRAGICOMEDY and BLACK COMEDY. A common distinction made is between HIGH COMEDY (clever, witty and graceful) and LOW COMEDY (crude, physical, blunt), which both provoke different kinds of laughter.

Comedy is more period-specific than tragedy, and makes us more aware of historical distance between TEXTS and later readers: many people today would find sitcoms funnier than Shakespearean comedies. This doesn't mean that Shakespeare isn't funny, just that tastes change over time. 'Comedy' is normally used to describe plays, sketches and other types of performance, but has close equivalents in LIGHT VERSE and comic PROSE FICTION. In literary criticism there is a general tendency to concentrate on the gloomier portrayals of life, but that doesn't mean that criticism is never serious about comedy. It is true, however, that comedy is a diverse, universal form of performance, and one that could never be simply classified and analysed as a tidy literary GENRE.

comedy of humours COMIC DRAMA featuring CHARACTERS based on the contemporary theory of the four HUMOURS, written around the turn of the seventeenth century and the following decades. It created STOCK CHARACTERS who were PERSONIFICATIONS of certain types of behaviour: e.g. melancholic or cowardly. Earlier FORMS of DRAMA (e.g. INTERLUDE and MORALITY PLAY) had presented ALLEGORICAL portraits of character; the comedy of humours added a physiological component to the tradition. The first major examples are Ben Jonson's *Every Man in His Humour* (1598) and *Every Man out of His Humour* (1599).

comedy of manners A COMIC DRAMA that makes fun of social CONVENTIONS and CHARACTER TYPES familiar from real life. The term is often used to refer specifically to RESTORATION comedies, which are elegant but cynical depictions of misunderstanding and mishaps in upper-class families (e.g. William Congreve's *Way of the World* (1700)). It was considered a morally suspect form of COMEDY and slowly gave way to more upstanding

SENTIMENTAL COMEDIES in the eighteenth century. However, the comedy of manners is really a much broader FORM, one which covers anything from Greek comedy and DRAWING ROOM COMEDY to American sitcoms like *Seinfeld* (1990–98). It often contains quick-witted REPARTEE, exposure of individuals' greed and lust, and comedy that is funny because the audience recognises the situations being shown.

comic relief A light-hearted moment within a serious-minded work. COMIC RELIEF could be a simple phrase, a piece of SLAPSTICK, a small FARCE or a whole SUBPLOT. The JIG at the end of Renaissance TRAGEDIES is similar in intention. They are often included by dramatists aware of the need to relieve tension in the audience. It can also comment on or PARODY the main action.

command-point The area of a stage where ACTORS are visible to the whole audience.

commedia dell'Arte A Italian form of COMEDY, particularly popular in late MEDIEVAL and RENAISSANCE Italy. It was based on STOCK CHARACTERS like the miserly old man, clever servant, and pair of lovers. It was partly improvised, and included plenty of MIME and FARCE. *Commedia dell'Arte* means 'comedy of the professional actors', and each player would play the same type of role in every production. Troupes performing *commedia dell'Arte* toured Europe in the sixteenth century, and influenced DRAMA in numerous countries, such as England. Critics have shown the influence of *commedia dell'Arte* on Shakespearean DRAMA, and it lives on in Britain through the Punch and Judy puppet show.

common measure A STANZA FORM consisting of four LINES (a QUATRAIN) with four STRESSES (TETRAMETER) in the first and third lines, and three (TRIMETER) in the second and fourth lines. Its RHYME scheme is usually *abab*, and sometimes *abcb*. It is almost identical to BALLAD METRE (and to rhyming FOURTEENERS), but common measure is often used to describe HYMNS, a FORM which grew out of popular BALLADS; indeed, it is sometimes known as the hymnal STANZA. See 'quatrain' for a comparison with the related forms LONG, POULTER'S and SHORT MEASURES.

commonplace book A collection of quotations and ideas, often gathered under chapter headings. Commonplace books were essential to the HUMANIST education, and taught school children to pick out and reuse memorable phrases from CLASSICAL AUTHORS. Desiderius Erasmus's *Adagia* (1500 onwards) helped establish commonplacing (see 'adage') as an educational technique. Most commonplace books were handwritten (John Milton's still exists, for example), though several appeared in print, such as Ben Jonson's *Timber: Or Discoveries* (1640). Commonplace books have been studied for what they tell us about how EARLY MODERN individuals read and thought. The principle isn't so different from modern writers who keep notebooks of their ideas.

Commonwealth (1649–1660) Relating to the period between the execution of King Charles and the RESTORATION of the monarchy. It is also known as the Interregnum ('between kings') period. Theatres were closed in this period because Oliver Cromwell's government was Puritan, and literature often addressed the political situation (see p. 365 for writing from this period). 'Commonwealth' once described writing by citizens of former British colonies, but in LITERARY CRITICISM the broader term 'POSTCOLONIAL' is now preferred.

comparative literature A critical discipline that studies the literature of two or more cultures alongside either other. Study of CLASSICAL influences on European literature is a form of comparative literature (or comp lit), as is, for example, comparing contemporary Chinese and American poetry. Literature in TRANSLATION and translation theory both fall within the category 'comparative literature' too. Comparative studies often look for underlying cultural similarities, or even the deeper truths that unify literature. In this sense, comparative literature could be understood as a successor of MYTHIC(AL) CRITICISM, ARCHETYPAL CRITICISM and the STRUCTURALIST concept of *LANGUE*. The idea of universal inborn linguistic COMPETENCE also supports truly comparative studies. It encourages globally aware CRITICISM that looks beyond national boundaries, and encourages sensitivity to other cultures. Many great scholars have written mould-breaking studies that could be categorised as comparative literature.

Yet comparative literature is not a fully established discipline. The top U.S. universities have departments, but few British ones do. Part of the problem is that INTERDISCIPLINARY research is often more convincing if scholars are recognised as having a single speciality. Rather than have a set of scholars dedicated to comparative literature, it makes sense for individuals to branch out of their area to consider wider questions, ones which may have productive connections with related fields. Comparative literature, in this model, is an approach you gravitate towards, rather than start from. All the same, T.S. Eliot was right to observe that comparison (along with ANALYSIS) remains essential to literary criticism.

competence A term used by the American linguist Noam Chomsky to describe our inborn understanding of language. Competence is an UNCONSCIOUS 'innate grammar' that suggests that all humans share a universal ability to use language. This is shown in the fact that small children can understand how GRAMMATICAL sentences work before learning the rules. It can also explain how readers can understand the CONVENTIONS of a work without previous knowledge of a GENRE: e.g. when reading a detective story, you automatically expect a great revelation (*DÉNOUEMENT*) in the final pages. Competence is similar to the STRUCTURALIST concept of *LANGUE*, i.e. the system of signs we used to communicate. Specific speech acts are known as *parole* in Ferdinand de Saussure's terminology, and 'performance' in Chomsky's thought. Both competence and *langue* claim to explain the essence of creative thought and literature. It has been criticised by POST-STRUCTURALISTS and others unwilling to accept that language has such inbuilt universal characteristics.

complaint A SONG or LYRIC POEM that bewails the cruelty of FATE. It is an ancient literary form: the Roman poet Catullus, for example, wrote numerous savage complaints directed at past mistresses. Complaints can be SATIRIC or DIDACTIC, and are more aggressive than related, more grief-stricken forms like ELEGY, LAMENT and DIRGE. Complaints were still being written in the seventeenth century; Edmund Spenser's book of *Complaints* (1591) is one of the last main examples. The closest modern equivalents are often DRAMATIC MONOLOGUES.

conceit An ingenious and elaborate METAPHOR that makes an unconventional comparison. A PETRARCHAN conceit draws an identity between two dissimilar physical phenomena (e.g. burning ice), while a METAPHYSICAL conceit takes an image that seems to have little to do with the emotion or theme being discussed. The conceit of John Donne's 'The Flea', for example, is that flea-bites mix blood in the same way that marriage does. Conceits can be contained within a single line, or can govern the structure of an entire poem. They can be combined with HYPERBOLE (exaggeration), PARADOX and OXYMORON. A conceit has an intellectual CONTENT that CATACHRESIS (far-fetched metaphor) lacks. In addition to displaying an AUTHOR'S WIT, conceits provoke questions about how suitable FIGURATIVE LANGUAGE is for describing truth.

concordance An index of all the words contained within a work or complete works of an AUTHOR. The words are listed alphabetically, and it is easy to find out how many times and where a word appears. There are many printed concordances, as well as easily-found internet versions—though as ever with online material, one should be sure that the source is reliable first. Concordances can be very useful when writing ESSAYS, particularly when paired with the *Oxford English Dictionary* to pin down the history of a word.

concrete language A form of expression suggesting something existing in a physical state, so can be sensed: e.g. 'duck', 'diamond' and 'doodle' are concrete nouns. For PLATONIC and literary CONNOTATIONS of 'concrete', see 'abstract language'. Unconnected with CONCRETE POETRY.

concrete poetry A verse form involving unusual LINEATION that gives a poem visual interest and can be more important than the SEMANTIC meaning of the words on the page. The term is sometimes used as a SYNONYM for PATTERN POETRY, but particularly refers to a group of post-1950 poets. Concrete poetry raises important questions about what 'READING' and 'INTERPRETATION' involve, and the border-line between POETRY and visual art.

confessional literature AUTOBIOGRAPHICAL writing that contains personal revelation. There are numerous prose examples in English, such as Thomas De Quincey's *Confessions of an English Opium Eater* (1822), which merge childhood experience and dreams. 'Confessional' describes poetry that seems to put the AUTHOR'S state of mind on paper, and implies thoughts of depression and despair. Indeed, three major 'confessional poets' who published major collections in the 1960s all killed themselves: Anne Sexton (AUTHOR of *To Bedlam and Part Way Back* (1960)), Sylvia Plath (*Ariel* (1965)) and John Berryman (*The Dream Songs* (1969)) all killed themselves. Though confessional literature is strongly personal, the BIOGRAPHICAL FALLACY still holds: such writing isn't just a transcript of someone's thoughts.

confidant A minor CHARACTER who provides opportunity for a PROTAGONIST or leading character to express his or her thoughts aloud in dialogue, instead of in a SOLILOQUY. A confidant is a literary DEVICE that gives a writer to provide further information. Confidants like servants or waiting women rarely influence the action. The most engaging confidants are those that seem to represent the audience's point of view. Arthur Conan Doyle, for example, constantly uses Dr Watson as a confidant to ask Sherlock Holmes all the questions on the audience's mind, to which Holmes tells the audience that the answer is 'elementary, my dear Watson!'(or something similar—Holmes never actually uses this phrase).

conflict A struggle in a literary work, whether between two CHARACTERS in a DRAMA (see 'agon'), or against FATE, an environment or something else. Most literary works involve a conflict/ structural TENSION of some variety that is usually brought to resolution by or at the conclusion.

conjunction A word that connects two CLAUSES: 'and', 'but', 'because', 'when', 'therefore', 'although', 'if', 'however', 'nevertheless' and 'yet' are the main ones. HYPOTACTIC writing uses conjunctions to show the logical progression of thought; PARATACTIC writing has no clear continuity because it omits conjunctions (ASYNDETON) or only uses simple 'and'.

connotation Associations suggested by a word, as opposed to its literal meaning (or DENOTATION). A word's connotation will be not be found in a dictionary; it is particular to a culture, group or individual. AMBIGUITY, PARADOX, and TROPES (e.g. METAPHOR, METONYM, IRONY) all depend on word-connotations: in fact, literature in general is more concerned with connotation than DENOTATION. Connotation and literature are both form of interpretation, and both uncover INTERTEXTUALITY. The counter-argument to this view is an extreme NEW CRITICAL position, that words have entirely integral meanings, and the reader has to uncover the fixed meaning in a literary text.

consonance The REPETITION of the same consonant(s) within nearby words where vowels differ. It is usually used in reference to POETRY, and is primarily an AURAL effect: e.g. 'tugging at a tiger', 'the curved river'. Consonance found at the beginning of words is termed ALLITERATION ('the chilled-out children'), and at the end of words it approaches, though isn't really, HALF-RHYME ('the Dutch torch'). RHYME occurs when both vowels and consonants match; in effect, simultaneous consonance and ASSONANCE. It is sometimes hard to tell whether the use of same or similar consonants is conscious or not (as in this sentence). The guiding rule should be whether it has an effect on you as reader. Consonance marks a point at which everyday speech becomes musical, and starts to possess a literary quality. Consonance can also mean 'harmony', and in either sense creates EUPHONY. This extract from Derek Walcott's *Omeros* (1990) reveals great subtlety in how consonance and ASSONANCE shape the everyday DICTION used:

> His kettle leaked. He groped for the tin chair and took
> his place near the saucepan to hear when it bubbled.
> It would boil but not scream like a bosun's whistle

to let him know it was ready. He heard the dog's
morning whine under the boards of the house, its tail
thudding to be let in, but he envied the pirouges [canoes]
already miles out at sea. (II.ii.7–13)

content Whatever is contained in a work; the meaning communicated. Content is commonly contrasted with STYLE and FORM: the distinction is between what and how meaning is expressed. It is widely recognised that content and style/form are inseparable, and a basic task of literary criticism is to study the interaction between the two. Criticism also investigates how content is influenced by other factors: for example, the AUTHOR'S attitude to ORIGINALITY/IMITATION, ANALOGUES and other related works, REVISIONS and new EDITIONS of a work, and CENSORSHIP. 'TENOR' is almost a SYNONYM, but is often reserved for the content of a METAPHOR.

context (adj. contextual) The situation and related writing from which a particular work or passage grows. A TEXT that is part of a larger work always needs to be placed in context of the whole—otherwise you risk quoting the TEXT 'out of context'. The AUTHOR'S other works, influences and circumstances are all relevant contexts. NEW HISTORICISM has disputed that a clear boundary exists between TEXT and context, preferring instead to assume that all texts are historical documents and are therefore relevant to others written at the same time. INTERTEXTUALITY too stresses how texts are connected to each other. Only a hard-line FORMALIST critic would insist that the complete text by itself is all that matters. Most critics would agree that texts remain unknowable because the precise context of a work—every detail of the AUTHOR'S situation and thoughts when writing—cannot be retrieved. Uncovering relevant new contexts generates fresh perspectives for critical appreciation.

contextual criticism A variant of NEW CRITICISM that approaches literature within the 'closed context' of its own structures, which exists independently of the wider world. It emphasised reading a poem's parts in relation to the whole, and was outdated by the 1960s. This idea of parts and whole (a timeless literary opposition) has remained with us, even as contextual criticism was overtaken by DECONSTRUCTION and other forms of CRITICISM in the twentieth century.

contrast The technique of bringing together opposing elements or ideas in a text to highlight the difference between the two. A sharper, more formal version of contrast is ANTITHESIS. Contrast should not be mistaken for a TENSION, in the sense of a deeper interpretative difficulty underlying a text.

convention (adj. conventional; Latin, 'coming together') In a broad sense it means something that is generally agreed. In LITERATURE, a convention can mean any of the following: a specific practice, especially in the theatre; a particular subject-matter or feature common to numerous works, often in the same GENRE; more broadly, it refers to cultural structures that have a bearing on literature. Ultimately all language depends on convention, and it influences the style adopted by a WRITER or SPEAKER. At the same time, convention is not something to be passively accepted: AUTHORS work with and against it as they seek to find a unique form of expression among existing traditions.

DRAMATIC conventions are particularly common because they provide convenient solutions to problems about realistic staging. Were conventions not in place, the dramatist would have great difficulty in immersing the audience in a FICTIONAL world. The ASIDE, for example, depends on the audience knowing that what is being said is supposed to be out of ear-shot of the other CHARACTERS; if it were actually inaudible, the audience would not be able to hear either. SOLILOQUIES, the PROSCENIUM ARCH, CHORUS, and TABLEAU all involve convention too. Aristotle described many long-standing DRAMATIC conventions in the *Poetics*: e.g. the three UNITIES of action, time and place and PLOT development. Conventions change with time, however, and are not passively accepted by major dramatists: conventions are there to be manipulated and discarded as desired. Bertolt Brecht's ALIENATION EFFECT was intended to remove illusions caused by conventions, because he felt they control an audience's emotions, and stop them thinking about reality.

Traditional poetic FORMS like the SONNET and HAIKU have conventions attached to them. These too are there to be adapted: e.g. LIMERICKS create expectations about FORM and SUBJECT-MATTER that can be subverted, as in the example on p. 166. Although some works are rightly described as 'unconventional', the adjective does not mean that those works are written without an awareness of convention. Lawrence Sterne's *Tristram Shandy* is a good example: it has the external appearance of a BIOGRAPHY, but is much else besides. Moreover, innovative works produce new conventions, just as striking language turns into CLICHÉ over time. Convention shows how central IMITATION and existing TRADITIONS are to literary creation. It raise questions about ORIGINALITY in literature, and whether NATURALISTIC writing, which seeks to free itself from customs and traditions, is really possible. STRUCTURALISM stresses that writing works within the bounds of certain cultural codes; POST-STRUCTURALISM emphasises that conventions are everywhere, and that all language only takes meaning in relation to other conventions (see 'intertextuality').

copia (Latin, 'abundance') Creative expansiveness understood as the hallmark of great writers. Copia was an important concept for European HUMANISTS, and grew from the methods catalogued in Erasmus' *De Copia* (1512). The skill of developing variations on a single theme (in effect, a form of PARATAXIS) was part of school curricula across Europe. Copia indicated a fertile mind that could draw on moral goodness for inspiration. The creative heights of copia can be contrasted with 'copying' as a purely mechanical act, though copia is nonetheless closely related to Renaissance notions of IMITATION.

copyright The legal right of a work's creator to make that work available, and authorise others to do so. It is a form of protection against PIRACY and PLAGIARISM. The copyright symbol is ©. A copyright library is one that is offered a free copy of every book published in that country. The Library of Congress is the copyright library of the United States. The UK copyright libraries are: the British Library, the National Libraries of Scotland and Wales, the Library of Trinity College, Dublin, the Bodleian library (Oxford), and Cambridge University Library.

copytext A text upon which a later EDITION is based. When other versions are available, an editor will often list variant readings, and EMEND the copytext in light of those versions. Even when COLLATING editions, the editor will still have a favoured version. Some editors will take the latest edition that the AUTHOR was involved in as copytext, for it is thought to represent the author's 'final intention'; others will take the first printed edition, because it seems the purest form of the author's vision. With increasing awareness of the SOCIOLOGY OF TEXTS, each version is valued as a potential copytext. In any case, both editor and reader benefit from being aware of which text is being used, and where that text fits into the history of a work's development.

corona (also 'crown') A DEVICE that joins together a series of SONNETS or poems through repetition of the final line of one poem as the first line of the next, returning to the beginning with the last line. Coronas can form an introduction to poetic works. The major example is John Donne's 'La Corona', which prefaces his *Holy Sonnets*. ANADIPLOSIS is a related rhetorical FIGURE.

corpus (Latin, 'body') A collection of works by the same AUTHOR or on the same subject. *OEUVRE* is a term specific to an author's works, and CANON has a similar meaning.

cosmic irony A form of STRUCTURAL IRONY in which destiny raises and dashes the PROTAGONIST'S or NARRATOR'S hopes to reveal the lack of justice in the world.

coterie A small and select group of individuals, united by friendship or shared interests. The term implies a exclusive circle of the social élite, such as a French salon. Not all coteries are famous, but the BLOOMSBURY GROUP is a well-known British example.

country house poetry A fairly small group of seventeenth-century poems that celebrated country estates of noblemen. It is a form of TOPOGRAPHICAL POETRY, and shared some of the concerns of PASTORAL POETRY in viewing the country as a retreat from political and other urban trouble. Andrew Marvell's 'Upon Appleton House' (written c.1651) and Ben Jonson's 'To Penshurst' (1616) are the key examples.

coup de théâtre A sudden and unexpected plot twist that changes the direction of the action. It is difficult to translate—which is why the French term is used—but its meaning is roughly 'theatrical bolt from the blue'. It is a particularly DRAMATIC form of CRISIS. A *DEUS EX MACHINA* is a CLASSIC *coup de théâtre*.

couplet A pair of consecutive VERSE lines that are connected, usually by RHYME. Its use has been widespread for centuries in English literature: Geoffrey Chaucer was among the first English writers to use it (if not the first); it provided a CONVENTIONAL way for ELIZABETHAN and Jacobean dramatists to conclude scenes (including Shakespeare); Dryden and Pope mastered the HEROIC COUPLET in the eighteenth century; and it has continued to be used in POETRY, song LYRICS and JINGLES. It also forms part of other stanza forms, such as RHYME ROYAL and *OTTAVA RIMA*. A useful way to begin analysing couplets is to identify them as either CLOSED or OPEN COUPLETS. In this CLASSIC closed couplet from Alexander Pope, the satisfying break after 'expressed' matches the meaning perfectly:

> True wit is nature to advantage dressed;
> What oft was thought, but ne'er so well
> expressed.
>
> (*Essay on Criticism*, ll.297–98)

courtesy book A work that offers advice about how to behave. In the medieval and Renaissance periods, courtesy books were taken seriously as a guide to civilised living. 'Courtesy' meant much more than 'politeness': it suggested an ideal of courtly gracefulness, sound morals and good learning. Baldassare Castiglione's *Il libro del cortegiano* (1528) was influential across Europe, including England (having been translated in 1561). Castiglione outlined the ideal courtier as someone who possessed moral, physical and intellectual virtues, yet was able to display them with graceful ease (*sprezzatura*). Thomas Elyot's *The Boke Named the Governour* (1531) is an important English example, which offered advice about education. Edmund Spenser's *Faerie Queene* (1590, 96) shows how seriously courtesy was taken by literary writers around this time. Courtesy remained important throughout the humanist period, and it wasn't until the late seventeenth century that literature began to mock social CONVENTION in COMEDIES OF MANNERS.

courtly love A concept found in MEDIEVAL and EARLY MODERN literature based on a man's noble adoration of an idealized woman. The lover pledges service to his object, and describes his condition as a form of illness. Courtly love is bound up with cultural codes, CONVENTIONS, and courtesy in a broad, moral sense—though it often accepts adultery as necessary to fulfil true ROMANTIC love (rather than marriage arranged for practical reasons). It was later integrated with the idea of Platonic love. Courtly love is typified in CHIVALRIC ROMANCES, and a work like Geoffrey Chaucer's *The Knight's Tale*. It's debateable whether courtly love reflected social practice, or is just a literary TROPE; it's clear, however, that the women admired are not treated like real people (as FEMINIST CRITICS and others have pointed out).

creole In general terms, a language that has developed from the mixture of two others. For the English language, it is specifically a language developed when the VERNACULAR language of the coloniser (English) mixed with that of colonised countries, which includes the West Indies, Nigeria, and Singapore (creating 'Singlish'). A creole language is not just a DIALECT FORM of English. It can have GRAMMAR independent both of English and the original native language. A good example of a literary writer who uses a creole language is Linton Kwesi Johnson, a Jamaican poet regarded as the founder of Dub poetry. Here are lines from 'Doun de Road' (lines 12–25):

> terror fire terror fire reach we;
> such a suffering we suffering
> in this burning age of rage;

no place to run to get gun
and the violence damming up inside.

so in the heat
of the anguish
you jus turn:
turn on your brother

an yu lick him
an yu lash him
an stab him
an kill him

and the violence damming up inside.

cretic Another term for AMPHIMACER, i.e. a FOOT with the pattern stressed-unstressed-stressed (– o –).

crime fiction (detective fiction) A FICTIONAL work in which an illegal act is committed, and the main CHARACTER (PROTAGONIST) must work out what happened. Literary works that are driven by suspense and mystery leading to a final revelation (*ANAGNORISIS* or *DÉNOUEMENT*) have been around for millennia: Sophocles' tragedy *Oedipus Rex*, for example, contains all these elements, as do most REVENGE TRAGEDIES. Fyodor Dostoyevsky's *Crime and Punishment* (1866) is another obvious example of literary FICTION centred around a crime (and its punishment).

Crime fiction settled into the modern GENRE of **detective fiction**, in which a highly intelligent or otherwise distinctive detective solves crimes with the assistance of a side-kick/CONFIDANT. Arthur Conan Doyle's *Adventures of Sherlock Holmes* (1891) are CLASSICS of the genre. Agatha Christie and Raymond Chandler were two best-selling crime fiction writers who helped turn detective fiction into a major popular genre, common now in TV DRAMA as well as NOVELS. As a result of its great popularity, detective fiction struggles to establish itself as a topic for serious literary CRITICISM, even though it often offers more than page-turning GENRE FICTION. Patricia Highsmith, AUTHOR of *The Talented Mr Ripley* (1951) and other acclaimed psychological thrillers/crime fiction, is a good example of a writer still regarded more as a successful popular writer than a CANONICAL figure in American literature. Related GENRES that make similar use of mystery and suspense are horror story, ghost story, spy story and thriller.

crisis (pl. crises) A structural turning point in a DRAMA, typically involving a moment of recognition (or *ANAGNORISIS*) or reversal (*PERIPETEIA*). It changes the course of the PLOT, leading towards a CATASTROPHE or *DÉNOUEMENT*. The crisis is sometimes a play's CLIMAX, and sometimes leads towards one. *COUP DE THÉÂTRE* is similar in meaning, but is more unexpected. Crises can be foreshadowed with DRAMATIC IRONY, or a tragic sense of inevitability.

criterion (pl. criteria) A common standard by which to judge something. A criterion can be a critical principle: e.g. 'sharp perception is a criterion for ORIGINALITY'. It can define a tradition: e.g. 'the essential criteria for any good LIMERICK are that it should be silly and vivid'.

criticism (critic; adj. critical; from Greek, 'judge') Reflection on a literary TEXT, which can take many forms: close reading or ANALYSIS, comparison with other works, drawing out THEORETICAL implications, or evaluation. A **critic** is a person who engages in this activity. Although '**critical**' has a negative CONNOTATION when used in everyday speech ('he's critical of everyone'), it is more balanced when used for discussion of the ARTS. Given the word's ETYMOLOGICAL meaning of 'judging', some critics find giving a judgment a key aspect of literary criticism, partly on the grounds that coming to an OBJECTIVE verdict that everyone would agree with is neither likely nor particularly desirable. Equally, literary criticism that is too opinionated doesn't usually go down well with teachers and academics—not that the first-person pronoun ('I think…') needs to be avoided altogether in critical ESSAYS. Criticism is a creative act of its own: indeed, it can be an art-form. It plays a vital role in generating fresh thoughts and perspectives on a work. T.S. Eliot touches on these issues in his ESSAY 'The Function of Criticism' (1923). He describes 'interpretation' as a form of FICTION:

> We must ourselves decide what is useful to us [as readers] and what is not; and it is quite likely that we are not competent to decide. But it is fairly certain that 'interpretation' […] is only legitimate when it is not interpretation at all, but merely putting the reader in possession of facts which he would otherwise have missed.

There are many varieties of criticism (see p. 355 for a list), each of which FOREGROUNDS one aspect of literature: e.g. the text (PRACTICAL CRITICISM); historical CONTEXT (NEW HISTORICISM); problems of expression

(DECONSTRUCTION); and male dominance in society and literature (FEMINIST CRITICISM). All critics could be identified with at least one school of criticism, but that doesn't necessarily mean they follow one. No critic is wholly unique, but equally no critic can be summarised just by associating them with a critical TRADITION. For general readers, criticism can seem filled with difficult terms (i.e. those contained in this book), and intimidating and pretentious in equal measure. All critics have their opinion on what criticism is for, and theories of criticism (METACRITICISM) is its own field. One general view is that it stimulates fresh ideas about literature, and prevents thoughts stagnating. This process of engagement and reassessment of literature nurtures creative diversity, and encourages readers to make sensitive and independent judgments of their own, whether student, academic or general reader.

critique A thorough ARGUMENT or ANALYSIS. It can describe full-length treatises (e.g. Immanuel Kant's *Critique of Judgment*), but applies equally well to a detailed analysis of a literary work. It is CRITICAL, in the sense of being reflective, but does not at all imply a negative judgment. 'Critique' is primarily a noun, but can also be used as a VERB—though some writers find it inelegant to use nouns as verbs (like 'impact') and prefer 'I wrote a critique on *Peter Pan*' to 'I critiqued *Peter Pan*'.

cross rhyme A form of INTERNAL RHYME in which rhyming words are paired in the same place within consecutive lines. It often occurs within rhyming COUPLETS to create a QUATRAIN (also called ARCH RHYME), though this is sometimes referred to as LEONINE RHYME too.

crux (pl. cruces) A difficult passage in a TEXT that has no agreed interpretation. A crux arises either because of AMBIGUITY or a textual problem (i.e. variant readings or corruptions). Its resolution will often reflect how the reader approaches the TEXT as a whole. In William Shakespeare's *Hamlet* the following phrase is a crux because no-one knows for sure what it means: 'the dram of eale | Doth all the noble substance of a doubt | To his own scandal' (Q2 text, 1.4.36–38).

cultural criticism An alternative term for CULTURAL STUDIES, only even more nebulous in what it covers.

cultural studies A wide-ranging area of LITERARY CRITICISM that treats 'high' and 'low' culture as equally deserving of critical attention. It moves beyond the traditional literary CANON to consider popular GENRES, media, the internet, sport and much else besides. The term is so broad as to be vague, like its twin, CULTURAL CRITICISM: it has leanings towards POSTMODERNISM,

MARXIST CRITICISM, CULTURAL MATERIALISM and DISCOURSE ANALYSIS. It looks to broaden and democratize the horizons of literary study into areas that matter in our times. Media studies is a particular area of cultural studies that has obvious relevance and value today: it is the field dedicated to ANALYSIS of how we receive information about the world, and traditional literary criticism can certainly contribute towards that. However, as an exam option in Britain, it has unfortunately gained a reputation for being a 'soft' subject. Thinking hard about the effects of the BBC or Twitter on how we communicate and learn about the world is clearly important. However, tension remains about where cultural studies belongs as an applied form of literary criticism. It's certainly a boundary worth pushing.

cultural materialism A field of criticism that shows how culture interacts with historical and political conditions over time. It is 'cultural' because its focus is on all areas of expression, but it tends to focus on CANONICAL works because these exert the greatest political influence. It is 'materialist' because its focus is on social, cultural and economic conditions of a period, rather than universal ideas. Its focus is on recovering historical information, particularly about how literature helps to control groups by promoting IDEOLOGY. This is a major difference from MARXIST CRITICISM, which is more interested in showing how literature is shaped by history (rather than vice versa).

It is known as the British version of NEW HISTORICISM, and shares with its American equivalent a refusal to recognise any difference between TEXT and CONTEXT, or to accept 'LITERATURE' as a category of its own. Cultural materialists range more broadly over history than NEW HISTORICISTS do: for example, only cultural materialists would consider why Shakespeare is included in today's school curricula, and what effect this has. Another difference is that cultural materialists are more engaged with how individuals shape culture, even if they are also affected by historical circumstances beyond their control. Also, although both approaches are allied to POST-STRUCTURALISM, cultural materialists consider themselves more broad-minded about its application; e.g. less inclined to follow Michel Foucault's ideas about the impersonal systems of thought that shape the individual. In other words, cultural materialism lays down theoretical foundations of CULTURAL STUDIES/CULTURAL CRITICISM.

curtal sonnet Gerard Manley Hopkins's name for a shortened ('curtal') FORM of the fourteen-line SONNET. It contains ten lines, divided into a six- and four-line stanza, with a half-line to finish. 'Pied Beauty' (quoted in the entry on SPRUNG RHYTHM) and 'Peace' are two curtal sonnets.

cybercriticism A vague term that has been used for a couple of different critical practices. It describes a companion to ECOCRITICISM; i.e. exploration of the relationship between humans and technology. Mary Shelley's *Frankenstein* (1818) is a seminal text here, in an approach that otherwise blends with literary NATURALISM. 'Cybercriticism' can also describe critical work on how contemporary digital culture affects reading (questions also are taken up by some TEXTUAL CRITICS and BIBLIOGRAPHERS), and criticism on works published in new forms (e.g. online or in E-BOOKS). Matters worth thinking about, but the actual term isn't much use.

cyberfiction (cyberpunk) A SCIENCE-FICTION work that examines the relation of humans and machines. Cyberpunk fiction depicts a DYSTOPIAN future world in which the machines have taken control, and it requires a group of anarchic rebels ('punks') to regain control. William Gibson's *Neuromancer* (1984) was an seminal work of cyberfiction.

cycle A group of works that can be experienced separately, but belong within a larger design. Homer's *Iliad* is a cycle of various sections of oral poetry, merged into an EPIC NARRATIVE; Geoffrey Chaucer's *Canterbury Tales* (1387–1400) have a FRAME STORY that turns the individual tales into a cycle; the MYSTERY PLAYS were arranged into cycles that related a biblical narrative from Creation to Judgment Day; and ELIZABETHAN SONNET SEQUENCES are all cycles. A group of three is a trilogy; a group of four is a TETRALOGY (as with Shakespeare's HISTORY PLAYS).

D

dactyl (adj. dactylic, Greek, 'finger') A METRICAL FOOT consisting of one STRESSED SYLLABLE followed by two unstressed ones. 'Gracefully' and 'fortunate' are naturally dactylic words. It is so named (and easily remembered) because fingers and dactyls are both formed from one long and two short sections. Along with ANAPAESTS they form the basis of TERNARY METRES; however, in sequence it is sometimes hard to tell dactyls and anapaests apart. A dactylic metre creates a FALLING RHYTHM. Dactylic HEXAMETER (lines of six dactyls) is associated with EPIC poetry and ELEGIES: Homer and Virgil both used it. However, dactylic metres have always been rare in English because they are so restrictive, and epic VERSE has more commonly been written in BLANK VERSE.

death of the author The title of a 1967 ESSAY by the French critic Roland Barthes that argued against the 'AUTHOR' having any control over the meaning of a TEXT. The phrase recalls Nietzsche's announcement that 'God is dead': Barthes maintained that the author's godlike presence over a work was a deceptive illusion. Instead, he emphasised the structures that create meaning (see 'structuralism'), and the reader's role in deciding upon an interpretation. Barthes was offering a more thunderous version of NEW CRITICISM's principle of INTENTIONAL FALLACY, and helped point the way to POST-STRUCTURALISM and NEW HISTORICISM (see 'author' for more detail).

débat A MEDIEVAL poetic contest on THEMES of morality or politics. It often involved PERSONIFIED CHARACTERS, as in the late-medieval poem *The Owl and the Nightingale* (c.1200). It is a form of literary dialogue that is like a FABLE or ALLEGORY, and was succeeded by DRAMATIC forms like the MORALITY PLAY and INTERLUDE. A quick poetic exchange between speakers is known as AMOEBEAN VERSE.

decadence In general, the term means a decline from former greatness, but with a capital 'D' it refers to a late nineteenth-century French literary movement (with Charles Baudelaire as its leading light) that promoted the superiority of the artist, and extravagant, sensation-filled indulgence. In its elitist pursuit of art rather than CONVENTION, it is connected to AESTHETICISM and PRE-RAPHAELITISM in Britain. Its general outlook holds a fair amount in common with the BEAT movement a century later.

decasyllabic An adjective describing a ten-syllable line. The term is rarely used in English PROSODY, because most decasyllabic lines are either IAMBIC or TROCHAIC PENTAMETER (five stress, ten syllable lines). Certainly the decasyllabic line is central to the development of English poetry, but for ACCENTUAL-SYLLABIC verse (i.e. where the number of stresses also matters) the term is not as precise as 'PENTAMETER' is.

deconstruction An influential approach to literary ANALYSIS developed by the controversial French philosopher Jacques Derrida (1930–2004). The term should never be used as a clever-sounding SYNONYM for 'destruction' because it carries lots of theoretical baggage with it. If anything, it is much closer to the ETYMOLOGICAL sense of analysis ('breaking down'). Deconstructionist criticism is typically sophisticated and difficult to read. This is no bad thing in itself, though it is sometimes criticised for being pretentious. Its basic principles aren't that hard to grasp, however.

Deconstruction ruthlessly unsettles meaning. Derrida sought to expose the basic instability of all language, in reaction to the fixed structures proposed by STRUCTURALISTS and FORMALISTS. It shows that any TEXT is saying something different to what it first appears to mean, but that its TEXTUALITY is inescapable. With AMBIGUITY apparently everywhere, meaning collapses and we are left with 'nothing outside the text' ('*rien hors du texte*'). A word has no DENOTATION, but endless CONNOTATIONS.

Derrida's work begins with Ferdinand de Saussure's CLASSIC distinction between SIGNIFIER and SIGNIFIED, and brings the principle that SIGNS only hold meaning in relation to others to an almost nihilistic conclusion. Deconstruction insists that all meaning is created from CONTEXTS: social, legal, linguistic and political (cf. NEW HISTORICISM). Western thought has always resisted this fluidity, Derrida argued, because of its fixation upon LOGOS. A LOGOCENTRIC culture—or PHALLOGOCENTRIC, if this thought is tied to male social dominance—is one that finds meaning guaranteed by this timeless concept of the Word. This is associated with the age-old priority given to speech over writing. This speech/writing dichotomy was one of many other TENSIONS that Derrida identified as artificial, including the crucial opposition of ABSENCE/PRESENCE. Presence indicates authority, and deconstruction claims that the presence implied by a speech act—someone being there to say something—doesn't solve any of the problems associated with language. Speech and writing are equally unstable. '*DIFFÉRANCE*' is the name given to this endless deferral of meaning (Derrida liked PUNS: this one plays on the French for 'defer' and 'differ'). Indeterminacy and indecision are the only options left open to the critic: a state of APORIA.

For literary studies, then, this encourages a form of close ANALYSIS that engages with this instability across all literary GENRES. It makes study of FIGURATIVE LANGUAGE important (because nothing is literally true), and in this regard deconstruction makes literature relevant to wider philosophical concerns. A group of critics at Yale University—Paul de Man, Harold Bloom, Geoffrey Hartman, J. Hillis Miller were the main players—did most to advance deconstruction as a serious form of literary analysis. Deconstruction has never called itself a theory—texts deconstruct themselves—but many people consider it an extreme form of literary theorising. It accepts itself as ultimately self-contradictory (it presents clear ideas about there being no final meaning), and this makes it peculiarly invulnerable to criticism. Like any school of literary thought, deconstruction is only something truly negative if it becomes so widely accepted that it frustrates other forms of debate—and this has not happened. Deconstruction has influenced other areas of criticism: in particular, it is central to POST-STRUCTURALIST thought, and is linked with the founding of POSTCOLONIAL CRITICISM. This is thanks in part to Gayatri Chakravorty Spivak, who translated Derrida's major work *Of Grammatology* (1976).

decorum In literature, the matching up of subject matter, CHARACTER and setting with an appropriate STYLE. Decorum is, in its basic form, an issue of clarity: if a window-cleaner spoke like an investment banker and vice versa for no reason, it would simply cause confusion. But decorum means more than this: it approaches literature with fixed notions of civility and seemliness. It is very much a CLASSICAL idea, which was described (but not introduced) by Horace in *De Arte Poetica*. This idea of appropriateness was later embraced by NEOCLASSICAL writers. The system of high, middle and low styles (see this entry for more) proper to the subject matter— HEROES were written about in EPICS, low-lifes in COMEDY—is a clear extension of principles of decorum.

Decorum is a conservative principle that reinforces social norms. It is unsurprising, then, that ROMANTICISM sought to overturn traditional decorum (see 'vernacular'). It poses an interesting question regarding IMITATION: on the one hand decorum is all about finding suitable ways to describe human beings in literature, and yet it perpetuates shared opinions about the world without questioning them. Perhaps, then, decorum is similar to CONVENTION: something that causes confusion and inconsistency if ignored, but which must be used mindfully.

defamiliarization (Russian, *ostranenie*) The process by which everyday language is made to seem unusual to the reader. It is an important concept in RUSSIAN FORMALISM (associated with Viktor Shklovsky) that accounts for the LITERARINESS of literature. Literary FOREGROUNDING of the use of language makes the reader aware of the techniques used by an AUTHOR to convey meaning (e.g. METAPHOR, SYNTAX). Russian formalism made a valuable connection between close reading and the creation of literary meaning: the reader is forced to pause when reading, and this creates a chance to view the world as if for the first time.

Defamiliarization is such an important concept that its implications are apparent in other approaches to literature too. READER-RESPONSE CRITICISM, ROMANTICISM and Bertolt Brecht's ALIENATION EFFECT, for example, also address literature's effect on the audience. Each suggests that LITERATURE (or DRAMA) suspends our assumptions about language, sharpens our perception, and allows us to come to our own judgments about the world. Instead of skimming over a word and automatically completing its meaning, literature makes us linger over individual letters. This process makes us alert to subtle distinctions in language. It doesn't just teach us lessons: it forces us to reconsider our ideas about the world.

deixis (deictic) A LINGUISTIC term describing the act of pointing something out. 'Look at that!' is a deictic expression.

demotic (noun and adj.; Greek 'of the people') Language that is everyday in its RHYTHMS, DICTION and SYNTAX. The word can be contrasted with 'hieratic', meaning stylized and formal (originally referring to priests). Now the term simply places a stress on language as it is popularly used, and is similar in meaning to VERNACULAR SPEECH. Related terms are DIALECT, COLLOQUIALISM and SLANG. As an adjective, it's a posh alternative for 'popular'.

denotation The literal meaning of a word, as opposed to its other associations or CONNOTATIONS. Denotation is a meaning that can be generally agreed upon, whereas connotations (which are basic to literary expression) are particular to individuals or groups.

dénouement (French, 'unknotting') The CLIMAX of a DRAMA or STORY; the point at which all is revealed. The mysteries and complexities of the PLOT are unravelled, and the CRISIS resolved. In a whodunnit it means finding out who done it: e.g. the moment in an Agatha Christie NOVEL when Hercule Poirot gathers everyone together and unmasks the murderer. The remainder of the story is a tying-up of loose ends. CATASTROPHE is similar in meaning, but is usually reserved for when things go wrong in TRAGIC plots, whereas *dénouement* applies equally well to COMEDY.

deus ex machina (Latin, 'god from a machine') A surprising and contrived intervention from a supernatural force in a play, usually to bring about resolution; in general terms, an unlikely plot twist. The term has its origins in Greek DRAMA, where a mechanism would lower a representation of a divine being onto the stage. This CONVENTION is occasionally found in EARLY MODERN drama: for example, Shakespeare (with tongue in cheek) brings Jupiter down onto the stage to help sort out *Cymbeline*'s convoluted plot. The term is used commonly for any plot development that hasn't been prepared for in the story, and seems to come from nowhere to bring about a (happy) ending. See the entry on 'alienation effect' for how the effect can be manipulated.

device A literary technique used for particular effect. The term itself is not very technical: FIGURE and TROPE are more specific.

devotional poetry Religious POEMS containing an expression of faith. The term covers a wide variety of poetry: PSALM, ANTIPHONAL, HYMN and LYRIC, for example. METAPHYSICAL POETS wrote some of the best-known devotional lyric poems, though there are many other great examples stretching from Old English to the twenty-first century. Some would say that religion and poetry naturally go together, while others would argue that approaching religious texts as works of literature misses the point. In either case, the Bible has had a great influence on Western literature, and so is indisputably an important text for English literary studies.

diachronic (Greek, 'throughout time') Something that lasts over time. It was used by the linguist Ferdinand de Saussure to contrast different types of LINGUISTIC study. PHILOLOGY is diachronic because it is interested in the historical change and evolution of languages over time. Saussure, by contrast, championed SYNCHRONIC linguistics; i.e. how language works at a single point in time.

diacritic Any sign placed above or below a word to indicate how it should be spoken. English is in a minority of European languages that uses few diacritical marks. Still, a reader may encounter the following diacritics, particularly in foreign loanwords: DIAERESIS (ë), acute ACCENT (à) or grave accent (é), cedilla (ç), circumflex (ê) and macron (ē).

diaeresis (di-**err**-ee-sis; Greek, 'separation') The pronunciation of two vowels separately, rather than as a single DIPHTHONG. It also refers to the double-dot symbol that indicates it: e.g. 'Zoë' and 'Chloë' contain two SYLLABLES each. In French it is called an 'accent tréma'. The equivalent German symbol is an umlaut, but that has a different function (it changes the vowel sound). *The New Yorker* magazine still uses diaereses instead of hyphens (e.g. 'coöperate', 'reëducation'), though this is a rare and fairly formal usage now. The term has a separate meaning in CLASSICAL PROSODY, where it refers to a pause at the end of a word and FOOT. It is close to the sense of caesura in English PROSODY (but different to the Latin or Greek 'CAESURA', which occurs within a FOOT).

dialect A FORM of a language distinct to a particular group, and which may not be comprehensible to other speakers of the same language. It differs from ACCENT only in that dialect can include distinct DICTION and SYNTAX, as well as pronunciation. Dialect forms are sometimes neglected, due to Anglocentric prejudices, which promote easy-to-read, 'standard' English. However, some VERNACULAR forms are established in the 'English' literary CANON: for example, dialects are used by the Scots poets (MAKARS) Robert Henryson and William Dunbar, and by some African-American writers like Alice Walker.

dialectic A method of learning based on a succession of questions and answers. Dialectic is found throughout Plato's dialogues (see also 'Socratic irony'), and remains a vital concept in Western philosophy. Here is an extract from Plato's *Republic* (VIII.532a-b) that discusses, and takes the form of, dialectic:

> In the same way [as sight], whenever someone tries through argument and apart from all sense perceptions to find the being itself of each thing and doesn't give up until he grasps the good itself with understanding itself, he reaches the end of the intelligible [i.e. truth], just as the other reached the end of the visible.
> Absolutely.
> And what about this journey? Don't you call it dialectic?
> I do.

This philosophical form is relevant to literature in numerous ways. First, it is relevant to that all-important THEME in medieval and Renaissance thought, RHETORIC. Dialectic was part to the discipline of logic, which formed part of the *trivium* (the three lower subjects) taught to students, along with GRAMMAR and rhetoric. Dialectic is a method of discovering truth; rhetoric is the art of persuading people that what you are saying is true. Second, dialectic describes the process of stating something (a THESIS), finding a statement that disagrees with the first one (ANTITHESIS), and then working out how to combine the two untrue statements into something closer to the truth (SYNTHESIS). Georg Wilhelm Friedrich Hegel argued that world history can be described as a dialectical progression. Karl Marx took up this idea, and argued that it is better applied to economic and political realities. This is called dialectic materialism, and is central to the socialist view of history. It is a principle worth knowing when approaching MARXIST CRITICISM.

dialogic criticism An area of critical enquiry based on studying the multiple voices present in a literary work. The term is strongly associated with Mikhail Bakhtin, whose major works were written in the 1920s and 1930s. Since these books were not translated into English until the 1980s, it is a relatively fresh idea in Anglo-American CRITICISM.

Bakhtin held that all language is shaped by the particular CONTEXT in which it is used. Where structuralists argue for an underlying system of signs (*LANGUE*) that controls all utterances, Bakhtin felt that meaning was pushed and pulled about by surrounding expressions. This thought can be brought to reading NOVELS, which were Bakhtin's primary literary interest. Fyodor Dostoyevsky was held up as a model dialogic writer, in contrast to the MONOLOGIC Leo Tolstoy. What this means is that in Tolstoy there is a dominant NARRATOR amongst the other VOICES, DISCOURSES and VIEWPOINTS expressed in the work. Such a controlling AUTHORIAL voice is absent from a work like Dostoyevsky's *Crime and Punishment* (1866): instead we find a range of competing VOICES, each vying for our attention and leaving the PROTAGONIST Raskolnikoff in a state of indecision. Note that Bakhtin did not label works as either purely monologic or dialogic: Tolstoy's *War and Peace* is less dialogic than *Crime and Punishment*, but it still contains a dialogue of voices. Important terms in the dialogic critic's vocabulary are 'polyphonic' (many voices), 'HETEROGLOSSIA' (indicating the presence of different voices) and 'CARNIVALESQUE' (referring to upturned hierarchies that allow popular voices to be heard).

Dialogic criticism is attractive because it is a fairly pure, non-ideological standpoint on literature. Dialogic critics usually recognise that their own viewpoint is one SUBJECTIVE opinion among many. Its emphasis on the PLURALITY of voices can be tailored to POSTMODERN and liberal democratic perspectives too. DECONSTRUCTION has developed the notion that meaning is never objective, and always undecidable. MARXIST CRITICISM has taken an interest in the tension between a dominant single voice that suppresses many others. Dialogic criticism has also been usefully linked to CULTURAL CRITICISM (which investigates what makes culture high or low) and DISCOURSE ANALYSIS (which explores the social CONTEXTS of language). Despite all these connections with other critical approaches, dialogic criticism has never been an earth-shaking movement—but part of its appeal is that it isn't intended to be.

diasporic literature (Greek, 'dispersion') Writing that describes the displacement of people from their homeland. It originally described the movement of Jewish people out of Palestine, but covers other forms of migration, both forced and voluntary; e.g. SLAVE NARRATIVES, which describe diaspora imposed by colonial powers. POSTCOLONIAL LITERATURE in general acts as a witness and critic of different global forms of diaspora.

dibrach An alternative term for PYRRHIC, i.e. two unstressed syllables next to each other.

diction The choice of words made by a writer or speaker. It also refers to the selection of words within a work, and to the way in which the words are delivered. It is an important component of STYLE, along with other features that determine how words are used: e.g. SYNTAX, PUNCTUATION, INTONATION, EMPHASIS and VOICE. Diction can be characteristic of individuals, groups and DISCOURSES, all of which may use particularly distinct word-choices in the form of NEOLOGISMS, SLANG and JARGON. The speaker or writer's vocabulary and anticipated audience cause English diction to be either more formal or COLLOQUIAL, LATINATE or VERNACULAR, and ABSTRACT or CONCRETE. POETIC DICTION is word-choice particular for verse, though it is disputed whether poetry really requires or has its own diction.

didactic (Greek, 'good at teaching') Writing that tries to teach its audience, or has the TONE of a teacher. Some didactic works explicitly concern NON-FICTIONAL subjects: two Latin examples that established the GENRE for later AUTHORS were Lucretius' *De Rerum Natura* (*On the Nature of Things*, c.50 B.C.E.) which describes a theory of physics based on atoms, and Virgil's *Georgics*, about working the land (see 'georgic' for more). ROMANTICISM has left the impression that a didactic tone is unwelcome in literary writing, but it's important to remember that this wasn't always the case. For example, Horace's insistence that poetry should both teach and delight was highly influential during the Renaissance period. ALLEGORY and SATIRE are just two literary GENRES that unavoidably combine the two.

A work that is narrowly didactic in making a specific point is known today as a 'THESIS' work, and as 'PROPAGANDA' if motivated by a particular IDEOLOGY or non-artistic purpose. Didactic and FICTIONAL writing can go together: explaining something or promoting a cause has been a key FUNCTION of literature for the past two millennia and more.

diegesis (**adj. diegetic**; Greek, 'narrative') An alternative term for 'NARRATIVE'; i.e. the telling of a STORY, or stating the facts in general.

différance An essential concept in DECONSTRUCTION, which indicates that there is no such thing as settled meaning. Derrida sprinkled his writing with PUNS, and this is his best known one. It comes from the French verb '*différer*' which can mean either 'to differ' or 'to defer'. '*Différence*' is the French for 'difference', and *différance* is a COINAGE that describes (and enacts) meaning slipping away from a word.

digression (also **excursus**) A section within a work that temporarily departs from the main topic. CONJUNCTIONS give a work a logical progression, and so writing with few conjunctions (PARATACTIC writing) is liable to appear digressive. Digressions can be frustrating when trying to follow a single NARRATIVE or ARGUMENT, but are often found in literature. PERIPHRASIS and STREAM OF CONSCIOUSNESS are two common FORMS. Digressions can make works more spontaneous, expressive, fluent, and obscure. Lawrence Sterne's *Tristram Shandy* is notoriously digressive—it takes many chapters for the narrator simply to get born. Here is Tristram digressing about digressions:

> For in this long digression which I was accidentally led into, as in all my digressions (one only excepted) there is a master-stroke of digressive skill, the merit of which has all along, I fear, been overlooked by my reader, —not for want of penetration in him,—but because 'tis an excellence seldom looked for, or expected indeed, in a digression; —and it is this: That tho' my digressions are all fair, as you observe,—and that I fly off from what I am talking about, as far and as often as any writer in *Great-Britain*; yet, I constantly take care to order affairs so, that my main business does not stand still in my absence.
>
> (I.22)

dimeter (Greek, 'two measures') A line of VERSE containing two FEET (RHYTHMIC units). Rare in English. It evokes the suspense of the hunt in the Robert Frost poem 'The Rabbit Hunter' (ll.1–6):

> Careless and still
> The hunter lurks
> With gun depressed,
> Facing alone
> The elder sways
> Ghastly snow-white.

diphthong A syllable that contains two VOWELS pronounced together: 'mail', 'treat', 'trouble', 'friend' and 'lion' all contain diphthongs. A double-dot DIAERESIS indicates two vowels are to be pronounced separately: 'Zoë' does not contain a diphthong, but 'toe' does.

dirge A public outpouring of grief sung or chanted at a funeral. The term derives from the Catholic mass, which contains the Latin ANTIPHON *Dirige, Domine, Deus meus, in conspectu tuo viam meam* (Guide, Lord, my God, my path in your sight). LAMENT, THRENODY, and MONODY are some related literary FORMS. An ELEGY is a more general term for FORMAL POETRY in commemoration of the dead that is primarily meant to be read, rather than sung. Dirges are found occasionally within PLAYS, while poetry concerning the *UBI SUNT* motif is often dirge-like.

disability studies An INTERDISCIPLINARY approach to disability as a social and cultural phenomenon. Disability studies combines elements of LITERARY CRITICISM, social sciences, history, psychology and CULTURAL STUDIES—but not medicine. It has a particular interest in the factors that construct an artificial idea of what disability is, and the problems that this causes. In *Aesthetic Nervousness* (2007), Ato Quayson sets out the terms in which literary critics analyse disability: 'the term disability is no longer taken as referencing the notion of a weakened ability deriving from impairment, but speaks to the built and social environments that generate difficulties for the disabled person's capacity to live a full and fulfilled life.' A goal of disability studies is to show that disability should be regarded as one of the myriad, equally valid ways in which humans experience the world. This PLURALITY is as natural as variations in race, GENDER, class and sexual orientation. It is still in its early days as a critical field, but there are lots of useful directions it is growing into: for example, how blindness is conceived by AUTHORS through history.

discourse (adj. discursive) Language as it is used in a particular CONTEXT; e.g. POETIC, medical, private etc. It also refers to a set of utterances: it can mean a manner of speaking, like FREE INDIRECT DISCOURSE, or can be a more formal SYNONYM for 'TREATISE'. The adjective '**discursive**' has contradictory meanings: it refers either to something that is DIGRESSIVE, or that proceeds by ARGUMENT.

The first definition given (language as used in context) is popular in literary discourse, having been introduced by POST-STRUCTURALIST critics (see also 'private language'). It places emphasis on the historical circumstances that combine to create a set of rules by which language works. Language is an ABSTRACT concept that becomes part of a discourse when used. Due to its focus on social forces affecting language, DISCOURSE ANALYSIS tends to treat language as essentially anonymous, and wouldn't acknowledge the existence of IDIOLECTS.

discourse analysis The study of larger patterns in written or spoken language as used in a particular situation. It examines how DISCOURSES (see directly above, and 'language games') mould together expression. Discourse analysis tends to be concerned less with LINGUISTIC detail than broader structures that are influenced by the environment in which they come about: for example, the difference between someone writing a NOVEL in sixteenth-century Spain and someone writing an email to someone in twenty-first-century England. Language is influenced, for example, by CONVENTIONS and DICTION used, and the interaction of writer and audience. This approach grew up in the 1970s, and has affinities with several other critical forms: POST-STRUCTURALISM in its interest in how discourse governs expression; HERMENEUTICS for how any utterance was created at a particular moment in history; STYLISTICS, the linguistic analysis of STYLE; SPEECH ACT THEORY for the function of expressions; and DIALOGIC CRITICISM for the presence of different, competing voices in speech.

discursive Moving between topics without a set structure. It's the adjectival form of DISCOURSE.

discussion play An alternative term for PROBLEM PLAY (or THESIS PLAY).

disinterestedness In LITERARY CRITICISM, the idea that all readers should try to see the work as it is really is. This idealistic concept is associated with Matthew Arnold, who desired CRITICISM to be purely OBJECTIVE, without intrusion from the reader's own opinions. Many critics since then have felt this is impossible, and some have argued that BIAS and PREJUDICE are essential to understanding (e.g. see 'hermeneutics'). It discourages readers from taking practical messages or benefits from works, which would seem a natural thing to do for many people. A related idea worth consideration is Immanuel Kant's talk of 'disinterested interest': an art-work is a product of its time, but feels like it transcends its historical situation. It can be contrasted with PERSONAL CRITICISM, which in (for instance) a FEMINIST interpretation argues that the desire for objectivity is a male impulse to dominate other, more feminine voices. Note that 'disinterest' meaning 'impartiality' is not SYNONYMOUS with 'lack of interest', suggesting dislike.

dissociation of sensibility T.S. Eliot's term for the separation of thought and feeling. Eliot believed that poets after Milton and Dryden did not bring their own experience to bear on their writing in the way that METAPHYSICAL POETS like John Donne had done. It seems a rather simplistic view of English literary history, and critics have pointed out that it conveniently justifies Eliot's own views on poetry. In itself, however, the mixture of thought and feeling in a work is something to have in mind (see also 'Apollonian/Dionysian' and 'abstract language').

dissonance Language that sounds discordant and lacks harmony. CACOPHONY arises when writers use dissonant language deliberately to modify the sense of a passage.

distich (Greek, 'two lines') A pair of VERSE lines in which the sense and SYNTAX are usually completed at the end of the second line. It is more useful for CLASSICAL PROSODY than English, where the term 'COUPLET' is more usual, particularly for RHYMED lines.

dithyramb (adj. dithyrambic) A form of Greek choral lyric, often of ecstatic violence. It has rarely been transferred into English, an exception being Dryden's ode *Alexander's Feast*. The adjective means passionately wild.

documentary (noun and adj.) In general, it refers to a television or film production on a NON-FICTIONAL theme. As an adjective, it can describe any creative work that incorporates a non-fictional DISCOURSE by using journalism, legal reports, articles or similar. This is often done in literary works to make a SATIRICAL point about society. It isn't a form of IMITATION as such—it directly transfers material into the literary work, so that a SUBJECTIVE point/opinion can be made about it, or FICTIONAL story woven around the non-fictional source.

documentary theatre A type of DRAMATIC performance that directly addresses NON-FICTIONAL themes, such as contemporary politics, current affairs, media or journalism. It arose in the second half of the twentieth century, and can be seen as an extension of EPIC THEATRE, and influenced by AGITPROP DRAMA. It is often DIDACTIC, and sometimes IDEOLOGICAL, in CONTENT: it's drama about the real world intended for real people.

doggerel Rough and unskilful verse, lacking depth in both sense and structure. Its METRE will be unsubtle, either highly irregular or tediously unvaried (with MONORHYME). It is a derogatory term, and expresses a CRITICAL judgment more than most terms do. When unintentional, doggerel implies that the poet is simply uninspired; however, it can also be composed for sharply COMIC or satiric effect. SKELTONICS are agreed to belong in this second category, as is Samuel Butler's *Hudibras* (known as Hudibrastic verse). Somewhere in between lie simple FORMS like the JINGLE and NONSENSE VERSE. Here is a taster of *Hudibras* (1663) which is rough in metre, rhyme and sense:

> To this town People did repair
> On dayes of Market and of Fair,
> And to crack'd Fiddle and hoarse Tabor
> In merriment did drudge and labour:
> But now a sport more formidable
> Had rak'd together the Village rabble.
> 'Twas an old way of Recreating
> Which learned Butchers call *Bear-Baiting*.
> (First Part, Canto One, 665–72)

domestic tragedy TRAGIC DRAMA in which the PROTAGONISTS are ordinary people. The distinction matters because Greek tragedy always concerned the nobility, and Aristotle's *Poetics* reflects this. HEROES and royalty were thought to be exemplary figures, which made it easier for an audience to feel compassion for them. This trend continued into the Renaissance, but already plays like *A Warning for Fair Women* (1599) and Thomas Middleton and William Rowley's *The Changeling* (1622) concerned the lower classes. However it was not until the eighteenth century that a dramatist, George Lillo, consciously decided that tragedies should be about everyday life, rather than the court. Lillo's *The London Merchant* (1731) is thus the first properly domestic tragedy in English. The need for upper-class tragic HEROES has been thoroughly weakened since then, particularly by now-CLASSIC works like Henrik Ibsen's plays (e.g. *Ghosts* (1881)) and Arthur Miller's *Death of a Salesman* (1949). Perhaps this marks the 'death of tragedy' (to quote the title of a study by George Steiner), or maybe our ideas about HEROES (and ANTIHEROES) have changed over time such that no figure, FICTIONAL or real, can be representative of us all. In this light, domestic tragedy is a more democratic form of drama.

double entendre (**doo-**blah awn-**tawn**-drh; French, 'double meaning') An AMBIGUOUS word or phrase with two meanings, the second of which is usually sexual; in other words, a dirty PUN. Here are a string of (the numerous) examples from *Hamlet*:

Hamlet	Lady, shall I lie in your lap?
Ophelia	No, my lord.
Ham.	I mean, my head upon your lap?
Oph.	Ay, my lord.
Ham.	Do you think I meant countrey matters?
Oph.	I think nothing, my lord.
Ham.	That's a fair thought to lie between maids' legs.
Oph.	What is, my lord?
Ham.	Nothing. (3.2.112–21)

double rhyme (also **feminine rhyme**) A rhyme based on two SYLLABLES, with the first stressed and second unstressed: e.g. monkey/ funky; ticklish/ liquorice; lawyer/ destroyer. It is less common than SINGLE (MASCULINE) RHYME. MOSAIC RHYME occurs when the rhyming syllables are spread across two words: e.g. hatchet/ catch it. See 'feminine' for more about usage of that word. The double rhymes (MONORHYMES) in this quotation from Alfred, Lord Tennyson's 'The Lady of Shalott' echo through the stanza:

Heard a canal, mournful, holy,
Chanted loudly, chanted lowly,
Till her blood was frozen slowly,
And her eyes were darkened wholly,
  Turned to toward Camelot. (ll.145–49)

doubling The practice of one ACTOR playing two or more parts within a DRAMA. It often makes practical sense during production, and isn't a new idea: some ELIZABETHAN and JACOBEAN plays seem written to double up parts. In *King Lear* (1604), for example, the boy who took the part of Cordelia (there were no actresses in Shakespearean England) probably also played the Fool, and the script allows this. Doubling, as in this case, may affect our interpretation; it's another aspect of staging that should be taken in consideration when reading plays.

drama (adj. dramatic; dramatics) A performance involving ACTORS taking the part of FICTIONAL or historical CHARACTERS in an imagined SETTING. It also refers to the art of performance in general. Most dramatic works can be called PLAYS, and most plays take place on a STAGE, often with scenery and props. Dramas are mostly divided into ACTS and/or SCENES. Literary forms of drama other than plays include CLOSET DRAMAS, POETIC DRAMAS and radio-plays. The adjective **dramatic**, like its SYNONYMS 'theatrical' and 'histrionic', is often used outside of its strict meaning of 'relating to drama' to describe something bold and unexpected. **Dramatics** is an alternative term for 'DRAMATURGY', (i.e. the theory and practice of drama) as well as meaning over-the-top behaviour. Most plays can be classed as COMEDY or TRAGEDY, although this important CLASSICAL distinction often now means little more than 'happy' and 'sad', as forms of drama have proliferated through the centuries (see p. 346 for a list).

Drama, along with POETRY and PROSE, is one of the main GENRES of literature. Unlike those two, drama is not intended to be purely read; a play-text or SCREENPLAY is better approached as a series of directions for a performance. In most cases, drama is meant to be both seen and heard: the ETYMOLOGIES of 'theatre' and 'spectator' are based on watching, but 'audience' and 'auditorium' both come from the Latin verb 'to hear'. Most academics would recognise that the audience to some extent affects how a play is constructed and how it should be interpreted. Another point to note is that there are two kinds of drama specialist: academics and people involved with the theatre, like directors, producers, ACTORS and acting coaches. Both groups bring a different, equally valid approach to drama interpretation, and there are sometimes attempts to make the two meet, in both performance and scholarly works.

dramatic irony A form of SITUATIONAL IRONY involving incongruence between the expectations of naïve CHARACTERS and the reality known to the audience. It has more general applications than TRAGIC IRONY does. It is often used in COMEDIES, and also in soap operas.

dramatic monologue A poem in which a single speaker addresses an imagined audience. It is never BIOGRAPHICAL, though is sometimes based on historical figures. The poem creates the imagined world in which the persona performs the monologue. A monologue delivered to an actual audience is a MONODRAMA if a complete play, a SOLILOQUY if not. Comparing these two other forms with the dramatic monologue is worthwhile, particularly to grasp its historical development. An INTERIOR MONOLOGUE, by contrast, is an unmediated account (in PROSE) of a person's thoughts, with no element of performance implied. Given that poetry always involves some element of language crafted for performance, it could be said that the dramatic monologue merely exaggerates something intrinsic to LYRIC POETRY, which is perhaps reflected in its relative prominence in the twentieth century. Notable practitioners include T.S. Eliot ('The Love-Song of J. Alfred Prufrock'), Philip Larkin ('Wedding-Wind') and Carol Ann Duffy (*The World's Wife*).

The FORM is especially associated with Alfred, Lord Tennyson and Robert Browning, who between them initiated the form in poems like 'St Simeon Stylites' and 'My Last Duchess'. Dramatic monologues often require persistence on the reader's part, first to grasp the FICTIONAL situation, then to assess how the speaker's emotions merge into that description, and to decide what the reader's relationship with the speaker is (e.g. is there an IRONIC distance from the speaker?). In this extract from Tennyson's 'St Simeon Stylites', the reader is taken into the locations occupied by the imagined (but historical) speaker—on top of pillars:

> Then, that I might be more alone with thee
> Three years I lived upon a pillar, high
> Six cubits, and three years on one of twelve;
> And twice three years I crouch'd on one that rose
> Twenty by measure; last of all, I grew
> Twice ten long weary weary years to this,
> That numbers forty cubits from the soil. (ll. 84–90)

dramatis personae (Latin, 'persons of the play') A list of CHARACTERS involved in a play, which usually appears at the beginning of a play-text or in a THEATRE programme. They are often supplied later, and are often not AUTHORIAL. As the term suggests, the characters are PERSONAS ('personae') given life by the ACTORS on the stage.

dramatic poem A VERSE composition containing the words of FICTIONAL CHARACTERS spoken in an imagined location. It is a play staged by the imagination. A DRAMATIC MONOLOGUE is a dramatic poem in which one CHARACTER speaks. The dramatic poem is not really a form of PERFORMANCE POETRY, since it is often written primarily to be published and read silently. When a dramatic poem is thought to have been intended for reading aloud in a group, the term 'CLOSET DRAMA' is usually preferred. These alternative terms are more commonly found than 'dramatic poem' is in critical writing.

dramatization The transfer of a non-dramatic work into a spoken (and usually visual) form. Though it sounds like a twentieth-century American invention, the concept goes back much further. Dramatizations can introduce people to a work who are unable or unlikely to read the original text: for example, the MEDIEVAL MYSTERY CYCLES were biblical dramatizations intended for people who couldn't read Latin. HISTORY and CHRONICLE PLAYS are also good examples. More recently, the BBC TV ADAPTATION of Jane Austen's *Pride and Prejudice* with a wet-shirted Colin Firth is a dramatization that has influenced how many readers think about and visualise that particular work.

dramaturgy (**dramaturge; dramaturgist**; Greek, 'drama-work') The art of producing plays. It emphasises the joint importance of composition and production in the DRAMATIC process. Bertolt Brecht is a exemplary **dramaturge/dramaturgist** in this respect, because he conceived plays in which writing and performance were inseparable. 'PLAYWRIGHT' also conveys a sense of the overall craft of theatrical production. Aspects of realising DRAMA that are creative but not literary concerns include: costumes, PROPS, scenery, SETTING, STAGE BUSINESS, music and audience reaction.

drawing room play A Victorian style of COMEDY, based in a middle-class domestic setting. It is a form of COMEDY OF MANNERS. Oscar Wilde's plays (e.g. *The Importance of Being Earnest* (1899)) are models of the form. Noël Coward's *Blithe Spirit* (1941) belongs to the group of later drawing room plays that John Osborne and other ANGRY YOUNG MEN reacted against in creating so-called KITCHEN SINK DRAMAS that focused on the lives of ordinary working individuals.

dream poetry A MEDIEVAL poetic GENRE in which a FIRST-PERSON NARRATOR reports a dream vision. Dream poems usually begin with a description of the landscape in which the poet falls asleep. The vision is often ALLEGORICAL or prophetic in outlook, and can be used to make political comments in an indirect manner. *Roman de la Rose* is a long French dream vision that was translated into English by Chaucer and others. Chaucer's *Book of the Duchess* (c.1369) is one of numerous that he wrote, while William Langland's *Piers Plowman* (c.1367), and *Pearl* (c.1400; author ANONYMOUS) are both CLASSIC examples too. John Bunyan's *Pilgrim's Progress* is a late example, which is written firmly in a Christian tradition.

dub poetry A form of West Indian PERFORMANCE POETRY that was originally accompanied by a BEAT (as in rap). Dub poetry is now spoken or chanted aloud without music, and is sometimes improvised; increasingly, it's also being written down and published. Dub poetry is often political and social in outlook, but not always. Benjamin Zephaniah and Linton Kwesi Johnson are two major practitioners of dub poetry (see 'creole' for quotation).

dumb show A mime that prepares the audience for the action to come. It is mostly found in pre-seventeenth-century literature, though the best known example is from *Hamlet* (c.1604), in which the players' performance is prefaced by a dumb show that silently tells the story about to be acted in brief.

duple metre An alternative term for BINARY METRE (RHYTHMIC patterns based on two-syllable FEET). It is a fairly old term that often causes confusion; e.g. it is sometimes thought to mean DIMETER.

dystopia (Greek, 'bad place') A nightmarish vision of a society, usually set in the future. Like UTOPIAS, dystopias can be SATIRICAL and are found in SCIENCE-FICTION writing. Most works regarded as dystopian were written after 1900: Aldous Huxley's *Brave New World* (1932), George Orwell's *1984* (1949) and Margaret Attwood's *Oryx and Crake* (2003) are three well-known examples.

E

-ean/ian A suffix used to form adjectives, such as 'VICTORIAN', 'Shakespearean' or 'JOHNSONIAN'. Many '-ean/ian' adjectives are perfectly respectable and convey clear concepts. Sometimes, however, their use is confusing, particularly when they are NEOLOGISMS and read like critical JARGON. Such uses indicate that a writer is hazy about the specific point he/she wants to make: e.g. 'Eliotian features', 'Foucauldian dilemmas' or 'Keatsian tone'.

e-books An electronic book, either a FACSIMILE or original EDITION available on e-readers or online. In literary studies, currently only facsimiles of printed books provide texts that are guaranteed to be reliable (because publication standards are higher); however, the quality of wireless readers (e.g. Kindle and iPad) will only improve over time.

early modern (c.1485–1660) An adjective used to describe anything relating to Tudor, Stuart and Civil War periods in Britain. It is roughly equivalent to 'RENAISSANCE', except that 'early modern' doesn't prioritise the rediscovery of CLASSICAL culture over other major developments, such as printing, the Reformation and, later, the Scientific Revolution. The term is potentially confusing given that 'MODERN' has many meanings, and some critics prefer using more specific terms like 'sixteenth- and seventeenth-century'. 'Modern' refers to the presence of important cultural, economic, socio-political, economic and scientific developments that look forward to today's Europe, rather than back to the MEDIEVAL period: e.g. the evolution of a standard English language and the increasing influence of parliament. All the same, the early modern period was in many ways very different to twentieth-century culture; for example, PATRONAGE was a major influence on literature of the period. See page 360 for a list of CANONICAL early modern works.

echo In poetry, a CONVENTION in which the line-ending repeats the previous sound, forming a new word that fits with the sense. It is sometimes connected to the myth of Echo and Narcissus. Most echo poems in English were written in the sixteenth and seventeenth centuries.

Here are the final four lines of an echo poem by George Herbert, called 'Heaven' (1633):

> Then tell me, what is that supreme delight?
> *Echo. Light.*
> Light to the minde: what shall the will enjoy?
> *Echo. Joy.*
> But are there cares and businesse with the pleasure?
> *Echo. Leisure.*
> Light, joy, and leisure; but shall they persever?
> *Echo. Ever.*

eclogue A short PASTORAL poem, particularly one that IMITATES or is influenced by Virgil's *Eclogues* (37 B.C.E.). Eclogues are central to the pastoral tradition that was taken up by Renaissance writers such as Mantuan and Spenser (see 'pastoral' for more discussion).

ecocriticism An INTERDISCIPLINARY approach that examines the relations between literature and the natural environment. It developed in the 1990s, and in part responds to the world's pressing environmental concerns. It has been combined with environmental and CULTURAL STUDIES: GREEN STUDIES is an alternative name for this approach. Some ecocritics focus their efforts on works that explicitly concern nature: Henry David Thoreau's *Walden* (1854), ROMANTIC poems and works of NATURE WRITING are favoured ecocritical texts.

This approach has gained more attention and influence as it has moved to encourage a truly 'global' interpretation of other works. Ecocriticism examines how humans interpret and represent nature, and how natural images are used in SYMBOLS. It encourages us to look outside, outside of social DISCOURSES that POST-STRUCTURALISTS hold are the foundation of all experience. Ecocriticism is a growing field, and its principles and methods may settle over time. It has been fused with FEMINIST CRITICISM to analyse how male dominance has encouraged the exploitation of natural resources (think Mother Nature). It has been criticised for isolating environmental concerns as a separate topic of study, rather than developing its ideas in relation to existing concerns: rather than see a critical approach like post-structuralism as 'non-green' and therefore of lesser interest, ecocritics should be showing where the environment fits into post-structuralist ideas. In any case, it can't be denied that ecocriticism has brought lots of fresh air to LITERARY CRITICISM.

ecphrasis (pl. ecphrases; ek-**frah**-sis; Greek, 'description') A set-piece description. The term is sometimes restricted to works of art only (e.g. Achilles' shield in Homer's *Iliad*, Book 18), or other objects that cannot speak for themselves. It is an important concept in sixteenth-century literature, because the writing of ecphrases was part of the HUMANIST school curriculum. The idea of literature as a 'speaking picture' (linked to Horace's '*UT PICTURA POESIS*') gave it a THEORETICAL attraction. Such description was marked by clarity and vividness (ENARGIA). Keats' 'Ode on a Grecian Urn' is a well-known example, as is the description of the tapestry depicting the Fall of Troy in Shakespeare's *The Rape of Lucrece*:

She throws her eyes about the painting round,
And who she finds forlorn, she doth lament.
At last she sees a wretched image bound,
That piteous looks to Phyrgian shepherds lent;
His face, though full of cares, yet show'd content;
  Onward to Troy with the blunt swains he goes,
  So mild that patience seem'd to scorn his woes. (ll.1499–1505)

écriture feminine The notion of a 'writing of the female GENDER' that exists independently of dominant masculine forms of language. This idea (in both theory and practice) was explored by the French writer Hélène Cixous and others in the 1970s, and developed from work by FEMINIST CRITICS on POST-STRUCTURALISM and LINGUISTICS. *Écriture feminine* resists the PHALLOGOCENTRIC logic of writing controlled by masculine STRUCTURES, and some of its general characteristics are: openness to PLURALITY, refusal of simple generalisations, basis in felt experience and its non-linear nature. This is a sweeping distinction to make, but it fits in with something like Molly Bloom's MONOLOGUE that closes James Joyce's *Ulysses* (1922), quoted in the entry for 'interior monologue'.

edition All copies of a work printed from the same setting of type. The front-matter of a book will always tell you when an edition was first published, and whether it has been reprinted since. New editions typically update, expand and correct a previous edition. 'RECENSION', 'REDACTION' and 'REVISION' are three terms describing aspects of the editorial process. New editions can also be brought out, for example, in paperback or in an ABRIDGED version.

When reading a later edition of a primary text, it's useful to know how the edition has been prepared, and which BIBLIOGRAPHICAL principles were followed (e.g. which COPYTEXT is used). One of the balancing acts editors perform, for example in punctuation (see 'period'), is being faithful to the original text whilst presenting the TEXT in an accessible way to general readers. An ISSUE is a modified version of an original, in which the changes aren't substantial enough to count as a new edition. Editing a work is never a neutral task, and there is seldom a truly definitive edition of a work. Indeed, the process is more of an art than science.

Edwardian (1901–1910/14) Relating to the period during which King Edward VII reigned in Britain. It is sometimes extended to cover the whole period between Queen Victoria's death and the beginning of the First World War. The term is something of a stop-gap: the period isn't large enough to have produced a set of defining characteristics. See page 374 for major writers of the period.

effective Something that performs a function well. A literary 'effect' could be anything from the use of FIGURATIVE LANGUAGE, to DICTION, VOICE, LINEATION or anything else. For this reason, it's usually better to be more precise in critical writing. Note also the potential confusion with 'AFFECTIVE', which describes how something is felt.

egotistical sublime A phrase used by John Keats (in a letter to Robert Woodhouse, 27th Oct. 1818) to describe what he thought made William Wordsworth's poetry unique: its self-centred and therefore fixed sense of higher truth (the SUBLIME). The term makes more sense if compared to that other Keatsian NEOLOGISM, 'NEGATIVE CAPABILITY'. In effect, Keats is saying that Wordsworth holds awareness of indescribable truth, but only knows one way to talk about it.

ekphrasis An alternative spelling of 'ECPHRASIS'.

elegiac stanza (also **elegiac quatrain**) An alternative term for the HEROIC QUATRAIN, i.e. a QUATRAIN in IAMBIC PENTAMETER rhymed *abab*. See 'elegy'.

elegy (**elegiac**; Greek, 'mournful poem') A lyric poem that expresses grief, usually at someone's death. In CLASSICAL Greek and Latin elegies were written in elegiac COUPLETS (a HEXAMETER and PENTAMETER line with a dominant DACTYLIC BEAT), but in English LITERATURE it refers to any sorrowful verse. Like DIRGE, LAMENT and COMPLAINT, an elegy is often an OCCASIONAL POEM inspired by a particular event. Where elegy differs is that it begins to come to terms with grief, and look forwards. The TONE of an elegy is perhaps its most important feature, and the adjective 'elegiac' is now broadly used as a synonym for 'mournful', though in literary criticism the term should only be used when referring specifically to an elegy.

Elegies are one of the most traditional of English poetic FORMS, and there are examples from right across literary history: Old English elegies, like 'The Wanderer' and 'The Seafarer' (well worth a look); EPITAPHS; GRAVEYARD POETRY; Alfred, Lord Tennyson's *In Memoriam A.H.H.* (1851); Gerard Manley Hopkins' *The Wreck of the Deutschland* (1875), and more recently, Douglas Dunn's *Elegies* (1985). The PASTORAL elegy is a particularly CONVENTIONAL FORM, in which a shepherd mourns the loss of a companion. Milton's 'Lycidas' (1638) is the crowning example of the English pastoral elegy.

elision (eh-**liz**-on; Greek 'striking out') The leaving-out of a word or letter, either by omitting or slurring it. It describes any occasion when two syllables become one: e.g. 'do not' to 'don't'; 'fish and chips' to 'fish 'n' chips'. It arises in everyday speech to simplify pronunciation, and in VERSE to fit words to the METRE. 'SYNCOPE' is a specific term for elision created by losing a letter from the middle (e.g. 'ne'er'); for this reason 'elision' is sometimes reserved to describe removal of letters from the beginning and end of words only (e.g. 'the air' becomes 'th'air'). SYNAERESIS is the merging of two vowels into a single sound (e.g. 'seest' pronounced as one SYLLABLE). An alternative to elision is HIATUS (a GAP created by pronouncing two vowels separately).

Elizabethan (1558–1603) Relating to the period during which Queen Elizabeth I reigned in England. It is part of the RENAISSANCE or EARLY MODERN period of English literature. It is known as a period in which English literature blossomed in both DRAMA and POETRY: Philip Sidney, Edmund Spenser, William Shakespeare and John Donne are some of the most celebrated names writing in this period (see p. 361 for a longer list). Elizabeth herself played a role in poetry of the period, partly because HUMANIST arts and culture became increasingly centred around court (see 'patronage'). CONVENTIONAL love poetry was written in her honour, and the title of Edmund Spenser's *Faerie Queene* (1590, 96) is a reference to Elizabeth, who is a constant presence behind the action. Along with the JACOBEAN period, it is at the heart of British literary tradition, albeit one overwhelmingly concentrated on white male writers.

ellipsis (pl. ellipses, adj. elliptical, Greek, 'omission') A FIGURE in which a word is left out that could easily have been supplied. ASYNDETON always involves ellipsis, and PARATAXIS often does. It is commonly found in MODERNIST poetry. When indicating an omission of some words from a text, it's usual to use either a dash '— ' or points '…'. When quoting selectively from a text, it is clearer to write '[…]' to show that you have left out words, rather than the original AUTHOR. Louis MacNeice carefully distinguishes between both kinds of pause in the opening lines of 'Brandy Glass' (1937):

> Only let it form within his hands once more—
> The moment cradled like a brandy glass.
> Sitting alone in the empty dining hall…
> From the chandelier the snow began to
> fall [….]

elocutionary Concerning how something is spoken. The adjective is useful for describing punctuation that indicates phrasing and pauses for breath.

emblem (Greek, 'throw in; inlaid') An image with SYMBOLIC meaning. In EARLY MODERN literature it particularly refers to a picture with an accompanying motto and verse, such as is found in Francis Quarles's *Emblemes* (1635). Andrea Alciato's book of emblems (first published in 1531) was a key source-text in the sixteenth and seventeenth centuries. ALTAR and PATTERN POETRY could be considered forms of emblem, and the general influence of emblems on Spenser (as an ALLEGORICAL poet) is undoubted. Emblems are often TOPOI commonly found across Western literature: e.g. a snake biting its own tail (called 'Oroborus') is an emblem for eternity.

emendation (verb, to emend) The editing of a text to remove errors, such as problems with the particular COPYTEXT being used (e.g. a typing error), or places where it is likely the AUTHOR made a mistake (e.g. an unintentional misspelling).

empathy (adj. empathic; from German *Einfühlung*, 'feeling into') The ability to identify with something, whether a person, animal, place or other object. Empathy allows you to get to the essence of an object by projecting yourself into it. Something empathic creates in the audience a feeling of immersion in an object; it implies a capacity to lose yourself in an environment. Empathy is an alternative form of interaction to scientific study and measurement. SYMPATHY, by contrast, is a shared feeling with others alongside you. The idea has an affinity to ROMANTICISM; for example, John Keats' idea of NEGATIVE CAPABILITY implies a similarly selfless kind of engagement. Gerard Manley Hopkins' notion of INSCAPE also argues for active involvement in the object being considered. 'Empathy' can equally, however, describe audience reaction to a weepie movie, or other ESCAPIST forms of entertainment. It is one way of thinking about the AESTHETIC DISTANCE between the viewer and viewed: i.e. how an audience interacts with a work.

emphasis (**adj. emphatic**; Greek, 'exhibit') Stress placed on a particular word(s) or idea to draw the audience's attention to it. Readers should always ask why something is being emphasised in a literary work, rather than accept it as the work's set meaning. Emphasis does much more than crudely point to a work's meaning (see 'intentional fallacy'). Like REPETITION it is essential to organising thoughts and constructing arguments. Writers constantly and often unconsciously place emphasis on some elements over others, as do readers. Emphasis is inevitable because it is tied to the SUBJECTIVE nature of all reading and writing. Observe the controlled emphasis in this extract from Jean Toomer's *Cane* (1923). The subject is a social outcast called Becky who lives in a cabin between a road and a railroad:

> Six trains each day rumbled past and shook the ground under her cabin. Fords, and horse- and mule-drawn buggies went back and forth along the road. No one ever saw her. Trainmen, and passengers who'd heard about her, threw out papers and food. Threw out little crumpled slips of paper scribbled with prayers, as they passed her eye-shaped piece of sandy ground. Ground islandized between the road and railroad track.
>
> ('Becky', p. 1)

empiricism (**adj. empirical**; from Greek, 'experience') The belief that observation and experience are the foundation of all knowledge. Empiricists pursue *a posteriori* knowledge ('from what comes after'), as opposed to logic and reason, which is *a priori* ('from what comes before'). The term is sometimes used negatively in literary CRITICISM to describe critics and readers who do not consider theoretical matters. However, much literature is based on empirical evidence, and its combination with other principles. It forms part of literature's engagement in forms of experience and SUBJECTIVE truth.

enallage (Greek, 'exchange') A FIGURE involving the switching of one GRAMMATICAL form for another. It is more commonly found in CLASSICAL languages than in English, where it is often an unintentional error. For example, it can involve change of tense ('I *goes* to school everyday'), singular/plural ('I saw my friend and gave *them* a wave'), or gender ('His mother did *his* best to help us').

enargia (en-**ah**-gee-ah; Greek, 'vividness') A general term for vivid description that recreates something as if members of an audience are actually experiencing it directly. It makes an appeal to the senses, particularly the eyes, and can work towards PATHOS (the arousal of emotion). It is a key aspect of ECPHRASIS. As a concept, enargia focuses the psychological issue of how audiences respond to literature. Note that **energia** with two 'e's is a related but different term; it means 'expressive energy'.

encomium (**pl. –a**; Greek, 'praise') A work written in praise of something; a eulogy. Encomia can take the form of (among others) PANEGYRIC, ODE and OCCASIONAL POEM, and isn't restricted to POETRY. Desiderius Erasmus's *Morias Enkomion* (*Praise of Folly*, 1512), for example, is a IRONIC PROSE encomium that apparently praises (but actually criticises) stupidity. In CLASSICAL theory, praise is associated with epideictic RHETORIC.

end rhyme A RHYME that occurs at the end of VERSE LINES. It is more common than INTERNAL rhyme, and is essential to the formation of RHYME SCHEMES. It is an important structural DEVICE in POETRY.

end-stopped A line of VERSE in which there is a break in the sense, METRE and SYNTAX at the line-conclusion. It was particularly in fashion during the eighteenth century, when succinct, self-contained CLOSED COUPLETS were in high fashion.

enjambement (also **enjambment**; French 'in-striding') The running over of a phrase from one line of VERSE to the next, without a GRAMMATICAL pause. It does not occur in END-STOPPED lines, since this requires a break in the sense and METRE. It was frequently found in sixteenth- and seventeenth-century verse, then fell from favour under NEOCLASSICAL influences in the eighteenth century (when CLOSED COUPLETS were preferred). It was later revived by ROMANTIC poets like Keats. It is another means by which FORM and METRE affect sense: it can create expectation and suspense, highlight the flow of thoughts down the page, and place EMPHASIS on the word at the beginning of the line. Ted Hughes uses enjambement and thudding full-stops in these lines from 'Sheep' (lines 1–4), to convey an outpouring of anguish. The enjambement after the second 'crying' modifies the sense of the first line:

> The sheep has stopped crying.
> All morning in her wire-mesh compound

On the lawn, she has been crying
For her vanished lamb. Yesterday they came.

Enlightenment A general term for the late seventeenth- and early eighteenth-century rejection of superstitious beliefs in favour of hard scientific facts based on EMPIRICAL evidence and logical argument. It is also known as the 'Age of Reason' in English. Enlightenment ideals have essential similarities with NEOCLASSICISM, and HUMANISM before that in its preference for clarity, order and balance. It marked part of the transition towards a fully secular literature in which religion plays a peripheral role. ROMANTICISM fought against the OBJECTIVITY and cold reason of Enlightenment thinking, in favour of more imaginative writing, with everyday LANGUAGE, SUBJECTIVE experience and spiritual rapture. These principles have stayed relevant to literature, and define the stark, age-old dichotomy of arts versus science.

envelope A poetic structure involving the REPETITION of a LINE or STANZA at the beginning and end of a POEM. Its function is similar to that of a REFRAIN or BURDEN, but because it encloses the poem (like an envelope), it provides a definite conclusion to a poem (though, PARADOXICALLY, it sometimes suggests that the poem should be immediately read over again from the start). Lewis Carroll's 'The Jabberwocky' contains an envelope stanza (quoted in the entry for PORTMANTEAU WORD).

envoi (also **envoy**; French, 'sending off') A short STANZA that concludes a poem. In English poetry, it is usually found in VERSE FORMS borrowed from French (e.g. SESTINA). It sometimes appears by itself in English; for example, as a final dedication.

epanalepsis (Greek, 'resuming') A FIGURE involving REPETITION of an initial word(s) at the end of a line, stanza or phrase. It can make phrases EMPHATIC, clearer and more succinct. It is a form of PLOCE, and similar to ANADIPLOSIS, which is repetition of the end of one phrase at the beginning of the next.

epanorthosis (Greek, 'straightening out, correcting') A rhetorical figure in which the speaker amends something just said to make the point more forcefully: e.g. 'I asked him—no, begged him—to tell me the secret.'

epic A long NARRATIVE POEM that relates the adventures of a HERO/HEROINE, and normally concerns the origins of a people or nation. It is written in a suitably GRAND STYLE (see also 'decorum'), and often concerns feats of superhuman strength, together with doubts about FATE and how

God/the gods shape our destiny. Epic has its origins in ORAL LITERATURE; the earliest surviving epic poem is the CYCLE of stories that together constitute Homer's *Iliad* (c.800 B.C.E.). This work has influenced the style of virtually every epic poem since, including Virgil's *Aeneid* (c.19 B.C.E.) and John Milton's *Paradise Lost* (1667). The epic *Beowulf* is the longest and most important surviving OLD ENGLISH POEM. CLASSICAL epics were written in DACTYLIC HEXAMETER; BLANK VERSE is the METRE most associated with English epics. Other distinctive epic/HOMERIC features include: EPIC SIMILE, INVOCATION, FORMULAE and starting *IN MEDIAS RES*. Several MOCK EPICS were written in the early eighteenth century, but there are very few examples after ROMANTICISM, which disregarded the need for epic grandeur and other literary CONVENTIONS.

Like 'TRAGEDY', the term 'epic' has a simplified everyday sense: it is used to describe any long and ambitious work. In literary criticism, however, it wouldn't be accurate to describe a work like Leo Tolstoy's *War and Peace* (1863) as epic; indeed, arguably the only accurate non-poetic usage is for cinematic epics like *Ben-Hur* (1959). More than length, it is the lofty style that defines 'epic' as a literary term, and it is the decline of stories about noble individuals doing remarkable deeds that has reduced its relevance for describing contemporary literary works (see 'domestic tragedy' for related discussion). However, it remains an important concept for understanding English literary tradition, particularly in the RENAISSANCE and NEOCLASSICAL periods.

epic simile (also known as **Homeric simile**) A detailed SIMILE found as a digression within EPIC narratives. Homer used them frequently, and epic authors ever since have used them to reflect upon the events being described. Here is Milton using an epic simile in *Paradise Lost* (1667) to relate the fallen angel's entry into Pandaemonium. It contains a double comparison—the bees and their 'straw-built citadel' are compared with the angels' situation:

As bees
In spring time, when the sun with Taurys rides,
Pour forth their populous youth about the hive
In clusters; they among fresh dews and flowers
Fly to and fro, or on the smoothed plank,
The suburb of their straw-built citadel,
New rubbed with balm, expatiate and confer
Their state affairs. So thick the airy crowd [of angels]
Swarmed and were straitened; (1.768–76)

epic theatre A movement in early twentieth-century THEATRE that desired plays to be DIDACTIC and non-realistic. It was a break with existing DRAMATIC practice: it reacted against DRAMATIC UNITIES, DECORUM, WELL-MADE PLAYS and the illusion of reality that a play was supposed to create. In short, it sought to rescue theatre from being a middle-class entertainment, memorable only for its lavish staging. It is called 'EPIC' because it aspired to relate a NARRATIVE that contained lessons for the audience, like a PARABLE. For this reason, most works of epic theatre use a CHORUS or NARRATOR. The DRAMATURGIST Bertolt Brecht was a leading theorist and practitioner of epic theatre, and the ALIENATION EFFECT is a key concept that he devised. EPIC THEATRE has similarities to such later forms as AGITPROP DRAMA, DOCUMENTARY THEATRE and TOTAL THEATRE, though its specific principles, particularly the Marxist ones, do not necessarily survive in those GENRES.

epigram (Greek, 'inscription') A short, witty expression that gets straight to the point. An epigram will be carefully worded and balanced, perhaps using ANTITHESIS or APHORISMS. It is often shaped into a brief poem. The Roman poet Martial's twelve books of *Epigrams* (86–120) confirmed the potential variety and literary merit of the FORM. Various CANONICAL writers in English have composed them, including John Donne, Alexander Pope, William Blake and Oscar Wilde. These examples all show that a short poem is not necessarily an insignificant one. 'Epigram' literally means inscription, but 'EPITAPH' is the term usually reserved for literary tomb inscriptions. Here is a Donne epigram called 'A Lame Beggar' (1607):

> I am unable, yonder beggar cries,
> To stand, or move; if he say true, he *lies*.

epigraph A quotation placed at the beginning of a work, often on a separate page (near the dedication). They're always there for a reason, and it's worth stopping to read and think about them.

epilogue (Greek, 'after word') A section that comes after the conclusion of a work, usually providing reflections or an after-thought on what has gone before. It is marked off from the rest of the TEXT, unlike a CODA. PROLOGUE is an equivalent section at the start of a work. In EARLY MODERN DRAMA, an epilogue was often spoken by a single ACTOR onstage, who had stepped out of CHARACTER. In the epilogue to *The Tempest* (1611), Prospero begins by asking the audience for applause:

> Now my charms are all o'erthrown,
> And what strength I have's mine own,

Which is most faint. Now 'tis true,
I must be here confin'd by you,
Or sent to Naples. Let me not,
Since I have my dukedom got,
And pardon'd the deceiver, dwell
In this bare island by your spell,
But release my from my bands
With the help of your good hands.

epiphany (adj. epiphanic; Greek, 'manifestation') A moment of sudden insight. With an upper case 'e', Epiphany is a Christian festival that celebrates the appearance of Christ in this world to the Magi, and is celebrated on January 6. In a literary CONTEXT, it retains a sense of higher, sometimes mystical awareness of how the world actually is (a form of SUBJECTIVE truth). There are many AUTHORS, such as George Herbert and William Wordsworth, whose poem seem to contain epiphanic moments. But the term is specifically associated with James Joyce, who used the term himself, and whose CHARACTERS (particularly those in *Dubliners*) undergo moments of epiphany. Joyce thought it was the writer's task to record these flashes of truth when they appear.

episode (adj. episodic) In LITERARY studies, it refers to an incident or story that is detached from the main narrative. An episodic PLOT contains a series of related DIGRESSIONS that have some unifying element, which is sometimes nothing more than that they involve the same main CHARACTER. PICARESQUE NOVELS (e.g. Mark Twain's *The Adventures of Huckleberry Finn*) slowly approach a goal by moving from one episode to the next. These works are also described as ROMANCES or PICARESQUE works. In such works the main PLOT only ties different threads together. EARLY MODERN romances are energetically episodic: e.g. Miguel de Cervantes's *Don Quixote*¸ Ludovico Ariosto's *Orlando Furioso* and, to a lesser extent, Edmund Spenser's *The Faerie Queene*. 'Episode' has a connected meaning familiar to viewers of American TV programmes: a section in a larger serialized work.

epitasis (from Greek, 'intensify') The middle section of a DRAMATIC work, in which the action develops and leads towards the CATASTROPHE. In plainer English, it's the part where the plot thickens.

episteme (epi-**stee**-mee; from Greek, 'knowledge') A system of thoughts, codes, CONVENTIONS that organizes ideas into a structure of power and knowledge. The term is associated with Michel Foucault's thinking about historical DISCOURSES that control our thoughts and actions.

Foucault identified RENAISSANCE and modern epistemes in his major work *The Order of Things* (*Les Mots et les Choses*, 1966). PARADIGM has a similar meaning, particularly as used by Thomas Kuhn in specific relation scientific knowledge. The concept leads into POST-STRUCTURALIST and NEW HISTORICAL approaches to literature.

epistle A letter, particularly one intended to be read by a group of people. The New Testament contains numerous epistles written by St Paul and others to groups of citizens (e.g. Paul's Epistles/Letters to the Corinthians). Many sixteenth- and seventeenth-century literary works contain a PARATEXTUAL dedicatory epistle that praises a PATRON or member of royalty. There are many examples of VERSE epistles too, especially around this same period. The PROSE equivalent is the EPISTOLARY NOVEL (see below).

epistolary novel A PROSE FICTION presented as a sequence of letters (EPISTLES, hence 'epistolary'). The letters can be a correspondence between two people, or written by a single individual (similar to FIRST-PERSON NARRATOR). The major examples in British literature are all eighteenth-century, and were all written following the massive commercial success of Samuel Richardson's *Pamela* (1740)—a work so popular that it was also the first novel to have its own commemorative merchandise, such as waxwork figures and playing cards. *Clarissa* (1748) was the sequel, and Henry Fielding's *Shamela* (1741) was an initial PARODY; both works are also epistolary novels. Alice Walker's *The Color Purple* (1982) is a more recent epistolary novel, which confirms that the form wasn't just an eighteenth-century fad.

epistrophe A FIGURE in which repetition occurs at the end of consecutive phrases. It is the opposite of ANAPHORA (see example), and is sometimes referred to as ANTISTROPHE. A subtle use of epistrophe from T.S. Eliot's *The Waste Land* (1922):

If there were water

And no rock
If there were rock
And also water
And water
A spring
A pool among the rock
If there were the sound of water only

Not the cicadas
And dry grass singing
But sound of water over a rock. (ll.346–55)

epitaph (**lapidary**; Greek, 'on a tomb') An inscription suitable for a tombstone. **Lapidary** is an adjective with the related sense 'suitable for inscription'. A few British writers composed epitaphs, such as John Dryden and William Wordsworth, who wrote an ESSAY on the topic. Some epitaphs could be considered miniature ELEGIES.

epithalamion (Greek, 'at the bridal chamber') A LYRIC POEM written in anticipation of a wedding. It is a type of OCCASIONAL POEM, and English examples primarily come from the late-sixteenth and seventeenth centuries: e.g. Edmund Spenser, John Donne, Andrew Marvell and Ben Jonson. 'PROTHALAMION' is a SYNONYM.

epithet An adjective or descriptive phrase that places EMPHASIS on some aspect of the being/thing described: e.g. 'Ethelred the *Unready*', '*high-speed* connection'. An epithet can also replace the noun described: e.g. 'the double-dealer'. It provides an opportunity for descriptive EXPANSION upon a subject: KENNINGS (condensed METAPHORS) are a good example. HOMERIC epithets (e.g. 'rosy-fingered dawn', 'grey-eyed Athena') set an influential precedent in their literary use. Most HOMERIC examples are FORMULAE that are regularly used to build up lines, and testify to Homer's roots in ORAL traditions. HYPALLAGE and TRANSFERRED EPITHETS are FIGURES in which epithets relevant to one being/thing are applied to another.

epizeuxis (Greek, 'fastening together') A FIGURE involving immediate REPETITION of words. It is used almost exclusively for EMPHASIS: e.g. 'Alone, alone, all all alone, | Alone on a wide, wide sea' (Samuel Taylor Coleridge, *Rime of the Ancient Mariner*, ll. 232–33).

eponymous (e-**pon**-ee-mus) An adjective that describes either a CHARACTER lending his or her name to the title, or a work named after its main character or creator. David Copperfield is the eponymous HERO of *David Copperfield*; *Dr Faustus* is eponymous because it takes its name from its PROTAGONIST.

epyllion A mini EPIC. Epyllia will normally use an EPIC METRE (typically BLANK VERSE in English), and will contain a short and poignant NARRATIVE. Christopher Marlowe's *Hero and Leander* (1598) is a good, though incomplete, example of an epyllion.

erotic literature In a strictly LITERARY sense, it describes love poetry that describes sexual pleasures, such as William Shakespeare's *Venus and Adonis* (1596). Such poetry usually possesses some sense of Platonic love that transcends physical beauty, almost like an ALLEGORY. This is how the Biblical Song of Songs has been interpreted, which is ostensibly a celebration of sexual love. In general, other forms of erotic writing, such as pornography, are not classed as literature. The assumption is that literature does more that provide instant gratification; it has intellectual interest that transcends sensual satisfaction and aims at truth. Or so the argument goes.

escapist In literary criticism, it describes anything that allows audiences to immerse themselves in a FICTIONAL world, and 'escape' from reality. Popular entertainment (such as Hollywood movies) is often described and derided as escapist; in contrast, literature confronts truth and reality head-on. Most CULTURAL CRITICS would find this distinction simplistic; for a start, escapism shares much in common with the serious literary concept of 'WILLING SUSPENSION OF DISBELIEF'. People approach culture in different ways and get different benefits from it—and there's nothing wrong with that.

essay (French, 'attempt') A NON-FICTIONAL work (usually PROSE) that presents the AUTHOR'S personal views on a topic. It is more SUBJECTIVE than an article, and not as formal or authoritative as a THESIS, TREATISE or dissertation. They are usually readable. Essays are often DISCURSIVE and contain ANECDOTES or personal/AUTOBIOGRAPHICAL asides. It's also a very flexible FORM, as two of the earliest essay writers show: Michel de Montaigne devised the term 'essay', and his *Essais* offer highly SUBJECTIVE accounts of philosophical and assorted topics, with increasing amounts of everyday detail in later essays (and they still make for good reading). Francis Bacon, by contrast, wrote a volume of *Essays* (1597, 1625) that offered considered, concise advice about matters of civil society. Alexander Pope's *Essay on Criticism* (1711) deserves mention as confirmation that not all essays are in prose.

Numerous literary writers have also been essayists, particularly in the MODERNIST periods: T.S. Eliot (see 'tradition' and 'criticism'), Virginia Woolf and W.H. Auden to name three. Essay-writing is a separate skill to other forms of critical or literary writing, and some writers are particularly celebrated for their ability to make the most of the freedom afforded by the essay: Susan Sontag, AUTHOR of numerous essay collections (such as *Against Interpretation* (1966)) would be a good example. For all these reasons, essays are often enjoyable and informative in equal measure...

though, admittedly, school and university essays are sometimes less exciting.

et al. (*et alii/alia,* Latin) And others. It is used to refer to a book with multiple AUTHORS: e.g. 'edited by A. B. Mayhew *et al.*'.

ethos (Greek, 'character') In RHETORIC, an appeal based on showing that the speaker is trustworthy and knowledgeable, as opposed to stirring emotion (PATHOS) or using reason (LOGOS). It displays the speaker's PERSONA to the audience to create the impression that the audience can easily sympathise with both the person and his or her argument. Writing about DRAMA in the *Poetics*, Aristotle drew a separate distinction between ethos (CHARACTER) and *muthos* (PLOT), arguing that CHARACTER is determined by its function within the PLOT.

etymology (Greek, 'true word') The formation and development of a word. This book gives the etymology of terms when it can help make a word's meaning clearer or more memorable It's useful, for instance, to remember that 'etymology' literally means 'true word'—though it is highly contestable whether language is natural or artificial (see 'metaphor' for more on this important topic). Knowing a word's history (with the assistance of the OED) is important for reading older literature closely: see the entry on 'wit' for an example.

euphemism (Greek, 'speaking well') A milder expression of something unpleasant or taboo: e.g. 'break wind' or 'pay a visit'. It is PERIPHRASTIC and a form of understatement (LITOTES). Its standard use is for politeness, but in literature it could be COMIC, or the result of an attempt to find a more evocative EPITHET when a word like 'sex' or 'death' seems too blunt. William Makepeace Thackeray suavely mocks Mr Crawley's appalling spelling in the following sentences from *Vanity Fair* (Chapter 10):

> She [Becky Sharp] read over with indefatigable patience all those law papers with which before she came to Queen's Crawley he had promised to entertain her. She volunteered to copy many of his letters, and adroitly attuned the spelling of them so as to suit the usages of the present day.

euphony (**adj. euphonious**, you-**foe**-nee; Greek, 'sounding well') The use of pleasant-sounding, harmonious language. There are no agreed CRITERIA for what makes language musical or euphonious, though it tends to involve ASSONANCE and/or flowing long vowels. Its opposite is CACOPHONY, and both can only be detected by readers who listen to the text, either by reading a text aloud, or speaking it to themselves. It also demands close attention to how euphony matches the sense of a passage.

euphuism (adj. euphuistic; from Greek, 'naturally well endowed') A highly elaborate PROSE STYLE crammed with rhetorical FIGURES. It is named after John Lyly's prose romance *Euphues* (1578; sequel 1580). Euphuism shows writers experimenting with what can be expressed in PROSE, and it is accepted that it played a role in the development of English STYLE. Nonetheless, the term is almost always used negatively, because its stylistic ornamentations often have no connection to the meaning of the text. ANTITHESES and ALLITERATION are perhaps the two DEVICES most associated with euphuism, though RHETORICAL QUESTIONS, REPETITION, PERIPHRASIS, and forms of AMPLIFICATION are also essential to the STYLE. Shakespeare parodied euphuism, particularly in *Loves Labours Lost*'s Moth and *Much Ado about Nothing*. A sample passage from Robert Greene's *Greenes Groatsworth of Wit* (1592):

> But as all mortall things are momentaries, and no ceraintie can bee founde in this vncertaine world, so *Gorinus* (for that shall be this Usurers [money-lender's] name) after many a goutie pang that prickt his exterior parts, many a curse of the people that mounted into heauens presence, was at last with his last summons, by a deadly disease arrested.

exclamation An expression of intense emotion, indicated with an exclamation mark (!). An APOSTROPHE is a highly literary form of exclamation. At the opposite end of the spectrum is the non-verbal ('Argh!') or involuntary exclamation, which approaches APORIA (an inability to find the right words).

excursus An extended DIGRESSION within a work, or separate discussion at the end. An excursus examines a specific point or ARGUMENT in greater detail.

exegesis (adj. exegetical; Greek, 'interpret') Detailed explanation of a passage, particularly from the Bible. As it is usually used, 'exegesis' is a SYNONYM for 'INTERPRETATION' that emphasises attention to detail. Critical APPARATUS in a modern EDITION of a text is one form of exegesis.

exemplum **(pl. –pla,** Latin, 'example') A brief tale that illustrates a moral idea. *Exempla* take the form of SHORT STORIES, FABLES, PARABLES, ALLEGORIES and FABLIAUX. They are traditionally found in HOMILIES as well.

exposition The initial setting-out of background information or ideas in an artistic work. An opening CHORUS or PROLOGUE sometimes does this directly; or an AUTHOR can include a CHARACTER who also needs a summary of what has gone before. With many writers the exposition is discreetly merged into the opening section of a work.

expressionism A term that primarily refers to a twentieth-century artistic movement, but also refers to a wider cultural preference for expression over FORM. This encouraged deeper psychological expression through imagery, DICTION, SYNTAX and other linguistic features. In literature, it is particularly associated with PLAYWRIGHTS like August Strindberg (e.g. *The Ghost Sonata* (1907)), and was incorporated into MODERNIST thinking.

expressionistic criticism Critical writing that examines how AUTHORS express themselves through their writing. PSYCHOANALYTIC and PHENOMENOLOGICAL CRITICISM are close relatives with firmer roots in psychology and philosophy respectively. Like IMPRESSIONISTIC and JUDICIAL CRITICISM, expressionistic criticism describes a natural way for general readers to approach literature, and is worth mentioning because of this. However, none of these three terms is often used in academic circles. It doesn't help that the term sounds like it is the critics who are being expressive—not, of course, that critics aren't or can't be expressive in what they write. 'Expressionistic' is one of those words that may be off-putting to the general reader, and in LITERARY CRITICISM it's often plain confusing, unless referring directly to literature linked to the early twentieth-century artistic movement, EXPRESSIONISM, which sought to convey emotional experience vividly.

extrametrical Similar in meaning to HYPERMETRICAL, it refers to the addition of a syllable, usually at the end of a line or half-line. ANACRUSIS is an extrametrical syllable at the beginning of a line. In English PROSODY, an added unstressed SYLLABLE creates a LIGHT (FEMININE) ending.

eye rhyme A type of RHYME formed from two words that seem to match when written down, but differ when spoken: e.g. 'eye/ eternity' or 'give/ receive'. Actually both these examples appear to have been FULL RHYMES in EARLY-MODERN literature, but have become eye rhymes (and also NEAR RHYMES) due to shifts in pronunciation. True eye rhymes, like water/ later, clarify the existence of real differences between seeing and hearing a written poem.

F

fable (Greek, **apologue**) A FICTIONAL SHORT STORY that conveys a useful lesson to the audience. A fable is a mini ALLEGORY with a clear moral message; animals commonly represent humans in them (see 'beast fable'). A PARABLE is shorter and more direct than a fable. Fables are used as EXEMPLA. Note that the adjective 'fabulous' derives from a slightly different sense of 'fable', to mean any story that isn't based on fact.

fabliau **(pl. –*iaux*; fab**-lee-oh; French, 'fable') A MEDIEVAL French poem with a bawdy, COMIC NARRATIVE, written in OCTOSYLLABLES. Like a FABLE it has a moral point, but is also SATIRICAL because it has a realistic setting, and STOCK CHARACTERS based on real-life TYPES. Students of English literature are most likely to come across the term when reading Geoffrey Chaucer, because *The Miller's* and *Reeve's Tales* in the *Canterbury Tales* are influenced by fabliaux, though they are written in PENTAMETER lines. In *The Miller's Tale*, a student gets together with his landlord's wife, and then continues to make a fool of him and a jealous clerk—which angers the Reeve, making him tell a story in reply. These tales are in deliberate contrast to the dignified, courtly *Knight's Tale* that precedes them.

facsimile (Latin, 'make like') An exact reproduction of a TEXT. Electronic facsimiles—scanned images of a printed book—available online are bringing big changes in the ways people access books. In LITERARY studies, the availability of early EDITIONS online (via websites like *Early English Books Online* (see p. 388)) is particularly useful.

faery (fairy) A magical other realm, otherwise known as 'faeryland', in which mysterious and magical events take place. Its association with little winged 'fairies' is a Victorian invention: J.R.R. Tolkien, writing as a literary critic, emphasised that 'faeryland' is a perilous, threatening place, filled with potential dangers (see *Tree and Leaf* (1964)). For example, *Gawain and the Green Knight* contains numerous faery elements, such as a giant who can carry his head in his hands, and a castle that suddenly appears from nowhere. It is with this richer sense of the word that the title of Edmund Spenser's *The Faerie Queene* (1590, 96) should be understood.

fairy tale An ANONYMOUS story with origins in traditional FOLK or ORAL LITERATURE. World cultures have separate fairy tales; traditional ones in the West include 'Cinderella', 'Little Red Riding Hood' and 'The Three Little Pigs', though it wasn't until 1812 that Jacob and Wilhelm Grimm finally published a volume containing many of these centuries-old stories. Fairy tales have attracted most critical attention from ARCHETYPAL or MYTHIC(AL) CRITICS. FEMINIST, POSTCOLONIAL and other critics have pointed out the prejudices inherent in some of these tales, as have PARODY/COMIC versions. They are usually grouped as CHILDREN'S LITERATURE, though elements of fairy tales often appear within other LITERARY works too. For information on the meaning of 'fairy', see 'faery'.

fallacy A mistaken and misleading belief based on unsound justification. TRAGIC HEROES possess such delusions and fallacies, and so do literary critics (so say other critics): PATHETIC FALLACY, INTENTIONAL FALLACY, AFFECTIVE FALLACY and BIOGRAPHICAL FALLACY are of particular note.

falling rhythm A METRICAL pattern in which unstressed SYLLABLES sound like they are moving away from a stressed syllable. It holds up the line, and sounds less natural than RISING RHYTHM, which is more common in English. It is associated with TROCHAIC and DACTYLIC metres, though the connection isn't automatic: the substitution of IAMBS/ANAPAESTS and word-placing can disrupt the effect. Though usually created by metre, it is worth remembering that falling rhythm is a general RHYTHMIC phenomenon that only exists when heard by the reader. 'Aimlessness' creates a resonant falling rhythm in this poem by W.B. Yeats, called 'The Table' (ll.1–6, from *The Tower*):

> Two heavy trestles, and a board
> Where Sato's gift,
> a changeless sword,
> By pen and paper lies,
> That it may moralise
> My days out of their aimlessness.

fancy The ability to arrange mental images in ORIGINAL ways. Ever since Coleridge drew a distinction between fancy and IMAGINATION (they were previously near SYNONYMS), fancy describes an ability to have unusual, often whimsical and unlikely ideas about things, which is separate from the creative impulse to produce new images. Calling something 'fanciful' in modern English stresses that it is unlikely to occur in real life: e.g. growing a lollipop tree by planting a lollipop stick in the ground. The term 'imaginative' recognises the creative input into an idea, without worrying about how it applies to experience. Fancy suggests an imaginative idea based on existing information, and so can be idiosyncratic, deluded and/or playful, but not necessarily creative. This is why most instances of fancy are found in LIGHT VERSE.

fantasy (noun and adj.) A composition whose setting and CHARACTERS are highly imaginative and non-REALISTIC. A fantasy work will often have a secondary meaning that does refer to reality (e.g. ALLEGORIES, FABLES, DREAM VISIONS and UTOPIAS), though this is not essential. It is commonly associated in English literature with the world of FAERY, and particularly with the world inhabited by elves, goblins and other supernatural creatures; J.R.R. Tolkien's *Lord of the Rings* trilogy (1954–55) is a seminal work of fantasy FICTION. Fantasy remains a popular GENRE, though these more recent works receive little critical attention (some are assumed to be ESCAPIST).

farce A fast-moving COMIC piece designed to provoke laughter through a series of mishaps, confusions, accidents and calamities. It usually relies heavily on visual jokes. It is very much LOW COMEDY, and similar to SLAPSTICK and BURLESQUE. Because it is such basic form of humour it can be found in all sorts of places, including SATYR PLAYS, MYSTERY PLAYS, COMIC RELIEF in TRAGEDIES, ANTIMASQUES and PANTOMIME.

fate The idea of an ultimate force or being that controls our lives. Fate implies that things have to happen in a certain way. 'Destiny' is a SYNONYM, and 'providence' suggests an idea of fate linked with religious belief. It is continually being discussed in Greek TRAGEDY, and has been pondered in many more recent works. It raises deep questions of our free will, justice in the world, and what protection we have, if any, against disaster. Fate shatters illusions. The related Christian notion of Fortune was particularly prominent in MEDIEVAL literature, and asserted a belief in an overarching justice: the Wheel of Fortune means that the rich will fall, and the poor will rise.

feminine As an adjective in PROSODY, it means light and unstressed. It is normally used in the terms 'FEMININE ENDING' and 'FEMININE RHYME'. Masculine, by contrast, means heavy and stressed. Since the English language does not have GRAMMATICAL gender (unlike most European languages), these terms are purely technical. There are gender-neutral alternatives: 'LIGHT ENDING' and 'HEAVY ENDING' for 'feminine ending' and 'masculine ending', and 'DOUBLE RHYME' and 'SINGLE RHYME' for 'feminine rhyme' and 'masculine rhyme'.

feminist criticism A movement in LITERARY CRITICISM that began in the 1960s by examining social inequality suffered by women, and subsequently grew to cover a large variety of critical standpoints. It is important to distinguish the different 'fem-' terms: 'female' is a biological description; 'FEMININE' concerns gender identity, which is influenced/created by cultural conditions (see 'gender criticism'); and 'feminist' describes someone/something which analyses or champions matters relating to 'female' or 'feminine', rather than 'male' or 'masculine'. Although a majority of feminist critics happen to be female, there are many male feminists. It is potentially the most ambitious of all critical movements: covering half the human population—though crucially far from half of the traditional literary CANON.

Feminism isn't a late twentieth-century movement: numerous AUTHORS had previously made important steps in uncovering the male-dominated (or patriarchal) basis of society. These include Mary Wollstonecraft's *Vindication of the Rights of Women* (1792); Virginia Woolf's *A Room of One's Own* (1929) and Simone de Beauvoir's *La Deuxième Sexe* (*The Second Sex*; 1949). As a movement in literary criticism, feminism initially sought to promote LITERATURE by and about women. Towards this end, it was necessary to show how society and culture had been historically dominated by men, and continues to be so. Feminist criticism began to define itself in relation to other critical styles: as a rejection of male-orientated structures (STRUCTURALISM); against the patriarchal aspects of PSYCHOANALYTIC CRITICISM (e.g. that women are 'Other', though later feminist criticism is more sympathetic); by arguing that DISCOURSES and systems of thought were created by men, and are masculine in character (STRUCTURALISM and POST-STRUCTURALISM), and that an obsession with such systems creates false security in social 'norms' (DECONSTRUCTION); finally, against the masculine domination of language (LINGUISTICS, and see '*écriture feminine*'). Feminism has also been hostile to the 'DEATH OF THE AUTHOR', which can appear to exclude the diversity of human experience.

Already we can see that feminist criticism's initial work in contesting institutional bias spread quickly into many other domains. POSTCOLONIAL CRITICISM, GAY AND LESBIAN CRITICISM and DISABILITY STUDIES similarly began by showing the narrowness of a prevailing mindset. Related to this, all these fields attempt to correct the literary CANON to respect this newly-perceived PLURALITY. This has been done through GYNOCRITICISM (that focuses on literature about women's experience), through publishing initiatives like 'Virago Classics', through CULTURAL CRITICISM that analyses the continuing male bias in all forms of culture, and by assessing the historical causes for neglect of women writers.

Later feminist CRITIQUES rightly argued against a universal notion of 'feminine' experience, and this has encouraged further examination different female forms of experience (e.g. WOMANISTS, who focus on women of colour). Feminist criticism has combined with virtually every critical movement of the twentieth century, from ecofeminism to an interest in disabled females in literature. These critical fusions all deserve to be heard, and literary criticism is stronger for them. But there comes a point at which 'feminist criticism' ceases to mean anything. Feminist criticism began by answering a specific need in literary criticism, and perhaps its ultimate success will be when the term becomes obsolete, because it cannot possibly represent the variety of critical work on women and literature.

fetish (adj. fetishistic) An object that inspires irrational adoration (or sexual desire). The word is occasionally found in LITERARY CRITICISM, mostly in MARXIST CRITICISM that describes how bourgeois individuals have a fetishistic longing to own objects. Be careful if you google this term for more information.

ff. In literary criticism, it means 'following pages' (not 'fortissimo'). It is often discouraged in favour of giving precise references: e.g. 'pp. 101–156', not 'p. 101 ff.'.

fiction (adj. fictitious, fictional; from Latin, 'to form') The term's standard meaning is an imaginative piece of PROSE, such as a NOVEL. However, it can refer to any creative writing that is based on invented, rather than true, events and CHARACTERS. Fiction may be more or less REALISTIC (or like FANTASY if it consciously isn't), but will usually be relevant to the real world in some way. METAFICTION is an imaginative piece that is about imaginative writing in some way. **Fictional** describes anything that is deliberately invented, whereas **fictitious** emphasises that something isn't true, and implies this is a bad thing. If I had a dream in which I started having a conversation with a dog, it would be a fictional story. If I told my friend about the talking dog, but didn't mention the dream, I might get told my story was 'fictitious'. Something true that provides the basis for a fictional work has been fictionalized: If a dog barked at me, a fictionalized version of this event would be one where I started having a thoughtful conversation with it.

figurative language Any LANGUAGE that deviates from literal meaning through use of FIGURES. It is commonly used in LITERATURE, especially POETRY, to create stirring and colourful impressions. A list of RHETORICAL FIGURES is provided on page 344. FIGURES allow language to hold additional CONNOTATIONS beyond its primary meaning (DENOTATION). It is also common in everyday speech; for example, the phrase 'she's got a mountain to climb' is figurative language when used to emphasise the size of the task ahead, and doesn't literally mean she's about to set off on an Alpine expedition.

Elizabeth Barrett Browning's *Sonnets from the Portuguese*, 43 begins with some memorable figurative language:

> How do I love thee? Let me count the ways.
> I love thee to the depth and breadth and
>   height
> My soul can reach, when feeling out of sight
> For the ends of being and ideal grace.

figure (noun; Latin, 'the made') Any phrase deviating from the literal or expected meaning. Many figures compress thought in elegant ways. FIGURATIVE LANGUAGE is extremely common in poetry, and is widespread in everyday speech too: 'roll on the floor laughing' ('rofl') and 'side-splitting joke' are figures of speech (METAPHORS) because they don't literally mean that someone is writhing about uncontrollably or needs abdominal surgery. CLASSICAL RHETORICAL THEORY drew a distinction between FIGURES that created effects by altering the meanings of words (TROPES, or 'figures of thought') or patterning them (SCHEMES, or 'figures of speech'). There is no firm agreement about how to distinguish between all three. The list on page 344 contains the most common rhetorical figures.

first-person narrator A CHARACTER who relates events in a story from the viewpoint of 'I', and participates in the action. First-person narrators are often the main CHARACTER, or PROTAGONIST, such as the EPONYMOUS HEROINE of Charlotte Brontë's *Jane Eyre*. Note also that first-person narrators inevitably drift sometimes into a style indistinguishable from THIRD-PERSON NARRATION. Some first-person narratives are AUTOBIOGRAPHICAL, but the VOICE will have been edited or reworked during the transfer into literature. For this reason, it is still preferable to describe all first-person narrators as PERSONAS; i.e. as identities assumed by the AUTHOR. See 'narrator' for related terms. Here is a section from Jane Eyre's narration (Volume 1, chapter 9) that shows how third-person description is made poignant by being framed by first-person narration:

> April advanced to May; a bright, serene May it was; days of blue sky, placid sunshine, and soft western or southern gales filled up its duration. And now vegetation matured with vigour; Lowood shook loose its tresses, became all green, all flowery; [...] unnumbered varieties of moss filled its hollows, and it made a ground-sunshine out of the wealth of its wild primrose plants;

> I have seen their pale gold gleam in overshadowed spots like scatterings of the sweetest lustre. All this I enjoyed often and fully, free, unwatched, and almost alone.

fit A division in a long-poem; the poetic equivalent of a chapter. It is seldom used now (CANTO is more common).

fixed form A general term describing any kind of poetry that can be defined by its METRE or RHYME scheme. The SONNET, for example, is instantly recognisable from its set structure. 'Fixed form' also covers STANZA FORMS that are repeated within a poem, such as the SPENSERIAN STANZA. It includes STICHIC (line-by-line) verse, like BLANK VERSE, that is also defined by its metrical features. A NON-FIXED FORM, then, is a type of poetry that has a recognisable structure based on neither metre nor rhyme.

Recognising fixed forms is not just about finding the right label for a poem. You always need to ask how a FORM is being used in a particular poem: e.g. how the meaning matches the form; how the poet exploits form and whether he/she modifies it for effect; and where the poem stands in CONTEXT of other poems in this form. Before the nineteenth century most poetry was written in fixed forms, since in general each poetic subject had an appropriate form (e.g. BALLAD for NARRATIVE verse; LIMERICK for COMIC). In sixteenth- and seventeenth-century British poetry there was a great deal of IMITATION of fixed forms, including those from other languages (e.g. the PETRARCHAN SONNET). It is important to be aware that this was happening, in order to be sensitive to how poets work within particular traditions.

fl. (*flourit*, Latin) he or she flourished. It is used to state when a writer was active, especially when the person's birth and/or death years are unknown: e.g. 'Humphrey Gifford (*fl.* c.1580)'.

flash-back (analepsis) A scene set in an earlier period in time than the main action. The term is a twentieth-century invention, which is associated with cinema as well as literature; the device, however, is much older. Breaking the chronological sequence allows an AUTHOR to emphasise part of the action, or force reflection on the narrative. Any narrative that begins *IN MEDIAS RES* (in the middle of things) will have a flash-back at some point to provide background information. **Analepsis** is the rhetorical term for flash-back; the opposite is PROLEPSIS, or flash-forward.

flat/round characters A distinction made by E.M. Forster between FICTIONAL personages with one main characteristic (who are flat) and those who are more complex and 'rounded'. Flat CHARACTERS are CARICATURES or TYPES, and are (so Forster thought) inferior to characters with sophisticated, shifting motivations. It is an influential distinction, but it has been disputed (for example, in James Wood's *How Fiction Works* (2008)) on the grounds that no character can be truly round, and that some 'flat' characters present a richer impression than ill-defined complex characters do.

flyting (from Scots, 'quarrelling, contending') A poetic exchange of insults, as practiced by some Scottish sixteenth-century poets (MAKARS). It is an early form of PERFORMANCE POETRY, though some written examples survive. The term is also used to describe heated arguments in EPIC poetry (e.g. *Beowulf*). AMOEBEAN VERSE is related, though not necessarily so aggressive. The Scottish poet Hugh MacDiarmid resurrected the form in the twentieth century.

foil A CHARACTER whose qualities emphasise another's (usually the PROTAGONIST's) by providing a sharp contrast. For example, the impulsive and aggressive Hotspur in *1 Henry IV* is a foil to Prince Hal, who spends much of the play messing around at a tavern.

folio (Latin, 'leaf') A page format created by folding a single sheet once, and a book containing LEAVES of that size. A folio EDITION is a grand, presentation copy of a work. Ben Jonson took the then-audacious step of publishing his own works in folio in 1616, and the Shakespeare first folio of 1623 is a vital document in English literary history. Smaller QUARTO and OCTAVO formats were used for more modest publications.

folk literature A composition that has an ANONYMOUS, TRADITIONAL source and has been passed on through generations by being retold orally. As literature, some of its surviving forms are in: LEGENDS, MYTHS, FAIRY TALES, FABLES, BALLADS, SONGS, LULLABIES, PROVERBS, MAXIMS and RIDDLES. Folk literature is part of a culture's heritage, and often contains accumulated pieces of wisdom. This is different to folklore, which is the traditional beliefs of a culture and now considered outdated. Folk literature is of particular critical interest as the source of later literary works; MYTHIC(AL) and ARCHETYPAL CRITICS are especially interested in it from an anthropological and STRUCTURALIST perspective.

foot A basic rhythmic unit of verse METRE consisting of STRESSED and/ or unstressed SYLLABLES. It is an important concept in PROSODY (study of VERSIFICATION); however, feet are not integral elements in most English verse, unlike the CLASSICAL QUANTITATIVE verse from which the terms originate). It remains helpful for SCANSION (metrical ANALYSIS) to divide up VERSE into feet. Although Shakespeare uses IAMBIC PENTAMETER with great frequency, he didn't consciously count out every line into feet himself, or consider the concept himself (though he would have known how CLASSICAL verse worked)—but it's still useful for later critics to make the distinction.

Feet are defined according to how many syllables they contain, and the position of their STRESSED (–) and unstressed (o) SYLLABLES. The most common feet are the IAMB (o –) and TROCHEE (– o), followed by the DACTYL (– o o) and ANAPAEST (o o –). Poems that predominantly use these feet are known as IAMBIC, TROCHAIC, DACTYLIC and ANAPAESTIC respectively, and terms like PENTAMETER and HEXAMETER describe how many feet are contained in one line (see entries on 'metre' and each of these terms).

However, it is equally important that a reader can identify, and describe, variations in that basic pattern. In addition to the terms above, SPONDEE (– –) and PYRRHIC (o o) are two feet that cannot form a basic metre (it is impossible to create a RHYTHM if each BEAT is the same) but are substituted into BINARY (two-beat) METRES—i.e. iambic and trochaic—for effect. There are a whole host of other feet needed to describe QUANTITATIVE VERSE, but which are rarely needed in English PROSODY. It would be difficult to identify most of the following feet with confidence, but for those who like obscure terminology, here are some more: CRETIC or amphimacer (– o –); tribrach (o o o); bacchic (o – –); amphibrach (o – o); molossus (– – –); choriamb (– o o –); paeon (– o o o or o o o –); ionic (– – o o or o o – –) and so on.

Finally, Samuel Taylor Coleridge's poem 'Metrical Feet. Lesson for a Boy' provides good examples of the major feet used in English. The foot mentioned in each line is echoed in the metre:

> Trochee trips from long to short;
> From long to long in solemn sort
> Slow Spondee stalks; strong foot! yet ill able
> Ever to come up with Dactyl trisyllable.
> Iambics march from short to long;—
> With a leap and a bound the swift Anapaests
>   throng;

It is not difficult to see that metre and sense are interlinked in this passage, but the VERSIFICATION of any major writer will also reflect (and indeed alter/ INFLECT) the meaning. It is useful to know the basic names for feet in order to hear when variations from the dominant pattern amplify the effects of metre.

forced rhyme (also **synthetic rhyme**) Strained usage or pronunciation of words to create a rhyme where one is required. It gives the impression, often COMIC, of a poet at the mercy of the RHYME SCHEME. It is characteristic of LIGHT VERSE, but can nonetheless be used for other purposes: the subtly forced rhymes in the opening lines of W.H. Auden's 'The Unknown Citizen' IRONICALLY evoke bureaucracy:

> He was found by the Bureau of Statistics to be
> One against whom there was no official
>   complaint,
> And all the reports on his conduct agree
> That, in the modern sense of an old-fashioned
>   word, he was a saint,
> For in everything he did he served the Greater
>   Community.

foregrounding The placing of EMPHASIS on something throughout a literary work. According to RUSSIAN FORMALISM, the LITERARINESS of work is created by foregrounding the use of language; i.e. drawing attention to the act of expression itself (through DEFAMILIARIZATION). According to the critic Erich Auerbach (in the CLASSIC work *Mimesis* (1946)), Greek EPIC poetry foregrounds the ACTION, leaving no SUBTEXTS or unspoken details in the background, which Auerbach contrasts with the Old Testament. All works foreground one element over another, because it is impossible to include everything. Similarly, all readers and critics foreground one aspect over another when encountering a work. In this sense, foregrounding is a form of BIAS integral to the act of literary creation. Equally, some AUTHORS and critics are better at hiding this fact than others are.

form (adj. formal) The shape or structure of a literary work. It is one of the most frequently used literary terms (quite possibly the most frequently used term in this book), and has multiple meanings. It refers to general kinds of writing (i.e. GENRES), such as BALLAD, SHORT STORY or MONOLOGUE. It also refers to specific structures or patterns (FIXED FORMS) found in poetry, like SESTINA or RHYME ROYAL. It can also mean the unique structure of a particular work of poetry or prose. The question 'What is the form of this work?' could be answered by understanding 'form' in any one of those three ways.

There is general agreement that form is not just a container for CONTENT, but influences its meaning. The STRUCTURALIST view is that form gives a literary work all its meaning, whereas a POST-STRUCTURALIST would argue that stable forms and meanings do not exist separately in the first place. FORMALISM (including RUSSIAN FORMALISM) is based upon an ANALYSIS of the techniques and structures that go into creating literature. Another distinction is that made by Coleridge (following August Schlegel) between mechanical (i.e. fixed) and ORGANIC FORM (which evolves naturally).

formalism An approach to literature that emphasises FORM, STRUCTURE and/or STYLE over CONTENT and CONTEXT. When used in this broad sense, it usually has negative implications: i.e. the reader is focused on cosy interpretations about a text's appearance without considering meaning or other relevant issues. Its meaning is neutral when used to describe the influential group of early twentieth-century critics known as RUSSIAN FORMALISTS. NEW CRITICISM emerged separately, but is essentially American formalism. 'NEW FORMALISM' marks a return to using FIXED STANZA forms, RHYME and other more traditional poetic techniques after the supposed excesses of FREE VERSE. Using these compound terms is more precise than simply describing something as loosely 'formalist'.

formula (pl. formulae; adj. formulaic) A phrase with the same basic meaning and metrical pattern repeated numerous times within a work. ORAL POETRY is widely thought to be formulaic in style, since it was a practical help to the rhapsode, minstrel or story-teller delivering the poem. For example, HOMERIC EPITHETS have been much imitated, and formulae (such as 'folce to frofre' (comfort to the people)) are common in the Old English *Beowulf*. Outside of oral composition, **formulaic** is a general descriptive term referring to a work that sticks closely to the CONVENTIONS of a GENRE: e.g. a ghost story involving a haunted house, bumps in the night, and the ghost of a murdered child may well be formulaic.

foul papers A term used to describe Shakespeare's HOLOGRAPH manuscripts; i.e. the original hand-written version of the plays. They are thought to have been written messily and so to have caused problems when used for printed EDITIONS of the plays—though it is disputed when editors are likely to have used the foul papers.

fount (**font** (American)) A type-face used for printing; e.g. Times New Roman, or Garamond. It is another aspect of a work's presentation (alongside TYPOGRAPHY and LINEATION) to be taken into consideration, though it is liable to vary between EDITIONS.

four-hander A play that requires four ACTORS to be staged. This typically means there are four CHARACTERS, though it may involve the actors DOUBLING parts. 'TWO-HANDER' and 'MONODRAMA' are the terms for plays with two and one actor.

four levels of meaning A model for criticism current in the Middle Ages. It has origins in MEDIEVAL reading of the Scriptures, and is described at the beginning of Dante's *Divine Comedy*. The four levels are literal, moral, allegorical and anagogical. Literal reading means appreciating such elements as PLOT, CHARACTERS, STYLE and VOICE. 'Moral' (or tropological) refers to grasping how the particular story describes something relevant to everyone. 'ALLEGORICAL' means interpreting the text in a particular way (e.g. for the Christian message it contains). 'Anagogical' means 'elevated' or 'spiritual', and comes at the beginning and end of all interpretation: the reader is transported to a higher state of consciousness.

fourteener A line of verse containing fourteen syllables. It is sometimes referred to as HEPTAMETER (i.e. seven STRESS, fourteen SYLLABLE-line); however, in sixteenth- and seventeenth-century English literature it seems to have been considered the closest equivalent to the DACTYLIC HEXAMETER, which was the meter used in CLASSICAL EPIC POETRY. It is occasionally found in rhyming COUPLETS, and in this form it closely resembles BALLAD METRE. It is found mostly in English narrative verse, including Henry Howard, Earl of Surrey's version of Virgil and George Chapman's TRANSLATION of Homer. Here is Neptune travelling to Greeks from Chapman's *Homer's Iliads* (13.28–32):

> The woods and all the great hills near trembled
> beneath the weight
> Of his immortal moving feet. Three steps he
> only took
> Before he far-off Aegas reached, but with the
> fourth it shook
> With his drad entry. In the depths of those
> seats he did hold; [dread]
> His bright and glorious palace built of
> never-rusting gold.

frame story A story that contains or introduces another. *The Canterbury Tales* is the major example in English, and it shows that frame stories are often left incomplete: the pilgrims never make it to Canterbury in the NARRATIVE. Frame story can also describe a 'Russian doll' (or CHINESE BOX) story-within-a-story; e.g. when a CHARACTER DIGRESSES to relate a separate tale. Both FORMS are centuries-old: Ovid's *Metamorphoses* contains multiple frame stories, in which a CHARACTER in one story starts telling another. Frame story shouldn't be confused with SUBPLOT, which refers to a second story running parallel to another. Some frame stories are SELF-REFLEXIVE (see '*mise en abyme*'): the different stories comment on each other.

Frankfurt school A group of critical theorists active in the first half of the twentieth century, who were initially based in Frankfurt University. The school shared an interest in the growth and significance of mass culture, and is broadly united by MARXIST CRITICAL interests. The writings of Jürgen Habermas (specialising in sociology) and Theodor Adorno (music) have been influential in ways that have overlapped with literary criticism. However, it is Walter Benjamin's work that holds most direct relevance to literature. His two best-known ESSAYS, which were only widely available in English translation from 1968 are: 'The Task of the Translator' (1923), which that argues that translation involves the attempt to discover a universal, pure language; and 'The Work of Art in the Age of Mechanical Reproduction' (1935), which examines the creation of new forms of mass-produced art, like the cinema, which lack the bourgeois 'aura' or uniqueness of earlier art-forms (e.g. fine art), but gives art greater revolutionary potential.

free indirect discourse A NARRATIVE style in which a FICTIONAL CHARACTER'S opinions are blended with description of events. It is 'free' because it allows AUTHORS to drift in and out of characters' heads fluidly in their writing without need for introduction. A 'DISCOURSE' is a style of writing. It is 'indirect' because it combines direct thoughts with indirect speech. Direct speech is the exact words being spoken or thought: 'he thought to himself, "it's a rainy day, but I don't mind getting wet". So he went out.' Indirect speech is a reported version of thoughts: 'he thought that it was a rainy day, but he didn't mind getting wet. So he went out.' Free indirect discourse still reports the character's ideas, but doesn't use the fixed 'he thought' or other indicators: 'it was a rainy day, but he didn't mind getting wet. So he went out.' James Wood provides a lucid description of the development and advantages of free indirect discourse in *How Fiction Works* (2008).

free verse A general term for POETRY that does not have a strict METRICAL pattern, but organises its sounds around flexible RHYTHMS and CADENCES. Its popularity as a verse FORM, particularly in the wake of twentieth-century MODERNIST poets, is in part due to its perceived resemblance to natural speech. Its rise was in some sense a reaction against IAMBIC rhythms prevalent in English verse: in a sense, BLANK VERSE is the opposite of free verse, even though neither FORM involves RHYME, and both try to replicate everyday speech patterns. Traditional SCANSION is difficult with free verse, though close attention to stress patterns and rhythms remains important. Forms of REPETITION, such as ANAPHORA and ALLITERATION often provide structure to free verse.

Poetry written in ALLITERATIVE METRE can be thought of as a form of free verse, and the psalm TRANSLATIONS in the King James Bible are considered a form of it too. Walt Whitman and Gerard Manley Hopkins (see 'sprung rhythm') were influential in promoting the spread of free verse in the twentieth century. It edges towards the boundaries of what most people would recognise as poetry (or PROSE POEM); at the same time, it often has a unique poetic energy, which is illustrated in this passage from *Jubilate Agno* by Christopher Smart, an eighteenth-century poet. The subject is 'my Cat Jeoffrey' (the section also contains ANAPHORA):

> For having consider'd God and himself he will
>   consider his neighbour.
> For if he meets another cat he will kiss her in
>   kindness.
> For when he takes his prey he plays with it to
>   give it a chance.
> For one mouse in seven escapes by his dallying.
> For when his day's work is done his business
>   more properly begins.
> For he keeps the Lord's watch in the night
>   against the adversary.
> For he counteracts the powers of darkness
>   by his electrical skin & glaring eyes.
> For he counteracts the Devil, who is death, by
>   brisking about the life.

Freytag's pyramid A system for describing the general structure of PLOTS devised by the nineteenth-century critic Gustav Freytag. He maintained that most plots had a pyramidal structure: a rising action leading to a CLIMAX, a CRISIS and then a falling action resulting in CATASTROPHE.

fringe theatre DRAMA intended for an alternative and smaller audience, compared to mainstream theatre. It is often experimental, AVANT-GARDE and breaks with CONVENTION. The term originates from performances that took place at the fringe of the main Edinburgh

International Festival in the 1950s, and the Fringe Festival has since grown into a huge performance festival in its own right (that has lost its independent feel, some say). There are now many other fringe festivals across the world.

full rhyme The matching of two words that have identical middle vowels and endings: e.g. dream/ scream, waiter/ alligator. Also known as PERFECT or TRUE RHYME, not that NEAR RHYME isn't imperfect or worse by comparison; it is just a different type of match. *RIME RICHE* is a full rhyme in which initial consonants also match: the pronunciation of both words is often the same.

function An action that has an effect on the plot: e.g. a delayed bus allows two people to start chatting at a bus-stop, who then fall in love. STRUCTURALIST critics (especially RUSSIAN FORMALISTS) employ the term to describe the way languages are used: e.g. to express emotion, refer to something else, or establish a link between speakers.

G

gap In literary criticism, a missing element that makes INTERPRETATION more difficult. READER-RESPONSE CRITICS hold that all literature contains such gaps, whether this be withheld information, AMBIGUITY, LINGUISTIC gaps (in SYNTAX or SEMANTICS), or something else. The reader has to be active in filling those gaps, and this makes interaction of CONTENT and FORM all the more important. METAPHOR arguably pays an indispensable role in this process. By contrast, a piece of journalism will try not to leave any gaps, so that meaning is clearly transmitted. Other theorists also argue for textual gaps: PSYCHOANALYTIC CRITICISM associates it with the UNCONSCIOUS, MARXIST CRITICISM with the gap in understanding between different classes, and DECONSTRUCTION with the ABSENCE of authority in all language (see '*différance*', 'aporia', and 'undecidable' meaning). A LACUNA occurs when part of a TEXT is physically absent.

gay and lesbian criticism A critical movement that examines the experience and portrayal of homosexuals in literature. It developed in the 1990s, initially as an off-shoot of FEMINIST CRITICISM that was dissatisfied with the universally heterosexual female experience that was predominantly discussed. It has since grown to address relevant homosexual aspects of literature that are either brushed under the carpet, or that critics tend to avoid writing about (both of which quietly reinforce a heterosexual 'norm'). This has been brought to readings of major writers, from Homer and Plato to William Shakespeare (especially in the sonnets), Emily Dickinson and W.H. Auden. QUEER THEORY is the more THEORETICAL wing of gay and lesbian criticism, and SEXUALITY STUDIES is a broader term for INTERDISCIPLINARY research in the field.

gender criticism An area of critical enquiry that focuses on the social and cultural distinctions between the sexes. 'Sex' is understood as a biological condition of being male, female or somewhere between. 'Gender' is often used as a SYNONYM, but this is potentially confusing: it refers to wider associations of 'MASCULINE' and 'FEMININE' and how these concepts are constructed. Gender criticism examines how literary works conceive and perceive gender. A distinction is made between essentialists, who hold that 'masculine' and 'feminine' describe natural characteristics of the sexes, and constructivists, who find that these are conditioned by society.

Gender criticism refines our understanding of 'masculine' and 'feminine', and helps us understand that these terms are being forced to describe a wide variety of experience. This is relevant to much work in FEMINIST CRITICISM, GAY AND LESBIAN CRITICISM, POSTCOLONIAL CRITICISM, DISABILITY STUDIES and other areas, and has also been taken up by critics wishing to show that there are different forms of 'masculinity'. This type of criticism is often closely historicised; for example, gender critics can assess how the Victorian period made a certain notion of masculinity or femininity appear normal. Another important strand is a DECONSTRUCTIONIST argument that masculine/feminine is one of many binary oppositions that have no basis in fact: gender criticism testifies to the wide spectrum of genders.

Geneva school A group of critics based in Switzerland who pursued PHENOMENOLOGICAL CRITICISM. Also known as 'critics of consciousness' because they maintained that the circumstances of AUTHORS' lives united their works. Without referring to the external details of the author's life, the critic attempted to retrace the author's consciousness. It was most popular in the 1950s, and its key figure is George Poulet.

genre (adj. generic; zhawn-rh; French, 'kind') A variety of literature. In the twenty-first century there is no agreed way to classify literature, and this is a good thing. The following could all be described as genres: TRAGEDY, EPIC, SCIENCE-FICTION, ROMANCE, HORROR and POSTCOLONIAL LITERATURE. In a general bookshop, genres usually describes what a work is about (e.g. WESTERN or ADVENTURE STORY). In a work of literary CRITICISM, by contrast, genre is more often defined according to who wrote the work, or how it is structured: e.g. African-American literature or BLACK COMEDY. The definition of genre involves both these elements: it doesn't just describe a set of STYLISTIC DEVICES or STRUCTURES (what is often called forms), a work's general atmosphere (MODE), or THEME/CONTENT. It involves aspects of all three.

Genres are socially constructed, and serve a particular purpose (compare with 'gender', which has the same ETYMOLOGY). A genre is a literary CONVENTION that generates criteria for truth and reality within a work. It offers a set of guidelines that an AUTHOR can use to convey meaning, without necessarily following them. A work in the RIDDLE genre, for example, carries a set of expectations in the reader that the AUTHOR can adapt to produce meaning. Works often combine expectations from different genres. The following stanza from William Blake's 'Spring' (lines 10–18) reads like a SONG or NURSERY RHYME, but there is also a pull to read it as 'serious' poetry:

> Little Boy,
> Full of joy;
> Little Girl,
> Sweet and small;
> Cock does crow,
> So do you;
> Merry voice,
> Infant noise,
> Merrily, Merrily, to welcome in the Year.

Genres are not just lists of rules; they are separate DISCOURSES that authors can select from to find expression. Genres are defined in relation to others, and are connected to wider cultural patterns. They are determined by social CONTEXT, and are inherited by new readers. Genres surround a work, and are central to the idea of a literary TRADITION that all writers work within.

For these reasons genre is an essential concept, and branches out into wider theoretical discussion of how writers create meaning within a particular historical and social context. In the eighteenth century, literary DECORUM meant that genre was a simple matter, for each kind of subject-matter was thought to have a appropriate literary form (e.g. SONNET for serious love poetry). There is currently no such agreement in English literature, and there won't be anytime soon: into the twentieth century, genres are more diverse and difficult to classify than ever. The thematic index to this work groups genres according to poetry, prose, DRAMA where possible, and lists poetic forms separately (though overlap is unavoidable). The index barely makes any distinction between genre and SUBGENRE.

genre fiction A popular prose work that meets readers' expectations based on similar works. CRIME FICTION, ROMANCES, HORROR STORIES, PULP FICTION and PENNY DREADFUL are all potential examples of genre fiction. It implies that the AUTHOR is being unambitious, and writing a work intended to be pleasing and entertaining to its audience. This is traditionally considered different to 'literary fiction', which pushes the boundaries, defies expectations, and seeks new forms of expression. This doesn't mean that works should be lumped in one category or the other: many writers work with and manipulate genres in distinctive ways. See 'readerly/writerly' for a STRUCTURALIST perspective on the issue.

Georgian (1910–36) Relating to the period during which King George V reigned in Britain. The adjective could also apply to the eighteenth-century King Georges I to IV (1714–1830), but it rarely does so in literary CRITICISM. 'Georgian' is mostly used in reference to a group of poets who did not follow a MODERNIST agenda: these Georgian poets include the WAR POETS Wilfred Owen, Siegfried Sassoon and others, as well as poets like Walter de la Mare and A.E. Housman.

georgic (**jaw**-jik; from Greek, 'earth-work') A DIDACTIC poem about working on the land. Its setting is the same as PASTORAL poetry, but georgic is more didactic and concerns labour rather than leisure. It offers practical information about farming, harvesting, bee-keeping and other pursuits, and this makes for compelling poetry. Virgil's *Georgics* is the essential example, and it is regarded as the middle stage in his career: he wrote ECLOGUES as an inexperienced poet, and his EPIC *Aeneid* in full maturity. Georgics were well-regarded by English poets from the seventeenth century onwards, but there are few CANONICAL georgics in English. John Dryden's translation of Virgil's *Georgics* are worth reading, and there are numerous eighteenth-century poems written in a georgic spirit, such as James Thomson's *The Seasons* (1726).

gesture A body-movement intended to express a thought or emotion. Gesturing (particularly of the hands) was an area covered by CLASSICAL theories of RHETORICAL performance, and advanced ideas about gestures were still around in EARLY MODERN Europe. Gesture is an important aspect of an ACTOR's performance, and worth remembering when reading a text. MIME and PANTOMIME are DRAMATIC FORMS based largely on gesture, along with expression and physical movements. Gestures sometimes follow embedded STAGE DIRECTIONS in the text. In this brief example from Ben Jonson's *Bartholomew Fair* (4.6.147–48), the script only makes sense unless Bristle strikes Trouble-All first:

Bristle	'Slid [by God's eyelid], madness itself. Hold thy peace, and take that. [*Strikes him*]
Trouble-All	Strikest thou without a warrant? Take thou that.

The madman fights with 'em, and they leave open the stocks

ghost-writer An AUTHOR who writes in the place of an another. A ghost-writer is often employed when celebrities and (less often) political figures need outside help to write AUTOBIOGRAPHICAL works.

gloss (verb, to gloss) A note that provides a brief explanation to a word or phrase. Glosses can appear in the margins of a text, in footnotes or in a GLOSSARY at the back. They are usually written by the editor, but sometimes an AUTHOR will provide glosses; e.g. Samuel Taylor Coleridge's *The Rime of the Ancient Mariner*. Edmund Spenser's *The Shepheardes Calendar* contains glosses written by 'E.K.' (but probably by Spenser) which are considered as much a part of the work as the poems are (see 'paratext').

glossary A list of words with which the reader may be unfamiliar, usually found at the back of a book.

gnomic (no-**mick**) Characterized by dispensing advice, particularly in the form of APHORISMS, PROVERBS and SENTENTIA.

gothic A term that originally referred to a second-century Germanic tribe, but is now used in an extended sense to refer to MEDIEVAL culture in general. MEDIEVALISM was fashionable in eighteenth- and nineteenth-century Britain, as the Gothic came to represent a 'ROMANTIC' alternative to CLASSICISM. This is apparent in neo-Gothic architecture, and particularly in the GOTHIC NOVEL (see entry below), which is the main literary context in which the term is used. The modern-day goth subculture has its roots in gothic literature (as well as in twentieth-century horror movies).

gothic novel PROSE FICTION characterized by an atmosphere of terror, mystery and gloominess. 'GOTHIC' has associations of superstition and settings like ruined castles or monasteries. Gothic novels normally contain supernatural goings-on in a dark, desolate landscape. It is an early FORM of the ghost or horror story, and was popular in Europe around the period 1760–1820: M.G. Lewis' *The Monk* (1796) and Mary Shelley's *Frankenstein* (1818) are two of the many examples from this period. It is PRE-ROMANTIC, and develops an interest in the dark, GROTESQUE and UNCANNY found in GRAVEYARD POETRY.

grammar (adj. grammatical) The rules of a language. Its linguistic components are SYNTAX, PHONETICS, MORPHOLOGY and SEMANTICS. This book contains short definitions of basic concepts for quick reference, and a checklist of the terms to know is on page 345. These entries are included for two reasons. First, it is very useful to have a sound knowledge of grammatical terms to describe how language works; many students, however, have little formal knowledge of English grammar. Second, in literary studies and most other professional domains, sound grammatical knowledge is vital to communicate with authority, clarity and precision. This doesn't mean that grammar is just a set of cast-iron rules on 'correct' language usage which doesn't reflect real-life: languages do evolve, and following CONVENTIONS doesn't necessarily make you a better writer. However, this doesn't make understanding the basics about how language works any less important, both for reading and writing.

grand style A FORMAL, monumental approach to writing, suitable for discussing lofty ideals and great CHARACTERS. 'Milton's grand style' is the most distinct example in all English literature, and Christopher Ricks made a persuasive case that this is a great strength of *Paradise Lost* in his book with that name. Milton followed the 'grand style' of Homer and Virgil, his great predecessors in EPIC GENRE, to write a great Christian EPIC about Adam and Eve's fall. Because of its CLASSICAL inheritance (from high, middle and low STYLES (see this entry)), the grand style is highly LATINATE: i.e. VOCABULARY derived from Latin, long PERIODIC sentences, formal TONE and inversion (HYPERBATON), particularly with delayed VERBS.

grapheme A basic unit of written CHARACTERS/letters that represents a spoken sound (a PHONEME). It describes the LINGUISTIC element from which all written language is created.

graveyard poetry A group of eighteenth-century poems (particularly ELEGIES) that take a melancholic look at change and human mortality. Thomas Gray's *Elegy Written in a Country Graveyard* (1751) is the central English example of what was a European trend. Graveyard poetry is of historical interest because its interest in emotional darkness and mystery is PRE-ROMANTIC: it foreshadows ROMANTICISM and the GOTHIC NOVEL.

great chain of being The idea that a global hierarchy of beings exists. Plato and William Shakespeare (e.g. in *Troilus and Cressida*) are two of numerous writers over history to have described a great chain. It argues that the world is varied and abundant, but possesses an overall order, usually with God or another deity placed at the summit.

great vowel shift A important change in English pronunciation that occurred in the late MEDIEVAL/EARLY MODERN period. The great vowel shift is crucial in understanding the LINGUISTIC development of modern English. These PHONETIC changes took place gradually over time, and regional variations in pronunciation remained.

green [cultural] studies 'Green studies' and 'green CULTURAL STUDIES' are alternative names for the area of criticism most commonly known as 'ECOCRITICISM'. These two names stress that ecocriticism does not just concern literature, but extends into other cultural forms like film and TV.

grotesque In literature, it means an absurd and often repulsive departure from expected order and STRUCTURE, often involving a freakish distortion of human features. It is often used for COMIC exaggeration. Like BAROQUE, it has specific CONNOTATIONS as an art historical term (e.g. to describe the paintings of Hieronymus Bosch), but has broader relevance to literature. The EARLY MODERN French AUTHOR François Rabelais is strongly associated with the grotesque (following Mikhail Bakhtin—see 'carnivalesque'), but the adjective could also describe BLACK COMEDY, THEATRE OF THE ABSURD, PARODY, and CARICATURE. This description of a traveller from Charles Dickens' *Pickwick Papers* has something of the grotesque about it:

> It was a care-worn looking man, whose sallow face, and deeply sunken eyes, were rendered still more striking than nature had made them, by the straight black hair which hung in matted disorder half way down his face. His eyes were almost unnaturally bright and piercing; his cheek-bones were high and prominent; and his jaws were so long and lank, that an observer would have supposed that he was drawing the flesh of his face in, for a moment, by some contraction of the muscles, if his half-opened mouth and immovable expression had not announced that it was his ordinary appearance.

gynocriticism A term created by the American FEMINIST critic Elaine Showalter to describe CRITICISM focused on literary works by women and about women. It tries to establish a continuous literary tradition that describes the historical experience of women. Showalter's books *A Literature of Their Own: British Women Novelists from Brontë to Lessing* (1982) and *A Jury of her Peers: American Women Writers from Bradstreet to Proulx* (2009) are model examples. It is one aspect of the explosion in feminist criticism that sought to do justice to the wide array of women's writing over history that has been subsequently neglected. Showalter's approach has been challenged by other, more theoretically-inclined critics, who argue that such work, by being solely about women, fails to address STRUCTURAL inequalities in the literary CANON.

hagiography (Greek, 'sacred writing') Writing about saints' lives that combines BIOGRAPHY and LEGEND. The term describes both the writing process and final product. It particularly refers to MEDIEVAL tales, which later provided subject-matter for MORALITY PLAYS. It is also used as a FIGURATIVE term for any writing that glorifies an individual.

half-rhyme An alternative term for NEAR RHYME; i.e. two words containing identical sounds, but not similar vowels and endings as in FULL RHYME.

haiku (Japanese, 'humorous') A Japanese verse FORM that has been assimilated into Western culture: it is a seventeen-SYLLABLE poem divided into three lines of five, seven and five SYLLABLES. In English it is rarely restricted to finding pleasure in everyday scenes, as is standard in Japanese. Numerous poets, particularly the IMAGISTS, experimented with the FORM in English. Like LIMERICKS, a relatively familiar form like haiku can provide a starting-point for thinking about how form affects sense, and that it is important to know the rules, if only to see how poets work within a tradition and adapt it. This COMIC example is by David Bader (from *One Hundred Great Books in Haiku*), and summarises Christopher Marlowe's *Doctor Faustus*:

> A scholar trades a
> few fun years for endless Hell.
> Maths was not his field.

hamartia (Greek, 'error') The ignorance or error of TRAGIC heroes. In TRAGIC plots (as Aristotle defines it), a moment of recognition (*ANAGNORISIS*) arises in which the HERO's *hamartia* is replaced by knowledge, and which leads to a reversal in fortune (*PERIPETEIA*). *Hamartia* does not mean an inherent 'tragic flaw' (a common translation) because Aristotelian tragic HEROES are ignorant victims subject to higher forces. *HUBRIS* (excessive pride) is one source of *hamartia*.

hapax legomenon (Greek, 'thing said once') A word with only one surviving written example, particularly in older literature, such as

OLD ENGLISH. It is an older, scholarly alternative for 'NONCE WORD'. Since comparing uses of a word is the main way to establish its meaning, it can be difficult to know exactly what a *hapax legomenon*'s meaning is. A *hapax legomenon*, unlike a nonce word, may not have been unique when it was written down; it only became so over time.

Harlem Renaissance (c.1920s) A group of African-American writers, many of them internal migrants from the South, who settled in the Harlem area of New York. As 'Renaissance' suggests, it was a period filled with creative renewal and optimism. Langston Hughes, Jean Toomer and Zora Neale Hurston are three of its leading figures.

heavy (masculine) ending A LINE that concludes with a STRESSED SYLLABLE. It marks a definite end to the line, which is often END-STOPPED. Heavy endings occur at the end of a regular IAMBIC line, and CATALECTIC TROCHAIC lines; i.e. ones that have lost their final BEAT. The effect is related to that of HEAVY RHYME. The opposite is LIGHT ENDING (also known as FEMININE).

Hellenism/Hebraism A distinction made by the Victorian critic Matthew Arnold between Ancient Greek and Hebrew worldviews. According to Arnold, the Greeks cherished INTELLECTUAL and AESTHETIC perfection, whereas the Hebrews sought to perform their moral duty. The difference is between contemplation of an ideal life (Hellenism) and virtuous action (Hebraism). In an ESSAY 'Hebraism and Hellenism' (in *Cultural and Anarchy*), Arnold holds that all individual are drawn more to one option than the other, and that this affects how we think, act and express ourselves.

hemistich (Greek, 'half-line') A technical term for half-line. VERSE in ALLITERATIVE METRE contains hemistichs created by the division of the LINE by a CAESURA. Hemistichs can be abrupt and EMPHATIC, an effect that often occurs in rapid DRAMATIC dialogue (a form of STICHOMYTHIA).

hendiadys (hen-**dee**-ah-diss; Greek, 'one through two') A FIGURE in which two nouns connected by 'and' are used to express an idea, instead of noun and adjective. *Hamlet* abounds in them: e.g. 'sulph'rous and tormenting flames' (1.5.3–4); 'whips and scorns of time' (3.1.69).

heptameter (Greek, 'seven measures') A line of VERSE containing seven FEET (RHYTHMIC units). BALLAD METRE can be described as heptameter. The FOURTEENER, since it has fourteen syllables, is sometimes described as heptameter (though this is disputed).

heptastich A set of seven verse lines, also known as a SEPTET.

hermeneutic circle An interpretative problem first described in the nineteenth century: in order to understand the separate parts of a work we need to anticipate what the whole is, but we can't know what the whole is until we've read the parts. At some level, then, we decide what the meaning is in advance if we are to take meaning from it. This applies to individual words (as part of a DISCOURSE), as well as to larger interpretative structures such as ALLEGORY. A possible solution is to remain conscious of both parts and whole while reading so that our sense of the big picture is constantly being adjusted by focused details, and vice versa. HERMENEUTICS examines these issues of INTERPRETATION, BIAS and PREJUDICE in great depth, and RECEPTION THEORY examines how readers approach texts in different ways over history (see 'horizon of expectations' for more on this).

hermeneutics The study of INTERPRETATION and its possibilities. The term originally referred to biblical ANALYSIS/EXEGESIS, but from the nineteenth century centred on problems of recovering meaning from a text. Hermeneutics examines how we understand texts, and how the AUTHOR'S experiences are relayed to the reader.

A major twentieth-century work of philosophical hermeneutics is Hans-Georg Gadamer's *Truth and Method* (1960, trans. 1975). This book made the argument that the AUTHOR'S intended meaning was not the source of understanding. Gadamer argued that PREJUDICE and BIAS are not only present in all understanding, but are necessary to create meaning. In other words, his view was that there is no such thing as an objective reading of a text: all meaning is SUBJECTIVE, since it is created by the reader. This is different from 'DEATH OF THE AUTHOR' because it argues that the author's psychological presence is inaccessible. This is different from the INTENTIONAL FALLACY, because that only argues against bringing in outside information about an author, and assumes that a text reflects an author's intended meaning. Gadamer, like other hermeneutic writers, argues that all meaning is created from particular historical circumstances that later readers have no chance of recovering. As an example, he contrasts literature with architecture: buildings usually remain in the original space and CONTEXT in which they were created, whereas I can read a Jane Austen novel in an airport departure lounge. This is likely to make my interpretation even more distanced from its original CONTEXT, and dependent on my VIEWPOINT. The literary implications of all this have been explored in READER-RESPONSE CRITICISM.

hero (heroine, pl. heroes; adj. heroic) The main CHARACTER in a NARRATIVE or DRAMATIC work. **Heroine** is the female equivalent. In its strict sense, the term does not DENOTE moral goodness, but under the influence of the EPIC and Christian traditions it often does imply courage, nobility and great achievements. The adjective **heroic** almost always has these associations. An ANTIHERO/HEROINE is a character who does not live up to these lofty expectations; it suggests failure, rather than wickedness or opposition to a HERO. Given this potential confusion, PROTAGONIST is a useful alternative term to 'hero' that has no moral CONNOTATIONS.

heroic couplet A pair of rhymed IAMBIC PENTAMETER lines (five STRESSES, ten syllables). Heroic couplets are either CLOSED or OPEN. The form is most associated with John Dryden and Alexander Pope, who are recognised as masters of COUPLET writing. From Dryden's *Absalom and Achitophel* (ll. 723–26):

> Youth, beauty, graceful action seldom fail,
> But common interest always will prevail:
> And pity never ceases to be shown
> To him who makes the people's wrong his own.

heroic drama A type of late seventeenth-century (RESTORATION) DRAMA composed in HEROIC COUPLETS (IAMBIC PENTAMETER) that deals with noble THEMES like love and honour. John Dryden pioneered the FORM, considering it an extension of EPIC POETRY, and so deserving of a high STYLE. Characteristic features are DRAMATIC UNITY, upper-class CHARACTERS BOMBASTIC in their rhetoric, and POETIC JUSTICE. It is also linked to the introduction of English OPERA, through such works as William Davenant's *Siege of Rhodes* (1552). Dryden's *Indian Emperor* (1665) is a heroic drama, and also a TRAGEDY. The form was already the subject of PARODY and BURLESQUE by the 1670s.

heroic poetry A NARRATIVE poem based around a HERO or HEROINE. 'EPIC' is a preferable alternative, and 'heroic' is better used when describing poetic form (i.e. HEROIC COUPLET and QUATRAIN).

heroic quatrain Four lines (QUATRAIN) consisting of IAMBIC PENTAMETER (five stresses, ten syllables) rhyming *abab*. Also known as 'ELEGIAC STANZA'/ 'QUATRAIN'. It gained popularity with Thomas Gray's *Elegy Written in a Country Churchyard*.

heteroglossia (Russian, *raznorechie*) Literally meaning 'different speech-ness', the term describes the presence of many voices within a text. It is an important component of DIALOGIC CRITICISM, associated with Mikhail

Bakhtin. It points to the presence of clashing DISCOURSES and CONVENTIONS, and encourages exploration into the relation between these voices. CARNIVALESQUE writing is particularly heteroglossic.

heterometric (Greek, 'of other measures') A series of LINES with different lengths and/or METRES. It can refer to verse forms and STANZAS that contain different line-shapes, such as the LIMERICK and SPENSERIAN STANZA. It is worth exploring how poets use flexible LINEATION in heterometric FORMS to structure meaning.

hexameter (Greek, 'six measures') A line of VERSE containing six FEET (RHYTHMIC units). In CLASSICAL PROSODY it is most associated with the DACTYL: DACTYLIC HEXAMETER was the METRE used by Homer and Virgil. In English, however, the IAMBIC hexameter is more usual, which has its own name, the ALEXANDRINE.

hiatus (hi-**eh**-tuss) In English PROSODY, it refers to the small break in pronunciation created by voicing two vowels separately: e.g. 'selection' pronounced 'selec-ti-on' (not selek-shun), 'being' (not pronounced 'bing'). Hiatus is sometimes marked with a double-dot above the word (called DIAERESIS; e.g. 'Zoë'). It is often removed by ELISION (or SYNAERESIS) to make pronunciation easier—the indefinite ARTICLE 'an' replaces 'a' to prevent hiatus in phrases like 'an apple'. It can also describe a GAP created when a sentence, argument or verse is left incomplete: 'And then right before my eyes there was—'. In this sense it is related to the rhetorical terms APORIA and APOSIOPESIS.

high comedy COMIC DRAMA that is witty, elegant and graceful, in contrast to LOW COMEDY. The term isn't used all that much, and isn't necessarily that helpful either. The Victorian writer George Meredith used the term in 1877 to refer to COMEDY OF MANNERS, and clever, non-physical humour in general. Clearly there is a distinction to be made here, but it's less obvious that intellectual COMEDY is always 'higher' than physical humour.

historicism A broad term for all attempts to understand the thoughts, ideas, events and other CONTEXTUAL influences that affect the creation of a literary text. It grew out of nineteenth-century ideas about HERMENEUTICS (i.e. how a text is to be interpreted), and marked a development from JUDICIAL or PERSONAL CRITICISM that essentially considered literature something to be enjoyed and debated.

Historicised readings use historical details to illuminate a reading of a literary text. This principle remains generally relevant today. NEW

HISTORICISM sought to take the idea further: it broke down the division between text and context to show how literary texts inform our historical knowledge of a period. E.M.W. Tillyard's *The Elizabethan World Picture* (1943) is a CLASSIC historicist work that became something of a punch-bag for NEW HISTORICISM. Tillyard explained what the ELIZABETHAN Age's notion of a world order looked like, which includes ideas like the 'GREAT CHAIN OF BEING' and 'FOUR HUMOURS'. The earlier historicist argument is that knowing what the Elizabethans believed takes us closer to understanding the literary text. New historicists argued that these ABSTRACT ideas have nothing to do with the everyday reality of ELIZABETHAN life: it just picks out one idea floating around in the period, and pretends that being aware of that is the same as understanding the historical circumstances of the text.

The greatest weakness of historicism is its settled idea of a historical 'PERIOD' (e.g. Elizabethan) that can be recaptured with some critical work. All the same, a historicising approach to criticism would be welcomed by most critics (other than strong FORMALISTS) and it was an important stage in correcting ANACHRONISMS and other naïve interpretations of its time. All literature possesses historicity (a historical quality) in its language and content, and this is not just relevant to 'historicist' critics.

historical novel A PROSE FICTION that contains a SETTING, CHARACTER, THEME OR PLOT based on past events. The accuracy of the historical recreation varies greatly, and depends largely on how AUTHORS are adapting a historical situation to their purposes. The historical novel is a GENRE of popular FICTION, but it also describes 'literary' CLASSICS like Leo Tolstoy's *War and Peace* (1864). Note that 'historical' is relative to the author, not the reader: C.S. Forester's *Hornblower* novels (e.g. *Mr Midshipman Hornblower* (1950)) are historical because Forester wasn't around during the Napoleonic Wars, but Jane Austen did not write 'historical novels', even though the reader may be interested in the period setting.

history play A DRAMA based on historical events. The earliest surviving example in Western literature is Aeschylus' *The Persians*, while Hollywood movies or TV ADAPTATIONS are modern equivalents of this popular form. History plays have always been more about making successful dramatic creations than historical accuracy. Sixteenth-century CHRONICLE PLAYS, for example, were written to be entertaining: they were generally EPISODIC, vivid, and featured onstage battles. Equally, history plays often use past events to explore present situations. For example, Arthur Miller's *The Crucible* (1953) uses the seventeenth-century Salem witch trials to examine contemporary anti-communism. DOCUMENTARY THEATRE often contains CONTENT about non-fictional events to make political or other points.

Shakespeare's history plays are largely based on Holinshed's *Chronicles* but are generally still known as 'history plays' because the word 'histories' is found on the contents page of the First FOLIO EDITION (1623), alongside 'comedies' and 'tragedies'. They are commonly divided into two TETRALOGIES (sets of four): the first tetralogy contains the three parts of *Henry VI* plus *Richard III*; the second is *Richard II, Henry IV, Part One* and *Two*, and *Henry V*. However, the boundaries between history, COMEDY and TRAGEDY are flexible, and when considering history plays, it's always advisable to look beyond the historical NARRATIVE into the wider CONTEXT of the play and its PERFORMANCE.

histrionic (from Latin, 'actor') A SYNONYM for DRAMATIC or THEATRICAL, with an EMPHASIS on acting. From this comes the broader sense of over-the-top behaviour.

holograph (Greek, 'whole writing') A document written entirely in the AUTHOR'S hand-writing. AUTOGRAPH is anything written in the author's writing (not necessarily his or her signature).

Homeric Characteristic of the works of Homer; i.e. *The Iliad* and *The Odyssey*. These are the oldest surviving works of Western literature, thought to have been written around the eighth century B.C.E.. EPITHETS, EPIC SIMILES, INVOCATIONS, FORMULAE, and beginning *IN MEDIAS RES* are the literary DEVICES most characteristic of Homeric EPIC. Homer has fascinated readers for centuries, and provides a foundation or reference point for many later works. Homeric influence can be found throughout English literary history, from Chaucer's *Troilus and Criseyde* (1385) to Derek Walcott's *Omeros* (1990). Homeric features are used for PARODIC effect in MOCK EPICS.

homily (adj. homiletic) A spoken address on a religious subject, often including moral instruction. SERMON is a SYNONYM. Delivering homilies requires RHETORICAL ability, which is one reason that literary scholars have taken a particular interest in the published sermons of the then-renowned seventeenth-century preachers John Donne and Launcelot Andrewes. '**Homiletic**' describes a speech or writing that has the feel of a homily, and is sometimes used to imply something is dull and/or excessively moralising.

homonym (Greek, 'same name') A word that has an identical sound or spelling to another (the 'same name') but a different meaning.

A HOMOPHONE is a homonym based on same sound; a homograph is a homonym based on same spelling. 'Bear' is a homonym (homophone) of 'bare'; 'mint' is a homonym (homograph) because it refers to a sweet and to the place where money is made. Homonyms are the source of many a one-line joke; they are also a FORM of RIME RICHE.

homophone (Greek, 'same sound') A word that has an identical sound to another but a different meaning: e.g. 'scene' and 'seen', 'flair' and 'flare'. It is a type of HOMONYM, and creates RIME RICHE (and MONDEGREENS).

homostrophic (Greek, 'of one turning') An adjective for all poetry containing repeated stanza units. The HORATIAN ODE and BALLAD are both homostrophic FORMS, for example.

Horatian ode A FORM of LYRIC POEM that adapts the regular structure of the CLASSICAL ODE. An Horatian ode is HOMOSTROPHIC; that is, each STANZA (and there is no fixed number) has the same length and METRE. Marvell's 'An Horatian Ode upon Cromwell's Return from Ireland' adapts the form well, to create a monumental but not deferential TONE.

Horatian satire An urbane, relaxed style of VERSE SATIRE that gently mocks failings in the world, as found in Horace's *Satires* (c.35 B.C.E.). See 'satire' for more discussion.

horizon of expectations (German, *Erwartungshorizont*) A term created by the critic Hans Robert Jauss to describe how the reading process is affected by collective assumptions and ideas. The horizon of expectation is always changing over time: it is affected by GENRE, CONVENTION, DECORUM, IDEOLOGY and much else. Some expectations are built into a text, but readers respond to them in different ways. It maintains that AESTHETIC DISTANCE (the GAP between reader and writer) is vital in interpreting a text. These ideas are linked to HERMENEUTIC considerations about the limits of how we can engage with the past, and with the 'horizon' of our own experience (see 'bias'). The horizon of expectations built towards RECEPTION THEORY, and the development of READER-RESPONSE CRITICISM.

hubris **(adj. hubristic**; Greek, 'presumption') Excessive pride, leading to self-delusion and ignorance (*HAMARTIA*). In Aristotle's description of tragedy, a moment of recognition (*ANAGNORISIS*) exposes *hubris* and *hamartia*, accompanied by a change of fortune (*PERIPETEIA*). This process breaks CHARACTERS' illusion that they have a godlike superiority, and forces a reassessment of their place in the world around them.

humanism In EARLY MODERN Europe, RENAISSANCE humanism was the cultural movement that encouraged individuals to improve themselves through education, in particular through exposure to CLASSICAL culture. It was combined with a general Reformation transition in which knowledge was centralised around court, rather than the church. Accordingly literature became more secular, and PATRONAGE more prominent. It has many different aspects, of which some of the most important for literature are identified below.

Early humanists like Desiderius Erasmus and Philip Melanchthon encouraged classical learning so that individuals could read the Bible for themselves, and receive religious inspiration from reading. They complained about pedantic SCHOLASTIC readings, and a situation in which congregations listened without understanding to what priests, the guardians of truth, wished to tell them. This was part of a wider movement to recognise the dignity of being human and secular achievements, though still with an awareness of God. It was not until the ENLIGHTENMENT that humanist standards for learning were detached from explicitly religious concerns.

Humanism led to sweeping changes in the school curriculum. Children received a comprehensive education in Latin, kept COMMONPLACE BOOKS, IMITATED CLASSICAL AUTHORS, and learnt about RHETORIC and ORATORY. The individual's public PERSONA began to assert itself more (a process described by NEW HISTORICISTS as 'SELF-FASHIONING', and the concept of the 'AUTHOR' developed further. In short, humanism helped literature to become more of a public performance, which was assisted by developments in printing.

In the twentieth century 'humanism' also came to describe a secular approach to life that focuses on human achievements and endeavours. There are definite conceptual links with Renaissance humanism, but they are fundamentally different concepts because, as noted above, humanism was guided by Protestantism, and is defined by the influence of classical culture. Its importance for English literary history cannot be ignored.

humanities Academic disciplines that study human culture and learning, seeking to increase awareness and understanding of the diversity of human experience. 'ARTS' is a synonym that emphasises that artistic creation, rather than the natural world or society by themselves, is a central concern of the humanities. LITERATURE is a core humanities subject studied across the world. The humanities sometimes come off badly in comparisons with the sciences, but professionals in the humanities would respond that although its uses are not always immediately visible, it nonetheless has far-reaching social and intellectual benefits. The British scientist and novelist C.P. Snow's published lecture *The Two Cultures and the Scientific Revolution* (1959) is a CLASSIC and much discussed account of the difference between the sciences and humanities, and is a good stimulus to further thought about why the humanities matter.

humours (Latin, 'fluid') The idea, widespread in Medieval and RENAISSANCE Europe, that the balance of four different fluids (humours) controls our behaviour. An imbalance would cause certain CHARACTER traits. Here are the four humours and their associations:

humour	characteristic	condition	element	adjective
blood	happy	hot and moist	air	sanguine
phlegm	cowardly	cold and moist	water	phlegmatic
yellow bile (choler)	stubborn	hot and dry	fire	choleric
black bile	sad	cold and dry	earth	melancholic

Some related terms survive in the modern English IDIOM, such as 'being yellow (i.e. scared)', 'green with envy' and 'temperament' (meaning 'balance'). Literary CHARACTERIZATION was affected by the idea of four humours while it was current as a medical principle; COMEDY OF HUMOURS is named as a separate GENRE that makes light of unbalanced characters.

hymn A lyric poem in praise of an elevated subject, with Christian associations in English literature. Protestant hymns, divided into QUATRAINS of various METRES (see entry for details) are an influential and popular form of hymn (with roots in the BALLAD STANZA), but there are other varieties. Many English hymns are written to be read, such as Henry Longfellow's 'Hymn to the Night' (1839):

> I heard the sounds of sorrow and delight,
> The manifold, soft chimes,
> That fill the haunted chambers of the Night,
> Like some old poet's rhymes.
>
> From the cool cisterns of the midnight air
> My spirit drank repose;
> The fountain of perpetual peace flows there, —
> from those deep cisterns flows. (ll.13–20)

hypallage (Greek, 'exchange'; pronounced 'hy-**pal**-ah-ge') A common FIGURE of speech that takes a term that describes or agrees with one thing and applies it to something else. TRANSFERRED EPITHET is a specific FORM of hypallage; so, arguably, is SPOONERISM. It sometimes suggests the speaker's confusion, and sometimes works like PERSONIFICATION. In line eight of 'Howl' Allen Ginsburg employs the hypallage 'unshaven rooms' while describing 'the best minds of my generation'

> who cowered in unshaven rooms in underwear,
> burning their money in wastebaskets and
> listening to the Terror through the wall.

hyperbaton (high-**pur**-bat-on; Greek, 'overstepping') A FIGURE involving disruption to expected word-order (SYNTAX). The *Star Wars* CHARACTER Yoda constantly uses hyperbaton: e.g. 'Rejoice for those around you who transform into the Force. Mourn them do not. Miss them do not.' FORMS of hyperbaton include HYPALLAGE, HYSTERON PROTERON, and ANASTROPHE. It is a means of stretching the capacity of language to create new forms of expression. It sometimes requires effort to understand, and can also be difficult to read sometimes. It is common across literary history, particularly in the EARLY MODERN period. Emily Dickinson uses it to provide EMPHASIS in this complete poem (c.1874):

> The Infinite a sudden Guest
> Has been assumed to be—
> But how can that stupendous come
> Which never went away? (Poem 1309)

hyperbole (Greek, 'overthrow') A TROPE where deliberate exaggeration is used to emphasise a point. 'I'm starving' or 'I'm freezing' are hyperbolic phrases of the type found in everyday English, neither of which are to be taken literally. It can be used for IRONIC effect or to create bombastic speeches. Its near-opposites are LITOTES and MEIOSIS, both forms of understatement.

hypermetrical (Greek, 'beyond the measure') A line of verse that contains more syllables than expected in the METRE. Hypercatalectic (i.e. the opposite of CATALECTIC) is an alternative term. EXTRAMETRICAL refers to the addition of one syllable, normally at the end of a line or half-line (though see 'anacrusis'). This sometimes creates LIGHT (FEMININE) endings. 'HYPOMETRICAL' is its ANTONYM.

hypertext An electronic text available on the internet (not a photo-facsimile). Hypertexts make works more accessible, and provide relevant information quickly. Whether they match the experience of reading the printed page is a personal matter. However, electronic resources aren't always reliable, if only because they are easier to publish than printed books. For this reason caution needs to be taken when using hypertexts. Research skills are just as important when using hypertexts as with printed material. See p. 385 for some recommended websites.

hypometrical (Greek, 'beneath a measure') A line of verse that contains fewer syllables than expected, based on the METRE. HYPERMETRICAL is its ANTONYM. ACEPHALOUS (missing at the beginning) and CATALECTIC (at the end) lines are hypometrical.

hypotaxis (adj. hypotactic) The use of CONJUNCTIONS (e.g. 'because') to make SUBORDINATE CLAUSES, in order to making the relation between phrases clear. 'I followed him, but he didn't know where to go' is hypotactic; 'I followed him. He didn't know where to go' is PARATACTIC. PERIODIC SENTENCES are always hypotactic. Hypotactic writing (or STYLE) always shows a clear progression, which is either logical (making an ARGUMENT), temporal or showing causes (making a NARRATIVE). Awareness of hypotaxis makes it easier to recognise how word-order creates MEANING.

hysterical realism A term coined recently by the critic James Wood to describe some POSTMODERN novels that contain lots of realistic details and JARGON. Wood suggests this obsession with detail is hyperactive, and that personal insight into CHARACTER is lost. Hysterical realist novels are typically long and encyclopedic as a result: e.g. David Foster Wallace's *Infinite Jest* (1996) and Thomas Pynchon's *Against the Day* (2006).

hysteron proteron (Greek, 'latter former') A FIGURE (specifically, a form of HYPERBATON) in which the logical order or time-frame is disrupted: e.g. 'Get dressed and have a shower'.

I

iamb (adj. iambic) A METRICAL FOOT consisting of an unstressed SYLLABLE followed by a stressed one (o –). 'Rejoice', 'alone', 'I went to school today' and 'I'd like to start again, if that's all right' are all iambic. The iamb is easily the most common FOOT in English, which is because it comes closest to matching everyday speech. It creates BINARY METRES (two-beat RHYTHMS) and RISING RHYTHMS. For variation TROCHEES and SPONDEES can be substituted into an iambic pattern. An example from Thomas Wyatt:

> From these high hills as when a spring doth fall
> It trilleth down with still and subtle course.
>
> (47.1–2)

So dominant are iambic metres in English that FREE VERSE was effectively an attempt to rebel against them, as was SPRUNG RHYTHM. Iambs have often been used five to a line, creating IAMBIC PENTAMETER. This sound-pattern is the basis of such common forms as BLANK VERSE (if unrhymed), HEROIC COUPLETS and SONNETS. It is found throughout Shakespeare's works, but ORIGINATED around Chaucer's time. Eight-syllable iambic TETRAMETER has also been widely used in verse, while iambic HEXAMETER is also referred to as the ALEXANDRINE. It's relatively easy to recognise the 'di-dum' iambic pattern without SCANNING a passage. Once you can hear the basic METRE, you can start hearing how poets depart from it to create poetic effects.

ibid. (*ibidem*, Latin) In the same place: in other words, within the same book or passage. 'OP. CIT.' is a SYNONYM, and 'LOC. CIT.' is used for reference to a specific passage.

ictus (**ik**-tus; Latin, 'a beat') An EMPHASIS placed on a syllable. It isn't that useful for SCANNING English verse: its meaning is covered by the terms STRESS and ACCENT.

ideology The shared beliefs of a group. An ideology affects the thought, custom and lifestyles of the group that holds it. Ideologies are held both consciously and unconsciously. 'Ideology' is found in common parlance as a negative concept (e.g. right-wing ideology; capitalist ideology), but as a term meaning 'idea-system' it is indispensable. In particular, MARXIST CRITICS have concerned themselves with the relation of ideology and literature, in order to assess the social function of literature. Literature reveals and exposes ideologies. Criticism too is adept at uncovering ideologies latent in literature: e.g. POSTCOLONIAL CRITICISM explores the presence of colonial assumptions.

Ideology is only 'bad' if it thrives on untested assumptions, and allows people (usually the dominant social class) to control others and avoid upheaval. Literature encourages critical thinking that makes readers come to independent judgments, and challenge the sort of complacency upon which ideology is based. Whether literature can contribute to social progress doing this is a separate question, but it does suggest that literary writing is likely to be welcomed in any liberal, democratic society.

idiolect The form of language used by a particular individual, which may involve distinctive use of GRAMMAR, SYNTAX and PRONUNCIATION. Though it may sound attractive, it often describes a STYLE that veers toward OBSCURITY and is uncommunicative. Most writers acknowledged as great would be said to have an individual style, rather than an idiolect. It is also widely agreed that a private language cannot exist, since language depends on shared CONVENTIONS about meaning. DIALECT is the equivalent term for groups of speakers, but for this reason is more neutral.

idiom (adj. idiomatic) A word, phrase or form of expression particular to a specific group or language, especially when its meaning is not apparent from the words alone. In other words, an idiom is a phrase that a non-native speaker could only understand after explanation: e.g. 'he's driving me round the bend and up the wall' is not about someone's adventures in a car, but being irritated. Other common English idioms are: 'on cloud nine', 'jump the gun', 'bite the dust', 'feeling wobbly' (is nervous), and 'in a pickle'. Idiomatic language includes everyday FIGURATIVE LANGUAGE, which usually passes unnoticed because it is CLICHÉD. SLANG and COLLOQUIALISM are both forms of idiom too. More generally, idiom also refers to the language, or DISCOURSE, used by a particular group; e.g. the idiom of hip-hop, or of Yorkshire. Idiom is primarily spoken, and its literary use is mostly to describe the successful replication of an idiom on the page. Idiom sometimes refers to a writing STYLE, but there it is just a vaguer alternative for VOICE, DICTION, TEXTURE or similar.

idyll (idyllic; Greek, 'little picture') A short poem set in the countryside. The term is firmly associated with the Greek poet Theocritus's *Idylls* (c. 200 B.C.E.), which are the earliest surviving examples of PASTORAL (BUCOLIC) poetry. Like later ECLOGUES, the idyll celebrates the peacefulness of rural life. The term is most often used as an ADJECTIVE, though in LITERARY CRITICISM the term is never a SYNONYM for 'ideal'.

image (imagery) In literature, an image is a mental representation of something formed from CONCRETE language. 'Image' is rarely restricted to the visual: any imagined sensation is usually regarded as a literary image (e.g. 'the smell of marmalade', 'the gobbling turkey'). Image refers to literal usages ('tree'), as well as FIGURATIVE LANGUAGE ('tree of life'); it is sometimes a SYNONYM for METAPHOR and SIMILE. 'Literal' involves physical description, sometimes of a particular scene; 'FIGURATIVE' incorporates SYMBOLISM and ALLEGORY.

NEW CRITICISM began a trend for studying images as a unifying principle of works. Critical analyses of imagery usually take greater interest in figurative images because they are not required by a text. Such studies have usually focused on MOTIFS and image-clusters, though other critics have suggested that it is an error to consider images outside of their direct CONTEXT. Some studies have even tried to study images to gain access to an AUTHOR'S IMAGINATION: e.g. analysing Milton's poetry for all the images he must have seen before he went blind. It's worth remembering that images in any work are always connected, and it can be misleading to concentrate on one image to excess. It's also easy to exaggerate the coherence of imagery throughout a work: just because William Shakespeare's *Richard II* contains lots of sun, earth and sea images, it doesn't necessarily mean that Shakespeare charges every single image with special significance.

imaginary order A term used by Jacques Lacan to describe an infant's conception of the world before it can use language. The child is uninfluenced by the social and cultural codes that language brings with it, and can make no distinction between itself and the outside world. Its worldview is a well-rounded fantasy. Once children begin to consider their own image in a mirror (at the 'mirror stage'), the imaginary order is disrupted, which leads them to consider the self as something separate to the world (though Lacan would hold this to be a fantasy). As children learn to use language they enter the SYMBOLIC ORDER, where they absorb the same DISCOURSES as everyone else. There is no direct literary application to these ideas—children who can't use language can't write literature, for a start—but it is part of a Lacanian take on PSYCHOANALYSIS that has exerted serious influence, and asks deep questions about how language affects thought.

imagination The ability to generate mental images and concepts that are not based on sense-impressions. Thinking of a tree when none is in sight requires imaginative effort, as does imagining that the tree in front of you is about to fly into space. Imagination is never a direct IMITATION of something, and can be considered essential to ORIGINALITY.

Like originality and WIT, the meaning of imagination has changed over time as our knowledge of the human mind and ideas about literature have shifted. In EARLY MODERN literature, imagination was contrasted with reason. It was generally considered unruly, noisy and untrustworthy. A passage in Edmund Spenser's *The Faerie Queene* (1590, 96), for example, represents the imaginative part of the brain as 'a chamber [which] filled was with flyes | Which buzzed all about, and made such sound, | That they encombred all mens eares and eyes' (II.ix.51.1–3). ROMANTICISM prized imagination as a source of individual creative energy, and Samuel Taylor Coleridge differentiated it from FANCY, which for centuries had been a near SYNONYM. Imagination has retained these positive associations today, and is often spoken of as a creative force that only a few utilise to the full by letting their 'imagination run wild'.

Imagists (c.1910s) A group of poets writing FREE VERSE who maintained that clear, solid images were essential to good poetry. Ezra Pound and H.D (Hilda Doolittle) are two of its key names. It was influenced by French SYMBOLISM, and is of particular interest for how it affected the STYLE of later MODERNIST writers, such as T.S. Eliot and Wallace Stevens.

imitation (mimesis) The process of following or reproducing a particular example of something. Imitation shows how writers relate to established traditions and the natural world around them. It has been a fundamental concept in LITERARY CRITICISM ever since the CLASSICAL period. Plato doubted that poetry could convey truth, and his reason was that it was imitative (see 'abstract language'). Aristotle was the first of many to defend poetry against this claim, arguing that it reflects a human inclination to imitate nature, and that this allows the inner qualities of things to be revealed. Horace's notion that poetry is a 'speaking picture' (see '*ut pictura poesis*') continues this line of thinking.

Imitation, then, was considered an attempt to reproduce the truth, goodness and beauty found in nature. Renaissance HUMANISM placed the imitation of CLASSICAL AUTHORS at the centre of a well-rounded education: some sought to recreate the STYLE of Virgil or Cicero as closely as possible (see 'Ciceronian'); others sought to digest the examples offered by classical authors, and ultimately to emulate them. NEOCLASSICISM upheld the intrinsic value of imitation, and it was only with the rise of ROMANTICISM, which promoted individual ORIGINALITY, that the modern distaste for imitation arose. PLAGIARISM and derivativeness are at the extreme end of the imitative spectrum, however.

Legitimate imitation remains important to literary writing. Any writing with a FIXED FORM (e.g. SONNET, SESTINA) is consciously imitative. Works that are described as REALISTIC or true-to-life are imitative too. The image of the writer as lone artist hides the essentially collaborative nature of writing; e.g. T.S. Eliot's *The Waste Land* consciously draws on tradition in order to draw upon the legacies of past literature. Another related idea is ANXIETY OF INFLUENCE, which suggests that all writers are worried about stepping out of the shadow of past works. In short, imitation is unavoidable because it describes an integral aspect of literary composition. All literature mirrors the real world at some level, and does so in a way that has continuity with how others have attempted the same.

imperative An utterance that expresses a command: e.g. 'Help me!', 'Tell her what you thought.' It is a GRAMMATICAL MOOD, alongside INDICATIVE and SUBJUNCTIVE moods. In literature, imperatives are reliably found in INVOCATIONS.

implied author The impression of a work's creator gained from reading the TEXT. The actual AUTHOR, by contrast, may have written other works using a different PERSONA, or have deliberately distanced him/herself from a NARRATOR. STRUCTURAL IRONY and SELF-REFLEXIVE thoughts are ways to draw attention to the implied author. The term allowed NEW CRITICS to acknowledge AUTHORIAL presence in texts without claiming this was the actual author's VOICE (thus avoiding the INTENTIONAL FALLACY). It is similar in meaning to VOICE (authorial presence), and has been used as evidence that multiple voices exist in a text (see 'dialogic criticism'). It has suffered criticism, however, for drawing a fine distinction that in many works barely exists.

implied reader The impression of a work's ideal reader gained from reading the TEXT. Actual readers inevitably bring their own circumstances and thoughts to a reading of the text, which is traced by RECEPTION HISTORY: the implied reader possesses only those assumptions essential to a full understanding of a work. The implied reader of English DEVOTIONAL POETRY, for example, is religious, or at least conscious of the relevant religious tradition. The term is allied to READER-RESPONSE CRITICISM. It is debateable, however, whether it is possible or desirable to establish the characteristics of an imaginary reader who has no BIAS. Modern terms like 'implied reader' or 'religious' may themselves reflect a twenty-first-century

VIEWPOINT different from that intended by the original text. The historical GAP cannot be fully bridged.

impressionism Primarily the name of a radical nineteenth-century artistic movement that sought to convey the fleeting impressions of a scene. It is more faithful to the viewing experience, and marked a shift away from artistic REALISM. Claude Monet was its leading figure. In literary criticism, 'impressionism' is sometimes used to describe related aspects of MODERNISM, such as INTERIOR MONOLOGUE, SYMBOLISM and Imagist poetry (e.g. Ezra Pound's poetry). Early twentieth-century novelists like Henry James, Joseph Conrad and Ford Madox Ford have also been described as 'literary impressionists'. However, like its counterpart 'EXPRESSIONISM', its meaning for literature is rarely clear, and is best avoided unless making a direct ANALOGY with works of art.

impressionistic criticism An approach to literature that prioritises the reader's own reactions (impressions). PERSONAL CRITICISM and AUTOBIOGRAPHICAL CRITICISM are near SYNONYMS, and emphasise the relevance of individual experience; 'impressionistic criticism' suggests ties with ROMANTICISM. In any case, such criticism makes no attempt at an objective interpretation. This has been taken up as a FEMINIST cause on the grounds that it is white male critics (like early NEW CRITICS and Matthew Arnold—see 'disinterestedness') who have placed OBJECTIVE interpretation as an ideal, which is more important than hearing individual, marginalised voices. Some GAY AND LESBIAN CRITICS have also promoted the need for personal testimony in criticism. Like JUDICIAL CRITICISM it is widespread and perfectly natural. Yet purely opinionated writing is generally held by examiners and many scholars as unsuitable in academic contexts, and any attempt at PERSONAL CRITICISM needs to be clear about what it is trying to achieve. The New Critics' idea of an AFFECTIVE FALLACY still holds sway.

incremental repetition The use of identical structures to develop a narrative or other idea, particularly in BALLADS. ANAPHORA is the form of REPETITION often used for this effect, but larger elements within the STANZA may also be repeated to create the effect. It is often more striking when read aloud. The second and final stanza of 'In my Dreams' by Stevie Smith repeats a single phrase at its ending, which becomes more complex and assured each time it recurs:

> In my dreams they are always waving their
>   hands and saying goodbye,

And they give me the stirrup cup and I smile
as I drink,
I am glad the journey is set, I am glad I am
going,
I am glad, I am glad, that my friends don't
know what I think.

incunabula (Latin, 'swaddling clothes') A European book printed in the first fifty years of Western printing, i.e. prior to 1501. Johannes Gutenberg was hard at the press from 1450 and William Caxton began printing in English around 1475/76. It shouldn't be forgotten, though, that the earliest examples of moveable type printing are Korean, and date from seven centuries earlier.

indentation Positioning of text further from the left margin than nearby text. It is used to mark PROSE and VERSE PARAGRAPHS. In poetry it can indicate the continuation of one line into the next (sometimes counted as two), for example in BALLADS. Poets who have experimented with LINEATION, particularly in the early twentieth century onwards, use indentation for effect, as the final lines of D.H Lawrence's 'End of Another Home Holiday' (1913) show (it describes the call of a bird, the corncrake):

With a hoarse, insistent request that falls
Unweariedly, unweariedly,
Asking something more of me
Yet more of me.

indeterminacy Uncertainty within a text, either as a literary feature or an inherent property. An AUTHOR may be deliberately indeterminate by introducing AMBIGUITY, rhetorical APORIA or a CRUX. DECONSTRUCTIONISTS contend that multiple meanings are always available, and that no definitive interpretation is possible. Faced with indeterminacy, a SUBJECTIVE interpretation is the only fallback; in other words, the AFFECTIVE FALLACY becomes inevitable.

indicative An utterance that expresses ('indicates') a fact: e.g. 'it's not a big deal'; 'that cat is overweight.' Most spoken and written English is in indicative MOOD; IMPERATIVE and SUBJUNCTIVE are much less common.

induction An alternative term for PROLOGUE, only more ARCHAIC. The best-known example in English literature is the METADRAMATIC induction to Shakespeare's *The Taming of the Shrew* (1594). It introduces a CHARACTER, Christopher Sly, who is about to watch a play. A messenger arrives at the end of the induction to announce to Sly that a COMEDY is about to begin. The final lines before Act 1 begins are:

> *Sly* Marry, I will let them play it. Is it not a
> comonty [comedy] a Christmas gambold,
> or a tumbling-trick?
> *Page* No, my good lord, it is more pleasing stuff.
> *Sly* What, household stuff?
> *Page* It is a kind of history.
> *Sly* Well, we'll see't. Come, madam wife, sit
> by my side, and let the world slip, we
> shall ne'er be younger. (Ind.2.137–44)

inflection Variation of a word to express a GRAMMATICAL feature, such as tense, number or gender: e.g. 'play' becomes 'played' in perfect tense; 'tooth' becomes 'teeth' in plural. Modern English has relatively few inflected forms compared to OLD and MIDDLE ENGLISH. POLYPTOTON is a rhetorical FIGURE involving multiple inflected forms of a single word.

inkhorn term A term deriving from older texts or Latin, as opposed to everyday VERNACULAR speech. An inkhorn was a device for storing ink that was associated with book learning. The term applies particularly to writers in the EARLY MODERN period who were mocked for reviving obscure terms and being generally fussy in their writing. Some words called inkhorn terms at the time have survived in modern English— 'ability', 'ANALYSIS', 'encyclopedia' and 'skeleton' for example—while others have not: 'eximious' (excellent), 'illecebrous' (enticing) and 'exolete' (faded) among others.

in medias res (Latin, 'in the middle of things') The technique of opening a NARRATIVE in the thick of the action. Most EPIC narratives begin *in medias res*, as do most James Bond movies. In both cases, the audience does not need to worry about where the opening (usually vivid) incident fits into the STORY, since background information will be provided later. Its enduring appeal is simply that a beginning *in medias res* is more likely to grab the audience's attention than a lengthy factual EXPOSITION is. It is a feature of so many works that it would be a CLICHÉ, were it not that it still creates dynamic, diverse PLOT STRUCTURES in different works.

innuendo (Latin, 'nod at') An expression that hints at a secondary meaning through ALLUSION or AMBIGUITY. The intended meaning is often critical or suggestive; sexual innuendo or *DOUBLE ENTENDRE* is probably the commonest form. Like SARCASM, it is often used to make a point sharply, and is rarely found in literary language.

inscape/instress Two terms used by Gerard Manley Hopkins to describe the individual essence of things (inscape) and the divine force that holds them together (instress). Instress is linked to the natural poetic EMPHASES in SPRUNG RHYTHM. Hopkins did not consider perception a one-way process: we should not just be struck by instress, but must actively immerse ourselves too. This union allows us to perceive the unique inscape of objects.

inspiration (from Latin 'breathe in') A creative influence that stimulates authors to write. People, situations, emotions, or ideas are all cited as forms of inspiration. External or divine influence has been thought a source of literary inspiration for many centuries, as far back as Plato's reference to poetic 'madness' in *Ion* (see '*vates*'). Indeed, the word 'enthusiasm' derives from a Greek term meaning 'possessed by a god'. In addition, writers have frequently appealed to the MUSES for creative assistance, particularly in INVOCATIONS. ROMANTICISM began a shift towards inward inspiration, coming from the individual, and this brought with it a renewed EMPHASIS on ORIGINALITY. Since then, despite attempts to show the psychological grounds of inspiration (see 'psychoanalytic criticism'), there has been a lot less interest in inspiration as something unique to the so-called genius of the writer, and POST-STRUCTURALIST CRITICS highlight that works come about from social and cultural DISCOURSES bearing down on a writer. Equally, there are certainly times when writers feel an instant urge to write something down.

intensifier A word or prefix that emphasises another word's meaning: 'very', 'much', 'all', and 'hyper-' are some intensifiers. QUALIFIERS are the GRAMMATICAL counterpart of intensifiers. Note the difference from SUPERLATIVE, which shows that an adjective applies to the greatest degree. Intensifiers are sometimes used as stop-gaps (CHEVILLES) in verse.

intentional fallacy The error (FALLACY) of reading a literary text in light of why we think the author wrote the work. 'The Intentional Fallacy' is the name of the 1946 essay in which the term was coined by the NEW CRITICS W.K. Wimsatt and Monroe Beardsley. They argued that literary texts are self-contained (AUTOTELIC) objects, and so the author's intention as manifested within the text was still deemed to be relevant for interpretation (though HERMENEUTICS has challenged this view). This is why they thought it was a mistake to draw on details from an AUTHOR'S life or thought outside the text: they were protecting the poem's OBJECTIVE value. The AFFECTIVE FALLACY—that readers shouldn't base interpretation on their personal reaction—had the same aim in mind. The so-called BIOGRAPHICAL FALLACY is slightly different to both: it describes a reading of a text that tries to tell us more about how the author lived and felt. The New Critical focus on the text rather than AUTHOR reached its logical conclusion twenty-one years later, when Roland Barthes, with STRUCTURALIST ideas in mind, argued for the 'DEATH OF THE AUTHOR'.

interdisciplinary An approach based on combining the methods and interests of two fields considered separate. Various academic 'STUDIES' encourage interdisciplinary work; e.g. SEXUALITY STUDIES analyses sexual orientation from literary, historical, sociological, psychological and other perspectives. Interdisciplinary research makes even more sense if you think about how thin the divide between some subjects is, and how little co-operation often occurs. It pushes the boundaries of literary criticism in a different way to COMPARATIVE LITERATURE.

interior monologue An account of an individual's thoughts and perceptions that is apparently written down directly. It is often ALLUSIVE, DIGRESSIVE and PARATACTIC as associations are made with little logical connection. It is a transcript of private thoughts, rather than a performance of them; all the same, by being transferred into language, the thoughts involved have inevitably been processed and edited. An interior monologue is seldom BIOGRAPHICAL. It can form part of a FIRST-PERSON NARRATION, where it is introduced without introduction, or THIRD-PERSON, where some indication is given. FREE INDIRECT DISCOURSE is a narrative style that naturally integrates interior monologue into description of events.

Interior monologue is strongly associated with STREAM OF CONSCIOUSNESS. That much is certain. Otherwise the only agreement is that people have varying opinions about whether interior monologue is a subcategory of stream of consciousness, or vice versa, or neither. One fairly simple distinction is to hold stream of consciousness as the flow of a CHARACTER'S conscious thoughts; in other words, one aspect of CHARACTERIZATION, alongside DESCRIPTION and ACTION. Interior monologue is similar to DRAMATIC MONOLOGUE except privately spoken, not performed. So stream of consciousness is CONTENT and interior monologue a literary form—though this is disputable. This definition has the advantage of reminding readers that interior monologue does not tap into characters' souls or provide psychological insight outright: it is a particular mode of writing. It is closely associated with MODERNISM, with James Joyce's *Ulysses* and the novels of Virginia Woolf being among the most celebrated examples. Here is an extract from the final section of *Ulysses*, 'Penelope', which contains a virtually unpunctuated monologue by Molly Bloom:

> [...] people were always going away and we never I remember that day with the waves and the boats with their high heads rocking and the swell of the ship those Officers uniforms on shore leave made me seasick he didn't say anything he was very serious I had the high buttoned boots on and my shirt was blowing she kissed me six or seven times didn't I cry yes I believe I did or near it my lips were taittering when I said goodbye [...]

interlude (Latin, 'between play') A short, light performance given during breaks in a larger entertainment or banquet. It is primarily a MEDIEVAL tradition, which was important before professional theatres were founded. An interlude could be COMIC, FARCICAL, DIDACTIC or something else. Henry Medwall's *Fulgens and Lucrece* (c.1490) is a well-regarded interlude that examines the idea of nobility.

internal rhyme A RHYME that occurs within a verse line; i.e. any rhyme that isn't an END RHYME. LEONINE and CROSSED RHYME are forms of internal rhyme. Like NEAR RHYME, it is a variation on more common rhyme forms. As a result, it sometimes sounds clumsy, but more often creates delicate and unexpected EMPHASES, as in the internal rhyme on 'still' in the final stanza of Henry Vaughan's '¶':

> Either disperse these mists, which blot and fill
> My perspective (still) as they pass,
> [telescope/viewing glass]
> Or else remove me hence unto that hill
> Where I shall need no glass.

interpolation The insertion of material into a work at a later date, almost always without the AUTHOR's consent.

interpretation (Latin, 'explain, understand, translate') An attempt to make sense of a TEXT. Interpretation usually involves ANALYSIS of difficult points in a text, such as AMBIGUITY, a CRUX or FIGURATIVE LANGUAGE. HERMENEUTICS is the study of interpretation. That term, like EXEGESIS, has its roots in interpretation of the Bible, which provides the foundation of the Western interpretative tradition (see 'allegory' and 'four levels of meaning'). Some PSYCHOANALYTIC CRITICS, READER-RESPONSE CRITICS and others besides have argued that all forms of reading involve writing/ interpretation. In this view, criticism is not a neutral act: it is more like a form of artistic creation in itself.

intertextuality The idea that TEXTS are interconnected. The term was introduced by Julia Kristeva and is widely used (even appearing in school exam guidelines). It helps explain how GENRES and DISCOURSES create meaning in a particular text: i.e. a detective story is meaningful because it draws on previous stories in its form and STYLE. It encompasses ALLUSION, PARODY, IMITATION and other forms of conscious reference, and is sometimes used as a posh term for 'influence'. However, the term has broader theoretical implications that it's worth being aware of.

'Intertextuality' suggests that texts are collages of quotations from other texts. It examines the complex interactions between texts, most of which happen without our knowledge. The AUTHOR does not control the production of meaning (see 'death of the author'), but gathers together bits of pre-existing language and ideas. Thus texts are not representations of reality, but merely repeat existing worldviews. All this has origins in the STRUCTURALIST idea that meaning in a text is created from the relation of different signs to one another. However, it is essentially POST-STRUCTURALIST because it argues that texts aren't individual containers that exist independently. Kristeva was interested in so-called 'structuration': the network of existing patterns that generate meaning. Texts are inseparable from the cultural forces that create them: in other words, texts and CONTEXTS are basically the same (this is an important principle of NEW HISTORICISM). In this situation, the reader's role in creating meaning is very important. All interpretation depends on recognition and response to the cluster of intertextual references in a text.

intonation The manner in which something is said; i.e. changes in PITCH, VOICE and EMPHASIS when speaking. The phrase 'pears are purple', for example, shifts its meaning depending on intonation: If 'pears' is ACCENTED, it stresses that pears, as opposed to apples or bananas, are purple; if 'are' is accented, it insists that pears really are purple; if 'purple' is ACCENTED, it could be a definite statement of fact (if the pitch stays flat), or become a question, hinting at disbelief: 'pears are purple???'. Intonation affects meaning in DRAMATIC and POETIC texts, and is worth bearing in mind. It is a key way in which ACTORS interpret play scripts. It is one aspect of thinking about drama and poetry as texts for performance, along with other features like volume, silence, GESTURE and how speakers interact with each other. As such, it is an important consideration when thinking about both the writer's and performer's STYLE.

intrusive narrator An OMNISCIENT (all-knowing) PERSONA telling a story who offers reflections and other personal DIGRESSIONS on the story. It is particularly found in THIRD-PERSON NARRATION, and is very common among nineteenth-century prose writers. Henry Fielding manages to be an intrusive narrator in the chapter headings of *Tom Jones* (1730), which is one of the earliest NOVELS. The AUTHORIAL persona comically conditions our reactions to such chapters as 'Chapter VII: Containing such grave matter that the reader cannot laugh once the through the whole chapter, unless peradventure he should laugh at the author' and 'Chapter XIV: A most dreadful chapter indeed; and which few readers ought to venture upon in an evening; especially when alone'.

invective (adj. and noun) A bitterly critical attack of something. It denounces a person, practice or place, and often reflects as much on the person making the invective as whatever is being criticised. It can involve BURLESQUE, LAMPOON, CARICATURE, SATIRE and unkind EPITHETS. Jonathan Swift's *Gulliver's Travels* (1726) contains numerous prose examples of invective. Invective DRAMATIC speeches are often powerful in performance. Timon of Athens, for example, expresses his anger at the world through invective in Shakespeare's EPONYMOUS play. Here are the first lines of his speech outside Athens in Act Four, Scene 1:

> Let me look back upon thee. O thou wall
> That girdles in those wolves, dive in the earth,
> And fence not Athens! Matrons, turn
>   incontinent!
> Obedience, fail in children! Slaves and fools,
> Pluck the grave wrinkled Senate from the
>   bench,
> And minister in their steads!

inversion The reversal of the normal order of something for literary effect. It is a basic means of providing EMPHASIS and originality of expression in literary language. 'HYPERBATON' is the related rhetorical term, and it covers various kinds of SYNTACTIC inversion. In PROSODY, inversion helps shape a metrical line; e.g. by inverting a IAMB to make a TROCHEE. More broadly, a dramatic *PERIPETEIA* is an inversion of a CHARACTER'S fortunes, for better or worse. Tragic HEROES suffer a cruel reversal of their circumstances, showing that their previous good fortune was based on chance and self-delusion.

invocation An appeal to a supernatural being (often a MUSE) for assistance in composing the work just begun. It is an EPIC CONVENTION: Homer's and Milton's epic NARRATIVES invoke muses at the outset. Note that this is not done by the AUTHOR, but a PERSONA (i.e. the author's VOICE in the poem, not the actual poet). It is a form of APOSTROPHE, and often involves PERSONIFICATION. It has never lost its grand epic CONNOTATIONS, and has been used in PARODIES of the tradition.

irony (from Greek, 'dissembling') A form of expression involving disparity between expectation and reality. This can be created in numerous ways for many different effects, and has been used by writers spanning Aeschylus to Jane Austen. Irony is often divided into three categories: verbal, situational and structural. VERBAL IRONY is an important rhetorical TROPE, which occurs when a speaker says one thing and means the opposite. SITUATIONAL IRONY arises when an outcome (known in advance by the audience) does not meet a CHARACTER'S expectations. STRUCTURAL IRONY is when a writer makes the audience aware of the FICTIONAL nature of his writing (see separate entries on these topics for further explanation). As expected, other kinds of irony do not fit easily into these categories. These are DRAMATIC IRONY, TRAGIC IRONY, COSMIC IRONY, COMIC IRONY, SOCRATIC IRONY.

In everyday speech irony is often taken to mean 'strangely apt' or 'coincidental', but this confuses its strict dictionary definition. Irony can be an element of SARCASM and SATIRE, but is distinct to both: sarcasm is a crude form of irony used by embittered speakers; SATIRE may make use of irony and WIT, but is always directed to making a particular, critical point. People who use irony (ironists) usually create an impression of subtlety and composure. Often irony informs a writer's whole perspective on the world, rather than being a DEVICE deployed in particular instances. The 'ironic gaze' on life's absurdities is one such posture, particularly associated with ROMANTIC IRONY. Irony is associated with POSTMODERNISM too, when used to view society from a distance and avoid committing to belief-systems. A DECONSTRUCTIONIST take on irony is that it can give a text unity where all other methods have been discounted.

irregular ode A form of LYRIC POEM that adapts the regular structure of the CLASSICAL ODE. Abraham Cowley is attributed with creating the irregular ode in his *Pindarique Odes* (1668), which modified its STANZA pattern. In the preface to that work Cowley explained that 'I have in these two *Odes* of *Pindar* taken, left out, and added what I please; nor make it much my aim to let the Reader know precisely what he spoke, what was his *way* and *manner* of speaking'. Many eighteenth- and nineteenth-century odes took these words to heart.

isocolon (Greek, 'of equal clauses') Like PARISON, it is a specific form of PARALLELISM: it refers to phrases that not only have a similar form, but have a similar length too.

isometric (Greek, 'of equal measures') A series of LINES with the same length and METRE. It can refer to verse FORMS that contain the same line-shape throughout, such as BLANK VERSE, COUPLETS and the SONNET, and to such STANZAS as RHYME ROYAL and *OTTAVA RIMA*. This creates great scope for variation within the basic line-structure (e.g. CATALEXIS) and the relationship between lines (e.g. ENJAMBEMENT). The opposite is HETEROMETRIC. In non-poetic examples, ISOCOLON is the RHETORICAL term referring to phrases of similar length.

issue A reprinting of an EDITION with improvements that are not large enough to count as a new EDITION. If an EDITION was printed without pages 100 to 102, for example, it would be re-issued with those pages restored.

J

Jacobean (1603–25) Relating to the period during which King James I reigned over England. 'Jacobean' comes from the Latin form of his name, 'Jacobus'. James was the first Stuart monarch, and was previously James VI of Scotland. The Jacobean and ELIZABETHAN periods saw a remarkable flourishing of literature: e.g. William Shakespeare's plays and METAPHYSICAL POETRY (see p. 361 for more). James played a part in intellectual life too: he styled himself as a wise monarch, which encouraged writers to seek patronage from him; he staged court MASQUES; and he was associated with one of the period's most important publications, the Authorized (King James) Version of the Bible.

jargon Vocabulary specific to a group of people, particularly in the same profession. Many jargon terms are NEOLOGISMS, are often PERIPHRASTIC or EUPHEMISTIC, and form distinct DICTION or IDIOM. The term 'jargon' implies, sometimes unfairly, that a word is exclusive and impressive but conveys little meaning. This dictionary of literary terms, then, hopes to show that terms like DECONSTRUCTION and DRAMATURGY are relevant concepts rather than pointless jargon.

jeremiad (from 'Jeremiah', a biblical prophet) A fierce expression of distress at the wicked ways of society. Jeremiads often follow up their condemnation with a prediction of imminent disaster. They sometimes contain long catalogues (LITANIES) of moral failings. Jeremiads are a self-standing form sometimes found in literature, and are also found within some LAMENTS and ELEGIES. 'TIRADE' is a general term for a lengthy aggressive speech.

jeu d'esprit (French, 'game of spirit') A witty, elegant and light-hearted piece, such as an EPIGRAM or LIMERICK. *Jeux d'esprit* have a playful TONE, and give the impression of having been prepared quickly.

jig A short COMIC performance (an AFTER-PIECE) given at the end of plays in the sixteenth and seventeenth centuries. It originally involved a lively song and dance routine, but later included brief FARCES. It particularly helped to lighten the mood at the end of TRAGEDIES.

jingle A short verse that uses catchy ALLITERATION and/or RHYMES. Now mostly used to describe memorable little songs in TV and radio adverts, but it can be used as a negative description for DOGGEREL or LIGHT VERSE.

Johnsonian Prose characteristic of Samuel Johnson (1709–84): DIDACTIC, sharp-witted, well balanced, polished, and erudite.

judicial criticism Any approach to a work based on judging its qualities. Note that this term could be confused with criticism concerning the law and legal systems. Most pre-nineteenth-century British literary criticism was judicial in some regard. The derivation of 'criticism', it should be remembered, is the Greek verb meaning 'to judge'. NEOCLASSICISM offered particularly clear guidelines about what was right and wrong with regard to STYLE (see 'decorum' and 'convention'). ROMANTICISM began a movement towards appreciating individual reactions, instead of determining the objective value of a work. It remained part of literary criticism into the twentieth century too (see, for example, Matthew Arnold's ideas about TOUCHSTONES). Later ideas, such as the NEW CRITICAL EMPHASIS on OBJECTIVITY, caused judicial criticism to fade, just as PERSONAL CRITICISM remains a niche area of academic criticism. This isn't to say that people aren't supposed to hold opinions, because it's an entirely natural thing to do (and is essential to CANON formation). Many professionals believe that literary criticism is about more than deciding which texts are better or more beautiful than others, though others think this risks making literary criticism irrelevant to the general reader.

Juvenalian satire An indignant, angry style of verse satire that mercilessly exposes human flaws. This voice is found in the Roman poet Juvenal's *Satires* (c. 100–130). See 'satire' for more discussion.

juvenilia (jew-veh-**nil**-iah; Latin, 'youthful things') An AUTHOR'S early writings. The term usually implies that a work isn't equal to later efforts, and reveals more about an AUTHOR'S development than his or her mature vision. Note two 'i's in the spelling, so as not to create confusion with the works of Juvenal (see above). Jane Austen's early works are among the best known juvenilia.

juxtaposition Placing two things next to each other. A basic literary technique that creates meaningful SYNTACTIC sentences, and can form REPETITION, ANTITHESIS and EMPHASIS. PARATAXIS describes phrases strung together without connecting words.

K

kenning A condensed METAPHOR, commonly used in Old Norse and OLD ENGLISH literature. It takes the form of a compound phrase that doesn't make the terms of the comparison explicit. It is a form of PERIPHRASIS. Kennings are richly evocative: e.g. *hleahtor-smiþ* (laughter-smith) for 'minstrel', or *banhus* (bone-house) for body.

kitchen sink drama A form of REALIST DRAMA about domestic life in Britain, particularly in the 1950s and 60s. You often literally get to see a kitchen sink, which was a radical break from the cosy, DRAWING ROOM comedies of Noël Coward and others popular at the time. Accordingly, John Osborne's *Look Back in Anger* (1956), which takes place in a small flat in the Midlands, was shocking for its time. This interest in gritty social realism has continued since then. It transferred well to the screen, and has become central to British cinema tradition. Alan Sillitoe's novel *Saturday Night, Sunday Morning* (1958) became one of the first successful film ADAPTATIONS, and *The Full Monty* (1997), based on an original screenplay, won international acclaim.

kitsch (noun and adj.) An art-work or object that appeals to popular tastes in a tacky, excessively sentimental and/or pretentious way. Tourist souvenirs provide a super-abundance of good examples; e.g. Leaning Tower of Pisa ashtrays. It has strong negative overtones of being derivative and tasteless, but is also taken to mean items that are 'so bad they're good'. This attitude of ironic admiration can be called 'CAMP', while POSTMODERNISM blurs the divide between high and low, original and repetitive art (see 'simulacrum'). The term isn't often used to describe whole literary works, but is potentially relevant to some GENRE FICTION, PARALITERATURE and MELODRAMAS. Mills and Boon romance novels are the height of literary kitsch.

Künstlerroman ('artist novel') A novel that describes an artist's development to creative maturity. It is a form of *BILDUNGSROMAN* and is often AUTOBIOGRAPHICAL (see also '*roman à clef*'): e.g. James Joyce, *A Portrait of the Artist as a Young Man* (1916).

L

lacuna (pl. lacunae) A GAP in a text, particularly in a manuscript. In a curious case of FORM matching meaning, the surviving version of the Old English poem 'The Ruin' contains numerous lacunae.

Lake Poets (c.1800s) A term originally used negatively to describe three British poets based in the Lake District, Cumbria: William Wordsworth, Samuel Taylor Coleridge and Robert Southey. The epithet is still used, normally with more neutral CONNOTATIONS.

lament A passionate expression of deep sorrow or loss. Laments are often SONG or LYRICS, and follow set CONVENTIONS; the OLD ENGLISH 'The Wife's Lament' is an early surviving example. Two other forms of lament are ELEGY and DIRGE.

lampoon An aggressively SATIRICAL portrait of an individual. Lampoons are gross, blunt CARICATURES designed for ridicule. They are often a feature of invective. The eighteenth century (Alexander Pope, John Dryden, Jonathan Swift) was something of a heyday for the lampoon.

language (from Latin, 'tongue') A form of communication, either written or spoken. Language is in effect a system of SIGNS (see 'semiotics'). See p. 345 for basic terms relating to GRAMMAR (rules of language). Literary language is not necessarily any different from everyday language (see 'poetic diction' for discussion), though in literature it is usually clearer that language affects meaning. For the relation of literary language to written and spoken forms of expression, see '*langue*', 'orality' and 'oral poetry'.

langue/parole A distinction made by Ferdinand de Saussure between language as used by a community (*langue*) and by an individual (*parole*). *Langue* is the whole social system of a language that a community shares. It arranges all the elements of a language so that SIGNS can possess meaning in relation to others. *Parole* is an individual's speech or words based upon the system. The French terms are used because the French *langue* has no suitable English TRANSLATION: it is not the same as 'language' (*langage* in French). As an early STRUCTURALIST, Saussure was more interested in *langue*, and the DIALECTIC or TENSION this creates with individual SPEECH ACTS. If SIGNIFIERS (signs' forms) gain meaning from their position in a system, then social CONTEXT has a great influence on individual utterances. The idea lingers on that social and cultural DISCOURSES control individual expression, in everyday speech as well as in literature.

language games A philosophical concept devised by Ludwig Wittgenstein to describe simplified uses of language that follow certain sets of rules. Words are like chess pieces that can only be used properly if you know the rules of chess—and the concept of language games holds that there are many alternative rule-systems. A word can be used in many different systems, and these are similar, overlapping and often difficult to tell apart. Related is Wittgenstein's earlier 'picture theory of language', which holds that language is not a tool that describes the world, but is more like a picture that represents someone's view of the world. The uses of these thoughts for literary criticism have not been fully explored, but connections with other literary concepts can be made: e.g. the influence of DISCOURSES on expression (which are like language games) and language's METAPHORICAL nature (i.e. language as artificial). STRUCTURALISM and POST-STRUCTURALISM both take up these concerns.

Language Poetry (c.1970s) An experimental form of American FREE VERSE that was interested in language and words, separate to their meaning and expressive capacity. Influenced by POST-STRUCTURALIST thought, language poetry does not attempt to communicate with the reader. The process of creation matters more than the product. It has affinities with PATTERN and CONCRETE POETRY.

latinism (latinate) A word, phrase or GRAMMATICAL construction taken from Latin and incorporated into English. A STYLE characterized by such usages is known as Latinate. 'INKHORN TERM' is an alternative for this meaning, which frees up 'Latinism' to describe words that require the audience to recall the Latin word in order to understand the English: e.g. 'erroneous' meaning 'wandering'; 'gem' meaning 'to bud'. It is one way in which literary writers can make their DICTION more or less formal as desired, though when done unskilfully it can sound pompous. Milton makes striking use of Latinisms, particularly in *Paradise Lost* (1667). 'Aureate diction' is a form of Latinate writing associated with fifteenth-century Scottish writers.

lay (Old French, *lai*) Often used as an ARCHAIC term for 'SONG', but it refers specifically to a form of MEDIEVAL verse composed in OCTOSYLLABIC COUPLETS and meant to be sung. Marie de France's twelfth-century lays are standard examples of the GENRE. It entered English literature as the 'Breton lay' ('Breton' refers to modern-day Brittany), and there are numerous surviving examples, mostly based on ARTHURIAN legend, such as *Sir Orfeo* (c.1320):

> Tho was ther wepeing in the halle
> And grete cri among hem alle;
> Unnethe might old or yong [hardly]
> For wepeing speke a word with tong.
> Thai kneled adoun al y-fere [together]
> And praid him, yif his wille were,
> That he no schuld nought fram hem go. (ll.219–225)

leaf A single sheet in a book; i.e. two pages. The RECTO is the 'front' of a leaf, and the VERSO the reverse; in other words, on a opening of a book the recto is on the right (usually odd-numbered) and the verso on the left (even-numbered). In EARLY MODERN printing the most common leaf formats were FOLIO, QUARTO and OCTAVO.

legend (from French, 'to be read') A story of a notable individual. Legends are often an exaggerated version of historical fact, and usually have more basis in human experience than MYTHS do. Most legends have origins in ORAL LITERATURE, and most of the early legends were tales of saints' lives (HAGIOGRAPHY). They are often culturally specific: Robin Hood, Beowulf, and the tales of King Arthur and his knights (e.g. in Thomas Malory's *Morte d'Arthur* (printed 1485) are some classic British legendary HEROES.

leitmotif (German, 'lead idea') A prominent idea, CHARACTER, IMAGE or situation that recurs throughout a work, or an author's works (OEUVRE). The term was created to describe the musical themes in Richard Wagner's operas; however, in literature a finer distinction between 'THEME' and 'MOTIF' needs to be observed. Leitmotif retains its musical sense to mean a central STYLISTIC preoccupation or even obsession within a particular work—in other words, a favoured MOTIF. This DEVICE intensifies the sense of a work's overall design and thematic interest—without giving a simple answer about what exactly the theme is. Literary SYMBOLS and DEVICES are used because no easy explanation of a work's 'theme' can be given. For example, in William Golding's *The Lord of the Flies* (1954) a conch shell is supposed to be held by whichever boy on the island wishes to speak. It can be considered a symbol of civility and shared power, but that doesn't mean the reader has to read those higher ideas into that image.

lemma In literature, a heading or title that indicates what the work is about.

leonine rhyme A form of INTERNAL RHYME in which a word placed before a CAESURA (break) rhymes with the one at the line-ending. The term is more useful in CLASSICAL prosody; in English it is effectively a SYNONYM for CROSS RHYME.

lexicon A dictionary; a list of terms relevant to a subject; or the vocabulary known to an individual, group or subject. Lexicon describes the words available to someone; DICTION the words actually used. This book is a lexicon of literary terms. Unlike this book, however, some lexicons include COLLOQUIALISMS, SLANG, NEOLOGISMS and JARGON.

libretto (librettist; Italian, 'little book') The text of an opera or other performance, which contains dialogue and speeches put to music. A **librettist** is someone who has written a libretto.

light (weak or feminine) ending A line that concludes with an UNSTRESSED SYLLABLE. It leaves the line open-ended, sometimes leading to ENJAMBEMENT. It occurs at the end of regular TROCHAIC lines, but more often in IAMBIC lines that are EXTRAMETRICAL; i.e. have an unstressed syllable added at the end. The opposite is HEAVY ENDING (MASCULINE), and LIGHT RHYME is a related effect.

light verse A catch-all term for non-serious poetry: PARODY, NONSENSE VERSE, PASTICHE, SATIRE, LIMERICK and BURLESQUE could all be described as forms of light verse. It often uses a tripping IAMBIC METRE and simple rhymes, but the most important characteristic is a gracefully witty TONE that keeps the poem relaxed. Just because light verse is not serious, that doesn't mean it shouldn't be taken seriously, or that serious writers don't write it. Richard Lovelace, e.e. cummings, John Betjeman and Dorothy Parker are among the wide range of AUTHORS who have written well-regarded light verse.

limerick A poem containing five ANAPAESTIC lines that rhyme *aabba*, with three stresses in the *a* lines, and two in the *b* ones. It is strongly associated with LIGHT VERSE, thanks especially to Edward Lear. 'Serious limerick' is not an OXYMORON, however. Like all verse forms, the limerick is adaptable. This is one of many ANONYMOUS limericks:

> There was a young poet from Milan
> Who wrote verses no one could scan.
> When he was asked why,
> He would always reply,
> 'Because I always want to make the last line
>   as long as I possibly can'.

The limerick is so familiar that it makes a good starting-point for thinking about how other verse forms work: the limerick metre, well-suited for COMIC/bawdy subjects, is one of many METRES that are associated by CONVENTION with a particular tone of voice. Like many poems, it is hard to separate the poem's meaning from its FORM. Once you recognise the pattern and internalise it, it is hard to read a limerick without hearing how it sounds. Although the limerick is a simple and unforgettable example, all poetry can be read with awareness of how its sound, sense and use of GENERIC expectations are inseparable.

line The basic structural unit into which all poems are divided. In English PROSODY lines are usually described in terms of the dominant FOOT and how many it occurs in the line: e.g. an IAMBIC PENTAMETER is a line that is expected to have five iambs (o –). The line itself can be expressive in several ways: in the arrangement of lines (LINEATION) on the page; by bringing the sense and metre to completion at the line-ending (END-STOPPING); allowing the sense to run over into the next line (ENJAMBEMENT); and adding, subtracting or substituting syllables in the METRICAL pattern (see p. 347 for a list of relevant terms). A half-line is also known as a HEMISTICH. Even in FREE VERSE, it is still correct to think of a poem in terms of lines and sentences. Division into lines affects how a poem is heard and seen, often concentrating the sense; in particular, it is worth considering how the appearance of a line affects the way you read, hear and understand the sense. For example, consider the masterful, self-conscious lineation in the first stanza of Charles Tomlinson's poem 'Lines':

> You have seen a plough
> the way it goes breeds
> furrows line on line
> until they fill a field?

line-break The point where one LINE stops and another starts. It marks a complete METRICAL unit. If the meaning also breaks, it is END-STOPPED; if the meaning runs over, it is ENJAMBEMENT. An essential resource for poets, though it's worth paying attention to other aspects of LINEATION too.

lineation The division of a poem into LINES, in particular the visual arrangement on the page. It's almost always worth considering how LINE-BREAKS, INDENTATION and spacing affect the sound and sense of a poem. When observing and writing about lineation in a literary work, always be sure that the effect produced is found in a reliable TEXT of the work, and hasn't just been supplied by accident in the EDITION you happen to be using.

linguistics The scientific study of languages. Linguists try to say what language is, and how it works. It has numerous branches relevant to literary criticism: PHILOLOGY is the study of a language's historical development; STYLISTICS is linguistic study of style; while indirectly relevant are language acquisition (see 'competence') and evolutionary theories of language (see 'literary Darwinism'), promoted by the well-known American linguist Stephen Pinker. Page 345 provides a list of basic linguistic terms. In all its varieties, linguistics describes language without coming to judgments or laying down a set of rules to follow. It includes study of how languages create meaning through agreed principles forming a GRAMMAR (based on PHONOLOGY, SYNTAX and SEMANTICS). The linguistic principles of Ferdinand de Saussure were a decisive influence on literary STRUCTURALISM: see 'langue/parole', 'signifier/signifier', 'diachronic' and 'synchronic' for more on this. Jean Aitchison, *Linguistics: An Introduction*, 2nd edn (London, 1999) is a good starting-point if you want to know more.

litany (Greek, 'prayer') A long prayer spoken aloud that involves lists of items and repeated responses (ANTIPHONS). It also describes non-sacred expressions that contain long catalogues. Though found most often in phrases like 'litany of complaints' and 'litany of woes', 'litany' doesn't imply that the list is about something negative (i.e. a JEREMIAD), though the actual listing may be tediously long.

literal (Latin, 'letter') Following the letters on the page. It means taking the primary meaning (or DENOTATION) of a TEXT, rather than looking for FIGURATIVE significance or other CONNOTATIONS. A literal interpretation of the sentence 'her brain is a computer' is that her skull contains electronic components; a figurative (and more sensible) interpretation is that she's good at calculations. In everyday English 'literally' is often used figuratively (non-literally) as an INTENSIFIER (i.e. meaning 'really' or 'extremely'), which creates HYPERBOLIC phrases like 'he's *literally* not stopped eating for a month!' 'Literal' is also one of the FOUR LEVELS OF MEANING.

literariness (Russian, *Literaturnost*) What it is that makes literary TEXTS different from other kinds of writing. RUSSIAN FORMALISM's stated aim was to examine what created literariness, rather than debate the CONTENT of works. Roman Jakobson and others argued that literary texts emphasise their own use of language. This FOREGROUNDING makes FORM as important as CONTENT, and forces the reader to process the text in a different way. A related concept is DEFAMILIARIZATION, which describes the process of making ordinary language strange. It emphasises the changing FUNCTION of language in different CONTEXTS.

literature (adj. literary) Works of FICTION or creative writing in POETRY or PROSE. The term has different meanings, but this is the sense closest to 'literary' as found on the front cover of this book. 'Literature' as a term was invented in the eighteenth century, which is also when 'culture' came about, as something that involved cultural products to be bought and sold. It's important to remember that before that time writers made no such distinction between 'literary' and 'non-literary', and NEW HISTORICISM works on the basis that there is no difference between a TEXT and its CONTEXTS. 'Literature' has come to describe any written work on a subject (e.g. 'I'll make up my mind about where I'll apply to after I've read all the relevant literature').

In the twentieth century, RUSSIAN FORMALISM sought to describe what 'LITERARINESS' was (DEFAMILIARIZATION is an important part of their answer), while English literature as an ARTS and HUMANITIES subject grew up to encourage serious study of non-classical literary works. CULTURAL CRITICISM still argues over the formation of a literary CANON, and at what point the term 'literature' ceases to be useful. Often challenged is the notion of 'high' culture that counts as literature, and popular works that do not (sometimes looked down on a PARALITERATURE). Ideas of special 'literary' topics and of POETIC DICTION also seem outdated. But 'literature' retains the sense of referring to 'CLASSIC' imaginative works that a culture wishes to preserve. It can be said that in most 'literary' writing, CONTENT and FORM affect each other; e.g. Plato's writing are appropriately described as literary because the dialogue form is intimately linked to DIALECTIC and an interest in human, rather than divine, affairs. Similarly Francis Bacon's *Essays* (1597) are literary in that they do more than simply communicate ideas like a piece of journalism. The experience of reading literature is also fundamentally different to other forms; one theory is that literature contains GAPS that other forms of writing do not have.

literary Darwinism An approach to literature that seeks to apply evolutionary theory to literary CRITICISM. It contends that biology provides the ultimate explanation of language and literary creativity, and so argues against the POST-STRUCTURALIST claim that social DISCOURSE is the foundation of all linguistic expression. It is interested in literature as being beneficial for human communities, and in how works depict sexual selection, the 'survival of the fittest' and other evolutionary ideas. While Darwinism certainly has relevance to LITERARY HISTORY (see Gillian Beer's study on Darwinist ideas in Victorian literature, *Darwin's Plots* (1983)), many traditional literary critics view importing such ideas to explain literature as being REDUCTIONIST: i.e. an attempt to turn literature into a sub-category of science. They would want to protect the HUMANITIES as offering an entirely different model for analysing human experience to science: Keats's term 'NEGATIVE CAPABILITY' expresses a need for poets to embrace the mysterious and unknowable in life, and similar resistance to all-encompassing theories survives in criticism today.

literary history Critical enquiry into the development of literary FORMS and GENRES. It was more common in the nineteenth to mid-twentieth centuries than it is now. It seems dated because CRITICISM generally prefers to look at individual works and what makes them unique, rather than sweeping narratives about literary TRADITION. All the same, it's still useful to have a general sense of changes in literature over time, and the timeline beginning on page 357 is included for this reason. A literary historian is someone studying the history of literature, which is separate to studying literature *and* history, for which see 'historicism' and 'new historicism' in particular.

litotes (Greek, 'simple') A TROPE in which understatement is used to intensify meaning, often through use of a double negative: e.g. 'it wasn't dull' to describe something fascinating. Like the PUN, it is most used now in everyday (particularly British) speech, but has subtle literary usages. It is a defining feature of the poetic style of *Beowulf*, where it is used to suggest humility or fatefulness: for example, Grendel has terrorised the Danes for years, and the narrator grimly notes that 'Ne waes þæt forma sið | þæt he Hroþgares ham gesohte' (ll.716–17; this was not the first occasion that he had visited Hrothgar's home).

liturgical drama A play performed as an act of public worship based on a sacred text. It specifically refers to dramatic performances of Biblical narratives that were incorporated into the MEDIEVAL mass, of which PASSION and nativity plays are two varieties. In the later medieval period, MIRACLE and MORALITY PLAYS saw DRAMA gradually move outside the church into open-air public spaces (e.g. the town square). It was not until the sixteenth century that DRAMAS were based on secular themes (e.g. CHRONICLE PLAY).

loan word A word incorporated into English directly from another language. The rise of English as a global language was greatly assisted by its ability to absorb new words (and NEOLOGISMS) into the language. 'Window' (from Old Norse), 'amok' (Malay) and '*Zeitgeist*' (German) give some sense of English's global borrowings. Particularly in English, then, literary writers can stretch their language and draw on different traditions by using loan words, though this leads to OBSCURITY if not explained. The final six words of T.S. Eliot's 'The Waste Land' are loan words from Sanskrit (as Eliot explains in a foot note):

> These fragments I have shored against my ruins
> Why then Ile fit you. Hieronymo's mad againe.
> Datta. Dayadhvam. Damyata.
> Shantih shantih shantih

loc. cit. (*loco citato*, Latin) In the passage already quoted. More specific than 'IBID.' and 'OP. CIT.'.

logocentric A term in DECONSTRUCTION that refers to an apparently deluded Western belief that words have guaranteed meanings. The idea of a LOGOS (informing principle) is linked to Platonism, Christianity and all secular thinking after that time (before deconstruction, that is). It is connected to patriarchal (male) dominance in society—seen in a religious term like 'Word of the Father'—and for this reason the term 'PHALLOGOCENTRIC' developed to stress the FEMINIST implications of deconstructionist ideas.

logos (Greek, 'word') In RHETORIC, an appeal based on logical reasoning, as opposed to emotion (PATHOS) or proving the speaker's good character (ETHOS). However, the phrase has deep philosophical resonance too. The opening verse of St John's Gospel—'In the beginning was the Word, and the Word was with God, and the Word was God'—contains the word '*logos*' in Latin TRANSLATION, and the term has CONNOTATIONS of 'universal principle'. A meaningful contrast is often made with *ergon* (deed). The word has lingered in Western DISCOURSE, particularly in the related form '-ology' to describe aspects of knowledge (e.g. 'technology', 'geology', 'PHILOLOGY'). It became a keystone of Jacques Derrida's thought (see 'logocentric').

long eighteenth century (c.1688–1832) Relating to the period between William III's coming to the throne in 1688 (the 'Glorious

Revolution') and the Reform Act of 1832, which changed the voting system just before the VICTORIAN PERIOD proper began in 1837. It is within this period that 'LITERATURE' starts to exist as a separate category of writing. The main value of making such a division for literary criticism is that the period covers the larger transition from NEOCLASSICISM to ROMANTICISM (via PRE-ROMANTICISM), without insisting that everything before such a time was 'neoclassical' and everything after suddenly 'romantic'. See page 367 onwards for major literary works and related entries for this period.

long measure A STANZA form consisting of four LINES (a QUATRAIN) with four stresses (TETRAMETER) in each line. Its RHYME scheme is usually *abab*, and sometimes *abcb*. It is a longer variation of COMMON MEASURE, also commonly used to describe HYMNS. It is similar to POULTER'S and SHORT MEASURES as well.

Lost Generation (c.1920s) A term used by the American writer Gertrude Stein to describe other writers who drifted, cynical and disenchanted with society after the experience of World War I. F. Scott Fitzgerald's *Tender is the Night* (1934) evokes this atmosphere strongly. It doesn't just refer to WAR POETS, or to others who died early; this burdened attitude to life feeds broadly into American MODERNIST literature.

low comedy Humour that is mostly physical and contains plenty of planned jokes. It often borders on FARCE. It doesn't depend on language, so isn't a particularly 'literary' form of humour, though it appears often in literary works; e.g. as COMIC RELIEF or SLAPSTICK. Without doubt, low comedy requires talented performers just as much as so-called 'high comedy' does.

lullaby A gentle song intended to send a child to sleep; e.g. 'rock-a-bye baby'. The word is thought to derive from soothing sounds made to relax babies. It's one of few genuinely universal forms of poetry: many languages and cultures have distinct lullabies.

lyric poetry (lyrical) In Greek, it referred specifically to a poem written to be accompanied by the lyre, but has a much wider meaning now: i.e. a fairly brief poem that contains an imaginative expression of the speaker's thoughts and emotions. It covers most poetry that is neither NARRATIVE (EPIC) nor DRAMATIC. The poet and the PERSONA of the poem are distinct, however: it shouldn't be assumed that a lyric is BIOGRAPHICAL. There is no restriction on subject matter, or METRICAL structure. It will feel musical in some sense (if only by having a metre), even if it is not intended to be set to music. In EARLY MODERN literature, the SONG emerged as a separate form to the lyric. The term now covers a wide variety of forms from across English literary history, including AUBADE, DRAMATIC MONOLOGUE, EPITHALAMION, HYMN, ODE and SONNET. 'The Wanderer' is one of the earliest lyrics in English; lyrics are widespread in EARLY MODERN literature; and from the late nineteenth century, as poetry increasingly centred on aspects of the poet's own existence (rather than narrative or DRAMATIC), most poets have at some point written poems that could be described as lyric.

'Lyric', particularly in the plural 'lyrics' can also refer to words that are intended to be sung. It could well be asked what kinship there is between EARLY MODERN lyrics, such as Walter Raleigh's, and their modern equivalent, such as Billie Holiday's songs (as a Cambridge English exam in 2008 in fact did). The sheer breadth of a term like lyric is daunting, but turns attention to matters of how much (or little) has changed in literary writing across centuries. Lyric poetry hasn't evolved into a higher art-form over time, and it never will; equally, CLASSIC literature need not be treated with greater respect simply because it is older. It is a writer's historical situation that creates great variations in how a vision of the world finds expression. The lyric, as both a personal expression and words set to music, shows how diverse the circumstances faced by poets are.

M

macaronic verse Poetry in which two or more languages are mixed together, though 'macaronic' originally referred to words in a language other than Latin that are given Latin endings. It was initially found in COMIC or SATIRICAL poems, but was taken more seriously in the twentieth century, thanks in particular to the MODERNIST poets T.S. Eliot and Ezra Pound. Macaronic verse is more than just importing a few LOAN WORDS; it's genuinely hard to understand if you don't know both languages that are being used.

magic (or **magical**) **realism** In literature, PROSE works that contain fantastic or supernatural elements grounded in an otherwise REALISTIC narrative. Magical realist works are to a degree comparable to the GOTHIC NOVEL and HORROR STORY, but are usually more innovative and imaginative, with complex PLOTS that do not follow a chronological order. Other generalisations are difficult to make, for it is an international GENRE: it generally absorbs traditional FOLK stories, and can be SURREAL and COMIC, or political and SATIRICAL. This breadth is shown by the wide range of works that have been described as 'magical realist': e.g. Toni Morrison's *Beloved* (1987), Gabriel Garcia Marquez's *One Hundred Years of Solitude* (1962) and Salman Rushdie's *Midnight's Children* (1981). A criticism of the term is that by associating 'international' (i.e. non-Anglo-American) with a 'magical' quality, it prevents serious engagement with those cultures beyond a fascination with its wondrous OTHERNESS, which, in a sense, is an extension of ORIENTALISM.

magnum opus (Latin 'great work') A major achievement within an AUTHOR'S works (OEUVRE). Also known as a 'masterpiece' or '*chef d'oeuvre*'. The term implies nothing about a work's length. George Eliot's *Middlemarch* (1871) is a *magnum opus*, and also happens to be a long novel.

madrigal A short SONG, usually intended to be sung by a small group of different voices. They are usually about love and PASTORAL ideals, and are sometimes gently SATIRICAL. They were most popular from around the fourteenth to sixteenth centuries in Europe.

maker (makar; scop) A poet. The term reflects the derivation of 'poet', which derives from the Greek verb 'to make' (a poem is a 'thing made'). It evokes a sense of poetry as something crafted and created through basic strategies in STRUCTURE, EMPHASIS and REPETITION. The Old English word for minstrel, **scop**, has the connected sense of 'shaper'. By contrast, a VATES is a divinely inspired poet. **Makars** is a collective term for a group of fifteenth-century Scots poets (sometimes called Scottish Chaucerians).

malapropism (French, *mal à propos,* 'inappropriately') An error made when trying to seem learned by using a sophisticated word. The term is named after Mrs Malaprop in John Sheridan's *The Rivals*: 'He is the very pine-apple of politeness!' (instead of 'pinnacle', 3.3.23–24). Dogberry in *Much Ado About Nothing* makes the same mistakes—'Comparisons are odorous' (instead of 'odious', 3.5.16–17)—not that 'Dogberryism' is an alternative term for 'malapropism'.

mannerism A distinctive habit, style or manner characteristic of an individual, often deliberate. Scratching your head whenever asking a question, or saying 'to be fair' at the end of every sentence would be mannerisms. It's possible to speak of literary mannerisms as an aspect of AUTHORS' style that reappears throughout their works, regardless of the subject-matter: e.g. John Milton's use of LATINATE vocabulary. Mannerism is also the name given to a form of BAROQUE art in sixteenth-century Italy, which was full of artificial detail and very intellectual in its approach to art; EUPHUISM is its closest literary equivalent. As with 'impressionism' art historical terms are usually only helpful if trying to make a specific comparison with works of art.

marginalia Material included at the edge of a page. There is no singular form of 'marginalia': 'marginal note' or 'annotation' are the words used. Marginalia can be printed or hand-written, be written by the AUTHOR or someone else, and can offer GLOSSES, summaries or interpretation. Though most libraries absolutely forbid writing in books, rare books are sometimes more valuable if they contain hand-written marginalia. It is another aspect of how words are presented on the page to bear in mind when reading books.

Marxist criticism A major critical approach based on the belief that literature is influenced by the economic and political circumstances of its production. It is only indirectly related to Marxism, and does not promote a single political viewpoint. In fact, the term 'Marxist criticism' covers many different approaches, and this entry only attempts to sketch out the major ideas. Terry Eagleton's short book *Marxism and Literary Criticism* (1976; reprinted 2002) is a good starting-point for further reading.

One of the major strengths of Marxist criticism is its firmly historicised sense of literary creation. It does not just place texts in a social CONTEXT to understand the work better (see SOCIOLOGY OF LITERATURE), but shows how texts are products of a certain period. This arises from the fact that Marxism is a materialist philosophy: it only considers the here-and-now, rather than a world beyond our reach. It focuses on the economic realities that have affected people's lives throughout history, and how this has shaped history (see 'dialectic'). In particular, it deals with the relationship between the workers who produce things, and the consumers who use products. Marxism finds that workers (the means of production) are always separated from what is produced. The comfortable middle-classes ('bourgeoisie') enjoy what workers produce without doing the work themselves. This unfair system exists because the middle-classes hold power. Unsurprisingly, the middle-classes don't want to change things. When reading literature, then, we can expect certain GENRES and AUTHORS to reflect the social period in which they were produced: an upper-class literary form will demonstrate its contentment with the existing situation, while the lower-class will want change.

There is great variation in how far a Marxist critic would follow or promote these ideas in interpretation. But the close connection between literary creation and the social forces bearing down on the AUTHOR is indispensable. A classic essay like Walter's Benjamin's 'The Work of Art in the Age of Mechanical Reproduction' (1935) is a Marxist work because it broadly explores how mass culture made art more democratic and less bourgeois. Marxist criticism has similarities to STRUCTURALISM, which shows how language is created from a set of cultural CONVENTIONS and CODES. Marxist criticism essentially has the same objective, only with a more hard-edged sense of political and economic reality. Because of this secure foundation on our material existence, its conclusions tend to be less AMBIGUOUS and ABSTRACT that those in POST-STRUCTURALISM. This is apparent from a key theme in later Marxist criticism that Louis Althusser developed: IDEOLOGY. Literature is said to be created from ideological beliefs, and reinforces them. By having these belief-systems as a well-defined object of research, the Marxist critic is placed to make firm conclusions about how a work's meaning is affected by ideologies, or attempts to subvert them. For example, Marxist critics have interpreted William Shakespeare's *Troilus and Cressida* as being full of indecision, disorder and baseness, and therefore championing disorder. This makes for a radical CRITIQUE of social order (it is a 'radical tragedy', to quote the title of Jonathan Dollimore's book on the topic). Marxist criticism has also identified AESTHETIC beliefs as being determined by ideology.

Marxist criticism has suffered because it can be easily caricatured. In truth, it covers a range of criticism, and has often been combined fruitfully with other approaches, like PSYCHOANALYTIC CRITICISM and FEMINIST CRITICISM. CULTURAL CRITICISM and CULTURAL MATERIALISM are two approaches that grew out of Marxist criticism. Bertolt Brecht's ALIENATION EFFECT, and notion of EPIC THEATRE showed what sort of literature serious Marxist thought could help create. Around this period, the FRANKFURT SCHOOL were developing serious Marxist interpretations of cultural progress as well. As with all critical 'schools' it is better to judge critics based on how persuasive and insightful their work is, rather than on the approach they are most commonly associated with. When practiced well, Marxist criticism forces us to bear in mind that literature engages in the wider world, and isn't just a source of carefree pleasure.

masculine As an adjective in prosody, it means heavy and stressed. Like the term FEMININE it has little basis in English GRAMMAR, but it is still widely used. As an alternative, 'heavy' can be used for 'masculine' and 'light' for 'FEMININE'.

masque An elaborate court entertainment that starred amateur, aristocratic ACTORS, and involved expensive costumes, scenery and music. They contain ALLEGORICAL CONTENT with a strong sense of POETIC JUSTICE. They were essentially private PAGEANTS. Masques were particularly in favour during the early seventeenth century, during the reigns of James and Charles I. Numerous DRAMATISTS composed them, and Ben Jonson was the most successful. He introduced the ANTIMASQUE as a COMIC counterpart to the main masque. Jonson worked with the architect and stage designer Inigo Jones to produce colourful and ostentatious spectacles. However, John Milton's *Comus* (1637) is now probably the best known play in the masque tradition.

Masques are of critical interest in two related areas. First, the masque tradition affected popular forms of DRAMA: William Shakespeare's *The Tempest* (1611) contains a short masque, and has a masque-like air throughout. Second, some NEW HISTORICISTS have examined the close association of power and theatrical performance in JACOBEAN masques.

maxim (Latin, 'greatest') A phrase widely held to be true. Maxims are often short statements that provide a set of rules to live by, or state a general truth. Similar in meaning to SAYING and the other terms listed after it on page 350.

measure An alternative term for metrical FOOT, and now used to describe certain patterns of RHYME and METRE found in QUATRAINS (see this entry for details), such as LONG, SHORT, COMMON and POULTER'S MEASURE.

medium (pl. media) The material or process used to communicate meaning. Newspapers and magazines are media, and so are theatre, cinema, books, music, dance, poetry and, crucially, LANGUAGE. Media matters because they are not neutral processes. Ideas are coloured by the medium used to express them. The medium comes between the person communicating and the audience. In this sense, literary studies are a basic form of media studies.

medieval (c.400–1485) An adjective describing anything relating to the Middle Ages (Latin *medium aevum*, leading to 'medieval'), which covers a whole millennium or more, from the Roman occupation of Britain to the beginning of the Tudor monarchy. The period is far too large to be easily summarised (think how different the twenty-first and eleventh centuries are), and there is still a great deal that is unknown about the period (hence the old name 'the Dark Ages' for the second half of the first millennium). The term 'Middle Ages' came about because these 1000 years came between classical culture and its revival in the Renaissance. This implies that medieval culture is less civilised, erudite and generally more barbaric that the periods either side of it—which only holds true if you believe CLASSICISM to be the last word on human achievement and culture. Christianity and court culture were two major influences on the literature that survives. In terms of the English language, the medieval period can be divided either side of the Norman Conquest after the Battle of Hastings in 1066, which brought more French and Latin vocabulary into English; see 'Old English' and 'Middle English' for more. MEDIEVALISM is the renewal of interest in medieval culture by later AUTHORS (see below). See page 359 for important literary texts and related entries.

medievalism An interest in the language, themes and principles of the Middle Ages (particularly the later period from around the eighth to fifteenth centuries), and the recycling of those ideas in later literary texts. Prominent examples of writers engaging with medieval TRADITION include: Spenser's ARCHAIC DICTION, Milton and Keats writing in Spenser's wake, and GOTHIC LITERATURE. A medievalist is a specialist on the Middle Ages (and not someone who's pretending to live in the fourteenth century). Kevin Crossley-Holland is a poet, translator and children's author whose work is a good example of modern-day medievalism: e.g. *The Seeing Stone* (2000) is the first book of his Arthur trilogy, and it shows how medievalism can be entertaining for a general audience.

meiosis (Greek, 'lessening') A TROPE involving understatement. Meiosis differs from LITOTES in that it is used to make something seem less, not more, important: e.g. 'boys' toys' to describe super-cars. It is the near-opposite of HYPERBOLE, and can be used for COMIC or IRONIC effect.

melodrama (melodramatic; Greek, 'song-play') The term specifically refers to a musical play as performed in the late-eighteenth and nineteenth centuries. Early melodramas are plot-driven, contain FLAT and STOCK CHARACTERS with obvious HEROES and VILLAINS, and have a strong sense of POETIC JUSTICE. It was a middle-class form of entertainment, often with expensive sets and costumes. There were a great number of different melodramas, mostly forgotten now: one exception is George Dibdin Pitt's fictional drama (based on a PENNY DREADFUL novel) *Sweeney Todd, the Demon Barber of Fleet Street* (1847). *Grand Guignol* is the name given to a particularly lurid French variety of melodrama.

The form died out in the twentieth century for two main reasons. One is a dramatic reaction against bourgeois art-forms by Bertolt Brecht and other advocates of EPIC THEATRE in Europe, and by the Provincetown Players in America. The other is the rise of cinema, which offered a similar form of entertainment for considerably less cost. The term has since come to describe anything that is sensational, SENTIMENTAL and wildly unrealistic (often with unexpected plot twists), such as some SOAP OPERAS or GENRE FICTION. Used as an adjective, 'melodramatic' is normally used to be dismissive of a work, though it's unfair to project these later assumptions onto its earlier forms.

memoir A person's written recollection of his or her life and experiences. Memoirs are often EPISODIC, and focus on notable incidents and ANECDOTES rather than telling the AUTOBIOGRAPHICAL narrative of a person's life. Some NOVELS (and NOVELLAS) have, however, been structured as a set of memoirs, particularly in early eighteenth-century novels: e.g. Daniel Defoe's *Moll Flanders* (1722).

Menippean satire A work that jumbles together different elements in a witty, energetic but confused manner. Francois Rabelais' *Gargantua* and *Pantagruel* (1532–52) is a good example, and see 'satire' for more information.

meta- (Greek, 'beyond') A prefix used to denote works that move 'beyond' themselves and invite self-conscious thoughts about their own nature; e.g. METATHEATRE draws attention to the artificiality of dramatic CONVENTION; METAFICTION to the fact that the work is a FICTION. It involves rational thought that looks down on the original idea. 'METAPHYSICAL' should, strictly speaking, be kept separate to this type of 'higher' thinking: originally it purely meant the work that came after Aristotle's *Physics*, not 'physics' itself. 'Meta' is sometimes used informally as an adjective itself. It describes a certain SELF-REFLEXIVE and POSTMODERN attitude to the world, which is characterised by IRONIC detachment from (and sense of superiority over) an environment. And as the American philosopher John Wisdom puts it, 'every day, and in every way, we're getting meta and meta'.

metacriticism CRITICISM that examines the principles, methods, scope and efficacy of literary criticism. Most critical theories involve some metacritical aspect, because they seek to define themselves against other critical models. In general, SELF-REFLEXIVE thought, in moderation, is good at stopping readers from becoming complacent.

metadrama (metatheatrical) An aspect of DRAMA that brings attention to its own FICTIONAL status. PROLOGUES, EPILOGUES, INDUCTIONS and sometimes CHORUSES offer reflections on the play. The play-within-a-play DEVICE is also a form of metadrama: in *The Spanish Tragedy* (and then *Hamlet*) the PROTAGONIST, Hieronimo, stages a drama in order to exact bloody revenge on his ANTAGONISTS, Lorenzo and Balthasar.

metafiction A self-conscious piece of writing that is aware of its own status as a FICTIONAL work. It occurs when CRITICISM is found within a creative work. Though associated with POSTMODERNISM (see 'meta-' above) and twentieth-century novels like John Fowles's *The French Lieutenant's Woman* (1969), SELF-REFLEXIVE appears much earlier in English: Lawrence Sterne's *Tristram Shandy* (1760) is wildly metafictional throughout.

metalepsis (Greek, 'substitution') A FIGURE (technically a TROPE) in which an indirect cause is given for an event. It is sometimes a form of EUPHEMISM: e.g. 'I failed the test because I'm so sociable (i.e. because I was out partying instead of revising).' Metalepsis requires the audience to make a logical connection in order to grasp the underlying cause.

metaphor (Greek, 'transfer') An important TROPE in which a word or phrase is used in an unfamiliar CONTEXT. It creates non-literal meaning (FIGURATIVE LANGUAGE) by making a surprising connection between two ideas. 'It was a total nightmare' is metaphorical, because it takes the idea of a nasty dream and reapplies it to describe a disastrous event. 'The ice-cube burnt my mouth' is a metaphor, as are the phrases 'a mind-numbing lecture' and 'the prince of pop'. Each example states that the subject (i.e. thing described, sometimes called TENOR) and the unusual metaphorical image (VEHICLE) are identical in some way. An implied metaphor does not make the subject clear: e.g. the phrase 'that was a bitter pill to swallow' often refers to something else, such as an exam failure, rather than foul-tasting medication.

Whereas metaphors are often implicit, SIMILES never are. Similes suggest that terms hold similarity, not identity, and is always signalled in English with 'like' or 'as'. Two other forms of metaphor: a 'dead metaphor' has lost its FIGURATIVE meaning through overuse—e.g. 'her head is in the clouds'. A 'mixed metaphor' combines two or more separate metaphorical terms. When unintentional it creates ridiculous and/or confusing phrases: e.g. 'She jumped in at the deep end, and is already skating on thin ice.' An exaggerated metaphor is known as CATACHRESIS, and a CONCEIT is a far-fetched but highly original metaphor.

Some thinkers believe that language is inherently metaphorical. The argument goes that there is no such thing as natural or 'literal' language, which is suggested by the absence of any common language (e.g. each language has its own word for water). If language is invented, rather than naturally occurring, then all words are applied to new CONTEXTS in order to create meaning whenever they are used. We live by metaphors, and all progress is simply a refinement of those metaphors (see 'paradigm' for more on this).This argument goes back as far as Plato's *Cratylus*, and holds affinities with DECONSTRUCTION, which suggests that all language is built on unstable foundations. Also, since metaphors express something 'OTHER' than the literal meaning, some critical schools seek to define what that 'Other' is which metaphors and language are really getting at: e.g. religious truth, 'reality' or unconscious desire (PSYCHOANALYTIC CRITICISM). There is at least agreement that metaphors are worth studying for the original connections and thoughts they generate.

metaphysical poets (c.1600–90) A term applied to numerous seventeenth-century poets, including John Donne, George Herbert, Henry Vaughan and Andrew Marvell. Donne's LYRIC POETRY is characterized by its WIT, unusual imagery, PARADOXES, CONCEITS, distinctive personal voice, humour, complexity, and shared interest in romantic and spiritual love. These same features are found to a greater or lesser extent in other metaphysical poets too, though 'metaphysical' doesn't have to be a synonym for 'Donnian'. The term 'metaphysical' was occasionally used at the time, and refers to these poets' general interest in ABSTRACT ideas beyond the everyday, typically religious or Platonic (see 'meta-' for the term's derivation). A defining characteristic, at least according to T.S. Eliot, is that metaphysical poetry combines thought and feeling in a way that has rarely been done since (see 'dissociation of sensibility'). One reason metaphysical poems are so personal is that many were written by hand and distributed in manuscript among friends; only later were they published in printed EDITIONS.

metastasis (me-**tast**-isis; Greek, 'change') A quick change of subject, or movement from one rhetorical FIGURE to another.

method acting An acting technique in which an ACTOR recreates the emotions and MOTIVATIONS felt by a CHARACTER. It requires the ACTOR to recall his or her past feelings and experiences (using 'AFFECTIVE MEMORY'). The classic image of a Method actor is someone who stays in CHARACTER off-stage or off-camera—which isn't often true, but makes the point that the Method is all about being immersed in character. Method acting has its origins in Konstantin Stanislavski's system, which was developed by Americans like Elia Kazan and Lee Strasburg in the 1930s. It is thought by some to have revolutionized American theatre, and was adopted by such big-name Hollywood ACTORS as Marlon Brando.

metonymy (Greek, 'name-change') A TROPE in which a name is replaced by something closely related with it. There are numerous kinds of metonym, many of which naturally occur in everyday speech: 'here comes trouble' referring to your little sister; 'listening to the Beatles', when actually listening to the Beatles's music; 'the press' meaning journalism; and 'I'll have a bowl' when you actually want some Cornflakes. Antinomasia (use of EPITHETS) is a rare example of a specifically literary usage of metonyms.

The difference between metonym and METAPHOR has been heavily theorized. Roman Jakobson (a leading RUSSIAN FORMALIST) explained that metaphor draws associations between things, whereas metonym shows how things are dependent on each other (are contiguous), so leads to more realistic forms of writing. Sigmund Freud, on the other hand, held that metonym was a form of displacement (or TRANSFERENCE) that deflected attention from uncomfortable psychological truths, symbolised in metaphors (see 'psychoanalytic criticism').

This distinction is at least more clear-cut than that between metonym and SYNECDOCHE. SYNECDOCHE is often considered a type of metonym, except that it refers to something that is part of the whole, rather than something associated with it. If I call a car as a 'Skoda', then that is metonymy because it refers to the car's maker, but if I call it my 'wheels', then that is synecdoche, because wheels are part of the car. The difference can be characterized by thinking of synecdoche as vertical, zooming in and out on different scales, and metonym as horizontal, connecting up things.

metre (**meter** (American); **adj. metrical**; Greek, 'measure') The pattern of stressed and unstressed SYLLABLES (or BEATS) in verse. RHYTHM is a general musical or beat-like quality found in VERSE; metre is the systematic arrangement of syllables. To put it another way: when reading a poem, rhythm may make you tap out the BEAT, and metre may make you start counting.

Most English verse is ACCENTUAL-SYLLABIC; i.e. lines have a set number of stresses and syllables. It is possible to have purely syllabic (e.g. HAIKU) and ACCENTUAL (OLD ENGLISH verse and SPRUNG RHYTHM) verse, but it is fairly rare in English. The terminology used to describe English VERSIFICATION is based on the CLASSICAL system of QUANTITATIVE metre, which depends on the natural weight of syllables (heavy or light). English syllables do not have these natural properties, and so the terminology is sometimes inexact when transferred for English PROSODY. As a general rule, metrical terms provide a way of thinking about verse in English, not a rigid system to which it must conform. In English, metre terminology is not so much a set of rules to be understood, but a means of describing rhythmic effects of verse. Metre is not an essential feature of poetry in English: FREE VERSE and PROSE POEM are verse forms without a set metre, although both still involve RHYTHMIC patterns.

The standard unit used to describe metre is the FOOT, which is a combination of stressed (–, 'dum') or unstressed (o, 'di') syllables. DUPLE METRE occurs when most FEET have two BEATS, and TRIPLE METRE is when most have three. The most common feet are IAMB (o –), TROCHEE (– o), DACTYL (– o o) and ANAPAEST (o o –). Verse can be described according to the dominant FOOT; e.g. as 'iambic' or 'dactylic'. Since much verse in English contains the same number of syllables and stresses in each line, there is often the same number of feet per line too. This can be described using the terms DIMETER (two FEET per line), TRIMETER (three), TETRAMETER (four), PENTAMETER (five), HEXAMETER (six) and HEPTAMETER (seven), with MONOMETER (one) and OCTOMETER (eight) being less common. So an IAMBIC PENTAMETER is a line with a basic pattern of five iambs (o –).

This is just the starting point for SCANSION (metrical analysis). It is unhelpful to think of metres as being regular, and therefore something that needs to be labelled and then forgotten about. It is monotonous to use the same FOOT, and most verse contains plenty of variation on the basic pulse (LIGHT VERSE is a notable exception). Identifying verse as iambic pentameter or dactylic hexameter may well reveal something about the type of poetry being written (e.g. EPIC poetry in dactylic hexameter is following the form that Homer used). However, the beauty of metre is in the individual effects that are created by varying and breaking the basic pattern and blending different types of ACCENT. This requires listening skills that can only be learnt through practice and careful reading, and it usually comes more easily to readers with an ear for music. The importance of metrical terminology in English is not so much to describe what poetry is, but how it affects the sense. Knowing the right terms is a starting point to hearing the subtleties of verse.

metrics The technical study of VERSIFICATION; i.e. how METRICAL verse is formed. It is an alternative term for PROSODY.

Middle English (c.1066–1500) The English VERNACULAR language as it was influenced by French and Latin after the Norman conquest in 1066. A variety of DIALECT forms existed around at this time with different vocabularies and SYNTAX. Even in later Middle English that initially appears more familiar to modern eyes, as found in Geoffrey Chaucer's works, it still takes patience and practice to be able to read it accurately. Middle English poetry was written using two contrasting models: ALLITERATIVE METRE (used by William Langland and the *Gawain*-poet) and RHYMED PENTAMETER, which was used by Chaucer and eventually prevailed. The English language continued to develop in the Tudor period under HUMANIST influences, and it is only really at the end of the sixteenth century that vernacular English has settled into something recognisably MODERN; i.e. that can be read today without too much extra effort. See page 359 for important literary texts and related entries.

Miltonic sonnet A variation on the PETRARCHAN SONNET used by John Milton. It differs from the Petrarchan by delaying the turning-point of the poem (which is expected after line eight), and by adopting a different rhyme scheme in the SESTET (Milton had no set alternative). The octave's rhyme scheme is *abbaabba*. In other words, when reading a sonnet by Milton, be aware of its departures from the Petrarchan form, and identify the effect this creates. Milton's example was followed by late eighteenth- and nineteenth-century sonnet writers, such as Thomas Gray, William Wordsworth and John Keats.

mime A performance based on physical IMITATION through silent movement, GESTURE and expression. In the European tradition, it is usually a form of COMEDY: in CLASSICAL times, the mime (or pantomime) was a type of FARCE; Italian *COMMEDIA DELL'ARTE* used mime for comic purposes; and in the twentieth century, MIME made a comeback through comic ACTORS in silent cinema like Buster Keaton and Charlie Chaplin.

mimetic criticism Interpretation based on the notion that all literature is an representation of reality. Where other forms of criticism take the work itself, or the AUTHOR, or higher ideas as a starting point, mimetic critics take the real world as a point of reference. It is not a critical movement of its own, but it lingers in the background of other critical debates: Plato's thoughts on literature were based on its relation to reality (see 'imitation'), and many modern readers naturally relate what they read to the wider world (particularly in REALIST or DOCUMENTARY works).

minstrel (rhapsode) A professional musician who performs poetry in different places. EPIC narratives, BALLADS and other ORAL poetry are standard minstrel repertoire. The importance of the minstrel as a literary figure declined in EARLY MODERN Europe as literacy grew and printing became widespread. 'Scop' is an Old English word for minstrel, meaning 'shaper' (see 'maker'). A BARD is, strictly speaking, a Celtic minstrel, but is often used as a SYNONYM. A **rhapsode** is the name for a minstrel in Ancient Greece, particularly someone who performed Homer. The rhapsode's techniques influenced the style of the HOMERIC poems, and so indirectly influenced later literature. More generally, the written texts of early and ancient poetry in the oral tradition were shaped and developed by minstrels before being written down: e.g. *Beowulf* may have been performed for many generations before it was recorded in the copy that survives today.

miracle play A form of MEDIEVAL drama based on saints' lives (HAGIOGRAPHIES), and performed in VERNACULAR English. It is a form of LITURGICAL DRAMA that came after the MYSTERY PLAY (based on Bible stories), and marked another stage in the transition towards secular dram in the sixteenth century.

mise en abyme A fictional DEVICE in which a literary work or passage is referred to within the work. Martin Amis's *Money: A Suicide Note* (1984) is presented as the extended suicide note of John Self, who encounters a CHARACTER called Martin Amis who obtains the memoirs forming the basis of *Money*. It is a SELF-REFLEXIVE device loosely associated with POSTMODERNISM.

mise en scène The visual composition of a scene in DRAMA or film. Like '*COUP DE THÉÂTRE*' the French term is preferred because there is no simple TRANSLATION: it means 'putting into a scene'. In DRAMA it refers to aspects of SETTING: scenery, props, costumes, lighting, ACTOR movement and so forth. It implies a director's (or DRAMATURGIST'S) complete vision for staging a play that is realised in performance. In film, the term refers to the look of a single shot, independent of the camera movement.

mixed metaphor A use of FIGURATIVE LANGUAGE that results in a confused or far-fetched IMAGE. It often arises from an unintended combination of two commonly used METAPHORS or CLICHÉS. 'A pinch of salt to help the medicine go down' and 'We can still hang our heads high' are two examples. 'CATACHRESIS' has the same basic meaning.

mnemonic A word, phrase or passage intended to aid the memory: e.g. 'My Very Easy Method Just Speeds Up Naming Planets' is a simple method for naming planets quickly. It counts as a literary term because there has been some interest (among anthropologists as well as critics) in the possible mnemonic function of ORAL POETRY (i.e. before writing was widespread). RHYME, METRE, FORMULAE and lists are all arguably intended to make thoughts more memorable and memorizable.

mock epic (noun and adj.) A SATIRICAL poem that adopts the stylistic features of EPIC poetry for a relatively trivial subject matter. It's a form of BURLESQUE, and a particular variety of PARODY. HOMERIC features such as INVOCATION, EPIC SIMILE and FORMULAE are used to generate BATHOS; i.e. the work doesn't live up to its GRAND STYLE. MOCK-HEROIC is a more general term for an exaggerated IMITATION of HEROIC tone. Alexander Pope's *Rape of the Lock* (1714) is a classic mock epic, in which the theft of a lock of hair is described in terms similar to Helen of Troy's capture that led to the Trojan War, as described in Homer's *Iliad*.

mock-heroic A general term for a PARODIC imitation of the style and TONE of HEROIC POETRY. MOCK EPIC is a specific type of mock-heroic poem that ridicules a subject unworthy of EPIC treatment. Mock-heroic writing is particularly associated with the early eighteenth-century AUGUSTAN POETS; a slightly earlier example is John Dryden's *MacFlecknoe* (1682), which uses mock-heroic features to criticise the poet Thomas Shadwell.

mode The manner in which something is done. It is a fairly vague term in literary studies, where its meaning is roughly equivalent to 'mood'. It describes mindsets and atmospheres that affect meaning (in a way that

TONE doesn't). So IRONY, SATIRE and PASTICHE could all be considered modes in this sense. Mode is sometimes taken as a SYNONYM for 'GENRE' and 'FORM', though this seems to take the term closer to its sense of 'fashion' (as in 'modish' or 'à la mode').

modernism A movement in early twentieth-century arts and culture that reacted against Victorian order and its associated artistic forms. 'Modern' here only means that modernism was new for its time. Literary modernism sought to get behind the social decorum and neat surfaces of Victorian literature. It sought real psychological insight within the deeper traditions that informed cultures. Modernism, as a whole, looked for fragments of a hidden unity behind surface appearances. This effort came from various directions, including PSYCHOANALYSIS, literary NATURALISM, STRUCTURALISM, war, and twentieth-century urban experience.

Modernism encouraged experimental writing that challenged traditional GENRES: e.g. FREE VERSE, non-realistic prose, and EPIC THEATRE. It looked towards the AVANT-GARDE for complex new forms that didn't have pleasing narrative progression. Its various forms sought to drive out complacency from literature, and make it address pressing issues. Modernist literature was tied to the SUBJECTIVE VIEWPOINT, and looked to offer a more direct and personal form of expression that could reach beyond social CONVENTIONS. ALLUSION, STREAM OF CONSCIOUSNESS and sometimes OBSCURITY are related writing strategies. The two works that typify 'high' modernism were both published in 1922: James Joyce's *Ulysses* and T.S. Eliot's *The Waste Land*. Virginia Woolf, Ezra Pound and Marcel Proust are three other leading pre-Second World War modernists. At some point in the second half of the twentieth century, modernism was overtaken by what is now known as 'POSTMODERNISM', not that this term implies that modernism suddenly became defunct.

mondegreen A misheard word or phrase with changed meaning. They are often HOMOPHONES, and are common with song lyrics. In the Beatles' song 'Yellow Submarine', for example, the quotation 'And our friends are all on board, | Many more of them live next door' is a mondegreen, because the line actually goes 'And our friends are all abroad, | Many more of them live next door'.

monodrama A play that contains one CHARACTER to be played by one ACTOR. The term tends not to be used for plays in which one ACTOR plays many parts: the unwieldy ARCHAIC term 'MONOPOLYLOGUE' has been used since the nineteenth century for these DRAMATIC one-man bands.

Samuel Beckett's *Krapp's Last Tape* (1959) and Alan Bennett's *Talking Heads* (1987) are well-regarded examples of monodrama. The difference between monodrama and DRAMATIC MONOLOGUE is that only monodrama is written to be performed to an audience, and is more likely to make use of movements, expression, GESTURE and PROPS.

monody (Greek, 'single ode') An ODE sung by one person, rather than a CHORUS. The term originates from Greek poetry, where its meaning is fairly technical, but it has since come to mean any personal ELEGY, LAMENT, DIRGE or THRENODY. 'DRAMATIC MONOLOGUE' is closer to the term's original meaning.

monograph (Greek, 'one writing') A book-length academic work devoted to a single, closely defined subject. *The Victorians and Old Age* by Professor Karen Chase (Oxford, 2009), for example, offers a suitably narrow subject for a monograph.

monologic A term associated with DIALOGIC CRITICISM that describes a work that resembles a MONOLOGUE: it has one dominant VOICE. Mikhail Bakhtin, who developed an opposition between monologic and dialogic, maintained that even works that were dominated by a single NARRATOR or AUTHORIAL voice (as with Leo Tolstoy's works) still contained many other voices to be heard. Although other CHARACTERS and their VIEWPOINTS were beaten down by the main voice, these other opinions were still heard and could still affect the reader's opinion. As such, no literary work is wholly monologic.

monologue A long speech delivered by an individual. If performed aloud, a monologue spoken as if the speaker were alone onstage is a SOLILOQUY; an extended monologue (usually involving movements and actions) that forms a complete performance is a MONODRAMA. A poem in which a CHARACTER delivers a speech to an imagined audience is a DRAMATIC MONOLOGUE. A record of an individual's thoughts in FICTION is an INTERIOR MONOLOGUE. Monologues are the most direct way for writers to provide more information about fictional characters (or an AUTHORIAL PERSONA), but sometimes it can be difficult to integrate them well into larger works, which is where CONFIDANTS can be a useful addition to the script.

monometer (Greek, 'one measure') A line of VERSE containing one FOOT (rhythmic unit). Mostly used for novelty value.

monopolylogue (Greek, 'single-many-speech') An awkward ARCHAIC term for a dramatic work in which one actor plays many parts. Not really a term to use, except that 'MONODRAMA' tends to be reserved for performances in which one ACTOR plays one ROLE.

monorhyme A verse passage with line-endings joined by the same RHYME. It describes the prolonged use of one rhyme, either in a single sequence of rhymes or throughout a work. However, it is not used for single two- or three-line passages, which are simply called 'COUPLET' and 'TRIPLET'. Given its potential monotony, monorhyme is most often found in poems considered DOGGEREL, though see the example given for DOUBLE RHYME for an exception.

mood In literature it has two meanings, one vague and one technical. The vague meaning is 'state of mind' and is similar to ATMOSPHERE and TONE. Its sense is connected to MODE, which can be thought of as a mood that affects meaning. Like those two terms it needs to be used with precision; e.g. calling a literary work 'moody' doesn't mean much. The term's technical meaning is GRAMMATICAL: mood indicates whether a verb expresses a fact (indicative mood), a wish (subjunctive mood) or a command (imperative mood). 'I *am* a champion' is indicative; 'I wish I *were* a champion' is subjunctive' and '*Be* a champion' is imperative.

morality play A late MEDIEVAL drama that addresses moral matters like temptation and salvation. Morality plays are DIDACTIC and ALLEGORICAL: the PROTAGONIST is a METAPHOR for the audience's own life situation, and the events onstage represent our own daily struggles. Vice and other PERSONIFIED figures were STOCK CHARACTERS for the GENRE; the Seven Deadly Sins were sometimes paraded in small PAGEANTS. It was a more secular version of LITURGICAL DRAMA (such as MIRACLE and MYSTERY PLAY), and shaped the development of EARLY MODERN drama; specifically, it influenced the MASQUE and INTERLUDE. *Everyman* (c.1510) and *The Castle of Perseverance* (1420) are two CLASSIC examples that are occasionally performed today.

morpheme A basic GRAMMATICAL unit, which creates different forms of a word. Prefixes (e.g. 'post-'), suffixes ('-ize'), PREPOSITIONS ('by') and CONJUNCTIONS ('and') are all types of morpheme with particular functions within a sentence. MORPHOLOGY is the LINGUISTIC study of how morphemes form words.

morphology The formation of words, and linguistic study of this. It works with SYNTAX (arrangement of words) to create meaningful sentences. For example, 'eat' adds an '-ing' to describe the act of consuming food, or '-en' for the past act of consuming (these are participle forms), while 'moth-eaten' is formed by combining the word with another idea. A MORPHEME is a basic GRAMMATICAL element, such as a prefix ('pre-', 'inter-') or suffix ('-ing' or '-en').

mosaic rhyme A rhyme of two or three syllables (DUPLE or TRIPLE RHYME), in which one of the rhymes is spread across more than one word: e.g. 'stegosaurus/really bores us'. It is different from phrases in Cockney rhyming SLANG, which are mostly based on a single-syllable rhyme: e.g. 'dog and bone/phone'. It is associated with LIGHT VERSE, and sometimes feels like FORCED RHYME.

motif (motive) A recurring element within or between artistic works. The repeated element could be a STOCK CHARACTER, IMAGE, RHETORICAL FIGURE, SETTING or other idea. It describes two phenomena in literature. First, a basic means of shaping meaning within a work through REPETITION that hints at an overall THEME. In this sense it is similar in meaning to 'LEITMOTIF'. Second, it refers to the INTERTEXTUAL reappearance of elements, not always in conscious IMITATION of another work. Certain TOPOI have been prominent across literary history: these includes named motifs like *UBI SUNT* ('where are?') and *CARPE DIEM* ('seize the day'), as well as unnamed examples, such as the garden retreat or world-weary detective. 'Motif' is sometimes spelt 'motive', which is separate but related to the meaning 'reason for doing something'.

motivation The reasons that a CHARACTER acts as he or she does. Personality, circumstance and self-protection/interest can all drive character. A FICTIONAL person with a sole motivating factor (a 'FLAT CHARACTER') may be a CARICATURE, STOCK CHARACTER or TYPE; alternatively, an author may study the complexities of that motivation (e.g. revenge) as found in a single character. Motivation is crucial in the creation of unified PLOTS with a convincing sequence of causes. The notion of motivation is also important in METHOD ACTING, which requires actors to engage with a character's emotional CONFLICT. Not all dramatic characters possess clear underlying motivation: Samuel Beckett insisted that his CHARACTERS just spoke the words in the script and didn't have separate unspoken motivations (see also 'character').

Movement, the (c.1950s) A trend in post-war British poetry that favoured a return to traditional FIXED FORMS of poetry (as opposed to MODERNIST FREE VERSE). Ironic detachment and general Englishness were two other recurring characteristics. Its key figures were published in the 1956 anthology edited by Robert Conquest called *New Lines*: e.g. Thom

Gunn, Kingsley Amis and Philip Larkin. Note that not all the writers involved were happy to be associated with a 'Movement'.

mummers' play A FOLK DRAMA featuring masked ACTORS (mummers) that was revived in Britain in the eighteenth and nineteenth century, and is still occasionally performed today.

muse An inspirational being, traditionally female and often divine. There were nine Greek muses, who were later assigned separate GENRES of art in the Renaissance. They are: Calliope (ka-**lie**-oh-pee; EPIC); Clio (**klee**-oh; history); Erato (eh-**rah**-toe; EROTIC poetry); Euterpe (u-**ter**-pee; music); Melpomene (mel-**pom**-ee-nee; TRAGEDY); Polyhymnia (pol-**ee**-him-nee-ah; LYRIC POETRY); Terpsichore (**turp**-sik-oar-ee; dance/CHORUS); Thalia (**tha**-lee-ah; COMEDY) and Urania (oo-**rah**-nee-ah; astronomy, later the Christian muse). Muses are often found in invocations to works, and can offer divine, VATIC INSPIRATION. The words 'music' and 'museum' are both derived from 'muse'.

mystery play A medieval DRAMA that enacts a Biblical narrative. It is a form of liturgical drama that differs from MIRACLE PLAY mostly in subject-matter: mystery plays are always based on Scripture. The plays are PAGEANTS which were performed at the festival of Corpus Christi (body of Christ). They are thought to have been performed on wagons, as THEATRE IN THE ROUND. 'Mystery' comes from the Latin *misterium* meaning 'profession'; this is because mystery plays were put on by guilds of tradesman. Individual plays were arranged into CYCLES that relate the entire sweep from Creation to Christ's Resurrection and Ascension. Four complete CYCLES survive: York, Chester, Wakefield (Towneley) and N-Town. In the York CYCLE, for instance, there were around fifty performances: Shipwrights performed the building of Noah's Ark, the Smiths dramatised the temptation of Christ, the Pinners (pinmakers) and Painters took the crucifixion (PASSION PLAY) and the Tailors managed the ascension of Christ to heaven. Mystery plays did not survive the Reformation and were not influential on the development of EARLY MODERN drama (unlike MORALITY PLAYS). However, they are still performed today, and a South African production of *The Mysteries* was particularly well received in London in the early 2000s.

myth (adj. mythical, mythic; Greek, 'speech, narration') A FICTIONAL NARRATIVE or STORY that has origins in ORAL tradition. Myths are usually ANONYMOUS, associated with a particular culture, and usually have a supernatural element. A mythology is a collection of stories that expresses some of the beliefs and ideals of a culture. By contrast, a LEGEND is a tale that is closer to historical fact, and usually centred around an exceptional individual. A FABLE is a story, often involving animals, that conveys a specific message. The word 'myth' is also used to describe any untrue story, with '**mythical**' as its associated adjective (e.g. a mythical unicorn). '**Mythic**' refers specifically to something connected to a myth.

The word-root of myth is the Greek word for PLOT, *muthos*, which implies that a myth is a story that can be told in many different ways. STRUCTURALISTS have tried to discover the universal patterns originally found in myth that are transferred into later NARRATIVES. This is known as MYTHIC(AL) CRITICISM, and is related to NARRATOLOGY and ARCHETYPAL CRITICISM (which looks more at images and motifs than at individual works). This has been criticised as being REDUCTIONIST: i.e. it turns rich cultural heritages into a set of templates. The origins of myths and their role in forming cultures remain mysterious. The Nigerian novelist Chinua Achebe has written that:

> The universal creative rondo revolves on people and stories. *People create stories create people*; or rather, *stories create people create stories*. Was it stories first and then people, or the other way round? Most creation myths would seem to support the antecedence of stories—a scenario in which the story was already unfolding in the cosmos before, and even as a result of which, man came into being.

Later writers have created separate mythologies, often based on pre-existing ones; MYTHOPOEIA is the name for this. Some writers have even composed personal mythologies in an attempt to express their ideas: William Blake created a whole host of mythical CHARACTERS, such as Tiriel, Urizen and Los; W.B. Yeats published *A Vision* (1926) which described the structures and geometrical figures that he claimed provided order in his writing and a sense of security, even if it was a personal myth.

mythic(al) criticism A critical approach that seeks to extract underlying patterns from MYTHS, and find them present in other literary works. It is closely related to ARCHETYPAL CRITICISM, which concentrates more on IMAGES, SYMBOLS and other elements common to works. It was most popular in the 1950s and 60s, when the influence of STRUCTURALISM was strong, which encouraged literary critics to join anthropologists in discovering the hidden order that determined culture. Karl Jung's notion of the COLLECTIVE

UNCONSCIOUS suggested a connection with PSYCHOANALYTIC CRITICISM. It has come under criticism for being REDUCTIONIST and failing respecting the uniqueness of world cultures. Northrop Frye was among the most prominent mythic(al) critics.

mythopoeia (Greek, 'myth-making') The creation or ADAPTATION of a MYTH in a literary work. *The Lord of the Rings* is a CLASSIC mythopoeic work, and has its roots in J.R.R. Tolkien's academic interest in Old Norse mythology.

N

narratee The person being addressed within a literary work. 'Narratee' is not the same as the reader: he/she is a CHARACTER known to the NARRATOR. Wordsworth's narratee in *The Prelude* (1805, 50), for example, is Samuel Taylor Coleridge: 'Thus from a very early age, O Friend! | My thoughts by slow gradation had been drawn | To human-kind, and to the good and ill | Of human life' (VIII.676–79, 1850 version).

narrative A STORY or collection of events told by a NARRATOR. Narrative material can be FICTIONAL, historical or a mixture of both; likewise, the audience envisaged in the text can be real or imagined. The PLOT is the progression of events within the narrative. Narrative, DRAMATIC and LYRIC are the three main strands of poetry, and in this context narrative particularly refers to EPIC or other long plot-driven poems. NARRATOLOGY is the study of narratives.

narratology The study of NARRATIVE structures, which includes varieties of NARRATOR (and NARRATEE). It developed as a separate field in the 1970s, but has precursors in RUSSIAN FORMALISM and, going further back, to Aristotle's *Poetics*. Roland Barthes and Gérard Genette are two of the most influential narratologists. It shares STRUCTURALISM'S interest in locating deeper patterns in forms of literature, and asks questions about VIEWPOINT, FORM and the act of telling a story. Narratology seeks to uncover the rules and conventions behind different literary FORMS. Some critics consider this disinterested approach to literature REDUCTIVE. An important distinction is made between the STORY (or *fabula*, as some critics prefer) to be told, and how it is arranged into a PLOT (or *sjuzhet*). FLASH-BACK and PROLEPSIS (flash-forward), for example, are structural devices that narratology would naturally focus upon. The status of the NARRATOR and implied audience are central concerns too. The term is typically associated with literary theory, but in practice it could refer to work ranging across ORAL LITERATURE, SEMIOTICS, LINGUISTICS and anthropology.

narrator The person telling a story (NARRATIVE). This figure is distinct from the AUTHOR: the narrator is a separate PERSONA with its own VOICE.

Some authors switch between narrators, and studying narrative structure (NARRATOLOGY) is a separate field of its own. At a simpler level, it's worth being able to identify the various kinds of narrator, which can be done by asking a few simple questions.

Question one: what is the narrator's relation to the action? A FIRST-PERSON NARRATOR is involved in the story, and describes events from his/her VIEWPOINT, as he/she experienced it. A THIRD-PERSON NARRATOR has no involvement in the action, though he/she may have a particular VIEWPOINT on it. Question two: can I trust what the narrator is saying? An OMNISCIENT NARRATOR knows all the details, and seems to look down at the action. He or she sometimes supplies information before the CHARACTERS know it, and knows their unspoken thoughts. An UNRELIABLE NARRATOR will make discoveries as the reader does, and may make mistakes. The reader has to process the information, often to learn more about the narrator's own personality. This depends on question three: how aware am I of the narrator's presence? INTRUSIVE NARRATORS possess personalities of their own, whereas UNINTRUSIVE narrators are neutral, allowing the audience to concentrate on the narrative.

Question four: what is the narrator thinking about? 'Self-conscious narrator' is a term used for narrators who are aware that they are telling a story, and are careful to present in a correct manner. STREAM OF CONSCIOUSNESS is the apparently spontaneous flow of a CHARACTER's thoughts (not necessarily the narrator's), and FREE INDIRECT DISCOURSE is a means of weaving opinions into description. Other questions to ask would be: who is the narrator addressing—is there a specific person being addressed (NARRATEE)? How far has the AUTHOR distanced him/herself from the narrator? Is the work a MONOLOGUE, or are there different perspectives?

These questions are intended to contribute to an overall impression of how narrators have a presence within works. Certain combinations often go together—in particular the omniscient third-person narrator and the intrusive first-person narrator—but there are no set rules, and it is important to establish how authors create a narrative VOICE and to what end.

naturalism (naturalistic) The idea that human lives are controlled by nature and society. This gives rise to a form of literary REALISM that envisages the world as a machine that controls our movements and decisions. It originated in late nineteenth-century French novels, and was taken up by numerous early twentieth-century novelists writing in English, such as Theodore Dreiser. The ADJECTIVE **naturalistic** is used to describe DRAMA that is realistic in its dialogue, SETTING, *MISE EN SCÈNE*, CHARACTER and PLOT. This quotation from the opening pages of Dreiser's *Sister Carrie* (1900) conveys well the naturalistic perspective in literature. The subject is the city:

> There are large forces which allure with all the soulfulness of expression possible in the most cultured human. The gleam of a thousand lights is often as effective as the persuasive light in a wooing and fascinating eye. Half the undoing of the unsophisticated and natural mind is accomplished by forces wholly superhuman. A blaze of sound, a roar of life, a vast array of human hives, appeal to the senses in equivocal terms.

naturalistic drama A theatrical production that tries to IMITATE reality as closely as possible onstage. The play must follow the dramatic UNITIES so that the stage represents a single time and place throughout. Its CHARACTERS must be believable, and the PLOT cannot feel artificial. THEATRICALITY and symbolism are not allowed. It arose in the nineteenth century alongside literary REALISM and NATURALISM, but was found by many producers and playwrights to be too restrictive. Bertolt Brecht and others found the concept flawed, because it tried to increase the DRAMATIC illusion; Brecht proposed that the only way to make DRAMA 'real' was to smash that FICTIONAL world together, and make plays that were directly about reality (see 'epic theatre' and 'alienation effect').

nature writing NON-FICTIONAL prose that offers close observations of the natural world. Nature writing is typically reflective and exploratory. It expresses respect and awe for the natural environment. Nature writing is particularly relevant to ECOCRITICISM, and is often popular with general readers too. Gilbert White's *The Natural History of Selbourne* (1789), for example, is an early work of nature writing that remains enjoyable to read today.

near rhyme The matching of two words that contain identical sounds, but not the similar vowels and endings necessary for FULL RHYME. It involves CONSONANCE, ASSONANCE, or a combination of both: e.g. 'glimpse/clinch', 'batter/flatten', 'smooth/truth'. It is also known as HALF-RHYME, SLANT RHYME or PARARHYME (which is slightly different). Many EYE RHYMES are also near rhymes: 'mind/wind'. Near rhymes can be unintentional, attributed to poetic license or used to introduce subtle connections between words.

A near rhyme isn't necessarily an inferior version of a full rhyme: it all depends on its use in CONTEXT.

negative capability A phrase used by John Keats (in a letter to George and Tom Keats, 21st Dec. 1817) to describe an ability to embrace what is unknown and unknowable: it 'is when man is capable of being in uncertainties, Mysteries, doubts without any irritable reaching after fact & reason'. Keats thought that William Shakespeare had a great deal of negative capability, but that Wordsworth didn't (see 'egotistical sublime'). Keats is arguing that writers and readers of literature should accept that it contains a special complexity that cannot be explained through reason. Poetic beauty brings fresh insight into our lives, but doesn't take us closer to knowing how the world works.

négritude A term used in 1930s France to assert that native African culture is unique, and should not just be assimilated into traditional French culture. Aimé Césaire, a francophone writer from Martinique, coined the term in 1935 to describe acceptance, appreciation and affirmation of African heritage. It was influenced by the HARLEM RENAISSANCE and SURREALISM (particularly among Parisian immigrants), and was tied to aspirations for African independence (and even black supremacy). It could loosely be described as 'POSTCOLONIAL', though it concentrated on existing colonial practices (rather than looking beyond them): it involved a stinging attack on the institutional racism suffered by people of colour across the world. The Nigerian writer Wole Soyinka's oft-quoted criticism of *négritude* is worth quoting again: 'the tiger does not proclaim his tigritude—he pounces.'

neoclassicism The revived interest in CLASSICAL principles in British literature in the period from around 1660 to 1800, distinct from developments in music, the visual arts and architecture across Europe at this time. Neoclassicism generally approved of balance, order, clarity of expression and use of appropriate POETIC DICTION (with lots of ABSTRACT LANGUAGE). Classical ideas of DECORUM made some GENRES more acceptable than others, and put forms like the ODE, EPIGRAM and SATIRE in fashion. Although neoclassicism promotes traditional and IMITATIVE literature, it nonetheless provides ample scope for creativity. Generating suitable material (literary invention) and expressing it in an appropriate way led to much thoughtful and eloquent writing. The height of British neoclassicism is found in the work of the AUGUSTAN POETS. Alexander Pope, John Dryden, Jonathan Swift and Joseph Addison were all prominent neoclassical writers.

'Neoclassicism' is routinely contrasted with a movement that followed it, ROMANTICISM. When used in this way, the terms take on more general thematic significance. In the broadest possible terms, neoclassicism encourages literature suitable for civilised society, whereas romanticism claims literature as the product of the individual artist. Neoclassicism is regulated, systematic, uncontroversial, and has a fixed purpose. Romanticism is exploratory, liberated, attuned with nature, and suspicious of social mechanisms. Neoclassicism encourages the use of reason to create happy and disciplined citizens, where romanticism argues that true happiness is only attainable if humans return to a state of natural goodness. In this dichotomy, neoclassicism is allied to ENLIGHTENMENT philosophy and the Age of Reason, and romanticism to imaginative powers.

As always when discussing such large ideas, it shouldn't be assumed that they accurately reflect the priorities of any individual writer: the reality is seldom so clear-cut. Be aware that twenty-first-century ideas about literature are still influenced by romantic principles, and it's hard to unthink these ideas when encountering neoclassical literature. In addition, it's not helpful to name the entire long eighteenth century as the 'Neoclassical period', since this name doesn't do justice to the range of artistic activity that went on: Lawrence Sterne's and Henry Fielding's works, for example, are hardly CLASSICAL.

neologism (knee-o-**low**-jizm; Greek, 'new word') A new word or phrase; also, the creation of one. COINAGE is an alternative term, while some varieties of neologism are: PORTMANTEAU WORD, NONCE WORD, INKHORN TERM and (often) SLANG. Neologisms contribute to the creation of DICTION and STYLE unique to the writer; in effect, granting the AUTHOR new resources for expression. Shakespeare created many neologisms, many of which have remained in the English language (though see 'nonce word'). He is the first cited AUTHOR for 256 definitions in the *OED*, which include some that are still used (like 'priceless' and 'puppy dog') and some that are not (like 'pajock', meaning a conceited person).

Neoplatonism A 'new' form of PLATONIC philosophy with added spiritual and mystical elements that originated in the third century through the work of Plotinus. Neoplatonism overlaps with Christian theology, and these connections were subsequently explored across the Middle Ages and RENAISSANCE. Marsilio Ficino, a fifteenth-century Italian HUMANIST, translated Plato's works into Latin, and allowed Plato to be read across Europe. The Neoplatonic is widespread in literature (see also 'Platonic love'): two prominent examples are Dante's *Divine Comedy* and ELIZABETHAN SONNET SEQUENCES, such as Edmund Spenser's *Amoretti* (1595). Spenser's *Fowre Hymns* are even more explicitly Neoplatonic: 'More faire is that, where those *Idees* on hie | Enraunged be, which *Plato* so admyred, | And pure *Intelligences* from God inspyred.' ('Hymne of Heavenly Beautie', ll.82–84).

New Criticism A movement in American literary criticism based on the assumptions that poems are self-contained (AUTOTELIC) objects, and that interpretation should uncover their OBJECTIVE meaning. It was current from the 1930s to 1960s, and got its name after the publication of John Crowe Ransom's *The New Criticism* (1941). New Critics were particularly interested in PARADOX, IRONY, METAPHOR and other forms of FIGURATIVE LANGUAGE. It argued against understanding poems in light of CONTEXTUAL and historical influences. New Criticism found it mistaken to read a work from the AUTHOR'S supposed intentions (INTENTIONAL FALLACY) or based on personal reaction (AFFECTIVE FALLACY). It considered the text an organic, AUTOTELIC object, and sought to gain a near-scientific understanding of how it worked.

New Criticism was a more theoretical and analytical version of PRACTICAL CRITICISM, which originally stressed the value of close reading. It is FORMALIST in its principles, but developed separately to RUSSIAN FORMALISM. New Criticism's importance is confirmed by the number of critical movements that later defined themselves against it: the CHICAGO CRITICS initially criticised the narrowness of the New Critical approach, while CONTEXTUAL CRITICISM placed more EMPHASIS on the total structure of a poem over its details; POST-STRUCTURALISTS (and DECONSTRUCTIONISTS) don't believe a text has the sort of unity New Critics claim it does; MARXIST CRITICS find political and economic factors too important to ignore; READER-RESPONSE CRITICS play up the reader's role in generating meaning. The principle that a text holds objective value has been assaulted from all angles, but the New Critical method survives: most critical styles still consider thorough readings of a text valuable. It is a form of CRITICISM that requires discipline and skill, but can be attempted by any literate person, regardless of their background or training.

new formalism A recent current in American poetry that champions traditional FIXED FORMS, METRES and RHYME. It began in the 1980s as a response to FREE VERSE and LANGUAGE POETRY that had put formal poetry out of fashion (and the NEW CRITICAL principles underlying it). New formalism is another chapter in the to-and-fro argument about how AUTHORS should respond to the TRADITION, and the virtues of IMITATION.

new historicism A major area of LITERARY CRITICISM that places LITERARY and non-literary texts alongside each other. New historicism considers TEXT and CONTEXT to be identical, with influences and energies flowing in and out of both. It stresses the TEXTUALITY (written character) of history. Literature and historical documents inform each other. This opened up literary study to a whole host of non-literary texts (e.g. legal, medical or official documents) beyond the traditional CANON.

The founding text of new historicism is Stephen Greenblatt's *Renaissance Self-Fashioning* (1980). Most chapters in that book begin with a historical ANECDOTE that are related to the concerns of a given literary text. New historical studies come to solid conclusions based on clear documentary evidence. This took literary criticism into completely new territory, rather than participating in previous critical debates. Nonetheless new historicism grew out of the critical conditions of its time. 'Old' HISTORICISM (see this entry) tried to embed a literary work in the thoughts, ideas and events of its time, whereas new historicism saw this as an artificial exercise, because it still regarded literature as created by universal ideas that transcend history. New historicism was a reaction against FORMALIST and STRUCTURALIST CRITICISM that believed a literary work existed as a self-standing object, created from an underlying pattern. Its origins are in POST-STRUCTURALISM, DECONSTRUCTION, and, to a lesser degree, PSYCHOANALYSIS. New historicists are typically interested in the social and cultural DISCOURSES present in a work. In particular, new historicists have worked on how literature is created from impersonal systems of power and IDEOLOGIES, not an individual AUTHOR'S voice. Here Michel Foucault's influence looms large: his interest in the 'panopticon', a circular prison where everyone is always in sight, is a crucial image in early new historicist CRITICISM.

New historicism grew out of EARLY MODERN studies, and its influence remained greatest for criticism in that period, partly because there are many historical documents available and issues about the inaccessibility of the past are prominent. Yet it has broadened out to other periods, and gave rise to CULTURAL MATERIALISM, a British extension of new historicism that identifies how literary works participate in larger political struggles. New historicism encourages close reading, but is criticised for stripping the text of its 'literary' characteristics and depicting the AUTHOR as a pawn of OBJECTIVE cultural forces. Certainly the movement towards a more integrated consideration of literature in its historical situation is valuable. However, new historicists can sometimes seem too convinced of their own conclusions. If taken to an extreme, you could well ask whether something called 'new historicism' moves too far into history and away from 'literary criticism', whatever we want that term to mean.

nom de plume An alternative term for PEN-NAME, taken from French (though for obscure reasons the French equivalent is *nom de guerre*).

nonce word (from Middle English 'than anes' meaning 'for the one') A word created for a specific occasion, often with no other recorded uses. Shakespeare created many nonce-words and other NEOLOGISMS (new words) besides. His nonce-words in the *OED* include 'overstink' (to smell more than) and 'fantastico' (an absurd person). PORTMANTEAU WORDS and INKHORN TERMS are sometimes also nonce words. *HAPAX LEGOMENON* is an older term with a similar meaning: it refers to words with one surviving recorded example, though this may be caused by absence of further evidence rather than the term being a conscious innovation.

non-fiction Factual writing, based on the real world and EXPERIENCES. In non-fiction, CONTENT usually matters more than FORM and STYLE, whereas in FICTION the way that imagined events are described is usually more important for consideration. Many non-fictional forms provide scope for creative writing and explicitly SUBJECTIVE VIEWPOINTS: AUTOBIOGRAPHY, ESSAY, MEMOIR, and even CRITICISM all stretch the boundaries of non-fiction. A fictional work described as DOCUMENTARY is one that directly imports elements of non-fiction. A historical work (e.g. HISTORY PLAY or HISTORICAL NOVEL) is based on actual events and CHARACTERS that have been fictionalized in some way.

non-fixed form A general term for any kind of poetry that does not have a set METRE or RHYME scheme. The term is vaguer than its opposite, 'FIXED FORM'. In this book it refers to types of poetry that are defined by a structural element other than metre and rhyme, as opposed to its CONTENT. FREE VERSE, ACROSTIC and CONCRETE POETRY count as non-fixed forms because they have distinctive formal properties, though no set patterns of METRE or RHYME.

nonsense verse A form of LIGHT VERSE that uses highly individual sounds and words. In principle 'nonsense' can describe prose as well, but the term is largely used to describe poems that make use of particularly unusual and surprising language, including NEOLOGISMS and phrases that cannot be PARAPHRASED. It is sometimes written in rough DOGGEREL, or in short JINGLES. 'Nonsensical' poems are not simply gibberish that make 'no-sense', and should not be confused with OBSCURITY. Nonsense verse is used for particular effect, usually COMIC or SATIRICAL. It can also be used when standard language just seems insufficient (see 'adynaton'). The most renowned examples in English are those by the VICTORIAN writers Lewis Carroll (author of *Alice in Wonderland*) and Edward Lear, who wrote many a nonsense LIMERICK (first published in *A Book of Nonsense* (1846)).

noun (proper) A word that names something: e.g. 'fish', 'friend' and 'fear'. A **proper** noun is an individual person's, place's or thing's given name, and is placed in capital letters: e.g. 'Florence', 'Finland'. Nouns are either CONCRETE or ABSTRACT.

novel A PROSE FICTION in which the CHARACTERS, PLOT and/or THEMES develop through the work. As a result it feels more substantial than either a NOVELLA or SHORT STORY. In addition a novel must be sufficiently large to allow it to be published alone. It is difficult to offer a more specific definition because novels can be written in many different GENRES and STYLES. The novel is often a fairly REALISTIC literary form, and is written to hold the general reader's attention—this can already be seen in the work traditionally considered the first English novel, Daniel Defoe's *Robinson Crusoe* (1719). Leading on from Gustave Flaubert's *Madame Bovary* (1856) the novel became increasingly serious about representing the world as it is. This developed into literary NATURALISM, which described the world as it affects individuals: Thomas Hardy's *Tess of the D'Urbervilles* (1891) is an example of this. However, it would be easy to offer counter-examples; e.g. from SCIENCE-FICTION or MODERNISM.

Because novels are often relatively long and intended for a popular audience, critical ANALYSIS can sometimes seem more difficult than it would for poetry, which contains obviously 'literary' DEVICES to spot like ALLITERATION, RHYME and so on. Rating a novel for its REALISM is no place to start either. However, as anyone who has tried creative writing will know writing prose is not easy and requires definite technical skill, and it contains elements that can be isolated and studied in detail. Once you understand the structure of a novel (i.e. you've read it), one way to start ANALYSIS would be to question why the AUTHOR makes certain choices: what PERSONA is used, and how does this VOICE relates to the AUTHOR; what type of NARRATOR is present; how selective or OBJECTIVE is the description; what DICTION is used; how long is each section; how many PLOTS and CHARACTERS are there, and do these develop; what is the novel's TONE, and is there a DIDACTIC/SATIRICAL/IRONIC/COMIC element; what is its AUDIENCE. By considering these sorts of question, it's possible to start thinking closely about how novels work, and the ways that STYLE shapes MEANING.

novelette A short piece of PROSE FICTION. The term is synonymous with NOVELLA, except that it is often used to suggest a work is trashy or shallow; e.g. like PULP FICTION or a Mills & Boon romance.

novella A short work of PROSE FICTION, which is longer than a SHORT STORY, but shorter than a NOVEL. Novellas are usually just long enough to be published as separate volumes; e.g. Joseph Conrad's *Heart of Darkness* (1902).

nursery rhyme A simple poem intended to be sung to and by children. It interests critics less as a form of CHILDREN'S LITERATURE, and more as an ancient and global form of poetry, with origins in FOLK LITERATURE, BALLADS and much else. Most contemporary nursery rhymes in British English are hundreds of years old: e.g. 'Ring a ring of roses', though some scholars dispute the popular belief that this rhyme is about bubonic plague.

O

object (direct, indirect) The person or thing having something done to it. A noun that names a **direct** object is placed in accusative CASE. A person or thing that is also affected by an action is an indirect object, and the noun is in the dative case: e.g. in the sentence 'I passed the apple to Doris', 'apple' is the direct object and 'Doris' the indirect object, since she benefits from my passing the apple.

objective (objectivity) Related to the world as it is, confirmed by fact. Objectivity involves a detached, uncommitted outlook on the world that is not affected by individual thoughts, opinions or BIAS. Science is usually thought of as the pursuit of objective truth and knowledge. Some literary writers write objectively; Henry James, Ernest Hemingway and some MODERNIST writers are renowned for it. OMNISCIENT NARRATION is a literary style particularly associated with objective thought. Literary critics regularly contest the opposition of objective and subjective—see the entry on 'subjective' for more.

objective correlative A term associated with T.S. Eliot (though he didn't create it) for objects, events or scenes in literary works that represent a specific emotion or MOOD: e.g. the dead albatross stands for the mariner's guilt and regret in Samuel Taylor Coleridge's *Rime of the Ancient Mariner*. An objective correlative occurs where FORM and CONTENT are well-matched: the IMAGES carry just enough SYMBOLIC meaning. It should be said that Eliot generally favoured precise imagery (as found in Eliot's work and also IMAGIST poetry) rather than vaguer description more typical to Victorian verse. Eliot first uses the term to criticise *Hamlet* for having no objective correlative, and thus leaving the PROTAGONIST'S EMOTIONS and MOTIVATION hopelessly cloudy, and the play messy and disordered. You wouldn't find many twenty-first-century critics who agree.

obscurity A lack of clarity in expression. Writers sometimes cultivate obscurity through ALLUSIONS, unusual language or private references. Though frequently used in a derogatory sense, there is no reason why literature should be easy to read. Obscurity is often necessary to convey sophisticated meanings: readers should be prepared to spend time and attention on words, phrases and passages before a work's meaning becomes clear. It is no bad thing to be made to read slowly. There are many accepted CLASSICS (like T.S. Eliot's *The Waste Land*) that require multiple readings and critical notes to make full sense. At the same time, some obscure work is plain uncommunicative, and reflects a writer's mental haziness. As a reader, an independent judgment needs to be made as to whether obscurity encourages perseverance to explore the TENSIONS it presents, or fails to convince you that extra effort will be rewarded. It is important to remember than obscurity is relative: what is obvious to a reader in one time and place may be impenetrable to someone somewhere else. Obscurity also refers to the fate of non-CANONICAL writers who are seldom read or written about. It is always worth asking why an AUTHOR has been ignored, and what this reveals about our own critical prejudices.

occasional poem A verse composition written for a particular event. This is traditionally a birth, death (e.g. DIRGE), marriage (EPITHALAMION) or other significant life-event. These forms were particularly common when PATRONS were influential figures to poets. More recently occasional poems often concern particular historical or political events. Occasional poems almost always announce themselves in the TITLE, which immediately creates a set of expectations: e.g. W.B. Yeats's 'Easter 1916' (about the Easter Uprising in Ireland) written in the summer in 1916. Occasional poems clearly benefit from HISTORICISED interpretation in a more specific sense than most poems do.

occultatio (also **occupatio, paralipsis**) A FIGURE that places EMPHASIS on something by pretending to ignore it: e.g. 'I won't say anything about how horrible that meal was.' It is often COMIC and/or IRONIC, but can also be manipulative. An example from Chaucer's *Canterbury Tales* (*The Knight's Tale*, ll. 2039–40): 'Suffiseth oon ensample in stories olde; | I may nar rekene hem alle though I wolde' ('That's enough examples from old tales; I cannot tell them all, though I would like to').

octave (also **octet**) The first eight lines of a SONNET (see this entry for common rhyme schemes), which is followed by a SESTET. It is unwise to use 'octave' in reference to other eight-line verse forms (e.g. OTTAVA RIMA), as it will usually be assumed that it refers to a sonnet. The octave and sestet are essential divisions in sonnets, and it is always worthwhile considering how an individual poem connects the two parts.

octavo A page format created by folding a single sheet three times, and a book containing LEAVES of that size. QUARTO and FOLIO are two other formats.

octosyllabic An adjective describing an eight-SYLLABLE line. It is rarely used in English PROSODY, since the alternative terms 'IAMBIC' and 'TROCHAIC TETRAMETER' (four stress, eight syllable lines) are more precise. Though the octosyllabic line is common in English poetry, it is better to describe a line of ACCENTUAL-SYLLABIC verse (i.e. where the number of stresses also matters) according to its syllables and stresses when possible.

ode (Greek, 'song') A long LYRIC POEM, formal in both structure and tone. In general, an ode in English is announced in the title. In its original Greek form, it was performed by a CHORUS and was divided into a STROPHE and ANTISTROPHE sharing the same length and METRICAL pattern, and an EPODE, which had a different structure and length. A PINDARIC ODE follows this three-part structure (often multiple times), whereas in an HORATIAN ODE each stanza has the same metrical pattern. The restrictions of the Pindaric ode were loosened by Abraham Cowley, who introduced the IRREGULAR (or Cowleian) ODE. The irregular ode discards the strict ode form but retains its monumental tone. This version of the ode was commonly used for a time, though eventually its ceremonial style lost its attraction, and there are fairly few twentieth-century examples. When reading odes, the expectations created by 'ode' matter as much as the actual form. This is seen in the TONE of Keats's odes, for example. Other forms of ode, such as the sapphic, have been imitated by English poets who possessed a knowledge of classical PROSODY, such as Philip Sidney.

OED An ABBREVIATED form of '*Oxford English Dictionary*, often used in secondary texts (such as this one). The *OED* is generally accepted to be the most authoritative English dictionary. This is both because of its size (over 500 000 entries and counting) and because it traces the history of terms through quotations. This makes it ideal for finding out the first known use of a term, and its subsequent development. Fewer people today would agree that the English language and its history can simply be catalogued than when the dictionary was first being compiled; nevertheless, the *OED* remains an essential research tool, and offers still more search options now that it is available online (through subscription, see p. 388). The dictionary you are currently reading follows *OED* spelling.

Oedipus complex In PSYCHOANALYSIS, a collection of repressed impulses that appears during early childhood based on the desire to be reunited sexually with the parent of the other sex, and to remove the parent of the same sex. It is named after the PROTAGONIST in the Sophoclean tragedy *Oedipus Rex*, who discovers he has unknowingly slept with Jocasta, his mother, and killed his father, Creon. This notion is among the most controversial of all Sigmund Freud's ideas, and has been ridiculed and admired with equal ferocity. Karl Jung found the Oedipus complex a flawed idea because it focused on individual desire, rather than finding truly universal patterns of thought in the COLLECTIVE UNCONSCIOUS (ARCHETYPES). Either way, it embodies the nature of psychoanalytic criticism, which is to claim scientific objectivity for moments of personal insight found in literary works: the rich artistic significance of Oedipus becomes classified as a psychological complex.

oeuvre **(err**-vr; French, 'work') The complete works of an AUTHOR. 'CANON' and 'CORPUS' have very similar meanings. A *chef d'oeuvre* is a masterpiece (or MAGNUM OPUS).

Old English (c.400–1066) The earliest form of VERNACULAR English before it was shaped by French after the Norman invasion. 'Anglo-Saxon' is an alternative term that is used in the twenty-first century. Old English is Germanic, and a knowledge of modern German GRAMMAR and vocabulary is helpful when trying to read it. Latin is also an influence: it was the language used in religion and official communications. In any case, readers of modern English need to learn to read Old English, as with any foreign language (see 'litotes' for a brief sample). It initially appears difficult because of GRAMMATICAL subtleties absent from modern English, and the characters 'ð' ('eth', a 'th' sound), 'þ' ('thorn', also 'th') and 'ʒ' as a letter 'g' (which became the 'yogh' character in Middle English). Old English literature has survived in four CODICES (named in that entry). See page 359 for important literary texts and related entries.

omniscient narrator (Latin, 'all-knowing') A PERSONA who tells a story knowing every detail of the story, as well as the MOTIVATIONS and thoughts of its CHARACTERS. It is a standard form of THIRD-PERSON NARRATION (though it can be FIRST-PERSON also), and throws emphasis onto events described. An omniscient narrator who also reflects upon the events described is an INTRUSIVE narrator. Even when omniscient narrators are UNINTRUSIVE, the VOICE telling the story is still a persona, rather than the AUTHOR'S own. From this description, omniscient narrators may seem to be 'unrealistic', but their use is so CONVENTIONAL that most readers would never question its use. Omniscient narrators are found in everything from *Harry Potter* to *War and Peace*.

one-act play A short theatrical performance; the dramatic equivalent of a SHORT STORY. One-act plays can be AFTER-PIECES or experimental works (FRINGE THEATRE), or serious dramas like John Millington Synge's TRAGEDY *Riders to the Sea* (1904).

onomatopoeia (Greek, 'word-making') A FIGURE involving the use of words that echo their meaning in their sound: e.g. 'crash', 'boom', 'quack'. It also describes words that resemble other sensations (i.e. have a SYNAESTHETIC effect): 'large' sounds bigger than 'little'; 'whizz' sounds quicker than 'bumble'; and (some would say) 'white' sounds more appropriate for the colour white than 'black' does. In fact, onomatopoeia has been shown to play a part in language formation. The term can also refer to language that bears a general correspondence to the meaning in some aspect (e.g. sound, FORM, STYLE, length). Onomatopoeia is language affected by what it describes. It is important, though, to remember that the effect of onomatopoeia is always linked to a word's meaning. It mixes language's appeal to thoughts (through its meaning) and feelings (through sensations). Onomatopoeic language is not a true IMITATION of what is being conveyed, which is shown by the different words for animal sounds between languages: the English 'purr' is 'ronron' in French, and this isn't because French cats speak a different language. The following example from Tennyson (*In Memoriam A.H.H.*, XI.1–8), contains delicate onomatopoeia combined with ALLITERATION. You can almost guess the meaning of 'furze' (line 6, an evergreen shrub) and 'gossamers' (line 7, what cobwebs are made of) from the sound:

> Calm is the morn without a sound,
> Calm as to suit a calmer grief,
> And only through the faded leaf
> The chestnut pattering to the ground.
> Calm and deep peace on this high world,
> And on these dews that drench the furze;
> And all the silvery gossamers
> That twinkle into green and gold.

op. cit. (*opere citato,* Latin) In the work already quoted: e.g. 'Mayhew op. cit'. 'IBID.' is a SYNONYM, and 'LOC. CIT.' is more specific alternative; e.g. to refer to the same page.

open couplet A pair of VERSE lines in which the sense, METRE and/or SYNTAX run on into the next line (usually into another COUPLET). An open couplet always involves ENJAMBEMENT, and the COUPLET is usually RHYMED.

Even though the couplet is not self-contained, it is worth exploring in what ways it is complete in itself, and how it structures meaning in a passage.

open form A poetic STYLE associated with the BLACK MOUNTAIN POETS, in which FIXED FORMS are rejected in favour of fluid structures that convey breathing patterns and creative energies. It's a form of FREE VERSE with distinctive lineation across the page and large spaces to indicate silence. Open form is also known as 'projective verse'.

opera (Italian, 'work') A musical work with DRAMATIC elements. It has associations with more literary/speech-based forms like MASQUE, MELODRAMA and HEROIC DRAMA. Some opera LIBRETTOS (scripts) are literary ADAPTATIONS, such as Benjamin Britten's *Turn of the Screw* (1954), based on a Henry James story. Literary figures have also collaborated directly in opera, Bertolt Brecht and Kurt Weill's *The Threepenny Opera* (*Die Dreigroschenoper*, 1928) being a notable example.

operetta (Italian, 'little work') A light-hearted COMIC OPERA. The Victorian operettas of the writer (LIBRETTIST) W.S. Gilbert and composer Arthur Sullivan are CLASSICS of the GENRE.

oral literature (orature) A work that reaches its audience and is passed onto others by being spoken or sung. Oral literature is often slightly improvised, or varies between performances; the work is likely to change over time, and any written version shows the work at a later point in time. Most oral literature is poetry, because that is easier to remember and has more impact when delivered aloud. Though it does incorporate modern forms like PERFORMANCE POETRY, oral literature largely refers to literature that was composed before people started writing it down. This was the time of the MINSTREL, who performed poetry for a living. Forms like EPIC POETRY and BALLAD are inseparable from their origins in such performance. Note also the difference between 'oral', concerned with the mouth, and the similar-sounding word 'aural', which means 'associated with the ear'.

Its associations with FOLK LITERATURE leave a tendency to believe oral literature to be primitive compared to modern literature, which is an over-hasty assumption to make. This isn't helped by the term 'oral literature', because 'literature' means something written. The Ugandan scholar Pio Zirimu coined the term 'orature' in an attempt to correct this, but 'oral literature' remains the commonest term used. The lost prestige of ORALITY ('spokenness') has been addressed by some critics. DECONSTRUCTION, however, argues that the presence of a speaker doesn't make the meaning of an utterance any clearer (see also 'absence/presence', 'logocentric').

Though the written word dominates our encounters with literature, it is good to recall that poetry is often intended for speaking aloud. Even if written poetry is no longer purely a set of notes for performance, even features like LINEATION and INDENTATION affect how a poem is heard. It's possible to read with your ears.

orality The state of being spoken or verbally communicated. It is contrasted to literacy, which refers to being written or printed. In literary criticism, it is particularly associated with the work of Walter Ong, who writes of the 'primary orality' of cultures that have no agreed writing system, and 'residual orality' for those that have oral literature existing alongside written LITERATURE. This opens up issues about how written forms of communication structure thought in ways that orality doesn't, and in what sense speech is original, natural and powerful in a way that has been lost in Western society (though DECONSTRUCTION argues that speech doesn't indicate true presence (see 'absence/presence' for more)).

oration (oratory) A public speech, usually intended for a large audience. In addition 'oration' and 'oratory' mean the art of writing and giving speeches. It has particular relevance to CLASSICAL times, when orations had great prestige. A classical oration had six basic components: exordium (opening), narration (giving the facts), division (putting forward points for debate), proof (arguing the case), refutation, and PERORATION (summing up). This structure was still used being used in EARLY MODERN Europe; the best known written example is Philip Sidney's *Apologie for Poetrie* (1595).

organic/mechanical form A distinction between works that grow and live naturally, and those that are produced by following rules. This opposition in found in Plato, and was developed by Samuel Taylor Coleridge. Organic FORM tends to be looked on favourably by critics who use the term, because it suggests that a work is a product of the AUTHOR'S imagination, rather than slavishly following existing forms. Works with organic form (e.g. William Shakespeare's plays) are considered unified, consistent and AUTOTELIC, in the same way that trees and animals are created from a natural force. All the parts of the work can be understood as part of a whole. GENRES and CONVENTIONS, on the other hand, create mechanical works, though use of FIXED FORMS like the SONNET could still be considered organic.

The terms were another way of expressing the difference between ROMANTIC and NEOCLASSICAL views of literature. Criticism has moved on since then, however, and organic/mechanical are not in current use. DECONSTRUCTIONISTS have no time for the supposed unity of the work;

STRUCTURALISTS would find that the AUTHOR'S influence is being exaggerated (see also 'death of the author'); many others would find the distinction too sharp—literary works are not solely the product of individual inspiration or existing writing CONVENTIONS.

orientalism An outdated term used to describe the study of the 'Orient' (East), particularly the Near and Middle East. It is closely associated with the work that put the term out of use, Edward Saïd's *Orientalism* (1978). Saïd argued that the 'Orient' conjures up images of an exotic, mysterious and little-understood culture filled with STEREOTYPES (think Disney's *Aladdin*). The West imposed this image on the East without ever engaging with Eastern cultures. It is a form of cultural imperialism that asserts Western dominance (HEGEMONY). Ideas about IDEOLOGY and DISCOURSE are important here: Saïd is talking about how Western discussion of the East has affected everyone's perception and understanding of it, in both West and East. Saïd's ideas were important for the creation of POSTCOLONIAL CRITICISM, which seeks to uncover and resist the colonial imposition of culture. It has also shown the complexity and diversity of peoples and power structures grouped under those general terms 'West' and 'East'.

originality (adj. original) The ability to have fresh thoughts. An original work is something that has made a new beginning (origin) in some sense. That could be through author's INSPIRATION, IMAGINATION, invention (finding), calculated innovation or artful IMITATION. The relation between imitation and originality is complicated. The two may appear to be opposites, yet writing that follows CONVENTION or established TRADITION can still be original. Only PLAGIARISM and straight copying are definitely not original. Also, originality can only be judged within the tradition in which an AUTHOR writes. A piece filled with novelty and idiosyncrasy may not feel as original as a new version of something that has been tried before. Some forms of imitation probe unexplored areas of literary expression, and do so with real originality. Original material is not necessarily unique; indeed, Johann Wolfgang von Goethe is attributed with the quotation that 'everything has been thought of before, but the problem is to think of it again'. POST-STRUCTURALIST critics would go further, and suggest that a person's entire DISCOURSE has its origins in social systems of SIGNS, and that the idea of an original text existing by itself is a fantasy.

'Original' or 'imitative' have held different meanings over time, and this makes it even riskier to use these terms to describe historical texts. As a rhetorical term INVENTION covered the use of TOPOI and other commonplace ideas. Imitation was essential for training and fashioning someone into being a good writer. It was only with ROMANTICISM that spontaneous, individual expression was cherished in itself, and this led to the positive CONNOTATIONS that the word usually holds today (while 'imitation' seems more negative). Originality is also SUBJECTIVE: readers can disagree about how original something is based on their own knowledge of previous works. With these complications around, there seem two options: locate originality in an individual's creative energy that is never complacent and breaks free of established practice, or else conclude that originality is an illusion.

Other A term found in PSYCHOANALYTIC CRITICISM for everything against which the self (ego) defines itself. The idea holds wider applications; e.g. IDEOLOGIES always describe themselves in relation to an Other, whether this concerns race, class, gender, sex or some other constructed division. The concept of the 'SCAPEGOAT' is related: communities define themselves by choosing outcasts to eject. The Other is often just a projection of a negative definition of the self: e.g. I like English literature, so all scientists are my Other. The Other is related to the idea of the unconscious as well: the undiscovered world of which I have no knowledge, and which FIGURATIVE LANGUAGE (especially METAPHOR) attempts to access. These ideas have no single literary application, 'Other' is often used with the capital, and can be a confusing, slightly pretentious theoretical term unless well-defined.

ottava rima An Italian VERSE FORM involving STANZAS with eight lines of IAMBIC PENTAMETER that RHYME *abababcc*. Thomas Wyatt introduced the form into English, and it was revived in the early nineteenth century by John Keats and Percy Bysshe Shelley. It is well suited for NARRATIVE verse, and was used by Byron in such works as *Don Juan* (1819).

oxymoron (**adj. oxymoronic**; ox-ee-**more**-on) A FIGURE in which two terms (often ANTONYMS) are placed together in apparent contradiction; in other words, a condensed PARADOX. 'Pretty ugly' and 'fast asleep' are two everyday oxymorons. There is plenty of IRONIC potential too: 'fun maths lesson', 'realistic soap opera'. It is particularly common in sixteenth- and seventeenth-century verse. Whereas ANTITHESIS identifies oppositions, oxymoron forces unity between those opposites. There is scope for critical dispute as to whether an oxymoron is a highly meaningful use of language, or is devoid of meaning. Philosophers have often debated this point over Immanuel Kant's use of language; for example, in his oxymoronic description of artistic genius as 'disinterested interest'. Here is a quatrain by Walter Ralegh containing an oxymoron in its final line (modernised spelling and punctuation):

> Fortune hath taken thee away, my love,
> My life's soul and my heaven above;
> Fortune hath taken thee away my princess;
> My only light and my true fancy's mistress.
> (ll.1–4)

P

paean A song of hope or thanksgiving. Like 'ELEGY' and 'IDYLL' the term originally referred to a specific type of Greek poetry but is now used more widely. 'Paean' can describe any celebratory song, but for literary criticism it's worth being aware of its more specific definition.

pageant A performance with striking visual effects. A pageant usually takes place outdoors, often on a moving vehicle. Pageants were fairly common in MEDIEVAL Britain, particularly in DRAMATIZATIONS of historical or biblical narratives, such as MYSTERY and MIRACLE PLAYS.

palaeography (Greek, 'ancient writing') The study of writing and documents, especially scripts (handwriting) and manuscripts.

palilogy (Greek, 'speaking again') A common FIGURE in which REPETITION is used for forceful EMPHASIS. It is sometimes used as a SYNONYM for 'ANADIPLOSIS' (repetition at the end of one line and the beginning of the next), and is similar to EPIZEUXIS (immediate repetition) in its effect.

palimpsest (Greek, 'smooth again') A manuscript or other writing material that has been written on more than once, after the original text has been removed. Many medieval manuscripts are palimpsests, because good writing material (e.g. vellum, which comes from calf-hides) was so costly. It is sometimes used as a metaphor for a word that has accumulated different meanings over time, or for a work that has multiple levels of meaning.

palindrome (Greek, 'running back again') A word that reads the same forwards and backwards, if punctuation and spacing are ignored: e.g. 'noon'; 'a man, a plan, a canal, Panama'. It is too restrictive to be of much use to literary writers; ACROSTIC, another trick with letters, can at least be applied to a poem's LINEATION without much difficulty.

palinode (Greek, 'again song') A poem in which the AUTHOR takes back something said in a previous work. It is a tradition with few major examples in English literature. The end of Geoffrey Chaucer's *Canterbury Tales* (c.1400) offers a retraction in the style of a medieval palinode, except that Chaucer writes about the current work he is just concluding.

panegyric (**noun and adj.**; pani-**dji**-rik; from Greek) A poem written in praise of a person or group of people, and intended for a public audience. Panegyrics were written, for example, in the sixteenth and early seventeenth centuries to praise Elizabeth I and James I openly. ENCOMIUM is a slightly more general term for the same.

pantomime The term originally referred to a performance in CLASSICAL Rome based on GESTURE and movement rather than words, often COMIC and concerning MYTHS. It could also refer to the performer. It later came to describe performances based on dance or MIME in general, and in Britain now describes the traditional Christmas performance of a old tale (like *Dick Whittington*, *Puss in Boots* or *Cinderella*) at theatres, which features celebrities, bad jokes and lots of DRAMATIC CONVENTIONS (such as a ghost creeping up on a CHARACTER and the audience shouting 'it's behind you!').

pantoum A Malay verse form similar to a VILLANELLE and composed in QUATRAINS, in which the second and fourth lines of one STANZA are repeated in the first and third of the next. The second line of the final stanza is the same as the third line of the first stanza, and the first line of the poem is repeated as the last line. It has been attempted a number of times in English, mostly by American poets (e.g. John Ashbery).

parable A brief STORY that draws a parallel between two things to illustrate a point. It is similar to FABLE and ALLEGORY, only more DIDACTIC. The best-known examples in Western literature are those attributed to Jesus in the New Testament: e.g. the parable of the Good Samaritan, in which a person is left for dead, and after two people walk on by, it is only the Samaritan, supposedly the least likely to help, who provides assistance. Parable is another of those literary concepts that has been ambitiously identified as being essential to how humans think. Mark Turner, in *The Literary Mind* (1996) argues that we create meaning by blending different stories together: 'The projection of one story onto another is parable, a basic cognitive principle that shows up everywhere, from simple actions like telling the time to complex literary creations like Proust's *À la recherche du temps perdu*'.

paradigm (Greek, 'pattern, example') A model or pattern that can be applied to other things or works. CONCEITS can be regarded as a literary type of paradigm: e.g. in John Donne's 'The Flea', a flea is taken as a perfect expression of how lovers meet. LINGUISTICS uses the term 'paradigmatic' to talk about elements that can be substituted for one another, in contrast to different units placed next to each other to create meaning (SYNTAX): it's like a slot machine, with the paradigmatic elements being on each spinning reel, and the three symbols being related by syntax. This idea of paradigm informs STRUCTURALIST conception of how units of language are exchanged and placed together to make meaning. Another relevant sense is as a scientific model of understanding, an idea promoted by Thomas Kuhn in the influential work *The Structure of Scientific Revolutions* (1962). Kuhn argued that science adopted one model for understanding at a time, and that every so often a 'paradigm shift' occurred, as a new model fell into place. There are similarities here with Michel Foucault's notion of EPISTEME, which encompasses social and historical DISCOURSES in general.

paradox (**adj. paradoxical**; Greek, 'contrary to opinion') A FIGURE involving a statement that seems to be CONTRADICTORY, but is true in a deeper, unexpected way. It was used frequently by sixteenth- and seventeenth-century writers (and notably by Petrarch before them), particularly METAPHYSICAL POETS, particularly John Donne. A condensed paradox is an OXYMORON, and both are often used in EPIGRAMS. Like AMBIGUITY, paradox is a means of stretching the expressive capacity of language. It bends language to fit meaning, which reaches towards what is unspeakable, SUBLIME, and lacks cognitive content altogether. It creates awareness of where language is insufficient.

Related to this thought, greater claims for paradox's importance were made by NEW CRITICS such as Cleanth Brooks, who claimed that 'the language of poetry is the language of paradox' (in *The Well-Wrought Urn* (1947)). Poetry is about more than comforting unities: 'the language of paradox' creates unusual structures that can only be comprehended if readers reassess their own language and thought. DECONSTRUCTION is fundamentally concerned with the paradoxical, UNDECIDABLE nature of language, and the moments of APORIA this creates.

paralipsis (Greek, 'disregard') The Greek equivalent for the Latin 'OCCULTATIO' or 'occupatio'; i.e. a FIGURE emphasising something by pretending not to mention it.

paraliterature An academicky collective term for writing that is commonly thought to be on the edge of LITERATURE, and definitely not part of the CANON. This hierarchy is difficult to enforce, and it's highly debateable whether you'd want to. CHILDREN'S LITERATURE, FAIRY TALES, modern FANTASY novels, pornography (see 'erotic literature'), DETECTIVE STORIES and other GENRE FICTION or ESCAPIST works could be classed as paraliterature.

parallelism The arranging of CLAUSES with similar structures in sequence to suggest a connection between them. It involves SYNTACTIC REPETITION to shape an argument, sometimes building to a CLIMAX. ANAPHORA and EPISTROPHE are types of parallelism, as is the relation between PLOT and SUBPLOT. 'ISOCOLON' (or 'parison') is the rhetorical term that describes parallel phrases that are of similar length as well. Parallelism occurs in poetry and prose alike, and can be found within local phrases, or as a structural device for a whole work (especially poems). Although it is a basic and easily-spotted way to shape language, it can have subtle effects on RHYTHM and EMPHASIS. Parallelism sometimes has an incantatory religious element. In this example, the beginning of Maya Angelou's 'Woman Work', parallelism suggests the burden of relentless chores:

> I've got children to tend
> The clothes to mend
> The floor to mop
> The food to shop
> The chicken to fry
> The baby to dry
> I got company to feed
> The garden to weed
> I've got the shirts to press
> The tots to dress
> The cane to be cut
> I gotta clean up this hut
> Then see about the sick
> And the cotton to pick. (ll.1–14)

paranomasia The Greek RHETORICAL term word for PUN.

paraphrase (noun and verb) A reworded version of a TEXT, more substantial than a SYNOPSIS, but not simply a TRANSLATION. Some critics, in particular NEW CRITICS, argue against the possibility of paraphrase, because this implies that CONTENT and FORM are separable. Literary paraphrases exist; for example, many variations on the biblical PSALMS have been written, particularly in the Renaissance.

pararhyme The matching of final and initial consonants of a word with different vowels: e.g. pocket/packet, 'launch/lunch', 'freed/fried'. It is form of NEAR (or HALF-) RHYME, and never FULL RHYME. Pararhyme and RIME RICHE are more elaborate forms of near rhyme and full rhyme respectively. The term is particularly associated with Wilfred Owen (1893–1918). Pararhyme of 'blind/blunt' creates an unnerving DISSONANCE in this carefully crafted stanza from 'Arms and the Boy' (ll. 5–8):

> Lend him to stroke these blind, blunt
>   bullet-heads
> Which long to muzzle in the hearts of lads.
> Or give him cartridges of fine zinc teeth,
> Sharp with the sharpness of grief and death.

parataxis (adj. paratactic) The placing of phrases next to each other without making the relation between them clear. It involves few CONJUNCTIONS: so ASYNDETON or lots of 'and's. 'I ate an avocado. I feel unwell.' is paratactic because the causes, logic and time-frame that links the phrases is unclear: maybe the avocado caused the illness; maybe the avocado is taken to cure the illness. Use of 'because', 'although' or 'now' would explain the progression, and this would make the complete phrase HYPOTACTIC. For this reason parataxis makes it difficult to string together a NARRATIVE or an ARGUMENT. It creates abrupt and compressed phrases, often with ELLIPSIS, or compact lists of items. These features can make paratactic passages difficult to read, and its creative uses have never been studied in depth. Parataxis spans literary history too: it is common in ORAL LITERATURE and early epics like *Beowulf*, as well as being found in INTERIOR MONOLOGUES written by MODERNIST writers. In general, it supports writing based on perception and association, rather than conscious connections and fixed PARADIGMS.

paratext All the material that surrounds the main TEXT in a printed book: preface, foreword, EPILOGUE, TITLEPAGE, dedications and dedicatory EPISTLES, list of ABBREVIATIONS used, EPIGRAPH, textual APPARATUS, front cover, contents page, blurb, and details about the AUTHOR to name the most common. When holding a book in your hand, it's worth asking how paratextual material creates expectations about the work, and affects how the main text is approached.

parison (Greek, 'evenly balanced') An alternative term for 'ISOCOLON', both of which are specific forms of PARALLELISM. It refers to a series of phrases that have similar form and length.

parody (noun and verb; adj. parodic) A work that imitates the distinctive characteristics and STYLE of another for COMIC effect. Its meaning is similar to 'BURLESQUE', but parody refers to specific, exaggerated copying of MANNERISMS, ideas and other features. This is known as 'PASTICHE' when done affectionately. 'Spoof' and 'send-up' are COLLOQUIAL alternatives. When used to describe a whole GENRE, 'parody' also refers to TRAVESTY, though this is specific to a weak IMITATION that mocks the higher tone of the original. Parody has been around for many centuries, and is still popular today: e.g. the Greek playwright Aristophanes parodied the Greek tragedians Aeschylus and Euripides by including them as CHARACTERS in *Frogs* (c.405 B.C.E.), while two millennia later the *Scary Movie* franchise parodies horror films.

particle A minor word or prefix that has a specific function within a word or sentence: e.g. 'of', 'for', 'a', 're-', '-ness'.

participle A verb form used as an adjective, or together with the verbs 'to be' and 'to have'. The form of a participle reflects its TENSE: e.g. 'running', 'ran'; 'entertaining', 'entertained'.

passim (from Latin 'scattered'). References to be found throughout the text.

passion play A DRAMA that depicts the crucifixion of Jesus Christ, often performed on Good Friday. Medieval passion plays came at the end of MYSTERY PLAY CYCLES.

passus (Latin, 'step') A division within a long poem. William Langland's *Piers Plowman* (c.1367) is the best-known poem in English literature with passus divisions. 'CANTO' and 'FIT' are alternative terms.

pastiche (pas-**teesh**) A work that borrows aspects of STYLE and/or THEME from another AUTHOR or GENRE. Its method is similar to PARODY, but pastiche is written out of respect to the original, not to ridicule it. Pastiche also refer to literary works that draws upon a number of different sources to create a patchwork of styles. Pastiche is arguably not properly 'LITERATURE', because it lacks originality and adds little that's new; it shouldn't, however, be classed as PLAGIARISM either, since the IMITATION is not disguised. A CENTO is an extreme form of pastiche, in which a work (usually a poem) is created out of quotations from other works. It has been said that pastiche is well suited for POSTMODERNISM, specifically the anxiety that there is no way to gain self-identity other than taking on aspects of other STYLES.

pastoral (or **bucolic; noun and adj.**; from Latin, 'shepherd') A small but significant GENRE in CLASSICAL and Renaissance literature, in which the simple rural life is celebrated. All the many pastoral CONVENTIONS and TROPES derive to some degree from the two earliest pastoral works: Theocritus' *Idylls* (c.200 B.C.E.) and Virgil's *Eclogues* (37 B.C.E.). The setting is a version of ARCADIA; i.e. an idealised setting in which shepherds work happily, sing and fall in love. Pastoral poetry typically expresses nostalgia for lost innocence, and anger at the corruption and greed of the court and city. Pastoral is usually written in short poems (known as ECLOGUES) that are MONOLOGUES or dialogues spoken by shepherds (see also 'amoebean verse').

Later readers of pastoral were influenced by the Christian association of Jesus Christ with a shepherd. Virgil's fourth eclogue, for example, was read as an ALLEGORY of Christ's coming. The fifteenth-century Renaissance poet Mantuan's eclogues had a strong Christian TONE, and were popular reading in schools. Edmund Spenser's *The Shepheardes Calendar* (1579) is the most extensive pastoral sequence written in English. This work also shows Spenser using pastoral to fashion his own public image as a poet, distanced from court but able to comment on it. There were more diverse versions too: Philip Sidney's *Arcadia* (1581) is a prose pastoral ROMANCE; Phineas Fletcher followed the Italian writer Iacobo Sannazaro in relocating the eclogue to the sea-side and writing about fishermen; there are numerous pastoral ELEGIES too, of which John Milton's 'Lycidas' (1638) is the prime example. This poem was still being imitated once the pastoral GENRE seemed otherwise outdated. Romantic poets were interested in the countryside, but wanted to describe it directly, unbound from MYTH and CONVENTION. Pastoral doesn't really count as an early form of NATURE WRITING or TOPOGRAPHICAL POETRY because it is rarely purely descriptive. It provides a poetic setting for thinking about love, society and companionship, which later poets IMITATED and adapted in original ways.

pathetic fallacy A CONVENTION that imagines nature as having human attributes and feelings. The term was coined by John Ruskin (in *Modern Painters*, 1856) to describe this supposedly irrational error ('FALLACY') creating a distortion of nature. The term is now more neutral. Its use is more substantial than METAPHOR, but less developed than PERSONIFICATION. It is often used for literary effect to convey human emotion, or suggest identity between humans and the natural world.

pathos (adj. pathetic; pay-thoss; Greek, 'emotion') The arousal of an emotional response in the audience through language, especially pity, sorrow and compassion. As a rhetorical term, it refers to an appeal to the emotions, which is the easiest way to win over a crowd. It is distinct to ETHOS (describing the speaker's own good CHARACTER) and LOGOS (an appeal to reason). Pathetic characters are usually thought of as innocent victims who deserve our sympathy; e.g. Desdemona in *Othello*. CHARACTERIZATION is not that important when arousing PATHOS, which is unlike TRAGEDY, where ETHOS is more prominent as it shows how the person deserves their fate through pride (HUBRIS) and ignorance (HAMARTIA) as a necessary function of the PLOT (*muthos*). The pathetic CHARACTER arouses emotions that move or persuade the audience, but in tragedy the purgation of emotion (CATHARSIS) is what matters. BATHOS occurs when the attempt to rouse noble feeling fails by becoming ridiculous.

patois (**pat**-wah) An informal DIALECT form of a language, specific to a region. It can involve SLANG and COLLOQUIALISMS, but can also have substantial differences from 'standard' language. PIDGIN ENGLISH and CREOLE languages can be described as forms of patois.

patron (patronage) A person who provides financial support to an artist. Until the commercial publishing market took off in the eighteenth century, many people wrote poetry to secure patronage. When works were published, they were accompanied by a flowery-worded dedicatory letter to a member of the nobility, containing lavish praise with the end of gaining lucrative support. William Shakespeare sought patronage before he made a career in the theatre, and the dedicatory letters to his early poems *Venus and Adonis* (1593) and *The Rape of Lucrece* (1594) are addressed to Henry Wriothesely, an earl known for patronising the arts. For centuries patronage held great influence over what was being written and how it was being published.

pattern poetry A VERSE FORM involving unusual LINEATION so that the visual shape complements the poem's concerns. It is mentioned in George Puttenham's *Arte of English Poesie* (1589), at which time the ALTAR POEM was one of the commonest examples of the form in English, and it remained so into the seventeenth century. Yet pattern poetry was being written centuries earlier, and is still composed today. Pattern poetry after 1950 is more often referred to as CONCRETE POETRY, which also counts as a literary movement of its own. These experiments with form emphasise that written poetry has interlocking visual and aural elements (cf. ORALITY). Pattern poetry sometimes creates editorial problems about remaining faithful to the original, and you should also check whether an editor has altered the LAYOUT or LINEATION in any way (George Herbert's 'Easter Wings' has suffered particularly in this regard).

pen-name A name adopted by an AUTHOR when writing or publishing works. 'NOM DE PLUME' is a French alternative, and a PSEUDONYM is a fictitious name. Charlotte, Emily and Anne Brontë published under the names Currer, Ellis and Acton Bell; Joanne Rowling publishes under the name 'J.K. Rowling'. Both cases demonstrate female writers disguising their gender when publishing; in this way, pen-names provide evidence of the cultural conditions within which a writer works.

penny dreadful A nineteenth-century work of popular crime FICTION that was sold cheaply, and dealt with horrific and bloody incidents. There was some overlap with theatrical MELODRAMAS.

pentameter (Greek, 'five measures') A line of VERSE containing five FEET (rhythmic units). It is the most frequent line length in English VERSE from Chaucer onwards. The IAMBIC pentameter (five sets of unstressed-stressed BEATS) is the common form: so popular in fact that once you recognise the rhythm there is a risk of finding it everywhere, even where it is not present. There are very few poems in trochaic pentameters.

pentastich A set of five verse lines. The terms QUINTAIN or QUINTET are more often used.

perfect rhyme An alternative term for FULL (or TRUE) RHYME; i.e. words connected through identical middle vowels and endings.

performance poetry Verse compositions composed (or improvised) to be spoken, chanted, sung or otherwise delivered aloud. Poetry has its origins in ORAL LITERATURE, but since the seventeenth century it has primarily been written to be printed and read privately. In the twentieth century this balance has slightly corrected itself, particularly as RAP and SLAM POETRY have entered the public consciousness. Performance poetry has helped get more people involved with poetry: it is refreshingly direct, energetic and highly personal. It may not be a great topic for literary CRITICISM (if only for practical reasons), but it has introduced people to literary/ LYRICAL writing who mightn't otherwise find poetry relevant.

performative A term used by J.L. Austin to describe spoken expressions that perform an act by speaking, such as promising, commanding, questioning, wishing, predicting, stating. It forms part of Austin's SPEECH ACT THEORY, and is applied to all aspects of speech and literature. The following song-titles are performative phrases: 'I Predict a Riot' (Kaiser Chiefs), 'I Believe I Can Fly' (R Kelly), 'Danger! High Voltage!' (Electric Six), 'Help!' (The Beatles), 'Don't Tell Me' (Avril Lavigne) and 'Who Let the Dogs Out?' (Baha Men).

period It has two distinct meanings in literature: a section of literary history, and a RHETORICAL unit equivalent to a sentence that involves multiple CLAUSES.

The periods of English literary history are convenient divisions. They group together AUTHORS writing under similar historical circumstances, and who are therefore likely to possess similarities in STYLE and/or THEMATIC concerns. Periods are often named after the ruler at that time. This is partly a matter of convenience, because there is no reason why English literature should easily fall into groupings according to the reigns of monarchs: it is just as worthwhile to looking between the boundaries of, for example, JACOBEAN, GEORGIAN or VICTORIAN LITERATURE than consider them self-contained periods.

A period, or PERIODIC SENTENCE, is also a complex form of expression containing multiple CLAUSES or COLA. A period is typically paragraph-length and punctuated with colons (':', see entry for the plural of 'colon') and SEMICOLONS (;), and the clinching phrase is often delayed until the end of the sentence. It is typical of the CICERONIAN style. It was only after 1700 that the modern sentence, recognisable for containing a capital letter and full-stop, and/or a SUBJECT, OBJECT and VERB replaced the period as the standard unit of prose. Because the period is now relatively unfamiliar, many modern EDITIONS now modernize punctuation to create shorter sentences in texts that originally contained periods.

periodic sentence A complex utterance, composed of numerous CLAUSES strung together in a single, paragraph-length sentence. It is often referred to simply as a PERIOD (see this entry for more detail).

peripeteia (**adj. peripeteian**; Greek, 'sudden change') Aristotle's term for a surprising turn of events that leads to a change in fortune, for better or worse. It refers both to tragic downfall as well as a comic upturn in circumstances. In either case, it is triggered by a recognition (*ANAGNORISIS*) that is supposed to be built into the PLOT so that *peripeteia* seems necessary. The adjectival form '**peripeteian**' is distinct to 'peripatetic' (with a middle 'a'), which refers to someone travelling around.

periphrasis (pe-rif-**rah**-sis, Greek, 'speaking around'; also called circumlocution) The use of several words instead of a more direct alternative. It can be a form of understatement (LITOTES) or can skirt around a delicate subject (EUPHEMISM). Double negatives are a good example: 'it wasn't easy' or 'I took the scenic route'. It can form the basis of an ORATORICAL style, particularly when improvised; the Victorian prime minister William Gladstone gave notoriously periphrastic, long-winded speeches. Periphrasis also creates space to introduce poetic DICTION: KENNINGS (condensed metaphors) and HENDIADYS (use of two nouns instead of a noun and adjective) are clearly periphrastic FIGURES, for example. Furthermore, the case could be made that all REPETITION, indeed all literature, is necessarily periphrastic, because it does more than give plain reports of experience. Yet one mark of classic literature is that every word feels necessary to the whole, regardless of how expansive and slow-moving the work is.

peroration A compelling summing-up that comes at the conclusion of an ORATION. It can also refer to an entire formal speech.

persona (pl. personas, personae; Latin, 'mask') The CHARACTER assumed by an AUTHOR in a work, usually the SPEAKER or FIRST-PERSON NARRATOR. In many works the persona will be clearly distanced from the AUTHOR, as in DRAMATIC MONOLOGUES. Even when the persona does not have a separate identity, however, it's still sensible to talk of personas because the VOICE is not necessarily the author's. It's perhaps helpful to think of the term's relation to DRAMATIS PERSONAE, because an ACTOR giving life to a dramatic character is akin to a writer creating a persona. The everyday use of 'persona' to mean 'public image' is related, since a individual's private side and public face are almost always distinct.

With this in mind, even something like the John Clare poem entitled 'I am' shouldn't be assumed to hold any psychological insight: 'I am: yet what I am none cares or knows, | My friends forsake me like a memory lost'. It's far safer to speak of a fictional identity that reflects some aspect of Clare's own situation. The persona or speaker may be lonely and in despair, but it does not mean that Clare was when he wrote this (this is the BIOGRAPHICAL FALLACY). Clare could adopt this TONE in one poem, and then have adopted an entirely VIEWPOINT for his next work.

personal criticism (autobiographical criticism) A critical approach that takes account of the critic's reactions to and reflection on a literary text. Almost identical to IMPRESSIONISTIC CRITICISM (see this entry for more discussion). **Autobiographical criticism** is an AMBIGUOUS alternative, since many people would assume it meant close reading of AUTOBIOGRAPHIES.

personification (also **prosopopoeia**) A TROPE in which human attributes are given to something nonhuman. 'Love is blind' is a personification based on the possibility of love having eyes. The personified object is sometimes addressed by the speaker, particularly in INVOCATIONS: e.g. 'Hail, holy Light, offspring of heaven first-born' (John Milton, *Paradise Lost*, 3.1). This FIGURE is sometimes used in ALLEGORY to indicate hidden meanings. It is a more general term than PATHETIC FALLACY, which refers only to description involving nature. Some eighteenth-century writers, such as Alexander Pope, used personification very naturally. Pope's *Dunciad* contains plenty of vivid personification, including the following passage. The subject is Dulness:

> She sees a Mob of Metaphors advance,
> Pleas'd with the madness of the mazy dance:
> How Tragedy and Comedy embrace,
> How Farce and Epic get a jumbled race.
>
> (ll. 63–67)

Petrarchan sonnet A fourteen line poem (SONNET) divided into eight lines (OCTAVE) containing two QUATRAINS rhyming *abba*, and six lines (SESTET) containing two TERCETS rhyming either *cde cde* or *cdc cdc*. The total scheme, then, is *abbaabba cdecde* or *cdccdc*. Petrarch was one of several Italian poets in thirteenth- and fourteenth-century Italy writing in the form, but he is the acknowledged master, and some of the earliest English sonnets in the form were TRANSLATIONS from Petrarch's *Rime* by Thomas Wyatt. The Petrarchan sonnet is more than a FIXED FORM; it carries with it an expectation that the sonnet will deal with the passion and anguish of love, set up a problem in the octave that is resolved in the sestet, and contain PARADOXES, striking images and CONCEITS. These principles were very much in the minds of ELIZABETHAN sonnet writers, such as Philip Sidney and Edmund Spenser. Milton (see 'Miltonic sonnet') and others later adapted the form.

phallocentric (**phallogocentric**; Latin, 'centred on the phallus (penis)') Containing an unnatural BIAS towards the masculine in society and culture. The term is used by FEMINIST CRITICS wishing to avoid a simple MASCULINE/FEMININE opposition when discussing a male-dominated/patriarchal institution (such as literature). PSYCHOANALYTIC CRITICS have used the term to identify the penis's engrained influence on (male) mental activity. Jacques Derrida fused this term with 'LOGOCENTRIC' to create '**phallogocentric**', which indicates the preference for the masculine gender in Western languages.

phenomenological criticism Critical enquiry into how AUTHORS describe their perceptions in their works: in other words, how the subject creates meaning by experiencing things. Phenomenology is a philosophy of consciousness and experience. Georg Wilhelm Friedrich Hegel's *Phenomenology of Spirit* (1807) approached this subject in terms of world history, but Edmund Husserl really founded phenomenology as a philosophical discipline. It is strongly associated with HERMENEUTICS, which examines problems of interpretation caused by our SUBJECTIVE condition. In literary criticism, it examines how literature expresses the AUTHOR'S worldview, and attempts to retrieve an impression of the author's consciousness. It's particularly associated with the GENEVA SCHOOL of the 1950s. Phenomenology encourages us to see the world with fresh eyes, unburdened by habit. In this way, it shares an affinity with the idea of DEFAMILIARIZATION: i.e. that literature presents the everyday (especially with CONCRETE LANGUAGE) in a strange and striking manner. It was an influence on READER-RESPONSE CRITICISM, but was buffeted by POST-STRUCTURALIST arguments against the possibility of unity based on an author's life experiences.

philistine (noun and adj.) With an upper case 'p', a people based in ancient Palestine who fought the Israelites and were reputedly obsessed with wealth and material objects, holding no interest in intellectual or artistic endeavours; as an adjective in the lower case, the word is used to describe any loutish person who doesn't appreciate 'high' culture. Matthew Arnold used the term in this sense in *Culture and Anarchy* (1869). CULTURAL CRITICISM and others with a non-elitist view of literary studies would want to contest the term's use.

philology (Greek, 'love of words') The historical study of languages. Philologists study ETYMOLOGY, linguistic evolution and the connections between languages. It can overlap with TEXTUAL CRITICISM (establishing an authoritative text of a work). Nineteenth-century linguistics was almost entirely philological. Ferdinand de Saussure, who provided the theories that inspired STRUCTURALISM, argued against DIACHRONIC ('through-time') study of language, and instead pushed linguistics towards language at one moment in time (i.e. SYNCHRONIC). RUSSIAN FORMALISM was also uninterested in philology, and this trend continued in twentieth-century literary criticism—though some scholarly journals for English literature, like *Studies in Philology* and *Philological Studies*, recall a period when philology was more in fashion.

phoneme A LINGUISTIC term for any sound made by a human, whether a noise or SYLLABLES forming words. Phonemes are fundamental to all languages, but each language has distinct phonemes (i.e. each language trains the mouth to make different sounds). There are about forty-five different ones in English, although many more combinations are possible. PHONETICS is the study of phonemes.

phonetics (phonetic) The study of sounds made by humans to communicate. A phoneme is an individual sound, and PHONOLOGY describes how human use these noises to form language. It isn't a field of research so much as providing the fundamental principles and terminology required for research into GRAMMAR (see 'semantics' and 'syntax') and broader areas (see 'pragmatics'). The adjective 'phonetic' usually refers to written characters that directly represent sound: so 'ruff' is a phonetic spelling of 'rough'. There is some debate as to whether it's easier for children learning English as their first language to begin by learning phonetic spellings, and then learn conventional spellings later.

phonology The study of how humans use sounds in patterns to communicate. A PHONEME is a basic unit of spoken sound, and PHONETICS is ANALYSIS of those sounds. Phonology describes the human ability to use these sounds to create GRAMMATICAL language, by forming words (MORPHOLOGY), arranging them into a sentence (SYNTAX) and giving them meaning (SEMANTICS).

picaresque novel A PROSE FIRST-PERSON NARRATIVE in which the main CHARACTER (PROTAGONIST) travels through a realistic landscape. Like prose ROMANCES the action is pacy, EPISODIC and often COMIC. The term's origins are in Spanish narratives with a *picaró* ('rogue') for a HERO/HEROINE, but it now describes novels from Miguel de Cervantes' *Don Quixote* (1606) to Mark Twain's *The Adventures of Huckleberry Finn* (1864) and Saul Bellow's *The Adventures of Augie March* (1945). Lord Byron's *Don Juan* could be described as picaresque verse.

pidgin English (from 'business') A simplified form of English used for basic communication between people not sharing a language in common (i.e. it is a *lingua franca*). The result could also be called broken English.

Pindaric ode A form of LYRIC POEM that follows the regular structure of the CLASSICAL ODE. It has no set length, but is divided into groups of three STANZAS, a STROPHE whose length and intricate metrical pattern are repeated in an ANTISTROPHE, then an EPODE follows, with its own line-length and metre. This form has not been used all that often in English literature: there are more examples of IRREGULAR and HORATIAN ODES. Thomas Gray is one of the few Pindaric ode writers in English (e.g. 'Progress of Poesy' and 'The Bard' (1757)).

piracy In literary terms, the distribution of a work without the AUTHOR'S permission, often in infringement of COPYRIGHT. PLAGIARISM is a related notion, but emphasises intellectual theft, whereas piracy connotes financial profit by printing a work. Printed books have been pirated for centuries.

plagiarism (from Latin, 'kidnapper') The passing-off of someone's work as your own; i.e. intellectual theft. PIRACY is related to plagiarism, but suggests a commercial enterprise. The term plagiarism has a moral element fixed to it. All students and professional writers are strongly prohibited from plagiarism: however, the boundaries between plagiarism and legitimate ALLUSION-making, literary borrowing, or IMITATION, are tricky to define. The research an AUTHOR does prior to writing is likely to affect how they write: so at what point does unattributed research become unauthorised copying? Ideas about INTERTEXTUALITY argue that texts are interlinked. Moreover, some argue that accusing a past writer of plagiarism imposes our moral values upon a previous era. For all these reasons, plagiarism is difficult to define closely, and it could well be argued that it has legitimate outlets. Perhaps plagiarism is really 'excessive imitation' or 'theft' in that it has a victim who stands to lose by the copying, whether it be other people sitting an exam or an unacknowledged writer. Either way, it is just as awkward as defining ORIGINALITY, and reveals a latent tension in describing what literary writing involves.

Platonic love The idea that physical beauty is attractive because it is a sign of higher, spiritual goodness. It is based on the PLATONIC 'Theory of Forms', and is explored in Renaissance love poetry (especially SONNET SEQUENCES) and in some romantic poetry. In an everyday sense, it means being 'just friends'—a relationship that isn't about sex.

Platonism (Platonic) The theories and doctrines of the Greek philosopher Plato (c.428–348 B.C.E.). The influence of his dialogues has been felt continuously to the present day, particularly through NEOPLATONISM and Christianity. Though his thought has provoked strong rebuttals too, Platonism is undeniably a cornerstone of Western philosophy. The influence of Platonic ideas was strong in the Renaissance (see 'Platonic love'), and it remains an undercurrent in literary discussion: see 'imitation' and 'abstract language' for Plato's attack on poetry. Plato is also mentioned in a wide range of other entries: e.g. 'METAPHOR', 'INSPIRATION', 'VATES', 'GAY AND LESBIAN CRITICISM', 'APORIA' and 'VERISIMILITUDE'.

All Plato's surviving works are composed as LITERARY dialogues between a number of speakers, often including Socrates, an older philosopher who Plato followed. It is Socrates who reaches conclusions (not necessarily shared by Plato) by a question-and-answer method known as DIALECTIC, and through use of SOCRATIC IRONY. As to Plato's ideas, the most fundamental concept to be aware of is the 'Theory of Forms', which is described in his *Republic*. This argues for a higher realm of universal concepts (Truth, Beauty and, above all, Goodness) of which we only experience diluted versions. Plato uses the ALLEGORY of the cave to introduce the concept: a group of humans are living in an underground cave, and have always lived there, fixed to one spot. A fire is behind them, and a wall is in front of them. Other people walk past the fire, and the people looking at the wall can see their shadows. Since this is all they have ever seen, they take these shadows as the ultimate reality and truth. If they could turn round to look at the fire it would dazzle them, but they would know that the shadows they have been watching only provide a part of the ultimate truth. In this allegory, the shadows are the things we sense and experience on earth, while the forms are the actual people walking past, while the fire and the sunlight outside are the final forms of revelation and higher truth.

play A performance in which ACTORS (or 'players') represent CHARACTERS to relate a STORY to an audience. Plays usually happen on a theatrical stage, but can take other forms, like a radio-play. It is SYNONYMOUS with 'DRAMA', though this second term also describes the whole tradition and art-form that is performance, whereas a play is a specific happening somewhere.

playwright A person who writes DRAMA with awareness of performance requirements. The term highlights that writing plays is like a trade (e.g. shipwright, wheelwright) with its own techniques, skills and CONVENTIONS that need to be mastered. Scholars tend to emphasise that Shakespeare was a playwright, and not just a playwriter. 'DRAMATURGIST' has essentially the same meaning.

pleonasm (adj. pleonastic; Greek, 'superficiality') Unnecessary REPETITION. It can be used for deliberate effect, as a form of PERIPHRASIS, but is more often involuntary and inelegant (a bland TAUTOLOGY): 'I cycled there on my bike'; 'I greeted my friend by saying hello'.

ploce (Greek, 'plaiting') A basic FIGURE of REPETITION involving recurring elements in close proximity. A shift in tone or meaning often accompanies the repeated words: 'I expect my oranges to be orange'; 'Stella oft sees the very face of woe | Painted in my beclouded stormy face'(Philip Sidney, *Astrophel and Stella*, 45.1–2). It is close to EPANALEPSIS (repetition at the beginning and end of phrases) and other related figures; however, these figures are more conspicuous, since they are found at the beginning and end of phrases. Ploce is potentially more subtle, as its ETYMOLOGY suggests, because it can be woven within lines. It is different from EPIZEUXIS (immediate repetition).

plot The organisation of events within a literary work. Most critics and readers expect a plot to make clear what order events happen in and what causes them; by contrast, a STORY is just a collection of events. A NARRATIVE is a story told, and is very likely to contain a plot. An EPISODIC plot is a loosely connected series of events that provides minimal information on how the incidents are linked. Other plots are more unified, and will offer a more convincing illusion of reality—to an audience who expects all effects to have a cause.

Aristotle argued for the primacy of plot (or *muthos*) over CHARACTER (or ETHOS) in his *Poetics*. Certainly they are interdependent, for it is characters who perform the events that are then arranged into a plot. Aristotle held that the three UNITIES of action, time and place were thought to make depiction of events more convincing, and a good character was one who acted in a probable, believable manner. This preference is linked to Aristotle's thoughts about TRAGEDY. A tight, unified plot is better able to describe the overarching forces acting on characters (such as FATE), and to direct the audience's emotions (see '*catharsis*'). A plot will have a turning point (or CRISIS), of which reversal (*PERIPETEIA*) and recognition (*ANAGNORISIS*) are two of the most common.

All this largely holds true for a well-plotted modern NOVEL; e.g. a DETECTIVE STORY: the reader is drawn into the progress of the action, and feels suspense, tension, anticipation as the story unfolds. E.M. Forster felt, though some would disagree, that character had to be sacrificed to create strong and engaging plots. Plots show an AUTHOR guiding the reader through a story; in some cases, the reader is led by the hand, whilst in other works readers have to navigate their own path. Critical reading begins at the point where the reader hesitates on this journey, notices incidental details, and starts asking independent questions.

plurality The presence of many things at the same time. In literary criticism, the idea of uncontrollable diversity is an aspect of POSTMODERNISM, while POST-STRUCTURALISM and DECONSTRUCTION argue that a plurality of meanings can be found in any utterance. DIALOGIC CRITICISM investigates the presence of multiple voices in literary works, while other critics argue for greater, more representative plurality in literary criticism (e.g. POSTCOLONIAL CRITICISM, FEMINIST CRITICISM and DISABILITY STUDIES. The notion of *ÉCRITURE FEMININE* implies that plurality is a broadly 'FEMININE' characteristic, and is restricted by a more masculine tendency for logical argument and single answers.

poet A person who writes POETRY. Ideas on what makes a poet vary between individuals, cultures and historical periods (e.g. see 'bard', 'minstrel', 'poetaster'). Imagination and technical skill (VERSIFICATION) are widely thought to be possessed by all great poets. The classical distinction between maker and VATES is also worth consideration: a maker is someone who can craft and consciously produce a poetic work, almost like an artisan; a *vates* is an INSPIRED individual who writes under spontaneous compulsion. Poets combine both elements in their work, and attentive readers are alert in some degree to both the thought and feeling present.

poetaster (poh-e-**tast**-er; **verser**) An inferior or unskilled poet. **Verser** is an alternative, emphasising that the writer has little to say (see also 'verse'). Ben Jonson coined the term in his play of the same name (1601). Caesar offers a nicely hyperbolic definition at the end of that play (Act 5, Scene 3): 'It is the bane, and torment of our eares, | To heare the discords of these iangling rimers, | That, with their bad and scandalous practices, | Bring all true arts, and learning in contempt.'

poetic diction The choice of words and FIGURES made by a poet, particularly as it differs from common usage and prose. DICTION is a basic element of poetic STYLE, but as important is how the chosen words are used; for example, in LINEATION, TYPOGRAPHY, SYNTAX, FORM and RHYME. Not every writer pursues appropriate poetic diction, and many critics over history have resisted the notion that poetry requires its own special diction. William Wordsworth and Samuel Taylor Coleridge felt this strongly (see 'vernacular'). They were reacting against eighteenth-century NEOCLASSICAL verse that was consciously poetic in its diction, in that it was refined, noble, LATINATE and PERIPHRASTIC. Such poets had a strong sense of DECORUM: they believed that language should be appropriate to its subject-matter and audience. At its heart, poetic diction insists that some forms of language are more suitable for poetry, and others less so (such as JARGON or SLANG). This is not to say that poets do not often use distinctive diction: for example, Edmund Spenser's diction, with its characteristic ARCHAISMS, is easily recognisable. There are also numerous FIGURES that are widely felt to be instinctively poetic, whether or not they actually are, such as ALLITERATION, ONOMATOPOEIA, APOSTROPHE and PERSONIFICATION. Poetic diction is certainly an important historical concept in English literature, but does not necessarily contribute to a twenty-first-century definition of poetry.

poetic drama A theatrical production with dialogue written in VERSE, usually BLANK VERSE. The term stresses that the DRAMA is meant to be staged, whereas 'dramatic poem' stresses that the work is a verse composition, printed on a page. HEROIC DRAMA, written in HEROIC COUPLETS for stage performance, is a good example of poetic drama.

poetic justice The idea that good must ultimately triumph and evil be punished. It is usually felt at the end of NARRATIVE works (not just POETRY), as the HERO defeats the VILLAIN. It presents a DIDACTIC view of the world as it should be, rather than as it is. This view of literature has often been mocked (more so than the related concept of POETIC LICENCE), but poetic justice is an enduring concept. A Christian view of FATE creates need for poetic justice, as does the NEOCLASSICAL preference for DECORUM over NATURALISM. Hollywood movies confirm that audiences today still expect poetic justice to prevail. Perhaps this shows that one function of literature is to provide reassurance (compare with CATHARSIS).

poetic licence A poet's freedom to depart from standard language use (as found in everyday prose) for effect. The term was coined by Thomas Rymer is 1678, who was writing about ELIZABETHAN drama. Poetic licence is found in the purposeful use of FIGURATIVE LANGUAGE, INVERSIONS, PROSODIC techniques and unusual SYNTAX; POETIC JUSTICE is sometimes also a form of poetic licence. The unspoken deal made with the audience is that poetic licence will expand the expressive range of the AUTHOR. Indeed, the term 'poetic licence' usually only comes into play when there is reason to suspect that certain language usage is only being 'poetic', rather than having a specific effect. Just as many critics deny the need for an exclusive POETIC DICTION, poetic licence is not essential to poetic or literary writing. 'Poetic licence' has taken on the wider meaning relating to writers who are not worried about factual accuracy. Again, this can be purposeful because literature does more than report facts; equally, it isn't an excuse for sloppy writing.

poetics The principles of writing poetry. 'Poetics' is a singular noun, and there is no plural form. It is a branch of literary THEORY loosely allied to FORMALISM, interested in the ANALYSIS of ABSTRACT concepts in poetry like: PROSODY, FORM, FIGURATIVE LANGUAGE, GENRES and so on. It is often applied to study of PROSE and DRAMATIC work as well ('the poetics of the horror story', for instance). Like the noun 'AESTHETIC', an AUTHOR or work can be said to have its own poetics, meaning a set of principles for writing: e.g. 'Dickens's poetics reveal the dirt and grime of Victorian London', while *First Pages: the*

Poetics of Titles by Giancarlo Maiorino and *The Sources of Chaucer's Poetics* by Amanda Holton are just two examples of recent MONOGRAPHS that use 'poetics' in the title. Aristotle's *Poetics* is the original description of literary principles, although its focus is on TRAGIC DRAMA, not poetry. 'Poetics' as a literary term may well have proved too fashionable for its own good: it is one of those terms often used imprecisely (like 'DECONSTRUCTION'), and so can be confusing for readers.

poetry (poem, adj. poetic; from Greek, 'to make') An intensified use of LANGUAGE that involves REPETITION and EMPHASIS. It arises when the sound and sense of words are closely united. FIGURATIVE (i.e. non-literal) LANGUAGE is of central importance, because poetry usually looks beyond simple meanings to explore CONNOTATIONS, often reaching towards the SUBLIME. Related to this, poetry is not usually thought of as being purely FICTIONAL.

VERSIFICATION describes the basic tools and techniques for poetry, which include METRE, RHYME, FORM and STANZA. These all help shape a phrase into a poetic utterance. PROSE is written language that doesn't contain the same degree of refined meaning: only in poetry does every word feel irreplaceable and unshiftable. FREE VERSE and PROSE POEMS are forms that explore the boundaries of poetry. 'VERSE' refers to writing that has metrical characteristics but is not considered to have been invested with meaning and profundity in the same way poetry is.

From this definition, it would be easy to conclude that poetry is a higher, more hallowed form of literature, and historically this has thought to be the case. However, this most 'literary' of forms is not aloof to other forms of writing. Many critics reject the idea that POETIC DICTION is ultimately different from everyday speech, and only the most conservative writers would argue that traditional forms such as SONNET or BLANK VERSE are more poetic than others outright. Poetry is formed according to its purpose, and the distinction between NARRATIVE, DRAMATIC and LYRIC poetry is still helpful. Poetry remains a group-based activity across the world, particularly in forms like CHANTS, SONGS and HYMNS. Any definition of poetry needs to represent the full diversity of creative endeavour that it denotes, without giving a list of restrictive rules. The force of poetry lies partly in an individual being freely expressive whilst conscious of others who have attempted the same (i.e. aware of literary tradition). See p. 348 and p. 351 for a list of poetic forms covered in this book.

polemic (po-**leh**-mik; **adj. polemical**) A forceful written assault on a person or idea likely to cause controversy. Polemics often take on theological, philosophical, political or critical standpoints. Polemics are seldom literary, but some literary writers have composed them, such as John Milton, who passionately defends freedom of the press in *Areopagitica* (1644).

polyptoton (pol-**ip**-toe-ton) A FIGURE of REPETITION involving different forms of related words. There are more opportunities for its use in other European languages than English; however, it can still be used in English with, for example, different tenses or singular and plural. It is a subtle form of PLOCE. Examples: 'I looked yesterday, I'll look today and I'll keep on looking until I've found the scoundrel'; 'How much better is it to weep at joy than to joy at weeping! (with added CHIASMUS, William Shakespeare, *Much Ado about Nothing*, 1.1.27–29).

polysemy The presence of multiple meanings. It is a more technical term for 'AMBIGUITY'. Some critics, notably DECONSTRUCTIONISTS, find that all languages and sign-systems possess polysemy.

polysyndeton (Greek, 'many connections') A FIGURE involving the frequent use of CONJUNCTIONS between CLAUSES. Toddlers who begin every sentence with 'and' when telling a story are using polysyndeton. It is less common (and usually less elegant) than its opposite, ASYNDETON, though it can give rhythm and momentum to a phrase.

portmanteau word A word created by combining the sound and meaning of two others. Two everyday examples are 'brunch' (breakfast and lunch) and 'smog' (smoke and fog). In literature, portmanteau words are used as a basic form of word-play, or PUN. They are found throughout James Joyce's experimental work *Finnegans Wake*. Even the AMBIGUOUS title contains one: with an apostrophe it is a song-title and can mean 'after Finnegan' (in his wake), without an apostrophe it can be a call to Finnegans to wake up, and Joyce apparently combines both meanings in his apostrophe-less title. Their use can create a highly individualistic STYLE (like other forms of NEOLOGISM), as is the case with Lewis Carroll's poem 'The Jabberwocky'. The first stanza (repeated at the end—an ENVELOPE) contains several portmanteau words:

> Twas brillig, and the slithy toves
> Did gyre and gimble in the wabe;
> All mimsy were the borogoves,
> And the mome raths outgrabe.

postcolonial criticism The area of critical enquiry that examines the culture and thought of previously colonized peoples, both before and after colonization. Attention is naturally given to POSTCOLONIAL LITERATURE, but if anything postcolonial criticism's theoretical leanings speak more generally about oppression relating to race and imperial attitudes. As with FEMINIST CRITICISM, early postcolonial criticism uncovered narrow-mindedness and blind PREJUDICE in CANONICAL works (Joseph Conrad's *Heart of Darkness* (1902) was one such target). Later criticism moved to unravel the complexity, sophistication and diversity of world cultures, freed from a Eurocentric bias. Its emphasis on cultural PLURALITY is one of numerous similarities with POSTMODERNISM. It's still a newish field, having only developed in the 1980s and 90s.

There are no fixed principles or methods that characterize postcolonial criticism, though it was decisively shaped by several critics, whose contribution is far greater and more subtle than can be explained here. Three major figures are: Edward Saïd, whose work *Orientalism* (1978—see entry on this term) was influential in showing how Western DISCOURSES formed exotic impressions of the East that showed little first-hand experience or sense of cultural diversity. Gayatri Chakravorty Spivak brought DECONSTRUCTION into play, and argued that race, gender and class could not be treated as separate causes. Homi K. Bhabha suggested that colonised peoples absorbed foreign cultures, but transformed them to create hybrid cultures and narratives that the West now ought to acknowledge. A POST-STRUCTURALIST distaste for hierarchy has also been brought into postcolonial criticism.

postcolonial literature Writing that looks beyond colonial occupation, either in its ideas or, more commonly, in being written by citizens of former colonies. It is a more inclusive equivalent to 'Commonwealth' literature, which refers to previous British colonies. There are troubling assumptions in the definition of both terms: North America is a former colony, but no-one would call American literature postcolonial; likewise, Australian and Canadian literature are not typically considered postcolonial. In truth, the term actually covers a wide range of non-white, non-American AUTHORS writing in English, particularly Caribbean, African and South Asian writers. Such literature written in WORLD ENGLISHES does often examine colonial legacies and independence, but are not explicitly postcolonial, in the way that POSTCOLONIAL CRITICISM (see above) is—though postcolonial critics encourage wider appreciation of texts that are not currently CANONICAL in 'English literature'.

postmodernism An approach to Western culture prevalent from the late twentieth century onwards. There is no simple definition of 'postmodernism', which fits with its central contention that the world cannot be described by a simple theory. Postmodernism abandons the idea of meaningful unity in the world, which includes psychological unity and the idea of a continuous literary tradition—both concepts that were important to MODERNISTS. Instead, the postmodern world is characterized as a set of fragments that can't be fitted together. There are different media, more information than ever, and images of things that have no original (called SIMULACRA). This mass of information and activity creates an identity-crisis: postmodern individuals have no clear sense of self, independent from the culture within which they exist. Accordingly nothing is original, and the techniques most associated with postmodern literature are IRONY, PASTICHE, and METAFICTION (see also 'meta-'). It is left to the audience to piece together meaning; AUTHORIAL intention matters for little (see also 'death of the author').

This sketch of a postmodern standpoint has definite similarities to aspects of contemporary theory like POST-STRUCTURALISM, DECONSTRUCTION, INTERTEXTUALITY and DISCOURSE ANALYSIS. However, postmodernism is not directly allied to any of these, and relatively few critics would identify themselves with postmodernism as a theoretical stance. Postmodernism also factors in an awareness of tremendous plurality in the world, and this has been helped by MARXIST, FEMINIST, POSTCOLONIAL, GAY AND LESBIAN and other forms of CRITICISM that expand our sense of diversity in society. Postmodern literature has a particular association with American consumer culture: e.g. Don DeLillo's *Underworld* (1994) contains lots about household waste. Postmodernism offers a fairly cold and cynical view of contemporary society, and perhaps is a form of expression right for its time. It's difficult to say what comes after postmodernism, except that it'll probably have happened before a name for it is found.

post-structuralism An intellectual approach based on the belief that meaning is never fixed or controlled by well-defined STRUCTURES and systems. There is a noisy mass of competing social and cultural DISCOURSES from which individuals create an illusion of self-identity. AMBIGUITY is everywhere amidst multiple possible meanings, CONNOTATIONS and DENOTATIONS. Post-structuralism rejects the STRUCTURALIST principle of an universal order in favour of contextual ANALYSIS: i.e. how meaning is created at a given moment in time. DECONSTRUCTION, which is linked to post-structuralism, specifically took aim at the structuralist belief in the importance of binary oppositions in creating meaning—it argues that such tensions are themselves created from cultural circumstances, and are therefore unreliable. For the post-structuralist, culture is too messy for scientific analysis. Where structuralists discuss texts, post-structuralists talk about TEXTUALITY and INTERTEXTUALITY (the idea that every text is inseparable from others).

A problem in using the term is that few post-structuralists have identified themselves as such, and some have actively resisted being called such. In addition, post-structuralism and POSTMODERNISM should be kept separate because very few scholars involved in these debates would identify themselves as being both. Post-structuralism can be associated with approaches such as MARXIST CRITICISM, FEMINIST CRITICISM and GENDER CRITICISM, in that these each identify how certain IDEOLOGICAL beliefs are artificial constructions that should be resisted. For literary CRITICISM, the most influential strand of post-structuralist thought remains DECONSTRUCTION.

poulter's measure A STANZA form consisting of four LINES (a QUATRAIN) with three stresses (TRIMETER) in the first, second and fourth lines, and four (TETRAMETER) in the third lines. Its RHYME scheme is usually *abab*, and sometimes *abcb*. For those wondering: a poulter is a chicken farmer, and refers to the old habit of counting out eggs in 'dozens' in alternate twelves and fourteens. See 'quatrain' for a comparison with COMMON, LONG and SHORT MEASURES. It is sometimes referred to as SHORT MEASURE. A COUPLET of a HEXAMETER and HEPTAMETER can count as a poulter's measure, as in the following example from the ELIZABETHAN poet George Gascoigne's *Hundreth Sundrie Flowers* (1573):

> The straightest tree that growes upon one only
> roote:
> If that roote fayle, will quickly fade, no props
> can do it boote.
> I am that fading plant, which on thy grace did
> growe.
> Thy grace is gone wherefore I mone, and
> whither all in woe. (31.1–4)

practical criticism An approach to literature that begins by studying the words on the page, rather than with preconceived notions about the work or its AUTHOR. Practical criticism is not so much a theory as a technical skill that readers develop over time. And it is far from easy: close reading demands concentration, patience and a clear head. It requires readers to slow down and weigh the effect of every word and letter. Technical knowledge of PROSODY is one aspect of practical criticism, but needs to be combined with responsive and sensitive reading and listening to TEXTS. A great attraction is that anyone can try close reading: there is no barrier of complex terminology or advanced concepts. Practical criticism places value on the individual's response, over and above knowledge of critical JARGON, the finer details of DECONSTRUCTION, or other overarching ideas and themes.

It was initiated in Cambridge in the 1920s, not that long after English came to be regarded as a serious academic subject. I.A. Richards showed poems to his students without giving them details about the author or date of composition, and this experiment grew into a whole model of reading. Some practical critics will still approach a text 'blind', but it's not essential to the method. Although its theoretical concerns are modest, practical criticism still fits well into broader critical currents around it. Practical criticism was a culmination of the type of reading practiced by Samuel Johnson, Matthew Arnold (see 'disinterestedness') and T.S. Eliot. Practical criticism also held an influence on NEW CRITICISM, which stressed the importance of studying the text in isolation. The critical rigour demanded by practical criticism has helped make it a part of the majority of English degree programmes: Cambridge University, for example, still makes its students write a paper based solely on unseen texts.

pragmatic criticism (rhetorical criticism) Interpretation of a literary work based on the effect it has on the audience. The Roman AUTHOR Horace (in *De Arte Poetica*) was an early pragmatic critic interested above all in literature's ethical and social impact (based on RHETORICAL theory). Critics remained interested in the social influence of literature for centuries afterwards. This attention waned in the twentieth century as CRITICISM became professional: **rhetorical criticism**, which examines how literature elicits certain responses from its audiences, is its closest equivalent.

pragmatics The LINGUISTIC study of how languages are used in practice. STYLISTICS, psycholinguistics (see 'psychoanalytic criticism') and sociolinguistics are three areas of pragmatics relevant to literary studies.

prague school A group of Czechoslovakian critics who continued the work of the RUSSIAN FORMALISTS in the 1930s onwards. Roman Jakobson was the common link between both groups.

précis A concise summary of the main points in a text. A SYNOPSIS is a more detailed outline of a work.

preposition A word stating the relation between one noun and another: e.g. 'to', for', 'by', 'at'. It is often used with an indirect OBJECT, with a NOUN in the dative CASE: 'I went to Lancaster', 'I did it for her'.

pre-Raphaelites A group of writers and artists in the late-Victorian period, who sought a return to creative simplicity and naturalness. The name refers to the inspiration found in art before the fifteenth-century artist Raphael, and MEDIEVALISM in general. Beauty and sensuous, dreamy detail (see 'aestheticism') are also associated with the pre-Raphaelites. It was influenced by the French DECADENCE movement as well. The poetry of Dante Gabriel Rossetti and Charles Algernon Swinburne are key literary examples.

pre-romanticism A collective term for different aspects of eighteenth-century literature that foreshadow romanticism, by rejecting of CLASSICAL structures and shifting attention towards individual artists and their emotions. Pre-romanticism covers forms including PRIMITIVISM, GRAVEYARD POETRY, literature of SENSIBILITY, and BALLADS. The term is a useful reminder that there wasn't a clean break from NEOCLASSICISM to ROMANTICISM: it had been in the making earlier in the LONG EIGHTEENTH CENTURY.

prescriptive criticism An approach to literature based on establishing the rules that determine what is correct, normal and essential for great writing. It's a companion to JUDICIAL CRITICISM, and an enemy of most forms of CRITICISM from the twentieth century onwards: e.g. STRUCTURALISM finds literature created from impersonal systems of signs that are just there, and are neither good nor bad, while POSTCOLONIALISTS, FEMINIST CRITICS and others would contest the definition of 'normality'. LINGUISTS are also generally agreed that there is no such thing as 'correct' language (though see 'grammar' for one explanation of why it's still worth knowing how to write 'well').

primitivism A yearning for the freedom of the natural world. Primitivism reacts against artificial social structures that contribute to supposed progress, whether in industry, science or culture. Instead, it advocates a return to the ideal, innocent condition of pure nature; to a paradise like the Garden of Eden. Jean-Jacques Rousseau, with his deep interest in natural goodness, was a leading mover in PRE-ROMANTIC primitivism. In literature, it supports spontaneous, unadorned creation. The CLASSICAL PASTORAL ideal is a STYLISED version of primitivism, but the term is more associated with ROMANTICISM. It is applied equally to later writers who reject a sophisticated, urbane style of writing.

problem play A play that portrays a particular social dilemma, and often suggests a solution. The terms 'discussion play' and 'THESIS PLAY' are also used. DOCUMENTARY THEATRE is often related, though it doesn't have to be. Caryl Churchill's *Top Girls* (1982), for example, is a non-NATURALISTIC examination of the sacrifices made by women in order to thrive in a male-dominated world. 'Problem play' is used as a general SYNONYM for 'TRAGICOMEDY', or any play that cannot be slotted easily into a GENERIC category. It is used specifically in reference to those Shakespearean plays that reveal flaws in human nature, and so generates doubts that are not resolved by a COMIC conclusion (e.g. *Measure for Measure* (1604)). These plays were written immediately before Shakespeare's great TRAGEDIES.

proem ('preface') An introduction or PROLOGUE that announces what is to come, and seeks to grab the audience's attention. Each book of Edmund Spenser's *The Faerie Queene* (1590, 96) contains a proem of between four and ten stanzas.

prolepsis (**adj. proleptic**, Greek, 'anticipation') A FIGURE involving a response to an anticipated objection before it has been stated. It also refers to a flash-forward in a PLOT (the opposite of a FLASH-BACK, or analepsis). The future event is imagined to have already taken place (which is ANACHRONISTIC). Prolepsis in this sense can become a form of HYPALLAGE (applying a term that agrees with one thing to something else).

prologue (Greek, 'fore thought') A section that precedes the beginning of a work, usually preparing the audience for what will follow, and perhaps supplying background information (an EXPOSITION). Like an EPILOGUE, it is separated from the rest of the text, but it is part of the literary work; a preface, by contrast, is written in an AUTHORIAL PERSONA. 'INDUCTION' is a rarely-used SYNONYM for 'prologue'. EARLY MODERN dramatists sometimes introduced plays with a single ACTOR onstage performing the part of prologue: e.g. *Henry V*, with a prologue that begins 'O for a Muse of fire, that would ascend | The brightest heaven of invention!' The general prologue to the *Canterbury Tales* (ll.1–4, 12) shows beyond doubt that prologues can have real literary merit:

> Whan that Aprill with his shoures soote
> [sweet showers]
> The droghte of March hath perced to
> the roote, [dryness; pierced]
> And bathed every veyne in swich licour
> [such liquid]
> Of which vertu engendered is the flour [...]
> [formed]
> Thanne longen folk to goon on pilgrimages.

promptbook The master copy of a play script that contains all the cues and stage directions, and is used by a prompter to help ACTORS who forget their lines during performance. The Shakespearean First FOLIO may have been partly based on a promptbook or performing copy of the plays.

pronoun (personal, demonstrative, relative, interrogative) A word that replaces a NOUN already used or known, to avoid repetition. **Personal** pronouns include 'him', 'I' and 'us'; 'this' and 'that' are **demonstrative** pronouns; 'who' and 'which' are **relative** pronouns; 'who' is **interrogative**. Also, 'herself', 'himself' and themselves' are **reflexive** and **intensive**, though they rarely need to be used (less often than they actually are used).

proof A means of supporting an argument. It formed part of the RHETORICAL theories influential on sixteenth- and seventeenth-century literary writers. There were three ways in which a speaker could create support (artificial proof): ETHOS (describing yourself to persuade the audience that you should be believed), PATHOS (appeal to emotion) and LOGOS (rational argument). Objective 'evidence' was known as inartificial proof.

propaganda (novel/play) A literary work that makes a specific point, and appears more motivated by IDEOLOGY than artistic ends. It spreads (propagates) a particular viewpoint to its audience. The majority of literary works described as 'propaganda' are NOVELS or PLAYS—presumably because poetry is less suited to making blunt points about reality. It particularly describes overtly political literature; e.g. SOCIALIST REALISM. The term has definite negative implications; 'THESIS' novel/ play is a gentler alternative.

propriety In literature, the valuing of good taste, accuracy and appropriate forms of expression. Propriety promotes DECORUM and CONVENTION in writing as positive influences. It was a principle cherished by NEOCLASSICAL writers; no surprise, then, that ROMANTICISM disregarded rules of propriety.

props An abbreviated form of 'stage properties'; i.e. items necessary for dramatic action which are not part of the fixed scenery. STAGE BUSINESS often involves props. Many productions use props not strictly required by the script.

proscenium arch (pro-**scene**-eeum; Latin, 'in front of the stage') The part of the STAGE from which the curtain hangs (if there is one), as found in most twenty-first-century Western theatres. The proscenium is the small section beyond the curtain, and this space allows ACTORS to interact with the audience more directly. However, the proscenium arch also divides the stage from the audience, acting like a picture frame. In doing so it creates distance between the action onstage and the audience, as if the stage represents an alternate reality. It emphasises that the audience is watching, rather than participating in, the DRAMA. Theatrical CONVENTION allows the proscenium arch to be a fourth wall during indoor scenes. THRUST STAGE and THEATRE IN THE ROUND are the main alternative types of stage.

prose (adj. prose/prosaic; from Latin, 'direct') Standard written language, usually grouped into sentences and having a loose rhythm. Its structure is not tight enough to be regarded as POETRY (PROSE POEMS and FREE VERSE often test the boundaries). 'Prose' can refer to spoken language too, but it doesn't often do so. Alongside DRAMA and poetry, prose is a major literary GENRE (see page 351 for prose-based forms). Because prose is so familiar to us in daily life—in everything from newspapers to emails—the assumption is often made that prose must 'easier' to read and understand than poetry, but this is not necessarily the case. It is worth asking why a given writer chooses to write in prose, and it is just as possible to speak of a writer's prose STYLE, as of poetic style. **Prose** is the standard adjective for writing in prose; **prosaic** means 'prose-like' and has the negative implication that something is dull and uninspired.

The following example shows how blurred the division between poetry and prose can be. It's taken from David Jones' *In Parenthesis* (1937), one of the great works about World War I (which also hints darkly at the war to come). It is still not read all that widely, and one reason may be its unique, challenging combination of prose and poetry. The following two paragraphs are set out as prose, but taken apart, could be read as a prose poem:

> So they would go a long while in solid dark, nor moon, nor battery, dispelled.
>
> Feet plodding in each other's unseen tread. They said no word but to direct their immediate next coming, so close behind to blunder, toes by heel tripping, file-mates; blind on-following, moving with a singular identity.
>
> Half-minds, far away, divergent, own-thought thinking, tucked away unknown thoughts; feet following file friends, each his own thought-maze alone treading; intricate, twist about, own thoughts, all unknown thoughts, to the next so close following on. (p. 37)

prose poem A short piece of shaped writing in continuous lines. It will make use of such poetic DEVICES as INTERNAL RHYME, RHYTHM, FIGURATIVE LANGUAGE, CONSONANCE and ASSONANCE. It may be divided into VERSE PARAGRAPHS, but each prose poem is a self-contained work—it's different from a chapter in a NOVEL. As the term suggests, it explores the borders of POETRY and PROSE (see this entry for discussion and example). It's not worth worrying about what exactly counts as a 'prose poem'; instead, each poem should be taken on its own merits, and read as slowly and thoroughly as its STYLE requires. Geoffrey Hill's *Mercian Hymns* (1971) are a set of prose poems to linger over.

prosody (**pros**-oh-dee) The study of VERSIFICATION, i.e. aspects of METRE, RHYTHM, RHYME and STANZA form and sound in poetry. METRICS is a more technical form of prosody. SCANSION (metrical analysis) is a particular area of prosody. Knowing the right terms is an aid to training the mind to hear poetic effects when reading. Understanding the concepts is far easier than hearing the subtle ways in meaning is affected by the way in which it is expressed.

prosopopoeia (pro-soe-po-**pay**-ah, Greek, 'face-making') The Greek term for PERSONIFICATION; i.e. regarding a non-human being or object as human. As a rhetorical term, it also refers to the impersonation of someone living, dead or imaginary (often in the form of an APOSTROPHE).

protagonist (Greek, 'first actor') The main performer or CHARACTER in a work, who is often opposed by a rival, or ANTAGONIST. 'Protagonist' is a more technical equivalent of HERO/HEROINE. However, it does not create expectations about character, and has no sense at all of moral goodness: Patrick Bateman, the serial killer businessman in Bret Easton Ellis's *American Psycho* (1991) is definitely an 'evil' protagonist. There can only be one protagonist in a work; 'main protagonist' is a TAUTOLOGY. In PROSE FICTION, the protagonist is sometimes also a narrator. Though it now covers all literary GENRES, the term's meaning has remained fairly close to its original meaning in Greek DRAMA. It is said that during a CHORAL performance in or around sixth century B.C.E., one member stepped out from the group and in doing became the first DRAMATIC protagonist. That performer was Thespis, which is why ACTORS are also known as THESPIANS. Second and third ACTORS (deuteragonists and tritagonists) were introduced by Aeschylus and Sophocles respectively.

prothalamion A OCCASIONAL POEM written in anticipation of a wedding. The term is variant form of 'EPITHALAMION', coined by Edmund Spenser in a 1597 poem of that name (and almost exclusively associated with that poem).

proverb A traditional saying that expresses a COMMONPLACE truth: e.g. 'Good things come to those who wait'. World cultures have their own proverbs, and the tradition of proverbs in the West began with the Biblical Book of Proverbs, which remains one of the most substantial collections of proverbs. Proverbs risk becoming CLICHÉS if used too often. See page 350 for a list of other terms for short expressions of wisdom.

Provincetown Players (c.1910s) A group of early twentieth-century American dramatists who challenged existing theatrical tradition by performing experimental theatre. They reacted against bourgeois MELODRAMAS and excessive THEATRICALITY, initially by performing in an old wharf in Provincetown, Massachusetts. They were influential pioneers in MODERNIST and EXPRESSIONIST DRAMA; Eugene O'Neill became especially famous.

psalm A sacred song recited during public or private worship, as found in the Biblical Book of Psalms. There have been numerous literary TRANSLATIONS and PARAPHRASES, particularly in sixteenth-century England, and the psalm tradition has had a wider influence on the FORM, STYLE and IMAGERY of DEVOTIONAL POETRY.

pseudonym (Greek, 'false name') A fictitious name adopted by a writer. It is a form of PEN-NAME (or *NOM DE PLUME*).

psychoanalytic criticism A critical approach based on the ideas of Sigmund Freud that draws connections between AUTHORS' works and their inner mental state. Freud's theories incorporated literary readings, and have probably influenced literary criticism more than psychology. It has certainly left its mark on Western culture. Psychoanalysis is easily stereotyped as reducing all literature to an expression of sexual desire. The following brief survey identifies why psychoanalysis needs literature, and what literary criticism in general can learn from psychoanalytic criticism.

Freud's breakthrough work was *The Interpretation of Dreams* (1899). It makes the crucial distinction between conscious thought (what I want, what I think) and unconscious desire. Freud was happy to accept that he did not 'discover' the unconscious: artists had been writing about it for centuries (even the word was being used in the nineteenth century). What

Freud did do was integrate these ideas into a scientific system. Dreams, for Freud, were fantasies of wish-fulfilment, which brought unconscious desire into a visual form. Imaginative literature is like dreams and can be analysed in the same way. In one of the most influential footnotes ever, Freud offers a psychoanalytic reading of *Hamlet* to gain access to Shakespeare's unconscious thought: 'what I have attempted here is only an interpretation of the deepest layer of the impulses in the psyche of the creative poet' (p. 204).

Freud's method for dream-interpretation is therefore directly relevant to literary criticism. Because everyone represses unconscious desire, it does not transfer directly to conscious thought. Unconscious thought is represented in dreams which are filled with FIGURATIVE LANGUAGE, in particular with SYMBOLIC IMAGES (METAPHOR) and displacements of desire (METONYM). This does not mean that works can offer a detailed mental picture of what Shakespeare or anyone else thought: Freud always maintained that the unconscious was dark and mysterious. The unconscious can project repressed impulses in a way that is pleasurable, healthy but not simple to interpret. Freud had different systems for describing the structure of the psyche. The best-known is the division into the id (the unconscious matter), ego (conscious thoughts) and the superego (the social and moral standards hardwired into us).

This system sharpened critical thinking about figurative language. Psychoanalysis was also influential in developing what eventually became READER-RESPONSE CRITICISM; i.e. how readers react to someone else's expressive act. Important here is the notion of the *unheimlich*, usually translated as the UNCANNY. The uncanny in literature is something familiar and strange at the same time. The effect is created, Freud says, by recognising our own unconscious desires in someone else's thought. This made a difference in AESTHETICS, because things that were uncomfortable, secret and dark were shown to hold their own importance, and demand our attention though discomfiting.

If only in terms of the history of criticism, psychoanalytic criticism deserves attention. Jacques Lacan (the 'French Freud') extended Freud's ideas into LINGUISTICS, with great (and deliberate) complexity. He argued that the unconscious is made up of language; i.e. that all of our thoughts and actions are influenced by existing social and linguistic structures. FEMINIST CRITICISM has responded at length to the prejudice towards men in Freudian psychoanalysis. Harold Bloom's idea of the ANXIETY OF INFLUENCE is based on psychoanalysis too. A strong argument against psychoanalytic criticism is that it turns the sort of subjective, artistic truth found in literature into something OBJECTIVE and universally valid. The insight offered by Sophocles in *Oedipus Rex*, for example, becomes the OEDIPUS COMPLEX. But this scientific approach brought with it critical rigour, and an awareness that much about literature remains unknown.

psychobiography An attempt to learn more about the mental make-up of historically significant individuals through their lives and works. It seeks to answer specific questions about motives and influences, rather than diagnose someone's condition or write a complete BIOGRAPHY. Both psychologists (e.g. Sigmund Freud) and literary critics have written biographical accounts of literary writers; for example, the question of whether Virginia Woolf was 'mad' has been a topic of some critical interest. Like the BIOGRAPHICAL FALLACY, literary psychobiography runs the risk of being REDUCTIONIST if its conclusions make blunt observations without accepting associated problems of literary interpretation.

psychogeography The study of a physical environment's effect on our thoughts, feelings and behaviour. It has become particularly associated with British AUTHORS writing about London. Iain Sinclair is the AUTHOR most associated with the term, and *Downriver* (1991) is one of his most-read novels about the British capital.

psychological criticism An approach to literature that tries to get inside the AUTHOR'S mind. It tries to pick out authorial intention as a basis for INTERPRETATION. PSYCHOANALYTIC and PHENOMENOLOGICAL CRITICISM are more focused versions of psychological CRITICISM. BIOGRAPHICAL and INTENTIONAL FALLACY are two possible reservations to this approach. STRUCTURALISTS and POST-STRUCTURALISTS would find it unworthy of consideration (see 'death of the author'), while some twentieth-century HERMENEUTIC philosophers have argued that discovering the AUTHOR'S state of mind through a work is simply impossible.

psychomachy (sigh-coe-**mach**-ee; Greek, 'soul battle') A moral struggle between forces of good and evil in the soul. The Roman Christian poet Prudentius first wrote about psychomachy as a battle in which only the faithful triumph. The same concept can be found in MEDIEVAL MORALITY PLAYS and other ALLEGORIES: e.g. the play *Everyman* (c.1510) depicts the forces of virtue of vice trying to claim Everyman's soul.

Ptolemaic universe The cosmic theory proposed by the Greek astronomer Ptolemy, which was widely accepted in Europe until the seventeenth century. In the Ptolemaic system, the earth was at the centre of the universe and was motionless. The sun, moon, planets and stars revolved around the earth attached to spheres, and the proportions of those spheres described perfect musical patterns, known as 'music of the spheres'. This PARADIGM informs a number of MEDIEVAL and EARLY MODERN literary works in English. The Ptolemaic system was gradually replaced by Nicholas Copernicus's theory of a solar system with the sun at its centre.

pulp fiction A type of American popular FICTION, sold on cheap paper (known as 'pulp') around the 1930s. It could also be described as a NOVELETTE. Pulp fiction covered different types of GENRE FICTION, such as western, science-fiction and crime. The title of Quentin Tarantino's film *Pulp Fiction* (1994) is a reference to the in-yer-face, crime pulp fiction material that provides the film's storyline.

pun (also known by the Greek term **'paronomasia'**) A TROPE that exploits AMBIGUITY in words that have two meanings (POLYSEMY), or similarity in spelling (homonyms) or pronunciation (HOMOPHONES): e.g. 'A man walked into a bar. Ouch.' and 'a pun is its own reword'. 'Equivoque' is a SYNONYM, and '*DOUBLE ENTENDRE*' is a particular form of pun. Although puns are most commonly used now for newspaper headlines or knock-knock jokes, they can have literary applications: for example, James Joyce continually puns in *Ulysses* and *Finnegans Wake*, and John Donne's 'A Hymn to God the Father' plays on the pronunciation of his own name: 'When thou hast done, thou hast not done, | For I have more.' A pun is the verbal equivalent of the silhouette image that either looks like a candlestick or two faces, and in this way can potentially unsettle an audience's sense of reality. In this sense, puns have the same effect as IRONY, ALLEGORY and other TROPES.

punctuation A system of marks used to organise written language. It also indicates spoken pauses. The main punctuation marks in English are: full stop (.); comma (,); COLON (:); SEMI-COLON (;); question mark (?); exclamation mark (!); quotation marks (" "); inverted commas("); apostrophe (' '); brackets (()); square brackets ([]); stroke (/) hyphen (-); en-dash (–) and em-dash (—). Punctuation should always be borne in mind, both when reading and writing. For readers it provides vital information about sentence structure, and reveals subtleties of expression. For writers it indicates control over language, which lends authority to an argument (spelling and GRAMMAR matter for the same reason). A note of caution: modern EDITIONS of CLASSIC texts often update the punctuation for clarity, which makes literary ANALYSIS of original punctuation impossible.

purple patch Writing characterized by great richness in STYLE, with abundant use of FIGURATIVE LANGUAGE, IMAGERY, structure, RHYTHM or other DEVICES. BOMBAST and FUSTIAN use purple patches for a reason, but often a purple patch (often 'purple prose') just indicates a section that has been very well-worked. Indeed, the term derives from Horace's *De Arte Poetica*, where it has definite negative implications: it describes sections that has been over-worked. Some people still use 'purple patch' as a derogatory term, and others use it neutrally; perhaps it depends in part on whether you like the colour purple....

pyrrhic (**noun and adjective**; also **dibrach**) A metrical FOOT consisting of two unstressed syllables (o o). There is some debate as to whether pyrrhics can occur in English. In SCANSION, if you think you've found a pyrrhic, check whether one of the syllables has slightly more stress than the other before labelling it.

Q

qualifier A word or prefix that removes EMPHASIS from a word's meaning: 'quite', 'fairly', and 'semi-' are all qualifiers. Intensifiers are similar words that provide emphases (such as 'very'). British English is littered with qualifiers.

quantitative verse METRICAL writing that is structured around relative duration (quantity) of SYLLABLES; i.e. how long it takes to say them. It is based on the natural length of vowels and weight of syllables. English PROSODY, by contrast, depends on stresses given to words. English poetry is more flexible, and is generally ACCENTUAL-SYLLABIC, i.e. based on a fixed number of stressed and unstressed syllables per line. Quantitative verse in English (by Edmund Spenser and Philip Sidney, for example) imitates CLASSICAL poetry. A large part of the terminology used to describe verse in English comes from the quantitative system; when transferred into English verse, it shouldn't be assumed that these terms provide the rules that poets are consciously following, though they can be useful for describing its structures and effects.

quarto A page format created by folding a single sheet twice, and a book containing LEAVES of that size. Quarto EDITIONS often contained single works, such as treatises, plays or poem collections. They are less grand than FOLIO EDITIONS, and more standard than OCTAVO or duodecimo editions. Twenty-one of Shakespeare's plays survive in quartos, which differ from the text of the FOLIO edition in varying degrees. *King Lear* and *Hamlet* have quarto versions that are well worth reading, particularly for comparison with other versions. They can all be viewed at the following website: http://www.quartos.org/.

quatrain A set of four lines of verse. It is the most common STANZA unit, and various permutations of METRE and RHYME SCHEME are possible. The quatrain has been used across literary history in many different CONTEXTS, too many to summarise here. English quatrains usually rhyme, and the most common schemes (in rough order of importance) are *abab*, *abcb*, *abba*, *aabb* and *aaaa*. A line with four stresses can be described as a TETRAMETER line (which assumes one unstressed syllable for every stressed), and three as TRIMETER, both of which would normally be IAMBIC. Different line lengths gives rise to four different types of quatrain, known as COMMON, LONG, POULTER'S and SHORT MEASURES:

measure	stresses per line
long	4-4-4-4
common	4-3-4-3
poulter's (short)	3-3-4-3
short (half)	3-3-3-3

And here is a complete quatrain poem in which the simplicity of the form is beguiling and unsettling. William Blake's 'The Sick Rose' (from *Songs of Experience*, 1794):

> O rose, thou art sick:
> The invisible worm
> That flies in the night,
> In the howling storm
>
> Has found out thy bed
> Of crimson joy,
> And his dark secret love
> Does thy life destroy.

queer theory A critical viewpoint based on the assumption that sexual identity cannot be reduced to a male/female or MASCULINE/FEMININE split. It is rooted both in GAY AND LESBIAN CRITICISM and POST-STRUCTURALISM (especially DECONSTRUCTION), and its major theoretical text is the first volume of Michel's Foucault's *History of Sexuality* (1976). 'Queer' is a formerly offensive term for homosexuals (and is often still considered derogatory when used by heterosexuals) that was reclaimed as a positive indicator of sexuality in the 1980s, and 'queer theory' as a term arose in the early 1990s. It forms part of a wider movement to acknowledge social PLURALITY in literature and CRITICISM, rather than accept a traditional literary CANON based on a hierarchy dominated by heterosexual, white, male, rich, able-bodied (and the list goes on...) individuals.

Central to queer theory is HERMENEUTIC ANALYSIS of how sexuality is fluid and very difficult to categorise. It is only society and culture that force sexuality to fit into a fixed number of permutations, each with their own associations. Transgender, polysexuality, asexuality, intersexuality, and many other sexual preferences and practices have been explored by queer theorists. Judith Butler's *Gender Trouble* (1990), a key work for both FEMINIST CRITICISM and queer theory, argues that gender is something performed, and so should be studied in terms of what people actually do, rather than what we suppose they do. Beyond academic CRITICISM, queer theory has given rise to other creative work, particularly in literature and film.

quintain (also **quintet**) A STANZA containing five lines, normally with a set RHYME and METRE. PENTASTICH is an alternative, though less commonly used. LIMERICK is the major English example.

q.v. (*quod vide,* Latin), also ***qq.v.*** (*quae vide*)) Which see. '*qq.v.*' is used for plural. 'See' is an English-language alternative.

R

rap A form of popular music involving lyrics (usually rhyming) sung or spoken over a BEAT. It was developed by African-American males as a form of hip-hop, but has diversified: as well as more aggressive gangsta rap, it has become more inclusive and international, with both women and white people embracing the form. Improvised rapping (freestyling) and competitive rap (battle rap) are variations. Not everyone would accept it as a type of PERFORMANCE POETRY, but it is surely the most widely heard form of complex lyrical utterance in the West today. That it doesn't fit traditional categories of literary criticism is exactly what makes it worthy of consideration. And it does receive critical acclaim too: *Original Pirate Material* (2002) by The Streets (aka the British rapper Mike Skinner) was compared to a Dostoyevsky novel by one English professor, and was named as the best album of its decade by a British national newspaper.

rationalism (adj. rational; from Greek, 'reason') The belief that logical reason is the foundation of all knowledge. Rationalists pursue *a priori* knowledge, as opposed to *a posteriori* (see 'empiricism' for more discussion).

reader-response criticism An critical approach based on the assumption that it is the reader that determines a text's meaning and not the AUTHOR or TEXT. It emerged as a specific critical movement in the 1970s, but the notion of reader-centred interpretation had been around decades before. STRUCTURALISM and POST-STRUCTURALISM had argued that AUTHORS do not control meaning, and HERMENEUTICS explored how readers interpret texts. These perspectives lead to the conclusion that meaning is UNDECIDABLE, and so it falls to each reader to fill in the GAPS and produce signification. RECEPTION THEORY is allied to this approach. PSYCHOANALYTIC CRITICISM, which discusses the relation between the psychoanalyst (critic) and the analysed (patient/text) also made a contribution. Further back, PRAGMATIC CRITICISM, which explored how authors create responses in the audience, is an early precursor. Reader-response criticism, in emphasising subjective response, formed part of a movement away from the NEW CRITICAL claim that all texts had an objective meaning. This leaves important questions open: whether shared or objective meaning exists; how texts shape our response; and whether texts create an IMPLIED READER.

readerly/writerly (French, *lisible/scriptible*) A distinction made by Roland Barthes between texts that are easy and difficult to read. A readerly text (*lisible*) is one that conforms to our expectations, contains recognisable elements, and can be read passively for enjoyment. Barthes particularly has REALIST novels in mind here. A writerly text (*scriptible*) forces the reader to be more active and 'write' their own interpretation. The reader has to produce meaning from the text. Many MODERNIST texts are writerly; e.g. James Joyce's *Finnegans Wake* (1939). Closely related is the 'DEATH OF THE AUTHOR', which handed responsibility for interpretation onto the reader (see also 'reader-response criticism'). Barthes supported writerly texts as a form of liberation for the reader.

reading (reader) The process of looking through written material to understand its meaning. There are different types of reading: we can skim quickly over words we already know, or we can weigh the importance of every single letter on the page. Or ask questions about how words are presented on the page (LINEATION and TYPOGRAPHY). These skills take great effort to acquire. LITERARY CRITICISM has lots to say about reading: PRACTICAL CRITICISM promotes close reading; READER-RESPONSE CRITICISM asks how readers create meaning; and PSYCHOANALYTIC critics, DECONSTRUCTIONISTS and others argue that all reading is a form of INTERPRETATION.

realism Representation of the world as it is. It is another of those terms that is widely used in a vague sense, but has specific uses in literary studies. A tighter definition is needed, since, broadly speaking, all literature is concerned with replicating some aspect of experience (see 'imitation'). Also, some would argue that it is naïve to think that OBJECTIVE description is possible. Realism involves reporting details taken from life to suggest VERISIMILITUDE, with the use of literary CONVENTIONS (e.g. ONOMATOPOEIA, three UNITIES). It can be contrasted with ALLEGORY, as a form in which CONCRETE details are given secondary meaning. It is also different from ROMANTICISM, which gave priority to an individual's view of things, rather than an faithful description of appearances. The tension between appearance and reality is extremely old and slightly CLICHÉD now, though it can still be a good way to start thinking about forms of reality.

Realism is often used specifically to describe a group of nineteenth-century novels that sought to provide a true account of the world. Jane Austen, Elizabeth Gaskell, and George Eliot all pursued this path. Close observation, detailed CHARACTERIZATION, and an interest in the lives of ordinary people became hallmarks of realist writing. It has always been associated with the novel: Daniel Defoe's *Robinson Crusoe* (1719), accepted as the first English novel, is a FICTIONAL diary of Crusoe's time on an island. Its attention to fictional detail was innovative at the time:

> Having fitted my Mast and Sail, and try'd the Boat, I found she would sail very well. Then I made little Lockers, or Boxes, at either End of my Boat, to put Provisions, Necessaries and Ammunitions *&c.* into, to be kept dry, either from Rains, or the Sprye of the Sea; and a little long hollow Place I cut into the In-side of the Boat, where I could lay my Gun, making a Flap to hand down over it to keep it dry.

Though MODERNISM reacted against this form of realism, it still provided the basis for many later novels, including works of MAGIC REALISM. NATURALISM is a variety of realism that portrays the effects of nature and society on humans. HYPERREALISM is a recent term used to describe POSTMODERN novels littered with realistic detail.

recension (Latin, 'review') The REVISION of a work, particularly to remove textual error, or the TEXT (often a new EDITION) arising from this process. It often involves TEXTUAL CRITICISM; i.e. comparing the available versions to create a new TEXT.

reception history (reception theory) The study of how readers have responded to a work over time. It's similar to SOCIOLOGY OF LITERATURE, but is particularly associated with READER-RESPONSE CRITICISM through its interest in how different cultures and groups respond to a work, rather than the individuals. **Reception theory** is a particular strand within this area that draws on HERMENEUTICS for inspiration (see 'horizon of expectations' for more).Taken to its extreme, critics have argued that an individual's response is only part of a wider community's shared reaction to a text. Reception history covers such issues as audience expectation, knowledge brought to a text (and hindsight), and changing tastes. Today, reception history is generally accepted as an insightful and uncontroversial way to approach a text, and most modern EDITIONS of a CANONICAL work will make some reference to reception (or, for plays, performance) history. The principle of a SOCIOLOGY OF TEXTS has encouraged a BIBLIOGRAPHIC take on reception history. Literary ADAPTATIONS also provide good case-studies.

recessive accent An unnatural STRESS placed on the first SYLLABLE of a word when the second syllable would normally be stressed. It usually occurs when the next word would also begin with a stressed syllable. It helps fit the words to the METRE. It is a type of WRENCHED ACCENT.

recto The 'front' of a LEAF; i.e. the right-hand, odd-numbered page of an opening. The other page is the VERSO.

redaction (Latin, 'bring back') The editing or revision of a work to prepare a new EDITION. It can include ABRIDGEMENT of a previous version.

reductionism (reductive) The process of explaining something complex through one fundamental idea or concept. In literary criticism this is usually considered something to be avoided. Accusations of being reductive have been levelled against numerous critical schools: those with a scientific connection, such as PSYCHOANALYTIC CRITICISM and LITERARY DARWINISM, are particularly vulnerable. In some sense, interpretation always demands that the reader FOREGROUNDS some aspects over others, and such BIAS is inescapable. A statement like '*King Lear* is a play about old age' is reductive, but it could still prove a fruitful starting-point for a broader interpretation. Equally, focused attention is also well-advised, since a reading that also took in nature, death, kinship, politics, cosmology and a string of other ideas wouldn't necessarily be more satisfying. Also reductive is the literary timeline beginning on page 357, and the keywords are especially limited, but again both are intended to encourage further research.

reference An allusion to another TEXT. Literary writers constantly make references to other texts, sometimes without knowing it. Such IMITATION is quite separate to what is thought of as PLAGIARISM. Especially in MODERNIST texts, there is a risk of becoming overburdened with the need to discover references: however difficult the TEXT may seem, the experience of reading *Ulysses* shouldn't be like watching a tennis match, with your eyes flitting between the text and notes.

Critics need to cite their authorities in references. Clarity and consistency are what matter here. When quoting primary texts, use references that could be used by readers with another EDITION. So DRAMAS are cited according to act.scene.line, and poems by line number whenever possible. Page numbers, in short, are a last resort (especially in EARLY MODERN books, where they are reliably unreliable (use SIGNATURES instead)). It should be clear whether lines ('l.' or plural 'll.') or pages ('p.' or 'pp.') are being referred to ('FF.' is usually avoided now), and changes should be made clear. There are numerous different practices for making footnote references, even within literary studies. See the MHRA style guide (p. 388) for one such system.

refrain A phrase repeated throughout a poem or song at regular intervals, usually at the end of STANZAS. It is an important form of REPETITION, with roots in ORAL POETRY encouraging audience participation (like modern-day church HYMNS). The refrain usually emphasises the main point of the piece, and often appears in slightly varied forms during the work. In terms of LINEATION, it can appear as a part of stanzas (like a CHORUS) or separate from them (like a BURDEN). It brings home the point in these opening stanzas of a Thomas Wyatt poem (the other stanzas use the same refrain):

I have been a lover
Full long and many days
And oft-times a prover
Of the most painful ways.
But all that I have passed
As trifles to this last.

By proof I know the pair
Of them that sue and save
And within can attain
Of that which they deserve.
But these pangs have I passed
As trifles to this last.

register The form of a language used in a particular situation. It is similar in meaning to 'STYLE', but emphasises appropriate use in CONTEXT. To greet someone in a formal register (e.g. meeting someone for the first time) you might say 'hello, it's nice to meet you', and in an informal register (to friends) 'hey, how you doing?' might be more appropriate. Register, like style, involves changes in DICTION, SYNTAX and VOICE. Like POETIC DICTION, it could well be argued that there is no such thing as a literary register, only something that pretends to be literary: a greeting such as 'salutations, yonder friend most cherished by my heart' would be more like a PARODY of literary register.

Renaissance (noun and adj.; French, 'rebirth') The renewal of European arts and culture caused by a revival of interest in CLASSICAL Latin and Greek models. 'Renaissance' is a wide-ranging term that describes a large cultural movement that originated in fourteenth-century Italy and can still be seen in eighteenth-century England as NEOCLASSICISM. For

English literature, it usually covers the period from about 1500 to 1660, roughly between Thomas Wyatt's and Henry Howard's TRANSLATIONS of Italian and Latin poetry, and John Milton's *Paradise Lost*. The term 'EARLY MODERN' is preferred by some academic critics because it acknowledges other important influences besides CLASSICISM, such as the Reformation. Some argue that using 'Renaissance' reinforces the prejudiced view that the MEDIEVAL period was a unenlightened 'middle age' during which classical ideas had been sadly 'lost'.

In English literature, the Renaissance is closely linked to HUMANISM, which promoted self-improvement through learning. In the sixteenth and seventeenth centuries all educated individuals had a thorough knowledge of Latin (it is only in the past fifty years that learning Latin and Greek has ceased to be part of the standard British school education), and increasingly classical standards were used to improve the prestige of vernacular English. Classical theories of RHETORIC were very influential, and so were forms like EPIC, ELEGY and PASTORAL. This all assisted in the formation of a British literary tradition in the ELIZABETHAN and JACOBEAN periods. The Renaissance was a European phenomenon, however, and it's important not to forget that English literature was influenced by French, Italian and other foreign literature, more than is sometimes acknowledged.

The list of classical AUTHORS on page 358 gives some sense of how wide-ranging classical influences are on English literature, and see page 360 for important Renaissance works. Note that 'Renaissance' is sometimes used as a general term for 'revival', as in 'HARLEM RENAISSANCE'.

repartee (re-par-**tea**) Dialogue containing quick, sharp-witted responses. It works particularly well when spoken aloud, and is most associated in English literature with RESTORATION COMEDY OF MANNERS.

repertory (rep) In DRAMA, a group of plays being performed by a company (also called 'repertory') in a given period, or available to put on at short notice. Few theatres in London's West End and beyond are repertory theatres; instead, they perform one play in a long run, and then stage another.

repetition A basic literary technique that occurs when an element appears twice or more. It is the most basic means of crafting language and organising thoughts. All poetry involves repetition of some kind (even FREE VERSE); indeed, 'VERSE' literally means 'turn', which suggests an ultimate return to the same point. All forms of repetition create some kind of unity, whether of sounds (RHYME), of RHYTHM (METRE), of SYNTACTIC structures

(PARALLELISM), of consonants (CONSONANCE), of vowels (ASSONANCE), ideas (MOTIFS), letters, words or phrases (e.g. ALLITERATION, see p. 344 for a list of FIGURES of repetition). It is a means of consolidating knowledge and creating meaning, and is thus essential to literature.

Restoration (1660–1700) Relating to the period after the restoration of the monarchy after the Commonwealth period. In literature the period is particularly associated with COMEDY OF MANNERS and the works of John Dryden (see page 366 for examples). 1700 is a particularly arbitrary cut-off point, and the Restoration period is often incorporated in a larger NEOCLASSICAL movement, or is described as the beginning of the 'LONG EIGHTEENTH CENTURY'.

revenge tragedy TRAGIC DRAMA involving some or all of the following: murder, ghosts, bloody violence, retribution, a PROTAGONIST who delays, agonising SOLILOQUIES and CATASTROPHE. Thomas Kyd's *Spanish Tragedy* (1594) and William Shakespeare's *Titus Andronicus* (1593) contain most of these elements, though many others were performed in the late ELIZABETHAN and Jacobean periods (c.1590–1625). Revenge tragedy grew out of SENECAN TRAGEDY and a popular taste for gruesome ACTION. John Kerrigan, in a well-regarded book called *Revenge Tragedy* (1996), has explored revenge tragedy as a broader cultural form, one which looks at questions of justice, anger and violence in society.

revision (Latin, 'see again') The reworking of a TEXT, either by the original AUTHOR or later EDITOR, in order to correct and improve the ORIGINAL.

revisionism Any form of literary criticism that seeks to overturn an existing principle or point of view. The history of literary criticism is a succession of revisions of existing opinions: e.g. POST-STRUCTURALISM and POSTMODERNISM are revisionist interpretations of STRUCTURALISM and MODERNISM. A post-revisionist interpretation is when a critic seeks to find middle ground between the two extremes of original and revisionist ideas—though these terms are more often used in historical and political CRITICISM, since arguments in literary criticism are not always so focused around a single issue.

revue A theatre production containing a mixed programme of song, dance, SKETCHES, BURLESQUE, COMEDY and other performances. The jokes are often written with a particular audience in mind. VAUDEVILLE is an American variety of REVUE that was most popular at the beginning of the twentieth century.

rhetoric (noun; adj. rhetorical) The art of persuasive speech or writing. Numerous CLASSICAL rhetorical treatises give highly systematised accounts of how language could move an audience. The most influential are probably Aristotle's *Rhetoric*, Cicero's *Rhetorica* and *Rhetorica ad Herennium* and Quintilian's *Institutio Oratoria*. These works retained their importance for many centuries: the MEDIEVAL university education required advanced knowledge of rhetoric, and it was an essential part of the HUMANIST curriculum in EARLY MODERN/RENAISSANCE Europe.

Shakespeare and his contemporaries would have had rhetoric drilled into them at school during Latin lessons. *Julius Caesar* Act 3, Scene 2 displays Shakespeare's knowledge of rhetorical FIGURES; Brutus gives a half-decent speech over Caesar's body which is followed by the dazzling rhetoric of Antony's speech, which begins 'Friends, Romans, countrymen, lend me your ears!' George Puttenham's *Arte of English Poesie* (1589) was one of numerous rhetorical treatises written in English around this time. People generally agreed that CLASSICAL rhetorical principles could make VERNACULAR languages like English and Italian more refined and prestigious. It was also important for social advancement: a good rhetorician was (in theory) a virtuous and influential person. Rhetoric eventually came to seem an artificial means of composition, particularly as ideas associated with ROMANTICISM spread, and today it is often used to describe language that is hollow and designed to elicit a particular response from the audience.

In CLASSICAL theory, there were three branches of rhetoric, depending on audience: deliberative (political), judicial (legal) and epideictic (ceremonial praise, which is most relevant to literature). Most treatises dealt with five aspects of oratory. The three concerned with composing an ORATION are most applicable to literature: invention (generating material), arrangement (structuring an argument) and STYLE. The other two parts concerned performance: memory and delivery. FIGURES and TROPES are basic elements of any rhetorical composition—many also survive in everyday speech.

A basic knowledge of rhetorical terms is still very useful for close reading in English literature, and not just for writers who were consciously using rhetoric. It is impossible to classify all possible uses of language for effect, but rhetoric still provides a helpful way to think about how FIGURATIVE LANGUAGE works in general. For this reason it's worth knowing some rhetorical terms, and a good place to start is the list of rhetorical terms covered in this book, starting on page 343.

rhetorical question Any question that is not asked to gain information. It does not expect a response, and often implies its answer. It usually emphasises the speaker's own knowledge: e.g. 'Are you joking?' is a rhetorical question usually asked to pour scorn on someone's suggestion. 'Would you mind passing the salt?' is a rhetorical question used to make a polite request. Neither are genuine enquiries, but express the speaker's thoughts in a more persuasive way. Rhetorical questions can be subtle, emphatic and DRAMATIC. This makes they RHETORICAL, and as a FIGURE they are often used in public speeches. For example, it can be used to give sharp criticism ('How much longer should we put up with this?') and/or followed with an immediate answer ('When do we need to act? Now!') They are frequently found in literature, particularly drama. When Macbeth asks 'Is this a dagger which I see before me, | The handle toward my hand?' (2.1.34–35), the audience is forcefully told that Macbeth thinks he has seen one.

rhyme (noun and verb) In general, two words that have same-sounding endings but different beginnings. It arises when two words at once sound similar and different. It is principally governed by sound, though it is linked to how words appear on the page (EYE RHYME is based on sight over sound). ASSONANCE (vowel-REPETITION) and CONSONANCE (consonant-repetition) cannot constitute rhyme alone, but the presence of both together does: e.g. swaggering/staggering; craft/daft; cake/opaque; parade/displayed. It usually occurs at line-endings and creates structure (through RHYME SCHEMES) in STANZAS and poems. INTERNAL RHYME (within lines) is also common, and rhyme is not restricted to poetry, though it is most closely associated with it. Rhyme is also taken to mean a complete rhyming poem, or any type of verbal echo (more like a chime).

Rhyme is central to the English poetic tradition, though BLANK VERSE (unrhymed IAMBIC PENTAMETER) and FREE VERSE are both important non-rhyming verse forms. The use of set rhyme schemes generally became less common by the second half of the twentieth century onwards, and more experimental when it was used. Because it has such rich traditions behind it, apparent from such venerable forms as the SONNET, BALLAD, LIMERICK, and RHYME ROYAL it is sometimes considered conservative. However, as with any literary feature, its effect depends entirely on how it is used. Admittedly, it does create a degree of artifice in a poem, and can lead to awkward word-choices to fit the rhyme scheme. Yet this is more about how rhyme has been used, rather than what it is. Subtle and fluent rhyming is shown brilliantly in this thirteen-word poem by Samuel Menashe:

I lie in snows
Drifted so high
No one knows
Where I lie

Rhyme is a basic form of REPETITION, which offers a wide variety of options in lending structure and EMPHASIS to poetic utterances. It is ultimately related to the word RHYTHM, but the two are distinct (though often complementary): prose and poetry always have some sense of rhythm, whereas rhyme is optional and almost always deliberate.

There are numerous forms of rhyme, though in English PROSODY there is no agreed terminology. FULL (or PERFECT or true) RHYME is what most would consider a standard rhyme: bear/scare. NEAR (or HALF-, SLANT or PARA) RHYME covers anything that is less than a full rhyme, and is often used with subtlety and ingenuity. RIME RICHE (rich rhyme) is a fuller-than-full rhyme, not so common in English, in which initial consonants are also identical (e.g. kissed/cost). Types of rhyme can be distinguished by the number of syllables involved: SINGLE (or MASCULINE) RHYME involves one syllable (e.g. bat/flat; away/stray); DOUBLE (or FEMININE) RHYME involves two (e.g. outrageous/contagious); TRIPLE RHYME three (e.g. 'battery/flattery'). Position within lines is another way: ARCH-RHYME (a CHIASTIC *abba* pattern); BROKEN RHYME (a word split between two lines to rhyme); CROSSED RHYME (within two consecutive lines); LEONINE RHYME (middle and end of line); MOSAIC RHYME (when one of the rhymes is spread over more than one word); TAIL RHYME (in short lines at stanza-end). MONORHYME is a sequence of lines with the same rhyme. The existence of all these forms, and combinations with ASSONANCE, CONSONANCE, shades of different meaning, LINEATION and other aspects of writing (particularly poetry) show how flexible and varied use of rhyme can be in different situations, and that its effects can't be easily predicted, or disregarded.

rhyme royal A STANZA with seven lines of IAMBIC PENTAMETER (five stresses and ten syllables) that rhyme *ababbcc*. Its creation is attributed to Geoffrey Chaucer, who used it in various works. Rhyme royal was picked up by various later writers, particularly in the ELIZABETHAN period: both Edmund Spenser (*The Ruines of Time*) and William Shakespeare (*Rape of Lucrece*) wrote in rhyme royal. This stanza from Chaucer's *Troilus and Criseyde* (3.1744–1750) is both shapely and fluid:

> Love, that of erthe and se hath governaunce,
> Love, that his hestes hath in hevene hye,
> Love, that with an holsome alliaunce
> Halt peples joyned, as hym lest hem gye,
> Love, that knetteth lawe of compaignie,
> And couples doth in vertu for to dwelle,
> Bynd this acord, that I told you and telle.

rhyme scheme The pattern of RHYMING line-endings in a POEM or STANZA. It is typically indicated by assigning a lower-case letter to each rhyme, and noting down the fixed pattern: e.g. *abab* for QUATRAIN; *ababcdcdefefgg* for SHAKESPEAREAN SONNET. Sometimes the number of syllables per line is also given: e.g. a stanza in COMMON MEASURE could be notated *a8b6c8b6*. Rhyme schemes are comparable to musical time signatures: both provide essential information about the basic structure of a verse form, and both are chosen to evoke a particular atmosphere, and are disrupted or varied for effect.

rhythm (**adj. rhythmic/rhythmical**; Greek, 'to flow') The patterns created by BEATS occurring at regular intervals. In literature, it refers to the musical quality created by sequences of stressed and unstressed SYLLABLES. These patterns are usually more structured in VERSE, and take the form of a fixed METRE. Some poetic forms (particularly FREE VERSE) and all PROSE ones do not have such systematic arrangements of beats. In these cases, general rhythmic features can still affect meaning. Forms of REPETITION (e.g. ANAPHORA and ALLITERATION) can create their own rhythm. Rhythm can only be detected by using your ears when reading. It requires skill and practice to hear rhythmic effects, and these usually come more easily to those with musical experience. FALLING RHYTHM, SPRUNG RHYTHM and CADENCES are specific forms of poetic rhythm.

riddle A short piece that asks its audience to guess its subject from a series of clues. The riddle is a traditional and global form of literature. The major literary examples in English are the set of Old English riddles recorded in the Exeter Book, where the answers include 'shield', 'swan', 'bible' and private body parts.

rime riche (ream-reash; French, 'rich rhyme') The matching up of two words, not just on identical middle vowels and ending (as in FULL RHYME), but in an earlier consonant or syllable in the words too. In English, examples are often HOMONYMS (same names): HOMOPHONES (same sound) such as bear/ bare and for/ four and homographs (same spelling) like lead/lead (a metal/ 'guide someone') and recreation/ recreation ('have fun'/ 'create again').

rising rhythm A metrical pattern in which unstressed syllables sound like they are moving towards a stressed syllable. It helps sweep the line along, and is far more common than its opposite, FALLING RHYTHM. It is associated with IAMBIC and ANAPAESTIC metres, though the substitution of TROCHEES/DACTYLS and word-placing can disrupt the effect. Although it arises from the METRE, it is not a formal pattern: it is a general aspect of RHYTHM that needs to be heard by the reader.

role A part played by a ACTOR in a play. The role involves bringing to life a CHARACTER as written in the script. In a DRAMATIC CONTEXT, 'role' and 'character' are similar in meaning, with role being perhaps preferable when the part is small (such as third sentry) and doesn't really involve much CHARACTERIZATION. There's no need to spell role with a circumflex in English ('rôle').

roman à clef (French, 'novel with a key') A prose narrative in which fictional CHARACTERS represent real-world individuals. It is sometimes done for satirical effect or to distance the AUTHOR from the text's meaning. It is sometimes AUTOBIOGRAPHICAL; e.g. the description of a girl's mental breakdown in Sylvia Plath's *The Bell Jar* (1963) is usually read as a key for the AUTHOR'S own condition.

roman-fleuve (French, 'river-novel') A series of separate novels that flow into one another, by following in sequence and sharing the same SETTING, CHARACTER and THEMES. An awkward term because it involves distinguishing between a set of related novels and a single novel published in several parts. For example, Marcel Proust's *À la recherche du temps perdu* (*In Search of Lost* Time,1913–27) isn't really a *roman-fleuve*; its seven parts are generally considered a single, extremely long novel.

romance A narrative that describes a sequence of adventures in an imagined landscape. Romances bear little direct relation to everyday life, and have always been written for entertainment (they are to an extent ESCAPIST). Romance differs from EPIC in that it concerns personal emotion, is more EPISODIC, DIGRESSIVE and is lighter in TONE, as opposed to the more serious EPIC themes of heroism, nobility and nationhood. Homer's *Odyssey*, which tells of Odysseus' struggle to return home after the Trojan war, has been described as the first romance.

MEDIEVAL CHIVALRIC ROMANCES are important examples in the European tradition; these particularly focus on matters of COURTLY LOVE and questing knights, and was BURLESQUED by Miguel de Cervantes' *Don Quixote* (1605). The PICARESQUE NOVEL shares many features of romance, and the term has come to describe an ever-broader range of literature: PROSE FICTIONS involving adventures driven by the PROTAGONIST'S passionate devotion for a single cause; any literature that is highly imaginative and plot-driven (similar to FANTASY); and any writing that concerns love (a form of GENRE FICTION). In addition, Shakespeare's last plays are known as 'romances' because they feature improbable events and happy coincidences in imagined settings. An unrelated meaning of 'romance' to mention is in reference to European languages derived from Latin, such as French, Spanish and Italian.

romantic comedy A vague term for a play that combines elements of love and humour. It's no different from the PORTMANTEAU word 'romcom', and only useful as a name.

romantic irony A form of STRUCTURAL IRONY that provokes self-conscious thoughts about a FICTIONAL work. It stresses the AUTHOR'S freedom from the limits of the fiction being created. Rather than being immersed in the fictional world, the reader is forced to reflect on reality. This destroys the WILLING SUSPENSION OF DISBELIEF, and often exposes the transitory, unstable nature of the world. Despite its name, romantic irony is used by earlier writers like Cervantes and Shakespeare. Lawrence Sterne's *Life and Opinions of Tristram Shandy* (1760) contains many internal features that achieve such an effect: its erratic page-numbering interferes with the experience of reading so it creates a discrepancy between thinking about reading the book, and just reading the book. Like other forms of IRONY it suggests deeper truth beyond the simple appearance of things.

romanticism (adj. romantic) A set of ideas about literature that promotes the individual artist's feeling and IMAGINATIVE powers. 'Romanticism' is a very general term, but represents an approach to writing literature that is still influential today. It argues for the importance of SUBJECTIVE expression and creative ORIGINALITY that arises naturally from the writer's emotions. It countered the ENLIGHTENMENT preference for RATIONALISM, OBJECTIVITY and impersonal truth, and sought reality in the natural world.

Romanticism developed in the late eighteenth century out of earlier ideas like SENSIBILITY (which associated sympathy and civility), the SUBLIME (an indescribable higher truth) and idealist philosophy. A key thinker was the political theorist Jean-Jacques Rousseau, who was writing around the 1750s to 1770s. Rousseau made the radical suggestion that a civilised education does not improve individuals but makes them more prone to cruelty and wickedness, because it takes them further away from their natural state of goodness—whereas, ever since Thomas Hobbes' *Leviathan* (1651) the general feeling had been that human instincts needed to be restrained. Rousseau's ideas helped along the French Revolution, while for literature it suggested that passionate expression and a return to nature could be the source of simple but awe-inspiring truth. As an ABSTRACT set of ideas, romanticism is in a binary opposition with NEOCLASSICISM—see this entry for discussion of this TENSION.

The great romantic poets grew up in this climate of ideas, and developed a radical literature to match. William Wordsworth explored beauty, memory and honesty of everyday language in his poetry, while John Keats used the terms 'NEGATIVE CAPABILITY' and 'EGOTISTICAL SUBLIME' when describing the sources of intense emotional encounters. Lord Byron's chaotic lifestyle provided a model of the maverick, temperamental Romantic poet. William Blake could be described as a early Romantic: certainly the visionary aspects of his prophetic poetry indicate his tremendous poetic freedom. As well as LYRIC POETRY, romanticism influenced prose writing: GOTHIC NOVELS explored instinct and mystery in a Romantic spirit. Emily Brontë's *Wuthering Heights* (1847) is a good example of this. Romanticism led to widespread changes in how CONVENTIONS, GENRES and POETIC DICTION were perceived. American TRANSCENDENTALISM arose out of romantic ideas, and the PRE-RAPHAELITES took a romantic interest in artistic beauty to an extreme. Literary REALISM (and NATURALISM) sought to bring literature back to real world in the late nineteenth century.

The adjective 'romantic' is used to describe any writer who displays an affinity to romanticism, regardless of historical period. William Shakespeare, for example, has often been said to possess a romantic turn of mind. It's easy to see that 'romantic' as in 'lovey-dovey' also describes an expression of feeling, but be aware than in literary criticism the term has much wider CONNOTATIONS. It isn't used to discuss the ROMANCE GENRE; 'romance' is both noun and adjective in this case.

rondeau (Old French *rond*, 'round') A three-STANZA poem, usually OCTOSYLLABIC and containing only two RHYMES. The first two words act as a REFRAIN. A *rondeau redoublé* consists of six quatrains, in which each line of the first stanza recurs in order as the first line of the following stanzas. Rondeaus were most popular in sixteenth-century France. Rondeau is a type of ROUNDELAY and a ROUNDEL is an English variation. Charles Algernon Swinburne has done most with the form in English.

roundelay A simple SONG (LAY) intended for dancing, normally with a REFRAIN and with accompanying music. Most popular in EARLY MODERN France: RONDEAU and VILLANELLE are the commonest forms.

Russian formalism An influential critical movement in the early twentieth century, particularly associated with Roman Jakobson, that developed methods for looking at the FORM of POETRY and other literary texts. It's similar to American-style formalism (i.e. NEW CRITICISM), but developed separately to it. Russian formalists were interested in LITERARINESS: what it is that makes literary writing special. Concentrating on poetry, they analysed STYLE, FORM, SYNTAX, FIGURATIVE LANGUAGE and other components of literature to show how it made writing strange to the reader. Viktor Shklovsky named this process 'DEFAMILIARIZATION'. Formalism stresses that sensitivity to language is essential to literature, and that as readers we should approach literature differently to everyday texts. This does not mean that literature exists on a higher plane, in the same way that the idea of POETIC DICTION often implies. Language has different FUNCTIONS when found in a literary CONTEXT. In literary works the reader is equally aware of *how* something is being said as *what* is being said. This FOREGROUNDING of language is essential to literariness.

These ideas grew out of linguistic work, and remained a fairly scientific approach to literature. Its rigour is one of its key strengths: it taught Western readers to look harder at literary texts. Mikhail Bakhtin's ideas grew out of Russian formalism (see 'dialogic criticism' and 'heteroglossia', for example), and it was a foundation for later studies of POETICS and NARRATOLOGY.

S

saga Prose EPIC narratives that belong to the ORAL LITERATURE of MEDIEVAL Scandinavia, and were later written down. Sagas related the stories of great HEROES and royal dynasties. The term was picked up to describe other works that describe different generations of a single family in a large-scale work; John Galsworthy's multi-volume *Forsyte Saga* (1906–21) is the clearest example of saga in this broader sense.

sarcasm (Greek, 'sneering') An exaggerated use of IRONY used to criticise something directly. Known as the 'lowest form of humour' it is more common in everyday speech than literature. It is usually obvious through the speaker's INTONATION. It is used skilfully by such literary writers as Charles Dickens.

satire (noun; satirize (verb); satirical (adjective); Horatian, Juvenalian, Menippean) A composition that pokes fun at individual or social failings. It holds up an unflattering mirror to something in the world. It's a literary GENRE, but is just as often an element within a larger non-satirical work. Satire is defined more by TONE than any formal or stylistic device, though it often involves ludicrous imitation (PARODY, BURLESQUE, LAMPOON, TRAVESTY). It requires the existence of a moral standard, such that the AUTHOR can point out flaws and suggest corrections.

Satire has diverse forms, but is typically divided into direct and indirect satire. Direct satire occurs when a first-person speaker/narrator ridicules the subject; indirect satire is everything else. Many verse satires are direct, and can be described according to their VOICE: **Juvenalian satire**, named after the Roman poet Juvenal, is savage and aggressive in condemning failure; **Horatian satire**, by contrast, is gentler and more amused at idiocy observed. Indirect satire is anything else, and often involves a sequence within a larger narrative, such as Jonathan Swift's *Gulliver's Travels* (1726), though MOCK EPIC poetry is indirect satire throughout. A particular kind of indirect satire is **Menippean satire** (named after a Greek philosopher whose works are now lost) in which different speakers and GENRES are mixed together to discredit a single VIEWPOINT. This use of 'satire' is close to the term's Latin ETYMOLOGY, *satira*, meaning 'medley' (though it has often been confused with 'SATYR'). A Menippean satire is learned, disordered, COMIC and a mixed bag of curious material. Robert Burton's *Anatomy of Melancholy* (1621) and Lewis Carroll's *Alice in Wonderland* (1865) were both identified as Menippean satires by Northrop Frye, the critic who reintroduced the term in the 1950s.

Satire has always been dominated by male writers (like most forms), and perhaps this continues to be the case. In the twentieth century, satire has become a wider cultural form, and there are few exclusively satirical literary works produced, except for light verse and writing that is specifically protesting against something. Nonetheless it is an important way in which literary writing is directly relevant to the real world, and though it's often topical, satire often identifies faults that are common to all ages, and does so in an original, COMIC manner.

satyr play A lively and humorous DRAMA performed in Ancient Greece. A satyr is half man, half goat, and associated with male lust. Satyr plays were performed as AFTER-PIECES or COMIC RELIEF to a trilogy of TRAGEDIES, and all four plays were written to be performed together at a drama festival.

saying A brief phrase that is commonly used, such as an ADAGE, APHORISM, APOPHTHEGM, PROVERB, maxim, dictum or axiom. For something so short, there are many different terms. This book lists numerous alternatives on page 350, all of which have potential literary value as felicitous combinations of FORM and CONTENT.

scansion (verb, to scan; Greek, 'to climb') The detection and description of metrical forms line-by-line. When scanning a passage, a basic starting-point is to mark stressed and unstressed syllables above the lines. There is no agreed system of marking: stressed are often marked x, –, •, ´ or / and unstressed o, ○ or –.Whichever you use, it needs to be able to be used quickly and clearly when reading. DIACRITICS (which mark pronunciation and ACCENTS) are also useful. You can mark CAESURAS and line breaks with a | sign. Then try to identify the dominant FOOT (if there is one), and count how many appear in the line.

Once you have identified a line as, for example, IAMBIC PENTAMETER, you should then scan other lines to see if this general pattern is maintained, and to start observing subtle differences that occur in the metre at particular points; for example, if a TROCHEE or SPONDEE is substituted, and whether a line is CATALECTIC or HYPERMETRICAL. In short, it is not enough to say that a metrical pattern is regular and then ignore it: scansion is about observing metrical effects that arise from that basic pattern. Having identified the basic trend, scansion (like other forms of PROSODY) is about seeing how this enriches your reading of a poem. Some poetry, such as FREE VERSE, does not SCAN, but in those cases you can still be attentive to RHYTHMIC features that arise.

The following extract from William Wordsworth's *The Prelude* (1850 version) has metrical interest for the different ways that the basic iambic pentameter pattern is adapted to depict the movement of a kite (e.g. 'pull', 'high', 'impetuous' 'dash'd headlong'):

> —Unfading recollections! at this hour
> The heart is almost mine with which I felt,
> From some hill-top on sunny afternoons,
> The paper kite high among fleecy clouds
> Pull at her rein like an impetuous courser;
> Or, from the meadows sent on gusty days,
> Beheld her breast the wind, then suddenly
> Dash'd headlong, and rejected by the storm.
>
> (I.491–98)

scapegoat A central concept in the writing of the French intellectual René Girard that has been applied to literary criticism. A scapegoat was originally an animal cast out into the wilderness, carrying the sins of a community; its popular meaning (someone blamed for others' faults) comes from this. Girard argues that cultures are created from such violent sacrifices. This is even more worrying in light of Girard's other major concept, mimetic desire, which states that our wishes are imitations of others'. So finding scapegoats and committing violent acts against them is a means to gain power for ourselves. This process has been observed in Greek TRAGEDIES, and Girard himself wrote a book (called *A Theater of Envy* (1991)) about all the places this occurs in William Shakespeare's works. It has been associated with numerous other literary works, and has been fused with PSYCHOANALYTIC CRITICISM (see also 'abjection').

scenario An outline or SYNOPSIS of a DRAMATIC work. It introduces the CHARACTERS and STORY, but is separate to the final product. A scenario can be instantly recognisable if it reworks familiar situations and STOCK CHARACTERS.

scene A division in a DRAMATIC work. An ACT is made up of individual scenes, though some plays are divided into scenes only. Scene changes can be indicated in various ways: change of location and/or scenery; the entrance or exit of CHARACTERS (see 'act'); or the lowering and raising of the curtain in the PROSCENIUM ARCH. It is more helpful to give act, scene and line numbers when quoting from dramatic works than the page numbers of the particular EDITION used.

scheme (Greek, 'form') A RHETORICAL term for FIGURE, often used to refer specifically to 'figures of speech' that rearrange word-order for effect without altering the meaning. The term is sometimes contrasted with 'TROPE', and this alternative is used more often.

science-fiction (sci-fi) A prose narrative established in the twentieth century that imagines a future world (on earth or elsewhere), and combines FANTASY with realistic, scientific description. CYBERFICTION concentrates on relations between humankind and machines. It stretches the imagination to contemplate the future, and often presents a UTOPIAN or DYSTOPIAN vision. All the same, it's usually classed as GENRE FICTION, and in many cases science-fiction is read for entertainment.

scholasticism A MEDIEVAL form of theological and philosophical research, based on traditional methods of ANALYSIS in which scholars reinforced existing truths. RENAISSANCE HUMANISM called for a more passionate, personal response to religious texts, and led the term 'scholasticism' to have its current, negative CONNOTATIONS.

screenplay A film-script, which also includes instructions about shooting the film (MISE EN SCÈNE). It never means the finished film.

self My CONSCIOUS mind, which is capable of SUBJECTIVE judgment and has existence in a body. The opposition of self and OTHER common in PSYCHOANALYTIC CRITICISM, and the status of the AUTHOR are good places to start thinking about the self's place in writing literature. The limitations of PERSONAL CRITICISM and its alternatives are a starting point for thinking about the self as READER.

self-fashioning A term coined by the American critic Stephen Greenblatt to describe the process of creating an identity, as explained in his seminal work of NEW HISTORICISM, *Renaissance Self-fashioning* (1980). The term refers particularly to practices associated with RENAISSANCE HUMANISM, all of which show how cultural CONVENTIONS (such as those described in COURTESY BOOKS) and DISCOURSES determined the formation of public PERSONAS. A sound education in literature was an essential requirement, and this ties in with the new historicist interest in how literature, history and power structures intersect. The term has been used more widely since, but remains associated with Greenblatt's original usage.

self-reflexive Something that consciously turns attention back on itself. In literature, a self-reflexive work may have the AUTHOR as a CHARACTER, may reflect on the process of composition, or may describe a work contained in another work (called *MISE EN ABYME*, which describes the work written within the work, which describes the work…). It questions the nature of the FICTIONAL world by supplying the VIEWPOINT of the AUTHOR'S reality, which is often shared by the reader.

Self-reflexive MODES of writing are associated especially with POSTMODERNISM, given its tendency to get wrapped up in problems about identity, representing reality and the nature of FICTIONAL truth. Yet self-reflexive and introspective writing has been around for much longer. It is easy to become preoccupied with self-reflexive language, particularly in poetry. There is a (not particularly good) piece of exam advice that says 'if you're not sure what a poem's about, then it's probably about writing poetry'. This isn't a great back-up plan for literary appreciation, but it makes the point that self-reflexive writing and reading can end up becoming a cold intellectual exercise. In extreme cases it becomes unproductive, with the paralysed writer unable to feel or communicate anything to the wider world beyond SOLIPSISTIC, self-conscious thoughts.

semantics (adj. semantic) The meanings of words. Together with SYNTAX (arrangement of words), PHONOLOGY (forming sounds) and MORPHOLOGY (forming words) it creates a language's GRAMMAR, and thus makes communication possible. The adjective's semantic meaning is 'concerning meaning': for example, there is semantic AMBIGUITY in the phrase 'I shot a parrot' because it could mean shooting with a camera or a gun.

semicolon (pl. semicola, semicolons) A PUNCTUATION mark (;) indicating a pause stronger than a comma (,) but weaker than a COLON (:). It divides CLAUSES in PERIODIC SENTENCES, and in modern English usually separates clauses that lead directly on from the main CLAUSE, without simply emphasising its point. 'He knew the lemon was bitter; nevertheless, he took a big bite.' Some writers avoid them, while others use them very frequently. Confusingly, the different senses have separate plural forms: 'semicola' for rhetorical clauses, but 'semicolons' for punctuation marks.

semiotics The study of how meaning is created from systems of SIGNS, which initially owed much to the principles and methods of STRUCTURALISM. It examines the relation of SIGNIFIERS and SIGNIFIED, and identifies the CONVENTIONS that govern their relation. Semiotics is interested in the cultural and linguistic GRAMMARS that control meaning. Roland Barthes is a notable figure associated with semiotics, and it is worth noting that he shifted towards POST-STRUCTURALIST ideas later in his career. Semiotics ranges across literature and other cultural forms. Barthes once wrote about Roman noses in films, for example. He pointed out that when spectators see an ACTOR with a prominent nose, they immediately make the connection that he is supposed to be Roman. The nose is not representing reality—it matches our conventional belief about what a Roman's nose should look like. The nose is a sign controlled by CONVENTION.

Senecan tragedy TRAGIC DRAMA written or influenced by the Roman AUTHOR Seneca. It was probably a form of CLOSET DRAMA (i.e. for recital rather than performance), and consequently contains dialogues and SOLILOQUIES that are sometimes highly rhetorical and HYPERBOLIC. It is also in Senecan tragedy that the five-act structure is first found, which gradually became a consistent feature of EARLY MODERN DRAMA. Senecan tragedies were being read in Renaissance Europe, even when Greek tragedies (which are better known today) were not. It influenced two GENRES of sixteenth-century English DRAMA: ACADEMIC DRAMA and REVENGE TRAGEDY. Thomas Sackville and Thomas Norton's *Gorboduc* (1561) is acknowledged as the first English tragedy, and is Senecan in FORM and CONTENT.

sensation novel A best-selling type of PROSE FICTION in late Victorian England, which contained dark, shocking subject-matter that dealt with criminal acts in a domestic setting. Wilkie Collins' *The Woman in White* (1859) was one of the first sensation novels, and remains popular today.

sensibility The ability to have an emotional reaction to something, as opposed to rational or intellectual. The term has become synonymous with 'sensitivity' in everyday speech, but it has a couple of uses specific to LITERARY CRITICISM. T.S. Eliot used the term to mean the capacity to feel, which Eliot believed had been successfully combined with intellectual thought by METAPHYSICAL POETS; since Milton, however, poets had separated or 'dissociated' feeling from their thought (see 'dissociation of sensibility').

Its other use pertains to a concept in the eighteenth and nineteenth centuries, as found in the title of Jane Austen's *Sense and Sensibility* (1811). In the previous decades it was thought civilised to feel EMPATHY and SYMPATHY, and this was even associated with a literary SUBLIME. This was partly a reaction to Thomas Hobbes' argument in *Leviathan* (1651), which argued that men were naturally violent, and felt no compassion towards each other. Sensibility and sympathy were proposed as the natural means to create a functional society. Crying was very much in fashion during this period, which is reflected in the literary GENRES now known as the LITERATURE OF SENSIBILITY, SENTIMENTAL COMEDY and SENTIMENTAL NOVEL. 'SENTIMENTAL' now suggests excessive emotion, whereas 'sensibility' remains a more neutral word for the same.

sentence A complete statement. It is defined either as containing a SUBJECT, VERB and OBJECT, or as beginning with a capital letter and ending in a full-stop. Before 1700 the PERIOD was the standard unit, and so it is more accurate to speak of PERIODIC SENTENCES. Obvious differences are that periodic sentences are usually longer, and punctuated differently to the modern sentence.

sententia **(pl. *–ae*;** Latin, also English **'sentence')** A wise thought or maxim. It is a SYNONYM for 'APHORISM' or 'SAYING', and is particularly associated in English with HUMANIST writers who borrowed from CLASSICAL sources. 'Sententious' is the related adjective, and tends to have a negative meaning: it describes someone very keen to display his or her moral goodness by giving patronising advice.

sentimental Characterized by strong feeling (sentiment). In the eighteenth century, sentimentality was commended as civilised and noble for the same reasons that SYMPATHY and SENSIBILITY were. Since that time, the term has come to imply indulgent emotion, often CLICHÉD. Like 'MELODRAMA', the term contains an element of judgment, and so is one to use carefully. Some CULTURAL CRITICS would argue that sentimental romances or tear-jerkers today should not necessarily be considered inferior to 'high' culture because they appeal to our feelings rather than thoughts (compare also with ESCAPIST).

sentimental comedy A form of eighteenth-century COMIC DRAMA in which virtuous people struggle against wickedness. It was a gentler, more moral successor to RESTORATION COMEDIES OF MANNERS. Sentimental comedies contain plenty of PATHOS, and encourage audiences to feel SYMPATHY towards the CHARACTERS. Because of this, its characters are fairly 'FLAT', and the PLOT usually contains numerous twists to create a happy ending. It was influenced by the emerging sense that SENSIBILITY was what held society together, and this made it virtuous to feel compassion and shed tears.

sentimental novel An eighteenth-century form of PROSE FICTION that portrays honourable individuals triumphing against cruelty and vice.

Samuel Richardson's *Pamela* (1740) is a story of great PATHOS, which describes (through letters) poor Pamela's battles against Mr B.'s advances. It was swiftly PARODIED by Henry Fielding's *Shamela* (1741), which mocks *Pamela*'s straight-laced morals and makes its point with IRONY and BATHOS. However, the sentimental novel stayed popular because it was aligned with the socially conservative view that SENSIBILITY and sympathy were virtuous characteristics: a person who knew how to cry was civilised. This is taken to an extreme in Henry Mackenzie's *A Man of Feeling* (1771), in which the PROTAGONIST repeatedly bursts into compassionate tears. A taste for tears can also be found some early GOTHIC NOVELS.

septet (also **heptastich**) A seven-line STANZA. RHYME ROYAL is a named variation of septet, but they appear in various other forms across literary history: e.g. in Robert Browning's *A Lover's Quarrel*.

serenade A song sung at night beneath a lover's window. It's also used in the title of numerous musical works that have no words.

sestet The final six lines of a SONNET (see this entry for common rhyme schemes), which is preceded by an OCTAVE. Although you could try referring to other six-line verse forms as sestets (e.g. SESTINA), it will usually be assumed that you're talking about a sonnet. The octave and sestet are essential divisions in sonnets, and it is always worthwhile exploring how the two parts relate.

sestina A sophisticated verse form, consisting of six six-line STANZAS with the same six words used to end each line, which are rearranged between stanzas according to a strict pattern. That pattern is (if each word is numbered): 123456; 615243; 364125; 532614; 451362; 246531; 531 or 135. The end-words do not usually rhyme. The sestina concludes with a three-line stanza (an ENVOI) that contains all six words, with three at line-ends. It is worth seeking out an example of a sestina: some notable examples are Rudyard Kipling's 'Sestina of the Tramp-Royal' and W.H. Auden's 'Hearing of Harvests'.

setting The place and time where a DRAMA is imagined to have happened, which is described onstage using scenery, costume, and PROPS. It is narrower in meaning than *MISE EN SCÈNE*, which suggests a director's conception for the performance. 'Setting' sometimes holds a more general sense of ATMOSPHERE and TONE.

sexuality studies An interdisciplinary field that spans medical sciences, social sciences and humanities to examine conceptions of sexual orientation, and its interaction with race, class, gender, nationality, religion and other aspects of identity. GAY AND LESBIAN CRITICISM, GENDER CRITICISM and QUEER THEORY are aspects of sexuality studies particular to literature.

Shakespearean sonnet (also **English sonnet**) A fourteen-line poem in IAMBIC PENTAMETER (SONNET) containing three QUATRAINS that rhyme *abab* and a rhyming COUPLET to finish. Its rhyme scheme can be summarised as: *abab cdcd efef gg*. The final couplet is particularly distinctive: it marks the turning-point of the poem, and is often a form of EPIGRAM. Its name is due to its association with William Shakespeare's sonnets, but Thomas Wyatt and Henry Howard, Earl of Surrey were using the form well before Shakespeare did. The reason for its departure from the PETRARCHAN SONNET, it is thought, is that the Italian form was difficult to compose in English, where rhyming words are harder to find. The SPENSERIAN SONNET is a sophisticated variation on the Shakespearean sonnet that links together the quatrains through rhyme.

short measure A STANZA form consisting of four LINES (a QUATRAIN) with three stresses (TRIMETER) in each line. Its RHYME scheme is usually *abab*, and sometimes *abcb*. It is mostly used to describe METRES in HYMNS; see 'quatrain' for a comparison with COMMON, LONG and POULTER'S MEASURES. POULTER'S MEASURE is sometimes called 'short measure', in which case short measure becomes 'half measure'.

short story A brief prose NARRATIVE that is published alongside other stories or within a magazine. Short stories vary as much in subject-matter as novels do. Certain kinds of short story can be identified by their FORM, TONE or purpose: e.g. PARABLE, FABLE, *FABLIAU* and TALE. It became an important literary form around the MODERNIST period. Short story writers struggle to receive equal publicity as novelists: they don't generally sell as well, perhaps because they require more concentration and it's difficult to become so engrossed or familiar with the CHARACTERS. There are, however, writers especially celebrated for their short stories, including Elizabeth Bowen (e.g. *The Demon Lover and Other Stories* (1945)) and Alice Munro (*Selected Stories* (1996)).

sibilance REPETITION of hissing consonant sounds for effect. It is a form of ALLITERATION based on the sound indicated most often by 's', though 'c' ('century'), 'z' ('zephyr'), 'sh' ('shush') and 'ch' ('chateau') also create sibilance. Whether its effect is more like a whisper, a threat, rustling leaves or something else depends upon the meaning of the passage within which it is found.

sic **(Latin, 'thus')** A term placed in brackets after a word or phrase to confirm that it has been spelt accurately, particularly if it looks like it contains an error. It clears up doubt when unsure whether a quotation originally contained a GRAMMATICAL or spelling error, or has been quoted incorrectly. For example, here is Vladimir Nabokov discussing butterfly names in *Speak, Memory* (1967): 'a butterfly, *Parnassius phoebus golovinus* (rating a big *sic*), has been described by Dr Holland'.

sigla Letters used as an ABBREVIATION, particularly as used by editors to indicate different manuscripts consulted.

sign A mark, object, IMAGE, GESTURE or similar that conveys information. A sign has a specific, unambiguous meaning. Signs possess meaning through CONVENTION (waving to greet someone) or a causal link (dark clouds are a sign of rain). They differ from SYMBOLS in that a sign's existence is connected to its fixed meaning (or signification), whereas a symbol has an open-ended, independent meaning. A 'stop' *sign* exists to give a specific message (i.e. 'stop!'), while a flag is *symbolic* of a nation and its values. There is a field of literary studies, SEMIOTICS, devoted to the study of signs. Two basic principles in the literary study of signs are: the STRUCTURALIST division of signs into SIGNIFIER (doing the expressing) and SIGNIFIED (being expressed); and the idea that the connection between signifier and signified is determined by CONVENTION, not nature (see 'metaphor'). Signs gain meaning from their relation to other signs. Critics, especially DECONSTRUCTIONISTS, would be quick to point out that signs are unreliable carriers of meaning, and that they conceal or distort meaning. For such critics signs only gain meaning from the social and cultural circumstances in which they are found (see 'post-structuralism' for more about this).

signified/signifier Two terms that describe both parts of a SIGN, as defined by Ferdinand de Saussure. The signified (*signifié* in French) is the concept being represented, and the signifier (*signifiant*) is the form that the sign takes. So the word 'bird' is a signifier, and the signified concept is an actual flying creature with feathers. When describing METAPHORS, 'VEHICLE' is an alternative term for signifier, and 'TENOR' for signified. In everyday speech, the speaker uses the signifier to stand in for the signified concept, so that 'bird' is the name for a bird. This might seem obvious; however, Saussure argued that the connection between signifier and signified was arbitrary. For Saussure, the word 'bird' is just a sound that has no inherent connection with actual birds: language is not natural, but is built upon CONVENTION (see 'metaphor' for more on this point). This encouraged literary critics to explore just what these social and cultural CONVENTIONS are, and how they affect literature. Saussure's SYNCHRONIC analysis of language (i.e. language at one point in time) was paired with an interest in STRUCTURES—in other words, the ordered systems (*LANGUE*) that create meaning. The distinction between signifier/signified remained important to POST-STRUCTURALISTS who contested this view, and remains an essential principle in SEMIOTICS (the study of signs). The ideas leading from these terms have led to such developments as DISCOURSE ANALYSIS and Lacanian PSYCHOANALYTIC CRITICISM (see 'symbolic order').

simile A TROPE that draws a comparison between two things, indicated by the use of 'like' or 'as'. Simile is more explicit than METAPHOR, but more tentative in its claims: simile suggests things are alike, whereas metaphor suggests they are identical in some way. Though similes are found in everyday speech ('he's as deaf as a doorpost') it still has the same literary feel as other TROPES: e.g. Mohammed Ali's line 'I float like a butterfly, I sting like a bee' is partly so memorable because it sounds poetic. An EPIC SIMILE is an extended, digressive simile. Here is an elegant and PARADOXICAL simile from the start of Henry Vaughan's 'The World (I)':

> I saw eternity the other night
> Like a great ring of pure and endless light,
>   All calm as it was bright [....]

simulacrum (pl. –ca; Latin 'similarity, likeness') A sign or symbol that represents something else, without having all the qualities of the original. The POSTMODERNIST critic Jean Baudrillard describes simulacra as imitations that have no original. He argued that culture consists of representations that have no basis in reality: we are living an illusion.

sincerity The act of being honest or sincere. It is an awkward critical term, and should be used with caution. This is partly because AUTHORS continually use shades of IRONY and other TROPES that twist meaning, and add shades of COMEDY or CRITICISM. It's also hard to distinguish between the authorial PERSONA, IMPLIED AUTHOR and the actual author. A narrator could be being insincere, but the actual author may be making a sincere point.

single rhyme (also **masculine rhyme**) A rhyme based on one stressed, RHYMING syllable: e.g. law/ claw; moan/ telephone. It is the commonest form of rhyme, and creates heavy, decisive line-endings (see also 'heavy ending'). DOUBLE (FEMININE) and TRIPLE RHYME apply to two- and three-syllable rhymes. See 'feminine/masculine' for more about those terms.

single-moulded line A line of VERSE that is independent in METRE, SYNTAX and SENSE from those around it. In other words, an END-STOPPED LINE that is also preceded by one.

situational irony A form of IRONY involving an outcome different from that anticipated by the deluded or misinformed CHARACTER. It is a basic ingredient of DRAMATIC IRONY, TRAGIC IRONY and SOCRATIC IRONY. Sophocles' Oedipus is the CLASSIC example: his realisation that he is his father's murderer is a stunning reversal (*PERIPETEIA*) that he is unprepared for. Situational irony is sometimes thought identical in meaning to STRUCTURAL IRONY; the difference is that situational irony concerns events within the works, while STRUCTURAL IRONY provokes questions about the surface appearance of the whole work.

Skeltonics An irregular and irreverent verse form, as used by John Skelton (a Tudor poet who was also Henry VIII's tutor). It has no strict METRICAL pattern, but Skeltonic lines are short, with only two or three stresses (i.e. are DIMETER or TRIMETER), bursts of rhyming words (MONORHYME) and parallel CLAUSES (PARALLELISM). It verges on DOGGEREL (i.e. clumsy and artless verse), but has a higher critical reputation than that association would suggest. Skelton's poetry is certainly worth seeking out, and here's a short sample, taken from 'Philip Sparrow' (c.1500):

> I wept and I wailed,
> The teares down hailed,
> But nothing it availed
> To call Philip again,
> Whom Gib, our cat, hath slain.
> Gib, I say, our cat
> Worrowed her on that [bit]
> Which I loved best. (ll. 23–30)

sketch A quick composition that doesn't offer much development in PLOT, CHARACTER or IDEAS. In DRAMA, sketches are often COMIC (some TV comedy shows are entirely sketch-based). In PROSE, a sketch is a brief piece that doesn't contain enough NARRATIVE to be described as a SHORT STORY. Charles Dickens' early work *Sketches by Boz* (1833), for example, outlines a selection of scenes and individuals encountered in daily life.

slam poetry PERFORMANCE POETRY recited at a competitive event (a poetry slam). Usually the performer has a stage, a microphone, and (hopefully) an audience but nothing else. It is a dynamic, fun and popular form of poetry that is both admired and criticised by scholars. Delivery, GESTURE and presentation count for as much as the words do, as they do for most forms of oral literature. Experiencing slam poetry is a good reminder that literature isn't restricted to libraries: it's something to be passionate and noisy about.

slang Very informal language that is usually particular to one social group. It often includes NEOLOGISMS for concepts that have no suitable term in existing language, or imaginative alternatives for common ideas: e.g. 'skint', 'broke' and 'potless' are all slang equivalents of 'penniless'. It also includes coarse or offensive language, which makes slang dictionaries an exciting read. Slang is sometimes created by literary writers, and sometimes finds its way into popular language. This happens when a term is useful or unique enough and is picked up by the national media, before eventually finding its way into dictionaries: a word like 'chav' no longer seems such a slang term now that it has an *OED* definition: 'In the United Kingdom (originally the south of England): a young person of a type characterized by brash and loutish behaviour and the wearing of designer-style clothes (esp. sportswear); usually with connotations of a low social status.' Slang is innovative and dynamic, but loses its force as it is repeated in different CONTEXTS. For example, Cockney RHYMING slang remains a distinctive IDIOM, but it is hardly understood by giving the age-old examples of 'dog and bone' for 'phone' and 'apples and pears' for 'stairs': it needs to be heard as it is used on the streets of London today.

Invented slang takes the reader more deeply into the CHARACTER'S world at the beginning of Anthony Burgess's *A Clockwork Orange* (1962). Equally, Burgess tries to make everything easy for the reader to understand by including parenthetical glosses (if you know some Latin, because 'viddy' comes straight from the Latin verb 'videre' meaning 'to see'). The reader has to make less effort as a result:

> The four of us were dressed in the heighth of fashion, which in those days was a pair of black very tight tights with the old jelly mould, as we called it fitting on the crutch underneath the tights, this being to protect and also a sort of design you could viddy clear enough in a certain light, so that I had one in the shape of a spider, Pete had a rocker (a hand, that is), Georgie had a very funny one of a flower, and poor old Dim had a very hound-and-horny one of a clown's litso (face, that is) [....]

slant rhyme A lesser-used alternative term for NEAR RHYME (or HALF-RHYME): i.e. two words containing identical sounds, but dissimilar vowels and endings (unlike FULL RHYME).

slapstick Physical COMEDY, as found in numerous cultural forms across history: e.g. MORALITY PLAYS (in the VICE figure), COMMEDIA DELL'ARTE and silent cinema.

slave narrative A PROSE FICTION relating an individual's life of slavery and subsequent escape. Numerous African-American slave narratives were written in the eighteenth and nineteenth centuries, and the crucial early work published in Britain was explicitly AUTOBIOGRAPHICAL: *The Interesting Narrative of Olaudah Equiano* (1789). Equiano was an early figurehead for the abolition movement, and many later slave narratives were also DIDACTIC.

soap opera A popular TV DRAMA shown a set number of times in the week. It is often MELODRAMATIC and PLOT-DRIVEN. Even if it doesn't suit close literary ANALYSIS, it's a form of DRAMA encountered by millions of people on a daily basis, and so makes an obvious subject for CULTURAL CRITICISM.

socialist realism A style of artwork promoted in Stalinist Russia, particularly during the 1930s. Its purpose was to glorify the working classes' daily fight for a socialist revolution against the bourgeoisie. It was a reaction to other forms of realism in art (like naturalism and modernism) that were complicated, and seen as aimed at the comfortable middle classes. Socialist realist art was supposed to show three types of spirit: *partynost* (party-spirit), *narodnost* (national spirit) and *ideynost* (ideological spirit). All this puts its function as PROPAGANDA beyond doubt. Socialist realism has very little to do with MARXIST CRITICISM.

sociology of literature The study of literary works within their direct social CONTEXT. Audience and circumstances of publication and/or performance are two obvious areas of interest. It is opposed to the NEW CRITICAL method of treating the text as a self-contained object. MARXIST CRITICISM, FEMINIST CRITICISM and other approaches sharpened the sense of a sociology of literature. NEW HISTORICISM differs by rejecting 'literature' as a special category, and instead treating texts of all kinds together. 'SOCIOLOGY OF TEXTS' is a related concept in bibliographic studies. It argues for treating each version of a work as worthy of study because it was created for good reasons within a particular CONTEXT.

sociology of texts A term from BIBLIOGRAPHIC STUDIES attributed to D.F. McKenzie that describes historical study of how texts are produced and disseminated. Rather than study a literary work as being timeless—and use COLLATION methods to produce an ideal text—the conditions within which a work emerged (its 'sociology') are relevant to reading that work. This is especially relevant to EARLY MODERN texts, but has broader theoretical implications. It is a rebuke to NEW CRITICISM and FORMALISM, which emphasised the intrinsic meaning of a text. By stressing the relevance of historical CONTEXT, it is akin to NEW HISTORICISM, but is otherwise completely separate: 'sociology of texts' treats books as historical documents, but tries to enhance interpretation of those texts, not learn more about society in general. In the second decade of the twenty-first century, the 'sociology of texts' is widely held to be a useful principle to keep in mind.

Socratic irony A form of SITUATIONAL IRONY found in Plato's dialogues. Socrates habitually feigns ignorance and asks simple questions that expose the flaws in his interlocutor's argument. Socratic irony professes to reveal truth rather than create subtle rhetoric (as VERBAL IRONY does). It is close to the original (ETYMOLOGICAL) meaning of 'IRONY', 'pretended ignorance'. The term remains attached more to philosophical than literary writing.

solecism (Greek, 'speaking incorrectly') A slip made when speaking or writing, particularly as it exposes the ignorance of the person making the error. It can be used deliberately by literary writers to expose a flawed side to CHARACTERS, either savagely or sympathetically. Thomas Browne describes them as inevitable when speaking of the divine:

> I remember I am not alone, and therefore forget not to contemplate him and his attributes who is ever with mee, especially those two mighty ones, his wisdome and eternitie; [...] for who can speake of eternitie without a solœcisme, or thinke thereof without an extasie?
>
> (*Religio Medici*, I.11)

soliloquy (pl. soliloquies; so-**lill**-oh-kwee; Latin 'speak alone') A speech delivered when a CHARACTER is alone onstage (or being overheard). It has its roots in Roman theatre, and was taken up by EARLY MODERN dramatists in a big way, though it has generally been less popular since then. It allows CHARACTERS to communicate their thoughts and motivations to an audience directly. There is no set rule on whether ACTORS should acknowledge the audience's presence. Richard III's opening soliloquy in

Shakespeare's EPONYMOUS play could be voiced to himself, or spoken to the audience, which is what Ian McKellan does in the 1995 film version by looking to camera. Instead of using this CONVENTION, a more naturalistic option available to dramatists is to use a CONFIDANT who asks the character questions. These options alter the way we hear the speech:

> Now is the winter of our discontent
> Made glorious summer by this son of York;
> And all the clouds that low'r'd upon our house
> In the deep bosom of the ocean buried.
> Now are our brows bound with victorious
> wreaths,
> Our bruised arms hung up for monuments,
> Our stern alarums chang'd to merry meetings,
> Our dreadful marches to delightful measures [....]
> (ll.1–8)

solipsistic (Latin, 'lone self') Based on the belief that only the self and self-consciousness exist. It is a term in general use, and can describe writers who are immovably self-centred, and whose writing often leads to OBSCURITY as a result. Unskilful SELF-REFLEXIVE writing runs a risk of being solipsistic, and thus being of little interest to other readers.

song A poem intended to be sung, chanted or otherwise set to music. A basic literary form with roots in ORAL LITERATURE: EPIC, ODE, BALLAD, MADRIGAL, ANTIPHON and ANTHEM are all forms of song. LYRIC POETRY literally means poetry accompanied by a lyre (see also 'lyric'), but has taken on a general sense of all poetry spoken from a personal VIEWPOINT. Songs are not always intended to have musical accompaniment, and it's worth bearing CONTEXT in mind: e.g. songs in ELIZABETHAN DRAMA probably would have been set to music, but Thomas Wyatt's songs are early examples of poetry that stand alongside his SONNETS. Songs also provide great examples of interaction between music and literature. There are many musicians who write both words and music, from John Dowland (a seventeenth-century lutenist) to Bob Dylan (a contemporary singer-songwriter), and other composers have set words to music: e.g. Franz Schubert's *Winterreise* (1827) is a setting of twenty-four poems by the poet Wilhelm Müller. These are all examples from Western culture, but the song cuts across cultures and historical periods: it is one of very few global literary forms.

sonnet (Italian, 'song') A CONVENTIONAL form of LYRIC POEM containing fourteen lines in IAMBIC PENTAMETER (in English) and a set rhyme scheme.

Here is a summary of the major rhyme schemes (See separate entries for fuller descriptions):

Name	Rhyme Scheme
PETRARCHAN	*abba abba cde cde* (or *cdc cdc*)
MILTONIC	*abba abba* (SESTET variable)
SHAKESPEAREAN	*abab cdcd efef gg*
SPENSERIAN	*abab bcbc cdcd ee*

Each type is named after its best-known practioner. With the exception of the Miltonic sonnet, a major SONNET SEQUENCE was written in each form by the authors in question: Petrarch's *Il Canzoniere* (c.1374), *Shakespeares Sonnets* (1609) and Edmund Spenser's *Amoretti* (1595). The terms are not restricted to these poets: e.g. the pioneering Thomas Wyatt and Henry Howard, Earl of Surrey were writing 'Shakespearean' sonnets over fifty years before Shakespeare was; Philip Sidney's *Astrophel and Stella* (1591) is a seminal sonnet sequence that uses the same form. William Wordsworth adapted the Miltonic sonnet, and numerous other nineteenth- and twentieth-century poets have used and adapted the sonnet as a CLASSIC literary form: e.g. George Meredith wrote sixteen-line sonnets; Gerard Manley Hopkins wrote CURTAL SONNETS with only ten-and-a-half.

If you come across a fourteen-line English poem, the chances are that it is either a SONNET or at least acknowledges the sonnet tradition. The rhyme scheme and structure will reveal itself during the poem, and this will make it easy to track the poem's development: what happens within each QUATRAIN (four lines), the OCTAVE (the first eight lines) and the SESTET (the final six)? Does a turning point occur at the octave/sestet division? How does the end relate to the start? What variations are there on the iambic pentameter? The sonnet in its most CONVENTIONAL form is about personal love, but this has been adapted ever since John Donne's *Holy Sonnets*. Sonnets are in no way predictable: all that can be said is that choosing to use sonnet form produces expectations that a poet may satisfy or subvert.

sonnet sequence (also **sonnet cycle**) A series of connected SONNETS (fourteen-line poems). The collection will concentrate on a single theme (usually love) that is developed and explored from different perspectives. The CANONICAL sonnet sequences in English were written during the ELIZABETHAN period, when sequences about PLATONIC LOVE were written by Edmund Spenser, Philip Sidney, Samuel Daniel and Michael Drayton amongst others. See the above entry for major sequences that use each sonnet form.

speech act theory A philosophical interpretation of language-use created by J.L. Austin that identifies three categories of utterance. A locutionary act makes a statement or describes something (this is also called a connotative expression): 'There's a bird sitting on your head.' An illocutionary act performs some function by speaking, such as a threat, promise, command, question or wish (also called PERFORMATIVE): 'Watch out—there's a bird on your head!'; 'Is that a bird on your head?'; 'I wish a bird would sit on your head!'. A perlocutionary act uses speech to create some other effect; e.g. surprise, persuasion or alarm: 'Seriously, there's a bird on your head!'

These ideas have mostly found their way into LITERARY CRITICISM through DISCOURSE ANALYSIS, which examines closely the purposes and rules that guide communication. Some DECONSTRUCTIONISTS like the idea that language is a set of performances that don't necessarily hold any meaning. More broadly, it raises the question of what exactly poets are trying to achieve by writing a poem.

Spenserian sonnet A variation on the SHAKESPEAREAN SONNET that links together QUATRAINS through RHYME by making the last line of each quatrain rhyme with the first line of the next. The pattern that emerges is: *abab bcbc cdcd ee*. The nine-line SPENSERIAN STANZA *ababbcbcc* is effectively a shortened version of the sonnet form. Unsurprisingly, the best examples occur in Edmund Spenser's SONNET SEQUENCE *Amoretti* (1595).

Spenserian stanza A VERSE FORM consisting of eight lines with five stresses (IAMBIC PENTAMETER) and a final line with six (an ALEXANDRINE) that rhymes *ababbcbcc*. Edmund Spenser used the form throughout the *Faerie Queene* (1590, 96), and it was revived by the ROMANTIC poets in the early nineteenth century. It is similar to the OTTAVA RIMA, but the Spenserian stanza is uniquely adaptable: in particular, it is worth paying attention to PUNCTUATION in order to observe the different ways of structuring the stanza.

spondee (adj. spondaic) A METRICAL FOOT consisting of two stressed syllables (– –). Many English compound words are naturally spondaic: e.g. 'forcefield', 'sweetheart'. In English PROSODY it is used for variation within a BINARY METRE; i.e. it substitutes for an IAMB or TROCHEE. A dispondee is two spondees together: four stressed BEATS in a row.

spoonerism Switching consonants (usually initial) of different words, often for COMIC effect. 'Flutterby' for 'butterfly' and 'this food is nearly rice' instead of 'the food is really nice' are both spoonerisms.

The term is named after the Reverend William Spooner (1844–1930), who probably didn't use as many spoonerisms as he is credited with: the *Oxford Dictionary of National Biography* thinks that classics like 'you have hissed my mystery lectures (missed my history lectures)' were made up by his students.

sprung rhythm Gerald Manley Hopkins's term for his METRICAL system based on ACCENTUAL VERSE; i.e. the number of STRESSES per line. It sought to allow the energy of everyday speech to 'spring' out from the predictable stresses of common English metres (which he called running rhythms). Each stressed syllable in sprung rhythm can be followed by a number of unstressed syllables, from none to three. Hopkins described this in terms of FEET, of which four are possible: monosyllable (–), TROCHEE (– o), DACTYL (– o o), or first paeon (– o o o). Sprung rhythm can create remarkable and passionate VERSE, as in the final four lines of Hopkins's 'Pied Beauty' (the ACCENTS are Hopkins's own):

> Whatever is fickle, frecklèd (who knows
> how?)
> With swíft, slów; sweet, sóur; adázzle,
> dím;
> He fathers-forth whose beauty is pást change:
> Práise him.

Sprung rhythm was based on, but is different from, Old and Middle English ALLITERATIVE METRE. It influenced numerous twentieth-century poets, such as T.S. Eliot and Dylan Thomas.

stage A performance space, sometimes containing scenery and props. There are various types of stage, the main ones being those with a PROSCENIUM ARCH, THEATRE IN THE ROUND and THRUST STAGE. The director Peter Brook discusses the power of the bare stage in his book, *The Empty Space* (1968). Its first two sentences set the tone:

> I can take any empty space and call it a bare stage. A man walks across this empty space whilst someone else is watching him, and this is all I need for an act of theatre to be engaged.

stage business A specific on-stage action that is necessary for the plot. In *Hamlet*, for example, the accidental exchange of weapons in the final Hamlet/Laertes showdown (Act 5, Scene 2) is a tricky, but essential, piece of stage business to carry out.

stage direction A description within a play-text about an aspect of performance: e.g. movement, acting, speaking, entrances/exits, or SETTING. Some stage directions are embedded in the text: in this section from William Shakespeare's *Titus Andronicus*, the writing makes it so obvious what happens after Titus's first speech that no stage direction is needed:

Titus Die, die, Lavinia, and thy shame
with thee,
And with thy shame thy father's
sorrow die!
Saturninus What hast thou done, unnatural
and unkind?
Titus. Kill'd her for whom my tears have
made me blind. (5.3.46–49)

In ELIZABETHAN DRAMA stage directions are usually concise, and have often been added later. Such directions record how the play has been performed, rather than stating the dramatist's wishes. Some dramatists favour detailed directions (like Tennessee Williams and George Bernard Shaw), while others provide very few. Either way, stage directions are always worthy of consideration—but only if the stated AUTHOR is known to have written them. Even if he or she didn't, stage directions are still important for putting aspects of performance at the front of the reader's mind.

stanza (Italian, 'room') A group of LINES that appears as a separate structure within a POEM. A stanza is normally marked on the page by having blank lines either side of it. Stanzas are often rounded off by making the final word of a stanza rhyme with another. They can be described according to the number of lines they contain, FEET per line, RHYME scheme, METRE or LINEATION. Poems are not always divided into stanzas, and some poems use different stanza forms (the terms STROPHE or VERSE PARAGRAPH is sometimes used for irregular stanzas). The term stanza is sometimes reserved for groupings of four lines (QUATRAINS) or more, but for convenience, the list on page 348 includes COUPLETS and TRIPLETS. When identifying stanzas, it is always worth asking why a poet has chosen to use a particular stanza, and what effect it has on the poem's meaning.

stichic (Greek, 'line-based') An adjective describing lines of VERSE that follow the same METRICAL pattern but are not divided into STANZAS. BLANK VERSE is the most common example in English verse. Stichic verse can be divided into VERSE PARAGRAPHS.

stichomythia (Greek, 'line speech') A rapid dialogue in alternate verse lines (or HEMISTICHS), often involving competition or interrogation. REPETITION and ANTITHESIS (opposites) are commonly found in stichomythic exchanges. It is often found in Ancient Greek drama, where stichomythia builds towards resolution in a longer speech known as stasis. It is found occasionally in EARLY MODERN DRAMA too, and has a close relative in AMOEBEAN VERSE.

stock character A CHARACTER that is familiar to the audience because it follows the CONVENTIONS of a GENRE. Stock characters are common in DRAMA (e.g. Volpone in Ben Jonson's EPONYMOUS play is easily recognised as the old miser character), and appear in PROSE as CARICATURES or TYPES. The Roman COMEDY writer Plautus created numerous stock characters that survived in later literature; e.g. the clever servant and lecherous old man are carried over into ELIZABETHAN COMEDY. The term implies that such characters are FLAT and underdeveloped, but they are standard part of writing for a popular audience, and show writers working within literary TRADITIONS.

stock response A reaction to a work that is routine, unoriginal and suggests shallow engagement with the text. Some works encourage such a response, and it's worth asking how far readers' expectations influence a reading, and how this changes over time (see 'horizon of expectations' and 'reader-response criticism' for more). A stock response to Jane Austen's *Pride and Prejudice* in the twenty-first century might be to read it as an early work of chick lit., without also considering the humour, IRONY or social observation that makes the work such a CLASSIC.

story A set of events that provides material for a literary work. FABLE, TALE and PARABLE are three traditional kinds of story. A PLOT is an arrangement of a story into a NARRATIVE form, which could involve several kinds of alteration: shifting the story's order of events (through FLASH-BACK or beginning *IN MEDIAS RES*); relocating the story to a different SETTING (see 'adaptation'); or modifying details of the story. SHORT STORIES are, generally speaking, more concerned with single events than plot development (as in a NOVELLA). Stories can be told in every MEDIA form, including NOVEL, radio play, cinema, or improvised out loud. NARRATOLOGY offers a theoretical perspective on how stories are created.

stream of consciousness The continual flow of an individual's thoughts. In literature, it refers to a MODE of narration that presents a CHARACTER'S emotions, perceptions, memories, fears, reasoning and/

or associations. Stream of consciousness gives the impression of tapping directly into someone's mind, even though the process of communicating unspoken thoughts through the MEDIUM of language inevitably modifies those ideas in the transfer.

Stream of consciousness is intimately linked in critical DISCOURSE with INTERIOR MONOLOGUE, but there is little agreement about their precise relation. One way to approach the two terms is to think of stream of consciousness as providing the raw material for interior monologue. It permits sophisticated and fluent CHARACTERIZATION, relatively freed from CONVENTION. Interior monologue, then, is one method of communicating stream of consciousness on the page, and FREE INDIRECT DISCOURSE is another. It is associated with MODERNIST prose writers, although the term was around in the nineteenth century and pertains to numerous works written after the Second World War. Stream of consciousness requires readers to have discipline and sensitivity to shifting frames of reference (e.g. when someone is thinking or speaking aloud, or a different narrator speaks). Such writing cannot be skim-read, and initially requires patience while the reader becomes comfortable with its RHYTHMS and the often dense and rapid accumulation of ideas. Here is an extract from Virginia Woolf's *To the Lighthouse* (p. 76, Penguin edition) that needs to be read slowly:

> Years ago, before he had married, he [Mr Ramsey] thought, looking across the bay, as they stood between the clumps of red-hot pokers, he had walked all day. He had made a meal off bread and cheese in a public house. He had worked ten hours at a stretch; an old woman just popped her head in now and again and saw to the fire. That was the country he liked best, over there; those sandhills dwindling away into darkness. One could walk all day without meeting a soul. There was not a house scarcely, not a single village for miles on end. One could worry things out alone.

stress The EMPHASIS placed on a syllable by pronouncing it with more intensity than those that surround it. It is basically an alternative term for ACCENT, but is usually used more specifically to describe emphasis given by the RHYTHM or METRE of a passage. In English PROSODY, most VERSE (which is ACCENTUAL-SYLLABIC) has a set number of stressed and unstressed syllables in a line. For SCANSION, then, it is important to be able to recognise stressed and unstressed syllables, and see how they form regular units called FEET. Note that 'stressed' and 'unstressed' are slightly misleading terms, because all words are given some stress when spoken; it would be more accurate to talk about 'strongly stressed' or 'weakly stressed' syllables.

strophe (**strow**-fee; Greek, 'turning') An alternative term for STANZA. It often specifically refers to divisions in FREE VERSE (also known as VERSE PARAGRAPHS). The term's original meaning is the first part of a Greek choral ODE, which was followed by an ANTISTROPHE with the same METRICAL pattern. It is sometimes used to describe the structure of an ode in English; e.g. PINDARIC ODE.

structural irony A form of IRONY that causes the audience to become conscious of the FICTIONAL quality of the work. It disrupts the audience's WILLING SUSPENSION OF DISBELIEF. It is often brought about by an UNRELIABLE NARRATOR, such as the rational economist of Jonathan Swift's *A Modest Proposal* (1729) who argues that Irish children should be sold to rich Englishmen to relieve Ireland's poverty and overpopulation. Readers catch on that they are meant to question the work because of Swift's use of irony. COSMIC IRONY and ROMANTIC IRONY are usually cited as species of structural irony.

structuralism An intellectual approach that examines systems of SIGNS, CONVENTIONS and cultural codes as they produce meaning. Its roots are in European LINGUISTICS, but it has branched out into literary studies in general and other fields like anthropology. Structuralism identifies the underlying rules from which language and culture are constructed. Its central contention is that texts never exist in isolation. This is because the connections between SIGNIFIERS (the actual word) and SIGNIFIED concepts are arbitrary: words only gain meaning in relation to others. It follows that the arrangement of objects into structures makes language meaningful. Saussure used *LANGUE* to describe the total system of language that generates individual speech acts (*PAROLE*). In particular, binary oppositions or TENSIONS give definition to ideas: e.g. 'white' means something because it is contrasted to black. Structuralists prefer to speak of TEXTS rather than WORKS because 'texts' conveys the network of connections involved, rather than an individual's labour.

Structuralism is central to the history of twentieth-century LITERARY CRITICISM. It was a reaction to the strand of MODERNIST thought that focused on psychological turmoil, and the dissolution of cultural standards—though T.S. Eliot's views on TRADITION is a precursor of structuralism, and some find that James Joyce's *Ulysses* is a STRUCTURALIST work. SEMIOTICS arose as a separate branch of structuralism devoted to the study of signs, while NARRATOLOGY developed as the study of NARRATIVE structure in works. Structuralism is also linked to ARCHETYPAL CRITICISM (and some forms of PSYCHOANALYTIC and MARXIST CRITICISM) in that it searches for the deep patterns controlling human behaviour and society. In arguing that texts are created from outside forces, structuralism contributed to the so-called 'DEATH OF THE AUTHOR', which brought attention onto the reader's role. In the 1960s structuralism began to give way to what became POST-STRUCTURALISM. Post-structuralism holds that it is impossible to identify individual structures: there is only a collection of different VOICES and DISCOURSES that imprint themselves on the individual's mind. DECONSTRUCTION and DISCOURSE ANALYSIS prospered as structuralism crumbled.

structure The ordering of a work's elements as they are held together in a complete whole. Structure is the concrete arrangement of a work into a PLOT, ARGUMENT, STANZAS, ACTS and SCENES, SENTENCES or other elements. FORM usually describes the more ABSTRACT intellectual shaping of a work. The status of structure was a key battle-ground in twentieth-century literary theory. The NEW CRITICS found that structure and TEXTURE are the two fundamental elements of literary works. FORMALIST critics also placed weight on structure, as it creates UNITY and makes a work AUTOTELIC (self-contained). Meanwhile, STRUCTURALIST critics believe that meaning is created from systems of SIGNS, and that these signs take meaning from their position in relation to others. POST-STRUCTURALISTS suggest this model of structure and meaning is too simple.

style The manner in which someone speaks, writes or performs. It describes *how* someone communicates, as opposed to *what* is communicated (CONTENT). DICTION, SYNTAX, REGISTER, PUNCTUATION, INTONATION, VOICE, use of FIGURES (see p. 344) and other DEVICES are all aspects of style; however, 'style' is such a comprehensive idea that it is impossible to describe all the features of someone's style. STYLISTICS is an approach to style based on linguistics. More specific to literature, RHETORIC is essentially a systematic attempt to describe possible ways of using language for effect, and covered everything—even avoiding the use of rhetorical FIGURES was known as the 'plain style'. It heavily influenced EARLY MODERN notions of style, and continues to provide useful terms for discussions of style. It is generally held that style and CONTENT are ultimately inseparable, and that this union is particularly clear in literature.

There are various ways to describe and classify style. Many terms connected to style are associated with an individual or group. Individual AUTHORS often have styles attributed to them: 'CICERONIAN', 'HOMERIC', 'SPENSERIAN' and 'Shakespearean' are widely used, as are terms like 'Dickensian', 'JOHNSONIAN' and 'Joycean'. Some historical periods and groups have styles associated with them, such as AUGUSTAN, VICTORIAN or METAPHYSICAL; certain DISCOURSES or groups also have a recognisable style: e.g. scientific, journalistic, legalistic ('legalese'), academic or management-speak all have specialist styles with their own JARGON.

In some cases, it's more helpful to specify which aspect of style is meant, rather than speaking vaguely about a shared style. This particularly applies when using very general terms, NEOLOGISMS, and author names. The term 'Shakespearean', for example, will mean something slightly different to anyone who's ever experienced a Shakespeare play or poem. There is a risk that grouping names together under a single heading will emphasise one shared aspect (such as time period, or purpose), and will pass over what makes an individual writer unique. Broad discussions of style are meaningless if not accompanied by a precise sense of what a style actually involves. In this sense, it can be preferable to focus on more technical terms, such as 'APHORISTIC', 'FORMULAIC', 'PARATACTIC' or 'HYPOTACTIC'. There remain many other adjectives that express what it is that a style conveys. Some terms carry some critical baggage (e.g. 'GROTESQUE' and 'BAROQUE'), but other adjectives can be just as useful: e.g. 'eerie', 'energetic', 'exacting' and 'elaborate' to name but four. Such adjectives allow a reader to be specific about a style without being weighed down by critical history.

The often-heard distinction between high/ grand, middle and low styles has its origins in CLASSICAL literature, and was revived in the Renaissance. It is based on a class-based sense of DECORUM, namely that the work's style should reflect its subject-matter: high style involves EPIC or TRAGIC narratives about HEROES and the nobility; low style involves SATIRE, FARCE and COMEDY featuring the lower classes. When a writer like Milton consciously creates a 'GRAND STYLE'—complete with such feature as LATINATE language, HYPERBATON and lengthy PERIODS—he selects a style fitting for a poem about the Fall. He is certainly gesturing to the great EPIC AUTHORS in using it. The three styles are a key example of literary DECORUM: i.e. the idea that certain styles and subject-matters belong together. Decorum was important to the NEOCLASSICISTS, but was superseded by the ROMANTIC idea that style is an expression of the individual. Most readers today find that a style is artificial if it is pure IMITATION. A superficial style is one that does not appear to be conveying any meaning. This returns us to the idea that style is unique to each writer, and it's extremely difficult to describe its effects in full—despite all the terms used in connection with style and its CONVENTIONS (see p. 343).

stylistics The application of LINGUISTIC principles and terminology to analyse literature. Where linguistics typically focuses on small units and details, stylistics looks at larger patterns—though without the interest in social CONTEXT that DISCOURSE ANALYSIS has. Stylistics is more scientific than most literary CRITICISM, and contains a technical vocabulary that makes it hard for the novice to understand (and hard to summarise here). See page 345 for a basic list of linguistic terms relevant to literature. The relation of literature to everyday speech, SPEECH ACT THEORY and STRUCTURALISM are all relevant to stylistics.

studies Used to describe an interdisciplinary area of research that combines insights from the humanities, social sciences and natural sciences. LITERARY CRITICISM has participated fully in this movement towards greater interaction between disciplines, particularly after the very theoretical and often inward-looking research in the 1970s. So GENDER CRITICISM is part of gender studies, GAY AND LESBIAN CRITICISM belongs within SEXUALITY STUDIES, CULTURAL CRITICISM (also CULTURAL MATERIALISM) is a specific part of CULTURAL STUDIES, ECOCRITICISM is part of GREEN (CULTURAL) STUDIES, and TEXTUAL CRITICISM is part of BIBLIOGRAPHIC STUDIES. This type of work is particularly useful in helping LITERARY CRITICISM learn from other areas of research and vice versa.

subaltern (Latin, 'under-other') A person of inferior rank, once used to describe junior British colonial officers, but taken up by POSTCOLONIAL CRITICS and others as a term for the suppressed voices of a colonized people. Gayatri Chakravorty Spivak made notable use of the term in her ESSAY 'Can the subaltern speak?' (1988), which argued that Western intellectuals should not try to speak for subalterns, and that no country has a single voice only: all individuals should be left to speak for themselves.

subgenre A specialised grouping within a larger GENRE: e.g. CAMPUS NOVEL and *BILDUNGSROMAN* are subgenres of the NOVEL. As with GENRE, there is no fixed arrangement of GENRES and subgenres. It can be useful to establish a hierarchy of traditions that a work is responding to, because it can help the reader be specific about the large- and small-scale traditions bearing on a work.

subject The person or thing doing/being whatever is indicated by a VERB. The noun naming the subject is in the nominative CASE.

subjective (subjectivity) Related to an individual's mind and consciousness. It could be said the humanities are concerned with subjective truth: i.e. the opinions, beliefs and personal knowledge that people live their lives by. These truths may be persuasive to other people, but they cannot be proved. Subjectivity expresses itself through feelings, emotions and inner thoughts, which makes LYRIC POETRY, INTERIOR MONOLOGUE and STREAM OF CONSCIOUSNESS natural forms for expressing creativity. Indeed, there may even be a psychological connection between creativity and lying, both of which require us to suspend rational thought.

This focus is sometimes accompanied by scepticism about the possibility of objective truth. Critical movements like POST-STRUCTURALISM, DECONSTRUCTION, HERMENEUTICS and READER-RESPONSE CRITICISM, and many literary writers before them have all taken apart the binary opposition of subjective/objective (which could be rephrased appearance/reality) and shown that our experience of the world is conditioned by language. They argue that a detached VIEWPOINT is impossible: our personal situation restricts and constrains our ability to perceive reality, and introduces a form of BIAS. Critics over history have argued that all 'objective' fact is seen through a subjective lens: everything we know we know because it's thought within the human mind and communicated to others. Even computers are just objects made by humans. This is one argument for how the ARTS and HUMANITIES can be associated with subjective truth without diminishing its importance as an area of research.

This subjective model of truth requires its own serious investigation in the diversity and fullness of human experience, in which everyone's experience is an equally valid form of truth. In other words, some (but not all) literary critics maintain that literature, the humanities and science should be held on equal terms in the human pursuit to understand the world and how we experience it. Although it's only the scientists who will physically change the world we live in, subjectively-orientated ANALYSIS can change the way we think about it, enrich our experience and make us tolerant of viewpoints different to our own. And we would be poorer without this. Equally, this is a particularly subjective definition of 'subjective', and there are lots of other opinions out there. Some other related topics are: AFFECTIVE FALLACY, AUTHOR, DIALOGIC CRITICISM, EMPHASIS, EPIPHANY and ORIGINALITY.

subjunctive A GRAMMATICAL mood for utterances that express a wish or possibility: e.g. 'What if I were?'; 'come what may'. It is rarely found in modern English: INDICATIVE and IMPERATIVE MOODS are more common.

sublime (Latin, 'elevated') Inexpressible beauty in art or nature, on a higher level to ordinary experience. The term was first used in CRITICISM by a writer said to have been called Longinus. Edmund Burke, an eighteenth-century philosopher, drew a distinction between the sublime and beautiful, writing of the delightful awe and horror that the sublime can inspire: 'Whatever is fitted in any sort to excite the ideas of pain, and danger, or is conversant about terrible objects, or operates in a manner analogous to terror, is a source of the *sublime*; that is, it is productive of the strongest emotion which the mind is capable of feeling.' ADYNATON, APORIA and PARADOX are related rhetorical forms. The idea of the timeless and transcendent influenced late eighteenth-century writing, and is said to have contributed to the transition from the AESTHETIC principles of NEOCLASSICISM to ROMANTICISM. Keats wrote of a self-centred, EGOTISTICAL SUBLIME (see also 'negative capability').

subplot A complete story running alongside the main PLOT of a literary work. The subplot often mirrors the plot (often with CHARACTERS of a lower social class), either for COMIC effect or to offer interpretation of the action. The subplot in Christopher Marlowe's *Dr Faustus* (1604) does both: the clowns PARODY the main plot, but also highlight Faustus's folly.

subtext An implicit idea or THEME in written or spoken communication that is never stated. If a child runs up to a parent and says 'You know how kind you are….' there may well be a subtext: the child wants something. Silences and gaps are a usual way of indicating that what is *not* being said may have particular importance. In literary works the effect requires AUTHORS attuned to their audience, and vice versa, since different readers may understand different subtexts if no hints are given. There is also a danger in assuming that a subtext is something very specific, because literature is not usually so clear-cut (see 'theme'). Harold Pinter's plays, such as *The Birthday Party* (1957), are generally thought to have subtexts, since there are no thematic cues in the texts themselves (except for silences).

surrealism A cultural movement that sought to escape oppressive CLASSICAL models of art, and to adapt expressive instincts to create surprising but profound expressions of the unconscious. It seeks liberation among the irrational reality of objects. It began in 1920s Europe, and is primarily associated with visual artists like Salvador Dali. It also had some poetic offshoots, mostly in French, and the notion of AUTOMATIC WRITING is faithful to surrealist tenets by showing how words have an existence beyond their obvious function within sentences. Surrealist traces can also be found in the THEATRE OF THE ABSURD and the works of Samuel Beckett amongst others. B.S. Johnson's *The Unfortunates* (1969), although its direct links to the movement are weak, is an example of a work that could be described as 'surrealist' in a more general sense, though it risks reducing the term to meaning 'experimental' or even 'eccentric'. *The Unfortunates* contains twenty-seven sections that are not bound together, and can be read in any order (except for the first and last).

syllabic verse (syllabics) METRICAL writing in which only the number of syllables (BEATS) per line is fixed. There is no limit on the number of stressed or unstressed syllables per line. Most English verse is ACCENTUAL as well as syllabic: it also has a fixed number of stresses per line (i.e. is ACCENTUAL-SYLLABIC). Unless it is written down, syllabic verse can be difficult for listeners to tell whether a passage really is VERSE, for the RHYTHM may not be apparent. HAIKUS written in English are syllabic, and some poets have experimented with written syllabics; e.g. Dylan Thomas, Marianne Moore and Thom Gunn. Some NEOCLASSICAL writers, like Alexander Pope, were also very careful about the number of syllables per line (though writing in iambic metre). Here is the first stanza of Thomas's 'Fern Hill', written in dreamlike syllabic verse paired with a certain but indistinct rhyme scheme (with HALF-RHYMEs too):

> Now as I was young and easy under the apple
>   boughs
> About the lilting house and happy as the grass
>   was green,
>   The night above the dingle starry,
>   Time let me hail and climb
>   Golden in the heyday of his eyes,
> And honoured among wagons I was prince of
>   the apple towns
> And once below a time I lordly had the trees
>   and leaves
>   Trail with daisies and barley
>   Down the rivers of the windfall light.

syllable (sill-ah-bul) A set of letters that can be pronounced without pausing. A syllable usually contains a vowel with consonant(s) before or after, and can form a whole word or part of one. 'Tab', 'set', 'go' and 'ing' are all syllables. Most English VERSE has a set number of syllables in a line (it is SYLLABIC; though also see 'ACCENTUAL' and 'ACCENTUAL-SYLLABIC' verse).

syllepsis (Greek, 'taking together') A FIGURE, closely related to ZEUGMA, in which one word (a verb or proposition) applies to two others, but only agrees grammatically with one of them: e.g. 'he lost his wallet, and his temper.'

syllogism (adj. syllogistic, sill-**oh**-jizm) An argument containing two propositions that lead to a logically valid conclusion. It takes the form 'if *a* equals *b* and *b* equals *c*, then *a* equals *c*': e.g. 'all good food is homemade and this food is homemade, therefore this is good food.' The deductive logic by which the conclusion is reached cannot be disputed; however, the propositions are vulnerable to attack. It is an important aspect of CLASSICAL thinking, and its influence extends to literary writers like Geoffrey Chaucer and William Shakespeare.

symbol (Greek, 'throw together') A mark, object, IMAGE, GESTURE or similar that is taken to represent something else. Unlike a SIGN, a symbol has a separate existence before its symbolic meaning is attributed to it. A rainbow is a sign that it rained recently, and a symbol of God's benevolence, and, more recently, gay pride. Symbols and METAPHORS both involve taking something from one CONTEXT and applying it to something else; the difference is that metaphors give a specific meaning, but symbols suggest an idea or value that is more open-ended: 'doll' can be a metaphor to suggest someone is youthful and cute ('she's a doll'), or a symbol to suggest innocence, fragility or something else.

Symbols are integral to literature. FIGURATIVE LANGUAGE is allied to symbolic meaning, since both removing language from its regular use to create new meaning. A symbol always needs to be understood in its direct CONTEXT; i.e. whether it exists in the FICTIONAL worlds regardless of its symbolic meaning, or whether it belongs within a series of ALLEGORICAL images. EMBLEMS and PATTERN POETRY use visual symbols in a text. IMAGERY and MOTIFS are of particular interest to various critical groups. Formalists are interested in how symbols generate structure in a poem, and possibly also give an insight to someone's IMAGINATION. PSYCHOANALYTIC critics may examine unconscious meaning brought to the surface by symbols, and POST-STRUCTURALIST critics would show that a symbol's meaning is fluid.

symbolic order A term used by Jacques Lacan to describe an adult's conception of the world, as it is strongly influenced by language. The symbolic element is the presence of SIGNIFIERS, which for Lacan have no essential connection to SIGNIFIED CONTENT. Unlike the infant's IMAGINARY ORDER, the adult draws a clear—but artificial—distinction between the self and the outside world. Lacan argues that our very 'soul' is manufactured from social DISCOURSES: the UNCONSCIOUS is composed of language, and there is ultimately nothing mysterious about it. The REAL ORDER is a worldview that accepts the pervasive influence of social and cultural systems on our lives, but Lacan has little to say about it because he claims that all adults live in the symbolic order. This idea influenced later strands of PSYCHOANALYTIC CRITICISM and has relevance to DISCOURSE ANALYSIS and NEW HISTORICISM.

symbolists A movement in French poetry CHARACTERIZED by a use of SYMBOLS and FREE VERSE (*vers libre* in French) to access a deeper reality beyond ordinary language and experience. Arthur Rimbaud and Stéphane Mallarmé were two leading figures. It was influential on writers in Britain and Ireland, in particular the IMAGISTS, some MODERNIST writers, and W.B. Yeats in particular.

sympathy (**sympathetic**; Greek, 'fellow-feeling') Compassion for other beings or things. Sympathy is the ability to feel for someone's thoughts and fears whilst remaining true to yourself; by contrast, EMPATHY suggests a loss of selfhood. In literature and DRAMA authors often encourage sympathetic feelings in the audience, which is often balanced with ANTIPATHY for a less likeable character (the ANTAGONIST). This approach has a social benefit if it creates considerate, civilised individuals who think of each other's well-being.

Aristotle's concept of *CATHARSIS* envisions sympathy as forming part of an audience's response to Greek tragedy, with the aim of bringing people closer together. Sympathy was a prominent idea in the eighteenth century. David Hume described sympathy as a moral good in his *Enquiry Concerning Human Understanding* (1748), which countered the argument of Thomas Hobbes' *Leviathan* (1651) that men are inherently violent and cruel to each other, and an absolute monarch is the only way to create society. Sympathy is apparent in literature of the period, particularly in works that addressed the related concepts of SENSIBILITY and SENTIMENTALITY. In the twentieth century, Bertolt Brecht's ALIENATION EFFECT was specifically intended to render sympathy and PATHOS impossible, which would break the bourgeois, civilising effect of DRAMA. Some FEMINIST and POSTCOLONIAL CRITICS have pointed out that the sort of sympathy called for in many literary works is between rich white men, which reinforces social discrimination.

The adjective **sympathetic** possesses all these CONNOTATIONS, as in a 'sympathetic portrayal'; however, it is often used in the more general sense of 'kindness'.

synaeresis (Greek, 'drawing together') The merging of two vowel sounds into one vowel or DIPHTHONG. For example, the 'ao' of 'extraordinary' is pronounced as one vowel, and the verb 'beest' is spoken as a single 'ee' rather than a double 'e-e' 'beëst' (a DIAERESIS). Examples in English either come from the natural evolution of language into simpler forms—e.g. 'hour' (as 'ow-uh') often becomes one SYLLABLE ('our')—or to fit words into a METRICAL pattern. Synaeresis is a form of ELISION. It has a similar effect to SYNCOPE, which is the shortening of words by removing letters, not by combining them. A HIATUS is the GAP in pronunciation created when synaeresis does not occur.

synaesthesia (Greek, 'perceive together') A neurological condition in which a real sensation in one of the senses (sight, hearing, touch, taste, smell) creates a imagined perception in another: e.g. letters of the alphabet evoking specific colours, or seeing someone brushing their teeth, and feeling that your teeth are being brushed. Some peoples' brains are naturally disposed to make these connections, and these people are often unusually creative. More generally, 'synaesthesia' describes a deliberate literary strategy of blurring language associated with different senses. It can be thought of CATACHRESIS (strained metaphor), and in some cases a twisted form of ONOMATOPOEIA (e.g. if the sounds of 'aroma' and 'stench' suggest pleasant and nasty smells to you). The following extract from John Keats' 'Ode to a Nightingale' (lines 11–14) becomes increasingly synaesthetic as the speaker reaches out to describe natural unity (he's not talking about eating grass):

> Oh, for a draught of vintage, that hath been
> Cooled a long age in the deep-delvèd earth,
> Tasting of Flora and the country green,
> Dance, and Provençal song, and sunburnt
> mirth!

synchronic (Greek, 'at the same time') A term associated with Ferdinand de Saussure for linguistic study that describes how a language works at one point in time. It is not DIACHRONIC or historical in its approach: it does not examine how languages develop and change over time. The synchronic approach opened up new possibilities for the interaction of

LINGUISTICS and literary CRITICISM. Saussure's notion of SIGNIFIER/SIGNIFIED and LANGUE/PAROLE are influential concepts for literary criticism that came from this approach. It led directly to the rise of literary STRUCTURALISM, which focuses on how systems of SIGNS create meaning.

syncope (Greek, 'cutting short') The removal of letter(s) from the middle of a word when pronounced or written: e.g. 'ne'er for 'never' or 'Nottingham' (pronounced 'Nott-nam'). It is a form of ELISION, a term which is used to describe letter-removal from the beginning or end of words. Both are often used in (ACCENTUAL) VERSE to fit words to the metre.

synecdoche (si-**nek**-dok-ee; Greek, 'taking things together') A TROPE in which something is named by referring to a smaller part of the whole, or (less often) to the larger whole to which the part belongs. As well as part and whole, synecdoche can switch around species and genus or individual and group. Some synecdoches: 'threads' for clothes; 'Yellow Pages' for the telephone directory; 'the West' for countries in the Western hemisphere; 'the law' to mean a policeman. The movie *Synecdoche, New York* (2008) takes its title from a New York warehouse that is made to represent the entire city. The Globe theatre, where most of William Shakespeare's plays were first performed, used the same idea four hundred years earlier.

METONYM is the general term for name-switching, of which synecdoche is one form. Synecdoche is another of those terms (like METAPHOR and ALLEGORY) that is thought by some to be essential to language; this idea is potentially supported by POSTMODERNIST who see disparate parts, rather than well-defined wholes, as being essential to human experience and culture.

synonym (adj. synonymous) A word which has the same meaning as another. 'Cool', 'chilly', 'freezing' and 'nippy' are all synonyms for 'cold'. ANTONYM is the opposite of synonym. Careful use of synonyms creates well-crafted descriptions, but careless use of synonyms suggests the writer has swallowed a thesaurus.

synopsis A summary of an ARGUMENT or PLOT. Synopses can be found in ABSTRACTS or arguments preceding a work, but are more often encountered in critical introductions to a work. A PRÉCIS is a concise summary of the main points. Synopses can be useful short-cuts when encountering a work for the first time. Nonetheless, the old but sensible piece of advice holds true: a summary is no substitute for reading the work itself.

syntax (adj. syntactic) The arrangement of words into sentences. Syntax is an essential component of any language's GRAMMAR, along with MORPHOLOGY (forming words), PHONETICS (voicing words), and SEMANTICS (giving meaning). Sentence construction is of interest to the literary critic: unusual word order (e.g. 'red were his hands') is a basic way to create surprising or striking deviations from normal language. HYPERBATON (see p. 344 for related terms), HYPOTAXIS and PARATAXIS are major variations in syntactic usage.

synthesis (adj. synthetic; Greek, 'putting together') The combination of two things into one. Its opposite is ANALYSIS, which means breaking something down into its parts. It has a more technical meaning in philosophy: it means the DIALECTICAL resolution of a THESIS and antithesis. It has no specific meaning in literary studies, but can be used to describe anything (such as a RHYME scheme or IMAGE pattern) that is artificially created from different elements.

T

tableau (pl. tableaus, tableaux; tableau vivant; French, 'little table, picture') A DRAMATIC still-image, created by having the ACTORS hold a single position. Tableaus normally conclude ACTS or whole PLAYS—the curtain falls while the actors remain still. A similar device is found in films: the frame freezes on the final image as the closing credits come up. A **tableau vivant** is a carefully composed scene involving elaborate costumes and props. A series of such scenes tells a story, and in this form the tableau vivant was a parlour game among the wealthy in the nineteenth century. An example of a tableau comes at the end of Samuel Beckett's *Endgame* (1957). Hamm's monologue winds down into immobility and silence, and finally the ACTOR freezes in a tableau:

> Since that's the way we're playing it...
> [he unfolds handkerchief]
> ...let's play it that way...
> [he unfolds]
> ...and speak no more about it...
> [he finishes unfolding]
> ...speak no more.
> [He holds handkerchief spread out before him]
> Old stancher!
> [Pause]
> You...remain.
> [Pause. He covers his face with handkerchief,
> lowers his arms to armrests, remains
> motionless.]
> [Brief tableau.]
>
> *Curtain*

tail rhyme RHYME found in two or more short lines ('tails') contained within a rhymed stanza of longer lines, particularly at the end. It is among the most common ways to vary line-length within a stanza for effect. It was often used in MEDIEVAL poetry, and is occasionally used by later poets, such as Robert Burns (see 'Burns stanza'), William Wordsworth and Alfred, Lord Tennyson.

tale Something intended for telling. Such STORIES or NARRATIVES are meant to amuse and (often) instruct. Tales take many forms (e.g. PARABLE or FABLE), and are the raw material for many kinds of literature.

tautology (Greek, 'saying the same things') A FIGURE involving REPETITION of the same ideas in different words. It is often used unintentionally in everyday speech, and its literary functions are limited: e.g. 'She's a scoundrel and a rogue'. It is generally something to avoid when writing, because it makes sentences longer, woollier and more convoluted than they need to be (like this sentence). Tautology can also be COMIC, as the CLASSIC Monty Python dead parrot sketch shows. Mr Praline is forcing the pet-shop owner to admit that the parrot he just bought is dead: 'This parrot is no more! He has ceased to be! He's expired and gone to meet his maker! He's a stiff! Bereft of life, He rests in peace! If you hadn't nailed him to the perch he'd be pushing up the daisies!'

tenor A term used by I.A. Richards to describe the SUBJECT of a METAPHOR, as opposed to the VEHICLE. 'SIGNIFIED' has a very similar meaning. In the film *Forrest Gump* (1994), the EPONYMOUS HERO uses the phrase, 'life is like a box of chocolates'. 'Life' is the tenor because the METAPHOR 'box of chocolates' is describing it. Tenor can be used to talk about other FIGURES and TROPES too.

tense (present; perfect; imperfect; future) The form of a verb that indicates when the action takes place. The main tenses are **present** ('I am swimming'; 'I swim'); **perfect** ('I have swum'; 'I swam'); **imperfect** ('I was swimming'); and **future** ('I will swim'). Other tenses include **pluperfect** ('I had swum'), and **future perfect** ('I will have swum').

tension The presence of opposed elements or ideas which hampers interpretation. A CRUX is a particular point of difficulty. All literature involves tension, and one way to begin analysing a text (particularly in PRACTICAL CRITICISM) is to locate a tension and work from there. THEMATIC tensions provide ready-made interpretative frameworks: for example life versus death, innocence versus experience, and appearance versus reality. This last one can be applied lazily to pretty much any literary text. However, it is always best to start with textual evidence, such as rhetorical ANTITHESIS, as is found in the opening lines of Sonnet 6 from Samuel Daniel's *Delia* (1592):

> Faire is my Love, and cruell as she's faire;
> Her brow shades frownes, although her eyes
>   are sunny,

Her smiles are lightning, though her pride
despaire;
And her disdaines are Gall, her fauours Hunny.

The poet deliberately opposes 'cruel' and 'fair' here, but that is the only tension that can be identified with certainty. There is no evidence that Daniel has larger ideas about appearance, innocence or love in mind based on the CONTRASTING elements. Neither Daniel nor any other writer can be assumed to be thinking in terms of larger oppositions, even when a text places two contradictory elements together. A literary text is not simply a VEHICLE for larger philosophical themes. DECONSTRUCTION helped reveal how artificial such binary oppositions are.

Thematic tensions ignore the distance between writer and reader, and the problems of communication this causes. Problems of understanding, or HERMENEUTIC tension, holds more critical potential. Such tension could be formed on a word the reader doesn't understand, a point of OBSCURITY, or another difficulty created by the historical GAP between writer and reader. This approach is ultimately more subtle and more rewarding than proclaiming about lofty ideas. It focuses attention on how meaning is expressed. Such tension is integral to all writing, and raises searching questions about how we communicate.

tercet A set of three lines within a poem. It is sometimes a SYNONYM for 'TRIPLET', but more often applies to lines that do not all RHYME. Tercets are found as *TERZA RIMA* or within SONNET SESTETS, if the six lines are divided into two sets of three. In both cases, the tercet usually rhymes *aba*. The rhymes are eerie in the opening lines of Robert Frost's 'I have been one acquainted with the night' (1928):

I have been one acquainted with the night.
I have walked out in the rain—and back
in rain.
I have outwalked the furthest city light.

I have looked down the saddest city lane.
I have passed by the watchman on his beat
And dropped my eyes, unwilling to explain.

ternary metre (triple metre) A rhythmic pattern (a METRE) based on standard units (FEET) of three SYLLABLES. A ternary metre can be based on DACTYLS or ANAPAESTS (or, very rarely, AMPHIBRACHS/CRETICS). Ternary metres are much less common in English than BINARY METRES are, and if

VERSE appears to have a natural three-beat RHYTHM, it's worth exploring what purpose it serves.

terza rima An Italian verse form consisting of interconnected TERCETS (three-line stanzas) that rhyme *aba bcb cdc* etc.. Dante used it in *The Divine Comedy* and it was picked up by Geoffrey Chaucer, and then Thomas Wyatt. It has been used intermittently since then, often with Dante still in mind, by such poets as John Milton and W.B. Yeats.

tetralogy A group of four works that form a single CYCLE. A trilogy is the equivalent for three works. William Shakespeare wrote two tetralogies of HISTORY PLAYS (see this entry for details).

tetrameter (Greek, 'four measures') A line of VERSE containing four FEET (RHYTHMIC units). It occurs frequently in English verse, particularly in IAMBIC metres. TROCHAIC metres are more often than not tetrameters. Alfred, Lord Tennyson uses this line-length throughout *In Memoriam A.H.H.* [Arthur Henry Hallam]. Each tetrameter QUATRAIN reads like a single, solemn breath:

> I climb the hill: from end to end
> Of all the landscape underneath,
> I find no place that does not breathe
> Some gracious memory of my friend;
>
> No gray old grange, or lonely fold,
> Or low morass and whispering reed,
> Or simple stile from mead to mead,
> Or sleepwalk up the windy wold. (100.1–8)

text (Latin, 'to weave') A basic literary term with various meanings: the main body of a text (as opposed to the PARATEXT, APPARATUS and supplementary materials); a complete book containing a work (e.g. 'a set text'); and words on the page, separate from how they are presented. It can also mean a bible passage selected for reading or discussion. The etymological sense of 'weave' is worth remembering: a text is something that is woven together and has coherence.

There are numerous associated terms that indicate how many critical approaches to the 'text' there are: 'TEXTURE' concerns the effects made by words and images; 'TEXTUALITY' describes the status of being a written work; 'CONTEXT' draws attention to related areas surrounding the text (NEW HISTORICISTS tend to argue that texts and contexts are fluid); 'INTERTEXTUALITY' to the existence of texts within a cultural matrix; 'SUBTEXT' to underlying issues; 'TEXTUAL CRITICISM' to the difficulties in locating authoritative texts; 'COPYTEXT' to selecting a preferred text; 'URTEXT' to earlier versions of a work; 'HYPERTEXT' to the existence of texts in electronic form as well as print; 'SOCIOLOGY OF TEXTS' to the production and reception of texts.

The difference between text and WORK is both contentious and profound. One possibility is that a 'work' (also 'OEUVRE') is the physical process of creation over time, while texts are the various products of that work. Or works could be fixed objects that belong to a certain GENRE and follow CONVENTION, whereas texts are open-ended structures that are not grounded in the same way. Roland Barthes, following this second option, described texts as either READERLY or writerly, depending on how easy it is for the reader to engage with it. POST-STRUCTURALISTS would go further and would deny stable meaning in the text at all; some DECONSTRUCTIONISTS take this idea further still, and argue that all culture is one single text (or DISCOURSE) that cannot be evaded when using language. The image of the text as something woven or web-like is widely used (remember the ETYMOLOGY), and these disagreements reflect widely varying approaches to literary studies. The key questions: How stable are texts? Who or what controls the meaning of texts? How text-centred should we be?

textual criticism A branch of academic literary studies that assesses the different versions of a work, and attempts to establish useful TEXT(s) for the reader. The method of COLLATING texts to generate an 'original' or 'definitive' text is not widely followed now, and textual criticism is as much about uncovering details about the circumstances in which a work was produced, and the way texts have been affected by errors, INTERPOLATIONS and republication. It applies BIBLIOGRAPHICAL knowledge to actual works: i.e. studying physical books to inform how we read the words on the page. Many developments in textual criticism originated in Shakespeare studies. Textual criticism and BIBLIOGRAPHIC studies in general are at the forefront of assessing how technological changes modify how we read a text: both manuscript to print (in the RENAISSANCE) and print to electronic (see also 'cybercriticism')

textuality The state of being expressed in written language. Textuality is a theoretical concept allied to POST-STRUCTURALIST and DECONSTRUCTION arguments that texts and their meaning are inseparable from their being written down. There is 'nothing outside the text' ('*rien hors du texte*'): all meaning is unstable, determined only by competing DISCOURSES that are present in all languages. Related to this idea, INTERTEXTUALITY describes the connectedness of all texts. NEW HISTORICISM pursues similar ideas when it argues for the textuality of history (and the historicity of texts).

texture The surface features of a TEXT; in other words, aural or visual effects. Someone who couldn't understand the text could still gain a sense of texture, but wouldn't be able to tell how texture is affecting meaning. Aspects of texture include: ASSONANCE, CONSONANCE, EUPHONY, CACOPHONY, ALLITERATION, ONOMATOPOEIA, DICTION, METRE and RHYME. 'Texture' does not concern STRUCTURE; indeed, it can be considered a rival unifying principle in a work. NEW CRITICISM particularly encouraged an interest in texture.

theatre in the round A DRAMATIC performance in which the STAGE is surrounded by the audience on all sides. An arena and the street are two possible venues for theatre in the round. Some or all of the MEDIEVAL MYSTERY PLAYS were probably played in the round, perhaps on wagons. It means the ACTORS always have their back to some spectators, but it does encourage audience interaction. Most theatre today is performed behind a PROSCENIUM ARCH.

theatre of the absurd A DRAMATIC production containing illogical, surrealist and/or bizarre elements that highlight the irrational (absurd) nature of human existence. It grew from Albert Camus's philosophical ideas, and led to strange creations like Eugène Ionesco's *The Bald Soprano* (1949). Theatre of the absurd deliberately breaks with CONVENTION, yet a classic play like Samuel Beckett's *Waiting for Godot* (1955) has since been welcomed into the European DRAMATIC CANON. The play is about two men waiting for someone who never comes. It retains its power as a creative expression, and no longer seems as shocking or 'absurd' as it once did.

theatricality The state of being consciously connected to the theatre and stage CONVENTION. It describes theatre that promotes its theatrical nature, as opposed to creating an illusion of REALISM. 'Theatrical' here means acting to the audience (rather than ignoring its existence), extravagant scenery, PROPS and music, unlikely plot twists (including *DEUS EX MACHINA*), and other DEVICES that make the most of theatrical traditions, but are not NATURALISTIC. William Shakespeare's late plays (sometimes called ROMANCES), such as *Cymbeline* (1609), are highly theatrical. Heavily theatrical performances are intended to make entertaining spectacles, and in this respect are the opposite of EPIC THEATRE, which breaks the DRAMATIC illusion to make serious points to the audience.

theme An ABSTRACT idea that seems central to a literary work's design. A work's structure and IMAGERY (MOTIFS) appear to support the theme. There is often little evidence, however, that many AUTHORS have specific thoughts about themes. It is much easier to claim that a work's theme is 'revenge', 'envy' or 'FATE' than to demonstrate that a work can or should be reduced to that single idea. In most cases, themes are covert precisely because they are difficult to express in simple language. Unless the work is consciously DIDACTIC, a work will not be reducible to a simple moral lesson or THESIS. Any attempt at a thematic approach ought to take into account how a given idea is being expressed.

theory A form of generalisation using ABSTRACT LANGUAGE that seeks to explain and/or make predictions about an aspect of literature. A theory brings consistency to a critical approach, the chance to reflect on one's own methods, and the ability to know what to look for when reading, and so dig deeper into a text. Some students and critics have a natural aversion to theory on the grounds that it imposes ideas on texts, and replaces the act of reading. It is a reasonable fear, and one partly founded on the perceived pretentious and woolly thinking that does sometimes hide in the clothing of theoretical thought.

However, theory is often sharp-toothed, sometimes surprisingly so, and has a broadly positive effect on reading: it challenges assumptions, and encourages diversity. It would be hasty, for instance, to reject MARXIST and PSYCHOANALYTIC CRITICISM out of hand because they initially sound weird; if serious minds have devoted lots of time to developing theoretical ideas on a subject, there is probably something worthy of serious consideration about them. Equally, literary theories will always be disparate and incomplete: as a rule, literary critics are content to leave physicists to ponder over ambitious 'theories of everything'. As such, there is always a need for new literary PARADIGMS, METAPHORS and THEORIES. Theory with a capital 't' is taken to refer to a body of thought in the HUMANITIES that brought this thinking away from discussion of metaphysical notions like truth, beauty (AESTHETICS) and goodness, and towards more scientific topics like psychology, economics and sociology. There are murmurings that the twenty-first century saw the arrival of a post-theoretical period—as is suggested by two recent books entitled *After Theory* (by Terry Eagleton in 2003 and Thomas Docherty in 1996).

This table offers a very rough outline of prominent critical movements in the past century. The individual entries for each term give a more thorough idea of the history of each school of thought.

1920s Russian formalism; psychoanalytic criticism
1930s
1940s New Criticism
1950s Chicago critics; mythic(al) criticism; archetypal criticism; structuralism;
1960s semiotics; feminist criticism; reader-response criticism
1970s post-structuralism; deconstruction; postmodernism; Marxist criticism; discourse analysis
1980s new historicism; cultural materialism; dialogic criticism (in English)
1990s gay and lesbian criticism, postcolonial criticism; ecocriticism; cultural studies
2000s disability studies; literary Darwinism

thesis (pl. theses) A statement to be proved or disproved. A thesis describes a long ESSAY or dissertation, usually one that will be examined. Literary works may contain theses, in the form of a PROTAGONIST'S (main CHARACTER'S) beliefs or initial expectation, but an ANTITHESIS will invariably be introduced to create CONFLICT. This could take the form of an ANTAGONIST (rival) or CRISIS. Most literary works explore a thesis's limitations rather than insist on its truth in a narrowly DIDACTIC manner. It's dangerous to assume that a work must have a universal THEME that is being explored. A thesis explored in Thomas Hardy's *The Mayor of Casterbridge* (1886) could be something like 'public standing counts for more than private morals'. While this thesis may focus a reader's response, it doesn't necessarily take us closer to understanding what the work is actually about. It says as much about our interests as what the text contains.

thesis novel/play A literary work that seeks to convey a particular message (THESIS) to its audience. SLAVE NARRATIVES, for instance, promote the thesis that slavery should be abolished. Novels and plays, as mass forms of literature. are best suited to this sort of direct communication. Propaganda is a stronger term for works that are directly political or ideological in CONTENT. A thesis play could also be called a PROBLEM or DISCUSSION PLAY.

thespian An ACTOR or actress. The term sounds a little pretentious, and that suggestion has become part of the word's meaning, particularly when abbreviated to 'thesp': e.g. 'That Tarquin, he's such a thesp!' See 'protagonist' for details about Thespis, the original thespian.

third-person narrator A CHARACTER who relates events in a story from the viewpoint of 'he', 'she' or 'it', and does not participate in the action. It is the simplest way of reporting events, and is more common than FIRST-PERSON NARRATOR. Third-person narrators often have their own personality, especially when they are UNRELIABLE. Even when a narrator is unobtrusive, the VOICE should be distinguished from that of the AUTHOR: in prose, a narrative is almost always told by a PERSONA; i.e. an assumed identity (which may well be similar to the AUTHOR'S own).

threnody (Greek, 'funeral lament') The term refers specifically to a Greek song of lamentation, but in English literary criticism 'threnody' is essentially SYNONYMOUS with a range of forms: DIRGE, LAMENT, MONODY, ELEGY and COMPLAINT.

thrust stage A STAGE that is surrounded by the audience on three sides. It 'thrusts' out into the audience, unlike the more usual arrangement today in which the action is performed behind the PROSCENIUM ARCH. Thrust stages encourage more engagement between ACTORS and audience, as does THEATRE IN THE ROUND, where the audience completely surrounds the stage.

tirade A long, abusive speech that violently condemns its subject. JEREMIADS are a form of tirade.

title The name given to a work. Titles create expectations and are a key method for directing the reader's attention towards one interpretation of the work. At the same time, one should be wary that titles are not always AUTHORIAL, particularly in pre-fifteenth-century works. The manuscripts of *Gawain and the Green Knight* and *Beowulf*, for example, do not have these names written at the top of the first page: these titles were adopted later. Poem titles are given in inverted commas ('The Jabberwocky'), and titles of everything else, including short stories and poem collections, are *italicised* or <u>underlined</u>. How does the title of this complete Ted Hughes poem (1968) affect our response?

> '?'
>
> Why Should Time be a road?
> Why should tomorrow be a distortion?
> Why should yesterday be another country?
> Everything is in the scales
> And every second weighs
> Exactly everything—as I can see
> With my see-saw brains.

tone In general, it means the quality of an utterance that expresses an attitude or emotion: e.g. nervous, sinister, IRONIC or delicate. It is often vague when used as a literary term. 'Tone' is used interchangeably with 'INTONATION' to describe physical changes in ACCENT, pitch or voice when speaking. It is also taken to mean the expression, often unconscious, of the speaker's personality and attitude to his or her audience (e.g. sneering, blithe, suspicious). A sarcastic tone will involve SARCASM, but in addition might involve a sneering and impatient quality in the voice.

In this broader sense, tone is associated with VOICE, PERSONA and ATMOSPHERE. 'Voice' is another unhelpfully general term that refers to someone's distinctive STYLE or VIEWPOINT as conveyed by his or her 'tone of voice'. Persona is the speaker's adopted CHARACTER, which is partly defined by the tone he or she adopts when addressing others. Atmosphere is equivalent to MOOD; i.e. the general impression something gives off, but not a precise characteristic of communicating with others. If you accept that it is impossible to say something in a neutral voice, then tone is how a speaker's style generally affects what they are saying without using intentional DEVICES.

topographical poetry A poem that describes a particular scene. It is a specific form of ECPHRASIS, and incorporates forms like COUNTRY HOUSE POETRY, some PASTORAL verse, and ROMANTIC poetry that meditates on a single location. A good example of the latter is William Wordsworth's 'Lines composed a few miles above Tintern Abbey, on revisiting the banks of the Wye during a tour, July 13, 1789' (the TITLE makes this an OCCASIONAL POEM). It can also be used to describe some NATURE WRITING or PSYCHOGEOGRAPHIC writing.

topos (or **topic; pl. topoi**) A set of commonly used THEMES or arguments. Like the Latin equivalent 'locus', the Greek word 'topos' literally means 'place', as if these ideas were stored somewhere. In CLASSIC RHETORICAL theory, writers were encouraged to stick to commonplace topics. In literary criticism, it usually describes recurring CLASSICAL themes, like the CARPE DIEM ('seize the day'), or the love-struck shepherd (e.g. in Marlowe's 'The Passionate Shepherd to his Love'). Topics are recurring themes between works; a MOTIF is an idea repeated within a work.

total poetry A concept described by the Nigerian poet Niyi Osundare in which poetry is combined with dance, music and percussion to create an effect like 'TOTAL THEATRE'.

total theatre A DRAMATIC spectacle that seeks to immerse the audience in the environment of a production. This can be done with bold sets, lights, music, film, and by involving the audience in the action. It was originally a German concept that evolved into EPIC THEATRE in the 1920s, but now refers more generally to vivid THEATRICAL experience.

touchstone Matthew Arnold's term for a brief quotation from an AUTHOR'S works that can easily be compared with other writers. It would be criticised by all sorts of post-Victorian critics for ignoring CONTEXTS of literature: RUSSIAN FORMALISTS would find this approach unscientific; NEW CRITICS would insist that the quotation needs to be understood within the work; NEW HISTORICISTS, MARXIST CRITICS and others would argue that all quotations need to be understood as a product of a certain historical period; CULTURAL CRITICS might question the point of comparing AUTHORS to choose the greatest. In fact, 'touchstone' is a good touchstone for the type of Victorian-era thinking about literature that now seems dated to most later writers.

tour de force (French, 'feat of strength') A great display of an AUTHOR'S skill. The work may also happen to be a masterpiece, or *MAGNUM OPUS*, or may be memorable for its particular strength and forcefulness. Euripides' *Bacchae* is certainly regarded as a masterpiece of Greek tragic DRAMA, and the label '*tour de force*' draws attention to the author's accomplishment in managing to write such a powerful work.

tradition The sum of past works and thinking available to an AUTHOR. All writers work within an existing tradition. This directly influences the FORM, CONVENTIONS and subject-matter of a work. Tradition refers to a nation's cultural heritage in general, and the CANONICAL works of a national literature. It also describes different groupings that testify to some shared element within a work: e.g. GENRE (EPIC tradition); MEDIUM (ORAL tradition) or historical PERIOD (VICTORIAN tradition). The adjective 'traditional' is sometimes used specifically to describe an ANONYMOUS FOLK song or story: 'London bridge is falling down' is a traditional English song.

Tradition plays an important role in literary MODERNISM and STRUCTURALISM. In his CLASSIC ESSAY 'Tradition and the Individual Talent' (1919), T.S. Eliot argued that Western writers need to draw on the past because that is where literary truth and the structures to express it lie (compare with Eliot's highly ALLUSIVE poem *The Waste Land*, published three years later):

> historical sense involves a perception, not only
> of the pastness of the past, but of its presence;
> the historical sense compels a man to write not

> merely with his own generation in his bones, but with a feeling that the whole literature of Europe from Homer and within it the whole of the literature of his country has a simultaneous existence and composes a simultaneous order.

tragedy (Greek, 'goat song') A key concept in Western DRAMA, though there is no agreed definition. In its most general sense, it means 'serious' play. If COMEDIES end with the ACTORS full of life and love, then tragedies end with multiple bodies lying dead on the stage-floor.

Tragedy has attracted a great deal of critical attention. Its origins are in Ancient Greek DRAMA, when the individual ACTOR (or PROTAGONIST) first began to represent CHARACTERS in the retelling of mythological or historical NARRATIVES (see 'chorus' for Friedrich Nietszche's version of tragedy's origins). The CHORUS was an important feature of Greek tragedy, and guided the audience's response to the unfolding CATASTROPHE. The most influential critic of tragedy is Aristotle, whose *Poetics* give a technical description of how he thought tragedy worked (little survives of Aristotle's thoughts on COMEDY). It corresponds well to the few surviving works of Aeschylus, Sophocles (Aristotle's favourite) and Euripides, but is not a definitive guide to the many later forms taken by tragedy. William Shakespeare, for example, couldn't have told you what Aristotelian tragedy was.

Aristotle held that tragedy was an IMITATION of an complete action in DRAMA that caused the washing away (*CATHARSIS*) of emotion through pity or fear. The imitation was made more convincing by observing the THREE UNITIES of action, time and place. The PLOT involves a change (through recognition or *ANAGNORISIS*) from ignorance (*HAMARTIA*) to knowledge that brings with it a reversal of fortune (*PERIPETEIA*), often leading to catastrophe. This emphasis on plot over CHARACTER makes the whole action seem necessary. Tragic HEROES are supposed to be noble, so that they provide a clear example to the audience of the workings of FATE.

All these principles have been challenged by later writers of and on tragedies. The adjective 'tragic' is, for a start, meaningfully used to described poetic and prose works. Two more examples: Shakespeare knew some of Seneca's later tragedies in Latin, but not the Greek ones. He writes tragedies with more emphasis on CHARACTER than PLOT, and often disregards the CLASSICAL UNITIES. By contrast, French CLASSICAL tragedy (particularly Jean Racine's) stick closely to the rules. Second, in modern times tragedy has become more domestic (e.g. in Henrik Ibsen's works) and introduced ANTIHEROES who are more representative of our common condition. As these examples suggest, tragedy is at the heart of the Western literary tradition.

The impact of tragedies depends in part in the major issues they address: knowledge, power, FATE, and the force on nature in human lives. Yet it also provokes a strong emotional reaction: as Mel Brooks put it, 'tragedy is when I cut my finger; comedy is when you fall in an open sewer and die'. Tragedy shows how some of Western literature's major writers have tussled with basic questions about human existence, and it has attracted similarly grand theories. But it remains a term that is used as often by news reporters as literary critics, and in English has become linked with any attempt to come to terms with suffering in language, whether literary or not. Tragedy resists a single definition, but remains a phenomenon that cannot be ignored.

tragic flaw A defect in a CHARACTER that leads to her/his downfall. A tragic flaw is an inherent fault that is set to explode into CATASTROPHE. It is an imprecise term, however, and is one to avoid. Despite its name, it isn't a structural element of TRAGEDY (as Aristotle defines it)—it is a poor TRANSLATION of '*HAMARTIA*' (ignorance). Tragic HEROES are partly victims, and their suffering is out of proportion with their error; characters with a 'tragic flaw', by contrast, get what they deserve thanks to POETIC JUSTICE.

tragic irony A form of SITUATIONAL IRONY where a CHARACTER is ignorant of impending CATASTROPHE. The situation arises from the character's arrogance (*HUBRIS*) and/or mistakes (*HAMARTIA*). Tragic irony is more specific than DRAMATIC IRONY: it results in the revelation of a truth that leaves the CHARACTER feeling helpless. In *Othello*, Iago's kindness to Othello creates tragic irony because it is completely at odds with his true hatred. The audience knows this, but Othello only makes this devastating realisation at the end of the play.

tragicomedy In general, any play that blends TRAGIC and COMIC elements—or, more vaguely, anything that makes the audience both happy and sad. A 'bitter-sweet' comedy, BLACK COMEDY or HEROIC DRAMAS that are tragic with a sense of POETIC JUSTICE might all be described as tragicomedies. In this broad sense, 'tragicomedy' could refer to anything from Euripides' *Alcestis* (438 B.C.E.) to Anton Chekhov's *Uncle Vanya* (1899). Tragicomedies may mix CHARACTERS from different sections of society, and the dramatist's intention may be to offer something more 'lifelike' than a play that offers a purely positive or negative view of life.

Tragicomedy is used in a more technical sense to describe a group of ELIZABETHAN and Jacobean plays that were influenced by the ideas of the Italian dramatist Battista Guarini, who tried to write plays that were between tragedy and comedy. Guarini's ideas were known in England, and the term 'tragicomedy' is being used around this time: Philip Sidney writes of 'mungrell Tragy-comedie' in his *Apologie for Poetrie* (1595). The major tragicomedy in this vein was Francis Beaumont and John Fletcher's *Philaster* (1609), which put so-called 'romance' DRAMAS in fashion, such as Shakespeare's late plays.

transferred epithet A form of word-exchange (HYPALLAGE) in which a descriptive term (EPITHET) is switched unexpectedly to refer to something else. For example, 'cruel sea' contains the transferred epithet 'cruel': the sea is just the sea, even if cruel things happen on it. Ben Jonson's 'To Penshurst' (1616) contains a transferred epithet in its closing couplet that transfers the lords' pride and ambition onto the house:

> Now, Penshurst, they that will proportion thee
> With other edifices, when they see
> Those proud, ambitious heaps, and nothing
>   else,
> May say, their lords have built, but thy lord
>   dwells.

transcendentalism A form of idealist philosophical thinking that sought a new form of literary independence, in reaction to the sterile rationalist thought of the period. Its leading figures were writers based in East-Coast America around the middle of the nineteenth century, such as Ralph Waldo Emerson and Henry David Thoreau. Individual expression, self-sufficiency and sense of wonder at the natural world are all important aspects of Transcendentalism. Its was influenced by ROMANTICISM and idealist philosophy (especially Immanuel Kant), and its presence was felt in the works of later writers, such as Herman Melville and Nathaniel Hawthorne.

transference In PSYCHOANALYTIC CRITICISM, the displacement of an AUTHOR'S emotions onto something else by METONYMY. In psychiatric terms, it describes the transfer of a patient's experience on the analyst.

translation Transferring a work from one language to another. It is often said that literature is untranslatable because its FORM and CONTENT are inseparable. In this way, translation and PARAPHRASE are at best METAPHORS for the original. Literary translators must decide how literal a translation should be: whether it should stick to the words of the original, which risks creating odd phrasing and SYNTAX in translation, or be faithful to the sense, which will produce something that reads more easily. Many find it essential to respect the difference between original and target languages. There is arguably no such thing as a perfect translation: instead, translations have a limited life-span, and need to be replaced once readers become too familiar with them, or as language and tastes change. On the other hand, Walter Benjamin argued coherently that translation is a search for an ideal language (see 'Frankfurt school').

Literary translation could be described as an art-form, though few translations are admired in their own right. Most of the time readers have no access to the original text, so are unaware of most decisions a translator has made, even if the work contains a translator's preface. Therefore well-known translations tend to be those based on classic texts, where the translator's innovations are more obvious. Translations from Homer, for example, are more likely to receive critical approval: e.g. George Chapman's *Homers Iliads* (1616) and Christopher Logue's *Kings* (1991). When reading a work in translation, it's important to bear the translator's role in mind, and be aware of differences in STYLE, DICTION and IDIOM created.

trauma theory An interdisciplinary field that examines the effect of horrific events on individuals, whether death, famine, war, assault, rape or something else. With regard to literature, trauma theory studies how individuals bear witness to trauma by creating a NARRATIVE of the event. Issues of memory, forgetting and psychological impact are also prominent, though trauma theorists would largely avoid generalisations, so as to respect the uniqueness of each case discussed.

travesty (noun, verb and adj.) An exaggerated, ridiculous IMITATION of another work or GENRE that doesn't do justice to the original. It's a form of BURLESQUE that lowers the tone for laughs, sometimes with a SATIRICAL edge. It typically involves PARODY. The term is sometimes used to describe a work that unintentionally misrepresents the seriousness of the original because it is simply bad; however, 'travesty' as a literary term describes a deliberate take-off of another work.

treatise A closely argued study of a particular subject. In MEDIEVAL English, it meant any descriptive writing or NARRATIVE, but it now refers specifically to a focused work of PROSE non-FICTION.

trimeter (Greek, 'three measures') A line of VERSE containing three FEET (RHYTHMIC units). Not very common in English PROSODY.

triple metre An alternative term for TERNARY METRE (RHYTHMIC patterns based on three-syllable FEET). The term is older and sometimes used inconsistently; e.g. it is taken as a SYNONYM for 'TRIMETER'.

triple rhyme A rhyme based on three syllables, with the first stressed and other two unstressed: e.g. Sunderland/ Wonderland, cosily/ dozily. It is almost always found in LIGHT VERSE, and often gives rise to FORCED RHYMES and MOSAIC RHYMES (when the rhyming syllables are spread across two or three words): e.g. 'secretly/ she peeked at me'; 'the hippopotamus/ didn't like the lot of us'.

triplet Three lines that have same METRICAL pattern. It particularly refers to lines that RHYME with each other; in effect, a rhyming COUPLET with an extra line. John Dryden and Alexander Pope used triplets to provide variation when writing HEROIC COUPLETS. In these cases, the triplet is often marked with a bracket. An example from Dryden's *The Hind and the Panther* (1687):

> When she, by frequent observation wise,
> As one who long on heaven had fixed her eyes,
> Discovered a change of weather in the skies;
> The western borders were with crimson spread,
> The moon descending loaded with flaming red.
> (II.665–69)

trochee (adj. trochaic; Greek, 'running') A METRICAL FOOT consisting of a stressed syllable followed by an unstressed one (– o). 'Female' and 'why did you not laugh?' are trochaic. It is the second most common FOOT in English VERSE, but is not found nearly as often as its opposite, the IAMB (o –). It creates a FALLING RHYTHM, which is heavy, jagged, and sometimes sounds like it is resisting the typical iambic BEAT. For this reason, it is rare to find an entire poems written in trochaic metres, and the trochee is more often used as a substitute for the iamb (since both create BINARY METRES).

Trochaic lines are sometimes CATALECTIC (losing the final unstressed syllable). It might be thought that this makes the distinction between iambic and trochaic metres even less clear in SCANSION, since they both consist of alternating stressed and unstressed syllables. In practice, it shouldn't be a problem if you listen to how the whole line sounds, and in particular whether the rhythm is leading towards or away from the stressed BEAT (i.e. has RISING or FALLING RHYTHM).

trope (noun, adj. tropical; Greek, 'turn') As a RHETORICAL term it means language that twists the meanings of words. It is sometimes identical in meaning to FIGURE. Many critics, however, think of tropes as 'figures of thought' in contrast to SCHEMES ('figures of speech'), which involve changing the order of words. The major tropes are METAPHOR, SIMILE, METONYMY, SYNECDOCHE, and IRONY, all of which are found in literary writing across historical periods and languages. Tropes are a basic way of stretching the possibilities of what language can express. A trope that exaggerates a point is called HYPERBOLE. For example, Nelly Furtado's song 'I'm like a Bird' uses an elegant trope in its title (a simile) to catch the listener's attention, but an alternative like 'I'm like a Soaring Eagle' would sound hyperbolic.

true rhyme An alternative term for FULL (or PERFECT) RHYME; i.e. words connected through identical middle vowels and endings.

truncation A general term referring to the shortening of a line of VERSE. This is typically achieved either by making the line CATALECTIC (removing the final syllable(s)), or ACEPHALOUS (the initial syllable(s)). Removing the final syllable of a TROCHAIC line to create a HEAVY ENDING is the most commonest form in English.

Tudor (1485–1558/1603) An adjective for the period of EARLY MODERN British history in which the Tudor monarchs reigned. It began as Henry VII came to the throne in 1485, which ended the Wars of the Roses and brought a period of relative stability. He was followed by his son Henry VIII in 1509, then his children Edward VI in 1547, Mary in 1553 and Elizabeth in 1558. Elizabeth's reign, though technically late Tudor, is often known as ELIZABETHAN, while 'early Tudor' refers to anything before Henry VIII's death in 1547. Major influences on the literature of this period are ideas linked to the Reformation and RENAISSANCE HUMANISM. See page 360 for a list of major AUTHORS, works and related entries for the period.

two bodies The theory that a monarch has political authority which is separable from his or her physical body. The notion of a 'body politic' and 'body natural' was a METAPHOR for the ruler's control. It was an orthodox RENAISSANCE view of monarchy, which supported the divine right of kings. Edmund Plowden's collection of law cases, *Reports* (1571), gives a standard account: 'Body natural (if it be considered in itself) is a Body mortal, subject to all Infirmities that come by Nature or Accident, [...] But his

Body politic is a Body that cannot be seen or handled, consisting of Policy and Government, and constituted for the Direction of the People and the management of the public weal'. William Shakespeare's *King Lear* (1604) is the classic work that dissects the idea of the king's two bodies.

two-hander A play that requires two ACTORS to be staged. It usually refers to plays with two CHARACTERS, but may involve DOUBLING of parts. 'FOUR-HANDER' is used for a four-actor play, and 'MONODRAMA' when only one is needed.

type A CHARACTER whose attributes represent those of another person or group. Types are sometimes STOCK CHARACTERS, but can also offer penetrating analyses of aspects of human character (see 'flat/round characters'). In a biblical CONTEXT, 'type' is an incident or person in the Old Testament that anticipates Christ in the New Testament (e.g. the suffering servant in Isaiah—see 'allegory'). More broadly, 'type' is another word for GENRE, MODE, or FORM.

typography The way words are arranged on the page. LINEATION and choice of FOUNT often combine with typography to create particular effects. PATTERN and CONCRETE POETRY make the most radical use of typographical possibilities. Examining typography is sometimes fruitful in analysis, particularly in poetry; however, be aware that later EDITIONS will not always replicate the typography used in earlier versions.

U

ubi sunt (Latin, 'where are they?') A commonplace theme (TOPOS) that considers the ruin and passing away of all human lives and achievements. '*Ubi sunt*' is a quotation from numerous medieval Latin poems, and two of the finest English examples are the Old English ELEGIES 'The Wanderer' and 'The Seafarer':

> Simle þreora sum | þinga gehwylce
> ær his tiddege | to tweon weorþeð:
> adl oþþe yldo | oþþe ecghete
> fægum fromweardum | feorh oðþringeð.
> ('The Seafarer, 68–71)
>
> [There are always three things that twist man's fate before he is due to die: disease, old-age or the sword's anger rip out the life of the doomed]

uncanny The most common TRANSLATION of the German word *unheimlich* (literally 'unhomely') when referring to its use by Sigmund Freud. It refers to something that is strangely familiar. An uncanny place, person or object feels known to us but mysterious at the same time, whether in literature or in life. Freud attributed this to the audience's recognition of the author's repressed desires that are projected through the uncanny idea/image. This has radical AESTHETIC implications: it argues that truth lurks in what is hidden, secretive and threatening, rather than the beautiful. Dark and repulsive images deserve our attention as much as something attractive. HORROR STORIES, the GOTHIC NOVEL, and dark novels like *Jane Eyre* have all been explored for elements of the uncanny. It connects too with Julia Kristeva's notion of ABJECTION, in that both centre on a reaction of horror to something unknown. Kristeva's term describes that act of repelling the object away from us. The impact made by the uncanny is summed up well by W.H. Auden in his poem 'In Memory of Sigmund Freud'(ll.97–103):

> But he [Freud] would have us remember
> most of all
> To be enthusiastic over the night

Not only for the sense of wonder
It alone has to offer, but also

Because it needs our love: for with sad eyes
Its delectable creatures look up and beg
Us dumbly to ask them to follow.

unconscious (adj. and noun) As an adjective, it describes anything of which we are unaware. It is routinely claimed that literature and the arts are uniquely suited to describing unconscious thoughts. This can be associated with sleep, death, DIONYSIAN ecstasy, FIGURATIVE LANGUAGE, divine inspiration (see '*vates*'), engagement with the OTHER, or pure feeling. As this list shows, the claim does not originate with Sigmund Freud; however, PSYCHOANALYTIC CRITICISM has thoroughly investigated it. Psychoanalysis also popularised 'unconscious' as a noun that names the place where such thoughts occur (also called the id). It is contrasted to conscious thought, which is indissolubly attached to our sense of self (ego). In whichever CONTEXT, unconscious thought implies loss of selfhood.

undecidable A term associated with DECONSTRUCTION that describes the inherent AMBIGUITY in language. READER-RESPONSE CRITICS argue that readers must create meaning for themselves from GAPS in a text. APORIA and PARADOX are relevant rhetorical terms.

unintrusive narrator An OMNISCIENT (all-knowing) PERSONA telling a story who simply reports the facts, and does not offer his or her opinions. An unintrusive narrator leaves readers to draw their own conclusions about CHARACTERS' thoughts and motivations. Although it sounds fairly neutral, no narrator adopts a truly impersonal perspective, and it is still worth exploring how details and events are being related, and what makes the narrative VOICE distinct.

unities The three unities specific to DRAMA are unity of action, time and place. Aristotle's *Poetics* only mentions that a drama ought to be a single continuous action, in which each part leads on from the other. This is unity of action. The two other unities were suggested in the RENAISSANCE. The unities of time and place state that a drama should take place in one location over the course of a whole day. The effect is to make the dramatic illusion more believable and so involve the audience.

Jean Racine's French NEOCLASSICAL tragedies, such as *Andromaque* (1667) and *Phédre* (1677) are highly unified dramas: the action is so controlled that the slightest sigh or movement can tragically disrupt the way we expect things to be. William Shakespeare played around with the possibilities of dramatic unities in his late plays. *The Tempest* (1611) is set on an island and takes place within a day; however, the REALISM this might suggest is set against the magical and fantastic elements of the plot (such as the banquet that suddenly appears and disappears in Act 3). On the other hand, *The Winter's Tale* (1611) deliberately wrecks dramatic unity: at the start of Act 4 a CHARACTER called Time walks onto stage and announces that sixteen years have just passed. The point is that in post-classical DRAMA the unities are not just something to be accepted passively. ROMANTICISM reacted against the restraints of formal unity, and Bertolt Brecht's ALIENATION EFFECT reflects his misgivings about using unities to create illusions of reality onstage.

unity Cohesion in a TEXT, such that all the parts are in an ordered whole. A fully unified text isn't DIGRESSIVE: each section is indispensable in making the same central point. CLASSICAL and NEOCLASSICAL ideas on unity (see the above entry) have been highly influential on literary writing. It is debateable how far unity is necessary for literature, even if an AUTHOR is aiming for VERISIMILITUDE or to make a particular ARGUMENT. Unity could perhaps be contrasted with energy: a calm, collected structure holds in place the messy creative impulses that go into writing a work. There is certainly a danger in assuming that a central idea or THEME unifies a text. Equally, all texts possess unity in some form, whether through NARRATIVE, PLOT, METRICAL STRUCTURE or some other means. The presence or absence of unity affects the reading experience. It creates interpretative difficulties too: readers and audiences often wonder where the action is going, and what something means. The term 'HERMENEUTIC CIRCLE' describes the need to anticipate the answers to these questions before you have experienced the whole work.

univocal An utterance with a single meaning; i.e. without AMBIGUITY or POLYSEMY. 'Unambiguous' is a more common alternative. Some POSTMODERN critics (e.g. DECONSTRUCTIONISTS) would argue that a univocal utterance is impossible.

unreliable narrator A PERSONA who tells a story from a limited perspective, either because he or she does not have access to all the facts, or distorts the story because of who they are. A BIASED VIEWPOINT could be based, for example, on circumstance, personality, or relation to the central CHARACTERS. The reader senses that only a partial account of events is being given, and this creates IRONY. It is often more unsettling than OMNISCIENT narration is, and forces independent reflection on events. For example, the use of young Scott and Jem Finch as innocent unreliable narrators is essential to the portrayal of racism in Harper Lee's *To Kill a Mockingbird* (1960).

urtext (from German *Ur*, 'primitive') An earlier EDITION of a TEXT that has not survived. Textual CRITICISM can speculate on, and in some cases attempt to reconstruct, the original EDITION. Based on documents from the time, *Hamlet* is thought to have an urtext. This Ur-*Hamlet* may have been written by Thomas Kyd.

ut pictura poesis (Latin, 'as picture, poetry) A phrase used by Horace in *De Arte Poetica* to compare poetry and painting that was later influential in the European RENAISSANCE. Poems were often described as 'speaking pictures' in this period. Numerous HUMANIST writers understood this idea alongside Horace's belief that poetry was intended to be sweet and useful (*dulce* and *utile*).The comparison describes a style of literary IMITATION that prioritises VERISIMILITUDE. See also 'ecphrasis', which is the rhetorical term for description of a scene or art-work.

utopia (Greek, 'no place') An imagined ideal society, usually based on a political system of communal living. Thomas More coined the term, playing on the senses of the Greek for 'no place' (*outopia*) and 'good place' (*eutopia*), for his subtly IRONIC work *Utopia* (1516). A DYSTOPIA is a nightmare vision of society. There are two related adjectives: 'Utopic' is a technical description of something which contains the ideals of a utopia. 'Utopian' is more commonly used and implies that the ideas are delusional. Utopic visions can be SATIRICAL or more fantastic, like SCIENCE-FICTION. Margaret Cavendish's *Blazing World* (1666) shows just how freely creative and philosophical the GENRE can be. Here is the moment when the Lady realises that the 'bear-like creatures' she has just encountered are friendly:

> they took her up in their rough arms, and carried her into their city, where instead of houses, they had caves under-ground; and as soon as they entered the city, both males and females, young and old, flocked together to see this Lady, holding up their paws in admiration; at last having brought her into a certain large and spacious cave, which they intended for her reception, they left her to the custody of the females, who entertained her with all kindness and respect.

V

vates **(adj. vatic**; Latin, 'prophet; poet') A divinely inspired poet with prophetic abilities. The idea of poetic madness leading to spontaneous creation has been around since Plato's *Ion*, and was still current in EARLY MODERN literature. Compare with 'MAKER'.

vaudeville A production consisting of numerous different acts, such as COMEDY, dance, song, and sketch. It was popular in North America in the late nineteenth and early twentieth centuries, before it declined as cinema grew in popularity. The British equivalent is 'music hall', while REVUE is a general term for variety performances.

vehicle A term used by I.A. Richards to describe a METAPHORICAL image that describes the SUBJECT (TENOR). In the phrase 'she's under a cloud', 'under a cloud' is the vehicle describing a feeling of melancholy (the tenor).

Venus and Adonis stanza A six-line stanza with a rhyme scheme *ababcc*. In addition to Shakespeare's poem of that name, it crops up in *Romeo and Juliet* and *Loves Labours Lost*, which were all written around 1593–95—though Philip Sidney had already used it in *Arcadia* (1590), as had Edmund Spenser in 'January' in the *Shepheardes Calendar*.

verbal irony (or rhetorical irony) A RHETORICAL TROPE in which IRONY is used by the speaker to imply a FIGURATIVE meaning opposite to what was actually said. It can be usefully compared to another trope, ALLEGORY: with irony the secondary meaning is guaranteed to be the exact opposite of what is being said, whereas in ALLEGORY you just know there's a secondary meaning. Irony can still be more complicated, if you can't tell whether a passage is intended to be ironic or not. INTONATION is often vital to detecting spoken irony. Understatement (LITOTES and MEIOSIS) and overstatement (HYPERBOLE) are both forms of verbal irony. Puttenham, in *The Arte of English Poesy*, characterizes verbal irony as 'drie [dry] mock', which vividly suggests its suaveness. William Makepeace Thackeray ironically undercuts the CHARACTER John Sedley in this passage by adding extra detail (from Chapter 59). The irony creeps in with the parentheses, then spreads to the whole sentence with '&c &c'. Sedley is tidying his papers:

> He had them in the greatest order—his tapes and his files, his receipts, and his letters with lawyers and correspondent; the documents relative to the Wine Project (which failed from a most unaccountable accident, after commencing with the most splendid prospects), the Coal Project (which only a want of capital prevented from becoming the most successful project put before the public), the Patent saw-mills and Sawdust Consolidation Project, &c &c.—

verisimilitude (Latin, 'true likeness') The quality of seeming true to life. It has provided a standard by which literature has been judged for centuries. This is of direct relevance to works described as REALIST or NATURALISTIC. Questions about whether a work is probable, likely or realistic are asked more widely, however. Ever since Aristotle's *Poetics* IMITATION of reality has been a crucial concept in thinking about what literature is. The UNITIES of CLASSICAL DRAMA and the inevitability of PLOT were intended to create illusions of reality. Others find the belief that reality can or should be represented onstage a huge illusion of its own. PLATONIC philosophy (see 'abstract language') and the ALIENATION EFFECT come to this conclusion in very different ways. Yet some degree of verisimilitude, however far-fetched, is inevitable in a literary work: even FANTASY novels have a basis in CONVENTION and worldly experience (think about how similar the faces of magical or alien beings look to our own). Verisimilitude is something that writers define in different ways: Jonathan Swift's *Gulliver's Travels* is hardly an accurate guide to world geography, but its SATIRE shines a bright light on realities of his contemporary society. The issue of verisimilitude could also be approached by asking how CONCRETE or ABSTRACT a work is in its depiction. Another important concern, perhaps, is how language (as a MEDIUM) deviates from life-likeness: the representation of verisimilitude is another large issue at stake.

verism The principle that representing reality matters above all in a literary work, regardless of how morally or AESTHETICALLY attractive it is.

vernacular (Latin, 'domestic, native') The common form of a language used in a country or region on an everyday basis. DIALECT emphasises a distinct form of a vernacular language: so English is a vernacular language, while Geordie and Cockney are dialects. DEMOTIC refers to a STYLE based on the vernacular.

The relation of English vernacular to literature is an important subplot in the development of the language. In the sixteenth century HUMANIST principles meant that Latin was an international language, with English a coarser alternative used for everyday communication. It was thought that the infiltration of CLASSICAL words, structures and ideas into English would help raise the standard of the vernacular, even if it could not attain the prestige of Latin. John Milton wrote his earlier poems (c.1625–40) in Latin because he had been schooled thoroughly in classical literature, and could gain readers abroad by doing so. He made a conscious decision to write *Paradise Lost* (1667) in English, albeit in LATINATE language, and he helped secure the prestige of English from that point onwards.

Eighteenth-century NEOCLASSICAL writers still maintained that the vernacular needed to be refined to create great literature, which would follow DECORUM and have suitably POETIC DICTION. William Wordsworth and Samuel Taylor Coleridge's *Lyrical Ballads* was an important step in reclaiming the sounds and RHYTHMS of everyday speech for literature. The 'Advertisement' to that work states that it is an 'experiment' because the poems 'were written chiefly with a view to ascertain how far the language of conversation in the middle and lower classes of society is adapted to the purpose of poetic pleasure.' SPRUNG RHYTHM and FREE VERSE explore similar territory. The term 'vernacular' has moved closer again to the sense of being a DIALECT or form of language that people actually use. Critics still debate how far vernacular forms like JARGON, SLANG and COLLOQUIALISMS are suitable for POETIC DICTION or literature, and conservative voices again defend the concept of literary language as being different in some way from language as everyone speaks it. Vernacular is irreplaceable because it can be so evocative, which we can see in the first half of Paul Muldoon's poem 'The Right Arm' (1983):

> I was three-ish
> when I plunged my arm into the sweet-jar
> for the last bit of clove-rock.
> We kept a shop in Eglish
> that sold bread, milk, butter, cheese,
> bacon and eggs,
> Andrews Liver Salts
> and, until now, clove-rock.

vers de société (French, 'society verse') Short, graceful pieces of LIGHT VERSE that SATIRIZE or make witty comments about middle- and upper-class life. It can take numerous forms, such as EPIGRAM , *RONDEAU*, *VILLANELLE* and LIMERICK, and has been popular since the late nineteenth century.

verse (Latin, 'turn') A piece of writing containing METRICAL features, but the term is difficult to pin down. Verse is distinct from PROSE: it has a consistent METRE, whereas prose at most has a clear RHYTHM. Verse generally has a stricter form (see p. 348 for a list) and often uses RHYME as a structuring feature. It follows rules of PROSODY and can be SCANNED. In its strictest sense, 'verse' means a single metrical line, and is often used to describe a group of lines, or a STANZA. When writing about poetry, however, it is clearer to use the terms 'line' and 'stanza' instead of 'verse'. Verse can also be used as a SYNONYM for 'poem'.

The difference between 'verse' and 'POETRY' is tricky to define. 'Verse' tends to emphasise a piece of writing's technical elements and VERSIFICATION; 'poetry', its intellectual elements such as intensity and sense of conceptual vision. Few would argue that METRICAL features are essential to poetry: FREE VERSE and PROSE POEM two varieties of poetry that are not organised according to metrical structure. Terms like 'COMIC VERSE' and 'LIGHT VERSE' imply that these 'verse' forms are not worthy of being called poetry. When using the terms 'verse', 'poetry' and 'prose', it's worth remembering that these do not describe fixed categories. But something in VERSE (unless it is free verse) will always have metrical interest that PROSE cannot have, and if verse is influencing a work's meaning, then it is probably also poetry.

verse paragraph A division that occurs in STICHIC (line-by-line) poetry, such as BLANK VERSE. Like a PROSE paragraph, it groups lines based on a single idea or theme, rather than following a set structure. In STANZAS, by contrast, the ideas have to be moulded around the form. William Wordsworth's *The Prelude* (1805, 50) and John Milton's *Paradise Lost* (1667) both contain verse paragraphs. It can also be applied to divisions in PROSE POEMS and FREE VERSE, though it is more awkward in these cases because it is not always clear what the standard unit is (equivalent to a sentence in a prose paragraph), and INDENTATION may be used for separate purposes.

versification The formation of METRICAL structures into VERSE, particularly in technical aspects like METRE, RHYME and STANZA FORM. PROSODY is the study of versification. The term can also refer to the process of turning prose into verse (as in 'to versify'), or to the structure of a poem (as in 'the versification of this poem is based on iambic pentameter').

verso The 'back' of a LEAF; i.e. the left-hand, even-numbered page of an opening. The other side is the RECTO.

vice A STOCK CHARACTER in MORALITY PLAYS who tempted the Christian HERO towards sin. In an example of Shakespeare's MEDIEVAL influences, Falstaff (whose major appearances are in the *Henry IV* plays and *The Merry Wives of Windsor*) is considered a descendent of the Vice CHARACTER. Both he and Vice are involved in SLAPSTICK COMEDY.

Victorian (1837–1901) Relating to the period during which Queen Victoria ruled Britain and the British Empire. The Victorian period introduced numerous social, economic and cultural changes that shaped the twentieth century, and which literary modernists reacted against. The Queen was not especially involved in literature herself, apart from association with the poet laureate (such as Alfred, Lord Tennyson). The majority of CANONICAL works from the Victorian period are prose, and novels in particular: see page 370 for a list of major works.

viewpoint The position from which events are described. If a work contains a single viewpoint, then it is more precise to talk about the type of NARRATOR found (e.g. OMNISCIENT, FIRST-PERSON). Viewpoint becomes useful to talk about multiple narrators in works that shift perspective: e.g. William Faulkner's *The Sound and the Fury* (1929). Making the effort to engage with a CHARACTER'S viewpoint is important, and potentially increases our SYMPATHY for lives different to our own. PERSONAL CRITICISM places the reader's viewpoint at the heart of an interpretation, and some critics of marginalised groups (such as FEMINIST CRITICS or GAY AND LESBIAN CRITICISM) would argue that testimony of individual experience is important.

Certainly viewpoint is an important aspect of interpretation. In Toni Morrison's *Beloved* (1987) both writer and reader need to make a great effort to grasp the perspective of the work's PROTAGONIST Sethe (based loosely on a historical character), an escaped slave who has lost her husband and child, and suffered much more besides. In passages like this one, it is difficult to comment on the absolute candour of Sethe's viewpoint—as a reader, I just have to try hard to understand what the character's situation is like:

> Sethe looked at her hands. her bottle-green sleeves, and thought how little color there was in the house and how strange that she had not missed it the way Baby [her mother-in-law] did.

> Deliberate, she thought, it must be deliberate, because the last color she remembered was the pink chips in the headstone of her baby girl. After that she became as color conscious as a hen. Every dawn she worked at fruit pies, potato dishes and vegetables while the cook did the soup, meat and all the rest. And she could not remember remembering a molly apple or a yellow squash. Every down she saw the dawn, but never acknowledged or remarked its color. There was something wrong with that: It was as though one day she saw red baby blood, another day the pink gravestone chips, and that was the last of it. (pp. 38–39)

vignette (vi-**njet**) The term originally referred to a small decorative pattern found on a blank page at the beginning or end of a chapter, but now usually refers to a short descriptive SKETCH that can stand alone, or exist within a larger work.

villain A CHARACTER who intends to commit wicked or criminal acts; the 'bad guy'. Many villains are ANTAGONISTS; i.e. opposed to the main character (PROTAGONIST). However, only 'villain' contains a sense of moral badness. An 'ANTIHERO' is a separate concept, which implies a failure to live up to HEROIC expectations.

villanelle A PASTORAL song consisting of five TERCETS rhyming *aba*, and a final QUATRAIN rhyming *abaa*. Normally the same two RHYMES are used throughout. The first and third lines of the first STANZAS are repeated in turn as a REFRAIN, and are found in the final COUPLET. It is a form of ROUNDELAY, popular in EARLY MODERN Europe. This form is similar to PANTOUM. A few writers in English, like Dylan Thomas, have experimented with villanelles.

viz. (*videlicet,* Latin) Namely, or in other words.

voice As a literary term, its meaning is vague: it can either mean the style adopted by a speaker within a work, or an AUTHOR'S voice (or ETHOS) as a viewpoint informing the text. In both cases, voice is meant figuratively—it is as if the CHARACTERS or author were actually speaking, and has little to do with the actual sound. The author's voice is usually heard when the audience is given more information than the characters; e.g. though

IRONY or reference to something outside the FICTIONAL world. In general, it is clearer to use another term, such as 'PERSONA', 'NARRATOR', 'IMPLIED AUTHOR', 'STYLE', 'TONE' or 'VIEWPOINT'. Voice is also a GRAMMATICAL term that describes a verb's relation to its subject: in **active** voice the SUBJECT does the action; in **passive** voice the action is done to the subject. 'She ate a radish' is active; its equivalent in passive voice is 'the radish was eaten by her'.

W

war poets (c.1914–45) A collective term for poets who were involved in the World Wars, in particular the First World War. The poetry typically explores the brutality and futility of war, often in a ROMANTIC manner. The CANONICAL war poets Wilfred Owen, Siegfried Sassoon and Rupert Brooke were all involved in the First World War. Later works of war poetry shouldn't be forgotten, however: e.g. David Jones's *In Parenthesis* (1937, see 'prose') and the poetry of Keith Douglas (who died at Normandy in 1944). 'LOST GENERATION' describes an attitude of disillusionment and cynicism among American writers after the First World War.

Wasp White Anglo-Saxon Protestant. The term refers to white middle-class Americans descended from the earliest European settlers. It is usually used in a negative light to describe a social élite who don't have to work to live the American Dream. In literature, it is found mostly in the works of non-WASPs; e.g. Jewish and Catholic American writers.

well-made play A term used to describe plays that have a tidy structure and a tight PLOT, but are perceived as dull. 'Well-made play' is usually used negatively to describe certain DRAMAS that were popular before the transition from MELODRAMATIC towards NATURALISTIC productions. It is a NEOCLASSICAL form of drama, and usually follows Aristotle's ideas about UNITIES, *PERIPETEIA* and *ANAGNORISIS* (often unconsciously). This is not to say that later plays were not well-crafted, only that neatly formal design doesn't control the outcome as it does in a well-made play. For example, Henrik Ibsen's *The Wild Duck* (1884) can be described as both naturalistic and well-made, but doesn't just follow the expectations of one or the other.

western A work (particularly a NOVEL or film) set in the desert Western areas of North America. The 'Wild West' is a kind of American mythology: it was seen as an unexplored expanse by the earliest settlers on the American East coast, inhabited by native Americans and later 'civilised'. James Fenimore Cooper's work, such as *Last of the Mohicans* (1826), contains numerous elements found later in the western novel. Though primarily a popular GENRE FICTION, the western explores larger questions of national identity.

willing suspension of disbelief Samuel Taylor Coleridge's term for an audience's readiness to enter the FICTIONAL world created by the AUTHOR, and to follow its CONVENTIONS. Coleridge describes it as 'poetic faith'. Put simply, it means that the audience will go along with what the author says without pointing out that 'that would never happen in real-life'. It allows a literary work to work its magic on an audience. 'Suspension of disbelief' could also describe a film-goer's willingness to be immersed in a film, and forget that it's only a film. This is both convenient and often desirable for popular audiences (see 'escapist'). The whole notion of illusions in literature has faced strong criticism from Marxist writers and Bertolt Brecht in particular, whose ALIENATION EFFECT was designed to remind theatre audiences that they were watching a wholly fictional production.

wit (Old English *witan*, 'to know') In general, quick-witted intelligence with an ability to make sharply succinct observations. More than any other term in this book, perhaps, 'wit' is a term that needs to be understood in historical CONTEXT, because its meaning has shifted considerably. In Old English 'wit' meant the mind, and the ability to think and reason, which survives in 'wits' and the modern insult 'half-wit'. In EARLY MODERN literature, it increasingly referred to displaying knowledge through use of ingenious, unexpected expressions and an engaging, original STYLE. METAPHYSICAL POETRY is associated with wit in this sense, because of its CONCEITS, FIGURATIVE LANGUAGE and distinctive VOICES. Part of T.S. Eliot's defence of these poets was that their style was both witty and serious, for in the nineteenth century 'wit' began to suggest a humorous quality, and it still retains that meaning. Before then, the eighteenth held a NEOCLASSICAL view of wit: it required judicious phrasing and sense of DECORUM. Now the most common vernacular use of 'wit' is to refer to someone who is learned and humorous, and perhaps possesses a large stock-pile of ANECDOTES, epigrams and other amusing tit-bits. Oscar Wilde remains the epitome of wit in this sense. The term's development is still worth knowing, however, in order to be sensitive to its CONNOTATIONS in particular contexts. It also shows how society's general sense of how intelligence can be most attractively displayed has changed. The *OED* is the place to look for more information on what the word means in different historical periods.

Here is an example of self-conscious Wildean wit, taken from *The Importance of Being Earnest* (1895), Act 1, lines 605–13:

> *Algernon* Allwomenbecomeliketheirmothewomanistrs. That is their tragedy. No man does. That's his.
>
> *Jack* I am sick to death of cleverness. Everybody is clever nowadays. You can't go anywhere without meeting clever people. The thing an absolute public nuisance. I wish to goodness we had a few fools left.

womanist Concerned with the experience and viewpoint of women of colour, particularly African-American women. The term was created by the novelist Alice Walker, and has since been adopted more widely in FEMINIST CRITICISM (and feminism in general). Walker wrote that 'womanist is to FEMINIST as purple is to lavender', to suggest that 'feminism' tends to focus on well-to-do white women. By contrast, 'purple' is more vibrant, rich and bold, all of which is relevant to Walker's best-known work, *The Color Purple* (1982). The term 'womanist' seeks to acknowledge how institutional hierarchies based on race and class need to be considered alongside oppression based on sex and gender. Womanist writers are witnesses to the experiences of a specific socially marginalised group, and contribute to the wider fragmentation of the catch-all field 'FEMINIST CRITICISM' into GYNOCRITICISM and other areas.

work In literary studies, a composition or group of compositions (see '*oeuvre*'). It is slightly different in meaning to text, but there is no firm consensus on the relation between both words (see 'text'). A work is often said to be the completed object that emerges from the text and is ready for distribution. Alternatively, if 'work' connotes the application of mental energy to a project, then 'text' seems to suggest the product of that effort. Perhaps these different emphases are ultimately compatible. Literary 'works', some have argued, could actually be a form of serious play: involving free exploration of ideas that is finally unproductive. This idea has been mapped onto the philosopher Immanuel Kant's notion of the 'free play of the imagination'.

world Englishes A term describing the presence of international localized variations of English. This is a legacy of the British Empire, and was assisted by the flexibility of English to mix with other languages (to form CREOLES). World Englishes mostly describe those forms associated with former colonies, such as India, the Caribbean and Malaysia. These are all legitimate alternatives to British (or American) English, and to argue that so-called 'standard' English is superior risks perpetuating the sort of colonial attitude that forced English on such nations in the first place. Some informal fusion languages are known by PORTMANTEAU terms like 'Spanglish' (English and Spanish) or 'Chinglish' (and Chinese).

wrenched accent An ACCENT in which METRE causes a word to have a STRESS that clashes with how the word would usually be pronounced. It is most common in BALLADS and LIGHT VERSE, and is generally thought something to be avoided in VERSIFICATION.

X/Y/Z

zeitgeist ('ei' pronounced 'eye'; German 'time-spirit') The general mood or atmosphere of a historical period. Works or phenomena are often said to 'capture the *Zeitgeist*', though such claims are often REDUCTIVE. Charles Dickens' *Bleak House* (1852), for example, is arguably filled with the spirit of Victorian London, but then who are post-Victorian readers to judge?

zeugma (Greek, 'yoking') A FIGURE in which a verb or preposition controls two different terms within a sentence: e.g. '*Good-Nature* and *Good-Sense* must even join; | To err is *Humane*; to Forgive, *Divine*' (Alexander Pope, *Essay on Criticism*, ll.324–25). It is a FORM of ELLIPSIS that creates elegant phrases. Its meaning tends to overlap with 'SYLLEPSIS': 'zeugma' is usually taken as the more general term, and describes instances where the first term has the same sense or grammatical connection with both others; 'syllepsis' when both uses are distinct. So 'he took the petrol can from him, and the matches from her' would be zeugma, but 'he took her by surprise, and the hand' would be syllepsis, because 'took her by' is being used in CONCRETE and ABSTRACT senses. Syllepsis is often more arresting.

Thematic Index

Any classification of literary terminology will be largely arbitrary, and this index is no exception. It only looks to provide a useful guide to the contents of this book, and not a comprehensive summary of literary criticism. It tries to help the reader locate new words by grouping together related terms under common categories: for example, if you already know the term 'alliteration', you can find eleven related terms under 'figures of repetition' in the rhetoric section. The guiding principle was to place terms where the reader is most likely to look for them; however, some could have appeared in more than one list, and others don't fit easily into any category. I have tried to put linked terms together, and the entries explain these connections. This provides a third form of cross-referencing in this book, in addition to the timeline and the capitalized words in the main text that point to other relevant entries. Main heading names are repeated if they have their own entry. Words in brackets are explained within the entry under which they are listed.

The index sketches out the different approaches to literature dealt with in this book. Its first two sections contain descriptive terms useful for reading literature and talking about its features, figures and forms. The second half, literary theory, contains concepts for thinking about literature and its approaches, contexts and key critical ideas. This doesn't mean that reading and thinking about literature are separate activities, but by dividing them up here, it should help the reader think about how to make best use of the terms on offer. I have grouped together critical terms associated with a particular writer for two reasons: it provides a useful checklist of some of the most influential writers on literature, and is a reminder that many important critical terms began as the work of one person writing in a specific context, and have since become more widely applicable. It is also worth bearing in mind that most terms used to describe English metre and rhetoric have been borrowed from classical theory, and so do not always map onto English exactly. Note that I do not italicise rhetorical terms (I have treated them as technical terms), and otherwise follow the *OED* in italicising foreign words and phrases. A summary of the contents:

I. TECHNICAL TERMS

A. LANGUAGE

1. KEY CONCEPTS

2. LITERARY LANGUAGE

- leitmotif
- motif
- originality
- persona
- poetic licence
- poetry
- prose
- sign
- subtext
- symbol
- synthesis
- theme
- thesis
- topos

3. SPECIFIC FEATURES (SEE ALSO 'RHETORIC' BELOW)

- abstract language
- anachronism
- anthropomorphism
- archaism (archaic)
- assonance
- blazon
- bombast (fustian)
- cacophony
- conceit
- concrete language
- consonance
- cliché
- colloquialism
- digression (excursus)
- dissonance
- *double entendre*
- euphemism
- euphony
- formula
- incremental repetition
- inkhorn term
- innuendo
- jargon
- juxtaposition
- kenning
- Latinism (Latinate)
- loan word
- malapropism
- mannerism
- medievalism
- *mise en abyme*
- mixed metaphor
- mnemonic
- mondegreen
- neologism (coinage)
- nonce word
- palindrome
- periodic sentence
- portmanteau word
- purple prose
- sibilance
- slang
- solecism
- spoonerism
- synaesthesia
- univocal

4. STYLES

- baroque
- burlesque
    - lampoon
    - mock epic
    - mock-heroic
    - parody
    - travesty
- camp
- Ciceronian
- classicism (classical)
- demotic
- euphuism
- Gothic
- gnomic
- grand style
- grotesque
- Homeric
- irony
    - cosmic irony
    - dramatic irony
    - romantic irony
        - sarcasm
    - situational irony
    - Socratic irony
    - structural irony
    - tragic irony
- obscurity
- self-reflexive
- solipsistic

5. RHETORIC

For a fuller list, see the website Sylva Rhetoricae or Richard Lanham's *A Handlist of Rhetorical Terms* (see p. 386).There are no agreed categories for rhetorical terms: they are grouped here for convenience only. Each term is listed once, though some fall within two or more categories:

general
device
dialectic
ethos
figure
logos
period
proof
rhetoric
scheme
trope

major tropes
allegory
hyperbole
litotes
meiosis
metaphor
metonymy
pun (paranomasia)
simile
synecdoche
verbal irony

figures of repetition
alliteration
anadiplosis
anaphora
antistrophe
epanalepsis
epistrophe
epizeuxis
palilogy
pleonasm
ploce
polyptoton
tautology

emotional appeals
anticlimax
aporia
aposiopesis
apostrophe
bathos
exclamation
pathos

unusual language-use
adynaton
antiphrasis
catachresis
hendiadys
hyperbaton
    anastrophe
    hysteron proteron
    hypallage
    transferred epithet
oxymoron
paradox
rhetorical question
syllepsis
zeugma

shaping an argument
anacoluthon
antithesis
chiasmus
    antimetabole
contrast
metastasis
occultatio (occupatio/ paralipsis)
oration
    peroration
parallelism
    isocolon
    parison
periphrasis
    circumlocution
prolepsis
syllogism

description
ecphrasis (ekphrasis)
enargia (energia)
epic simile
epithet
personification
    prosopopoeia

adding, subtracting and replacing words
amplification
asyndeton
copia
ellipsis
enallage
epanorthosis
metalepsis
polysyndeton
syncope

'figures of sound'
onomatopoeia
synaeresis

6. LANGUAGE/SYNTAX

7. LINGUISTICS

B. NARRATIVE

C. DRAMA

D. PROSODY

1. METRE

2. FORM

The following terms all concern poetic structures/aspects of performance. After terms for parts of stanza, forms are ordered by stanza length, followed by other fixed forms.

For different types of poetry, see page 351.

envelope
envoi
fit
homostrophic
passus
refrain
stanza
strophe
verse paragraph

two-line
closed couplet
couplet
distich
heroic couplet
open couplet

three-line
tercet
terza rima
triplet

four-line
ballad stanza (metre)
clerihew
quatrain
  common measure
  elegiac stanza
  heroic quatrain
  long measure
  poulter's measure
  short measure

five-line
limerick
pentastich
quintain (quintet)

six-line
Burns stanza
sestina
Venus and Adonis stanza

seven-line
rhyme royal
septet (heptastich)

eight-line
ottava rima

nine-line
Spenserian stanza

other fixed forms
ballad
ballade
blank verse
haiku
hymn
  ode
  Horatian Ode
  irregular ode
  Pindaric Ode
pantoum
rondeau (roundel)
Skeltonics
sonnet
  curtal sonnet
  Miltonic sonnet
  octave (octet)
  Petrarchan sonnet
  sestet
  Shakespearean sonnet
  sonnet sequence
  Spenserian sonnet
stichic
villanelle

lineation/visual effect
acrostic
altar poetry
amoebean verse
concrete poetry
open form
pattern poetry
prose poem

performance
antiphon
dramatic poem
flyting
performance poetry
rap
slam poetry
total poetry

3. RHYME

rhyme
rhyme scheme

arch-rhyme
broken rhyme
cross rhyme
double (feminine) rhyme
end-rhyme
eye-rhyme
forced (synthetic) rhyme

E. TEXTS/EDITIONS

II. TYPES OF WRITING

Terms that are mostly associated with one form of writing (poetry, prose, drama) are grouped under that section. Terms that are used more broadly are listed under general. This list is a common-sense guide, and there are many works that do not fit easily into one genre (e.g. Pope's *Essay for Criticism*).

form
genre
mode
subgenre

A. GENERAL

anecdote
apology
autobiography
automatic writing
biography
carpe diem
cento
children's literature
chivalric romance
confessional literature
cycle
débat
diasporic literature
didactic
documentary
dystopia
encomium
epistle
erotic literature
exemplum
fable (apologue)
  beast fable
fairy tale
fantasy
fiction
folk literature
hagiography
invective
jeremiad
jeu d'esprit
lament
legend
litany
literature (literary)
memoir
metafiction
monologue
myth
non-fiction
oral literature (orature)
palinode
panegyric
parable
paraliterature
pastiche
pastoral (bucolic)
propaganda (novel/play)
psychomachy
repartee
riddle
romance
saga
satire (Horatian, Juvenalian, Menippean)
saying
  adage
  aphorism (apophthegm)
  axiom
  epitaph (lapidary)
  maxim
  proverb
  sententia (sentence)
science-fiction (sci-fi)
sketch
tale
tetralogy
thesis novel/play
tirade
ubi sunt
utopia
vignette
western

B. PROSE

C. DRAMA

D. POETRY

Forms with specific fixed features (i.e. structure, lineation or performance) are listed from page 347 onwards.

abstract poem
anthem
aubade (alba)
carol
complaint
country house poetry
devotional poetry
dirge
dithyramb
doggerel
dramatic monologue
dream poetry
dub poetry
eclogue
elegy (elegiac)
epic
epigram
epithalamion
epyllion
fabliau
georgic
graveyard poetry
heroic poetry
idyll (idyllic)
jingle
lay
light verse
lullaby
lyric poetry
macaronic verse
madrigal
monody
nonsense verse
nursery rhyme
occasional poem
paean
prothalamion
psalm
roundelay
serenade
song
threnody
topographical poetry
vers de société

E. HISTORICAL PERIODS/MOVEMENTS

In chronological order. See timeline starting on page 357 for lists of associated writers and works.

medieval (c.400–1485)
Old English (c.400–1066)
Middle English (c.1066–1500)
Renaissance/early modern (c.1485–1660)
Tudor (1485–1558/1603)
Elizabethan (1558–1603)
Jacobean (1603–25)
Caroline (1625–49)
Commonwealth (1649–60)
long eighteenth century (c.1688–1832)
restoration (1660–1700)
neoclassicism (c.1660–1780)
romanticism/Romantic (c.1780–1830)
Victorian (1837–1901)
Edwardian (1901–1910/14)
Georgian (1910–36)

F. GROUPS OF WRITERS

Angry Young Men (c.1950s)
Augustan poets (c.1700–50)
Beat Generation (c.1950s)
Black Mountain poets (c.1950s)
Bloomsbury Group (c.1910s)
bluestockings
cavalier drama/poets (c.1630s)
Celtic Revival (c.1880–1940)
coterie
Decadence
expressionism

III. LITERARY THEORY

A. CRITICAL CONCEPTS

B. HISTORICAL CONCEPTS

C. CONCEPTS ASSOCIATED WITH A PARTICULAR WRITER

D. APPROACHES

Timeline of Works Cited

This timeline contains all the works mentioned in the entries, plus a few more. Partly because literary terminology originally developed to describe 'classic' works of English literature, the examples cited in this book are mostly canonical texts, and male writers are over-represented. Though the timeline is fairly conservative, it at least gestures towards other areas of English studies, and also mentions influential European and American works. Dates give the first publication or performance of a work where known, and not necessarily the final version (for which I only give the dates in a few exceptional cases). The final column gives the main entries where each author is cited, which does not always refer to the specific volume listed. Also, don't assume that each term directly describes the work appears alongside: for example, Alan Sillitoe's *Saturday Night, Sunday Morning* (1958) isn't actually a kitchen sink drama, but it's still worth following up the link. Other notes: for living poets, I usually cite collected editions, rather than individual publications; period headings have separate entries in the main text; an asterisk indicates works and authors often considered 'non-literary' (i.e. they are critical, philosophical, musical works etc.). I have mostly quoted from Oxford editions throughout the dictionary, though I used the Riverside editions of Shakespeare and Chaucer, and other authoritative texts (e.g. Longman) where convenient.

CLASSICAL LITERATURE/POST-ANTIQUITY

c.800 B.C.E.	Homer	*Iliad*	cycle, ecphrasis, epic, Homeric
	" "	*Odyssey*	epic simile, Homeric, narrative, romance
472 B.C.E.	Aeschylus	*Persians*	history play
458 B.C.E.	" "	*Oresteia*	protagonist, tragedy
438 B.C.E.	Euripides	*Alcestis*	tragicomedy
c.430 B.C.E.	Sophocles	*Oedipus Rex*	detective fiction, protagonist, psychoanalytic criticism, situational irony
c.405 B.C.E.	Euripides	*Bacchae*	*tour de force*
	Aristophanes	*Frogs*	parody
c.400 B.C.E.	*Plato	**Republic*	dialectic, literature
	" "	**Apology*	apology
c.330 B.C.E.	*Aristotle	**Poetics* *Rhetorica*	Chicago critics, rhetoric
c.200 B.C.E.	Theocritus	*Idylls*	idyll, pastoral
c.190 B.C.E.	Plautus	Comedies	academic drama, stock character
c.170 B.C.E.	Terence	Comedies	academic drama
c.120 B.C.E.	*Cicero	**Rhetorica/ Rhetorica ad Herennium*	rhetoric
c.60 B.C.E.	Catullus	Poems	complaint
c.55 B.C.E.	Lucretius	*De Rerum Natura*	didactic
37 B.C.E.	Virgil	*Eclogues*	Arcadia, bucolic, eclogue, pastoral
c.35 B.C.E.	Horace	*Satires*	Horatian satire
29 B.C.E.	Virgil	*Georgics*	didactic, georgic
c.20 B.C.E.	Horace	*De Arte Poetica*	decorum, didactic, *ut pictura poesis*
c.19 B.C.E.	Virgil	*Aeneid*	epic

c.2	Ovid	*Metamorphoses*	frame story
c.50	Seneca	Tragedies	academic drama, act, closet drama, Senecan tragedy, tragedy
86–103	Martial	*Epigrams*	epigram
c.100	*Quintilian	**Institutio Oratoria*	rhetoric
	Plutarch	*Parallel Lives*	biography
	(Phaedrus/ Aesop)	*Aesop's Fables*	beast fable
c.100–130	Juvenal	*Satires*	Juvenalian satire
397	Augustine	*Confessions*	autobiography

MEDIEVAL (C.400–1485): OLD ENGLISH (C.400–1066)

c.730	Bede	*Ecclesiastical History*	chronicle
c.750	(anonymous)	*Beowulf*	alliteration, epic formula, flyting, kenning, litotes
	(from *The Exeter Book*)	'The Wanderer', 'The Seafarer'	elegy, lyric, *ubi sunt*
	" "	'The Wife's Lament'	lament
	" "	'The Ruin'	lacuna
	" "	Riddles	riddle

MIDDLE ENGLISH (C.1066–1500)

c.1135	Geoffrey of Monmouth	*Historia Regum Britanniae*	chronicle
c.1200–1500	(anonymous)	Mystery Plays	dramatization, mystery plays, theatre in the round
c.1200	(anonymous)	*The Owl and the Nightingale*	*débat*
c.1310	Dante Alighieri	*Divine Comedy*	four levels of meaning, Neoplatonism

c.1320	(anonymous)	*Sir Orfeo*	lay
c.1350–52	Giovanni Boccaccio	*Decameron*	
c.1350–1400	(anonymous)	*The Cloud of Unknowing*	anonymity
c.1367–80	William Langland	*Piers Plowman*	allegory, alliterative metre, dream poetry
c.1369	Geoffrey Chaucer	*Book of the Duchess*	allegory, dream poetry
c.1373	Julian of Norwich	*Revelations of Divine Love*	
c.1374	Petrarch	*Il Canzoniere*	sonnet, sonnet sequence
c.1385	Geoffrey Chaucer	*Troilus and Cressida*	aubade, rhyme royal, Homeric
c.1387–1400	" "	*The Canterbury Tales*	analogue, beast fable. courtly love, cycle, frame story, occultatio, palinode, prologue
c. 1400	(anonymous)	*Sir Gawain and the Green Knight*, 'Pearl', 'Cleanness', 'Patience'	bob and wheel, dream poetry, faery
1420	(anonymous)	*The Castle of Perseverance*	morality play
1431–38	John Lydgate	*Fall of Princes*	
c.1432	Margery Kempe	*The Book of Margery Kempe*	autobiography
1485	Thomas Malory	*Morte d'Arthur*	chivalric romance, legend

RENAISSANCE/ EARLY MODERN (C.1485–1660): TUDOR (1485–1558/1603)

c.1490	Henry Medwall	*Fulgens and Lucrece*	interlude
1500	Desiderius Erasmus	**Adagiorum collectanea*	adage

c.1500	John Skelton	'Philip Sparrow'	Skeltonics
c.1510	(anonymous)	*Everyman*	morality play, psychomachy
1512	Desiderius Erasmus	*Morias Enkomion* (*Praise of Folly*)	encomium
1513	*Niccolò Machiavelli	**The Prince*	
1516	Thomas More	*Utopia*	utopia
1525	William Tyndale	New Testament translation	
1530s	Thomas Wyatt	Poems	iamb, refrain
1531	*Thomas Elyot	**The Boke named the Governour*	courtesy book
1532–52	François Rabelais	*Gargantua* and *Pantagruel*	carnivalesque, Menippean satire
1533	John Heywood	*Play of the Weather*	
c.1537	Henry Howard	*Aeneid* translation	blank verse
1549	Ludovico Ariosto	*Orlando Furioso*	episode
	(no single author)	**Book of Common Prayer*	
1552	Nicholas Udall	*Ralph Roister Doister*	academic drama
1557	(no single author)	*Tottel's Miscellany*	anthology

ELIZABETHAN (1558–1603)

1561	Thomas Sackville and Thomas Norton	*Gorbuduc*	chronicle
1570	*Roger Ascham	**The Scholemaster*	
1571	*Edmund Plowden	**Reports*	two bodies

1573	George Gascoigne	*Hundreth Sundrie Flowers*	poulter's measure
1577	*Raphael Holinshed	**Chronicles*	chronicle drama, history play
1579	Edmund Spenser	*The Shepheardes Calender*	amoebean verse, analysis, archaism, gloss, pastoral
1580	Michel de Montaigne	*Essais*	essay
1581	Philip Sidney	*Old Arcadia*	Arcadia, pastoral
1587	Richard Hakluyt	*Voyage made in Florida*	
c.1587	Walter Raleigh	'Fortune hath taken thee away, my love'	oxymoron
1589	*George Puttenham	**Arte of English Poesie*	rhetoric, pattern poetry
1590 (1596)	Edmund Spenser	*The Faerie Queene*	allegory, archaism, argument, canto, courtesy book, faery, imagination, proem
1591	Philip Sidney	*Astrophel and Stella*	blazon, ploce, sonnet
	Edmund Spenser	*Complaints*	complaint
1592	Samuel Daniel	*Delia*	tension
	Robert Greene	*Greenes Groatsworth of Wit*	euphuism
1593	William Shakespeare	*Titus Andronicus*	revenge tragedy
1594	Christopher Marlowe	*Edward II*	
	Thomas Kyd	*The Spanish Tragedy*	metadrama, revenge tragedy
	William Shakespeare	*The Taming of the Shrew*	induction

1595	" "	*Richard II*	anachronism, image
(written c.1580)	Philip Sidney	**An Apologie for Poetrie (A Defence of Poesie)*	abstract language, apology, oration, tragicomedy
	Edmund Spenser	*Amoretti and Epithalamion*	architectonics, epithalamion, sonnet, sonnet sequence
1596	" "	*Fowre Hymnes*	Neoplatonism
	William Shakespeare	*Venus and Adonis*	erotic literature
1597 (and 1625)	Francis Bacon	*Essays*	essay, literature
1598	Ben Jonson	*Every Man in His Humour*	comedy of humours
	" "	*Every Man out of His Humour*	" "
1599	William Shakespeare	*Much Ado about Nothing*	polyptoton
	" "	*Julius Caesar*	anachronism, rhetoric
	" "	*Hamlet*	aporia, catachresis, hendiadys, objective correlative, quarto
	(anonymous)	*A Warning for Fair Women*	domestic tragedy
c.1600–90	metaphysical poets		
1601	Ben Jonson	*Poetaster*	poetaster
1602	Robert Southwell	'The Burning Babe'	carol

JACOBEAN (1603–25)

1604	Christopher Marlowe	*Dr Faustus*	haiku
	William Shakespeare	*Measure for Measure*	problem play

	" "	*King Lear*	quarto
1605	Miguel de Cervantes	*Don Quixote*	picaresque novel, romance, romantic irony
1606	William Shakespeare	*Macbeth*	rhetorical question
1607	Ben Jonson	*Volpone*	
	Thomas Middleton	*Revenger's Tragedy*	
	Francis Beaumont	*The Knight of the Burning Pestle*	burlesque
	William Shakespeare	*Timon of Athens*	invective
1609	" "	*Shakespeares Sonnets*	antimetabole, antithesis, sonnet
	" "	*Cymbeline*	theatricality
	George Chapman	*Homers Iliads*	fourteener, translation
	Ben Jonson	*Masque of Queens*	antimasque
	Francis Beaumont and John Fletcher	*Philaster*	tragicomedy
1611	(no single author)	Authorized Version of the Bible (King James Bible)	
	William Shakespeare	*The Tempest*	epilogue, masque
1612	Michael Drayton	*Poly-Olbion*	alexandrine
	Ben Jonson	*The Alchemist*	acrostic
	John Webster	*The White Devil*	
1614	Ben Jonson	*Bartholomew Fair*	city comedy, gesture
1616	Ben Jonson	'To Penshurst'	country house poetry, transferred epithet

1621	Robert Burton	*Anatomy of Melancholy*	satire
1623	Thomas Middleton and William Rowley	*The Changeling*	domestic tragedy
1625	John Webster	*Duchess of Malfi*	

CAROLINE (1625–49)

1629	Launcelot Andrewes	*XCVI Sermons*	homily
c.1630s	cavalier drama/poets		
1633	John Donne	*Poems*	anadiplosis, epigram
	George Herbert	*The Temple*	altar poetry, echo, pattern poetry
1635	Francis Quarles	*Emblemes*	emblem
1637	John Milton	*Comus*	apostrophe, masque
1638	" "	'Lycidas'	catachresis, elegy, pastoral
1640	Ben Jonson	**Timber, or Discoveries*	commonplace book
1642	Thomas Browne	*Religio Medici*	cadence, solecism
1644	John Milton	*Areopagitica*	polemic
1645	Edmund Waller	*Poems*	
1648	Richard Crashaw	*Delights of the Muses*	anastrophe
	Robert Herrick	*Hesperides*	*carpe diem*

COMMONWEALTH (1649–1660)

1650	Henry Vaughan	*Silex Scintillans*	internal rhyme, simile
c.1650	Andrew Marvell	'To his Coy Mistress'	adynaton
	" "	'On the Definition of Love'	cheville
1651	*Thomas Hobbes	**Leviathan*	sensibility, sympathy

	Andrew Marvell	'Upon Appleton House'	country house poetry
1652	William Davenant	**Siege of Rhodes*	heroic drama

RESTORATION (1660–1700) (NEOCLASSICISM (C.1660–1770))

1663	Samuel Butler	*Hudibras*	doggerel
1665	John Dryden	*Indian Emperor*	heroic drama
1666	Molière	*Le Misanthrope*	
	Margaret Cavendish	*The Blazing World*	utopia
1667	John Milton	*Paradise Lost*	epic, epic simile, grand style, Latinism, personification
	Jean Racine	*Andromaque*	unities
1668	John Dryden	*Essay of Dramatick Poesie*	
	Abraham Cowley	*Pindarique Odes*	irregular ode
c.1670	Thomas Traherne	Poems	
1671	John Milton	*Paradise Regained*	
	" "	*Samson Agonistes*	closet drama
1675	William Wycherley	*The Country Wife*	
1676	George Etherege	*Man of Mode*	caricature
1677	William Wycherley	*The Plain Dealer*	
	Jean Racine	*Phédre*	unities
	Aphra Behn	*The Rover*	
1678	John Bunyan	*Pilgrim's Progress*	allegory, dream poetry
1681	John Dryden	*Absalom and Achitophel*	heroic couplet
	" "	*MacFlecknoe*	mock-heroic

1687	" "	*The Hind and the Panther*	triplet

LONG EIGHTEENTH CENTURY (C.1688–1832)

1690	*John Locke	**Essay concerning Human Understanding*	
1694	William Congreve	*The Double Dealer*	
	John Dryden	*Love Triumphant*	
1697	" "	Virgil translations	georgic
1700	William Congreve	*Way of the World*	comedy of manners
c.1700–50	Augustan poets		
1711	Alexander Pope	*Essay on Criticism*	couplet, essay, zeugma
1712 (1714)	" "	*Rape of the Lock*	canto, mock epic
1715	" "	*Iliad* translation	
1719	Daniel Defoe	*Robinson Crusoe*	realism, novel
1722	" "	*Moll Flanders*	memoir
1724	Eliza Haywood	*Fantomina: Or, Love in a Maze*	
1726	Jonathan Swift	*Gulliver's Travels*	allegory, invective, satire, verisimilitude
1728	Alexander Pope	*Dunciad*	personification
1729	Jonathan Swift	*A Modest Proposal*	structural irony
1730	James Thomson	*The Seasons*	georgic
1740	Samuel Richardson	*Pamela*	epistolary novel, sentimental novel
1741	Henry Fielding	*Shamela*	sentimental novel
1742	" "	*Joseph Andrews*	

1748	*David Hume	**Enquiry Concerning Human Understanding*	sympathy
	Tobias Smollett	*Adventures of Roderick Random*	
	Samuel Richardson	*Clarissa*	epistolary novel
1749	Henry Fielding	*Tom Jones*	*Bildungsroman*, intrusive narrator
1751	Thomas Gray	*Elegy Written in a Country Churchyard*	graveyard poetry, heroic quatrain,
1757	*Edmund Burke	**A Philosophical Enquiry into the Origins of our Ideas of the Sublime and Beautiful*	sublime
1759	Samuel Johnson	*Rasselas*	
	Voltaire	*Candide*	
1760	Lawrence Sterne	*Life and Opinions of Tristram Shandy*	digression, metafiction, romantic irony
1763	Christopher Smart	*Jubilate Agno*	free verse
1771	Henry Mackenzie	*A Man of Feeling*	sentimental novel
1773	Oliver Goldsmith	*She Stoops to Conquer*	
	John Sheridan	*The Rivals*	malapropism
1777	" "	*The School for Scandal*	
1779	Samuel Johnson	*Lives of the English Poets*	biography

ROMANTIC (C.1780–1837)

1789	Olaudah Equiano	*Interesting Narrative of the Life of Olaudah Equiano*	slave narrative
	Gilbert White	*The Natural History of Selbourne*	nature writing
1791	James Boswell	*Life of Samuel Johnson*	biography
1792	*Mary Wollstonecraft	**Vindication of the Rights of Woman*	feminist criticism
1793	Robert Burns	*Poems*	
1794	William Blake	*Songs of Innocence and Experience*	quatrain, genre
1795–96	Johann Wolfgang von Goethe	*Wilhelm Meisters Lehrjahre (Wilhelm Meister's Apprenticeship)*	*Bildungsroman*
1796	M.G. Lewis	*The Monk*	Gothic novel
1798	Wordsworth/ Coleridge	*Lyrical Ballads*	ballad, epizeuxis, vernacular
c.1800s	Lake Poets		
1805 (also 1850)	William Wordsworth	*The Prelude*	autobiography, narratee, scansion
1807	Charles and Mary Lamb	*Tales from Shakespeare*	children's literature
1811	Jane Austen	*Sense and Sensibility*	sensibility
1812	Lord Byron	*Childe Harold*	
	Wilhelm and Jacob Grimm	*Grimm's Fairy Tales*	fairy tale

1813	Jane Austen	*Pride and Prejudice*	
1815	Lord Byron	*Hebrew Melodies*	anapaest
1816	Jane Austen	*Emma*	character
1817	Walter Scott	*Rob Roy*	
	Samuel Taylor Coleridge	**Biographica Litteraria*	
1818	Mary Shelley	*Frankenstein*	cybercriticism, Gothic novel
1819–24	Lord Byron	*Don Juan*	*ottava rima*, picaresque
1820	John Keats	*Poems*	assonance, ballad stanza, ode, synaesthesia
	John Clare	*Poems*	persona
	Percy Bysshe Shelley	*Prometheus Unbound*	closet drama
1821	Thomas De Quincey	*Confessions of an Opium Eater*	baroque
1826	James Fenimore Cooper	*Last of the Mohicans*	western
1827	*Franz Schubert (Wilhelm Müller)	**Winterreise*	song
1830s	Transcendentalism (Ralph Waldo Emerson, Henry David Thoreau)		
1832	Alfred, Lord Tennyson	*Poems*	double rhyme
1833	Charles Dickens	*Sketches by Boz*	sketch

VICTORIAN (1837–1901)

1837	Charles Dickens	*Pickwick Papers*	grotesque
1839	Henry Longfellow	*Voices of the Night*	hymn
1843	Alfred, Lord Tennyson	*Poems*	dramatic monologue

	Thomas Carlyle	**Past and Present*	
	Alexander Dumas	*The Three Musketeers*	
1845	Edgar Allen Poe	*Tales of Mystery and Imagination*	
1846	Edward Lear	*Nonsense Songs*	nonsense verse
1847	Charlotte Brontë	*Jane Eyre*	first-person-narrator
	Emily Brontë	*Wuthering Heights*	Chinese box, romanticism
	William Makepeace Thackeray	*Vanity Fair*	euphemism, verbal irony
	George Dibdin Pitt	*Sweeney Todd, the Demon Barber of Fleet Street*	melodrama
1849	Charles Dickens	*David Copperfield*	
1850	Elizabeth Barrett Browning	*Sonnets from the Portuguese*	figurative language
	William Hawthorne	*The Scarlet Letter*	
	Alfred, Lord Tennyson	*In Memoriam A.H.H.*	elegy, onomatopoeia, tetrameter
1851	Henry Melville	*Moby Dick*	
	George Meredith	*Poems*	
1852	Charles Dickens	*Bleak House*	character, *Zeitgeist*
1854	Alfred, Lord Tennyson	'Charge of the Light Brigade'	
	Henry David Thoreau	*Walden*	ecocriticism
1855	Robert Browning	*Men and Women*	dramatic monologue
	Elizabeth Gaskell	*North and South*	
	Walt Whitman	*Leaves of Grass*	anaphora, free verse

1856	Gustave Flaubert	*Madame Bovary*	novel
1857	Anthony Trollope	*Barchester Towers*	
	Elizabeth Gaskell	*Life of Charlotte Brontë*	biography
1859	Charles Dickens	*Tale of Two Cities*	
1860	" "	*Great Expectations*	*Bildungsroman*
1861	George Eliot	*Silas Marner*	
1863	Leo Tolstoy	*War and Peace*	dialogic criticism, epic
1864	Fyodor Dostoyevsky	*Notes from Underground*	historical novel
	Mark Twain	*The Adventures of Huckleberry Finn*	episodic, picaresque novel
1865	Lewis Carroll	*Alice in Wonderland*	satire
1866	Charles Algernon Swinburne	*Poems and Ballads*	
	Fyodor Dostoyevsky	*Crime and Punishment*	dialogic criticism
1868	Louisa May Alcott	*Little Women*	
	Christina Rossetti	'Remember'	accent
	*Matthew Arnold	**Culture and Anarchy*	disinterestedness, philistine, touchstone
1871	George Eliot	*Middlemarch*	*magnum opus*
	Lewis Carroll	*Through the Looking Glass, and What Alice Found There*	envelope, portmanteau word
1872	Harriet Beecher Stowe	*Uncle Tom's Cabin*	
1873	Leo Tolstoy	*Anna Karenina*	

1874	Thomas Hardy	*Far from the Madding Crowd*	
1875	Gerald Manley Hopkins	'The Wreck of the Deutschland'	alliteration, elegy, free verse, sprung rhythm
1877	Henry James	*The Europeans*	
	Thomas Hardy	*Return of the Native*	
c.1880–1940	Celtic Revival		
1880	Fyodor Dostoyevsky	*The Brothers Karamazov*	
1881	Henrik Ibsen	*Ghosts*	domestic tragedy
1884	" "	*The Wild Duck*	well-made play
1886	Thomas Hardy	*The Mayor of Casterbridge*	thesis
1889	Jerome K. Jerome	*Three Men in a Boat*	
1890	Emily Dickinson	*Poems by Emily Dickinson*	hyperbaton
1891	Arthur Conan Doyle	*Adventures of Sherlock Holmes*	confidant, crime fiction
	Thomas Hardy	*Tess of the D'Urbervilles*	novel
1892	Alice James	*The Diary*	
1896	A.E. Housman	*A Shropshire Lad*	
1898	Oscar Wilde	*Ballad of Reading Gaol*	
1899	" "	*The Importance of Being Earnest*	aphorism, drawing room play, wit
	Anton Chekhov	*Uncle Vanya*	tragicomedy
	*Sigmund Freud	**The Interpretation of Dreams*	psychoanalysis

1900	Theodore Dreiser	*Sister Carrie*	naturalism
1901	Rudyard Kipling	*Kim*	

EDWARDIAN (1901–1910/14); GEORGIAN (1910–36); MODERNISM

1902	Joseph Conrad	*Heart of Darkness*	novella, postcolonial criticism
1903	Henry James	*The Ambassadors*	
1904	Joseph Conrad	*Nostromo*	
	John Millington Synge	*Riders to the Sea*	one-act play
1906–21	John Galsworthy	*Forsyte Saga*	saga
1907	August Strindberg	*Ghost Sonata*	expressionism
c.1910s	Bloomsbury Group; Imagists; Provincetown Players; war poets (c.1914–45)		
1910	E.M. Forster	*Howard's End*	
1912	George Bernard Shaw	*Pygmalion*	
1913	D.H. Lawrence	*Sons and Lovers*	autobiography
	" "	*Love Poems and Others*	indentation
1913–27	Marcel Proust	*À la recherche du temps perdu (In Search of Lost Time)*	*roman-fleuve*
1914	James Joyce	*Dubliners*	
1915	John Buchan	*The Thirty-Nine Steps*	
	G.K. Chesterton	*Poems*	ballade
1916	James Joyce	*A Portrait of the Artist as a Young Man*	*Künstlerroman*
1919	Siegfried Sassoon	*War Poems*	

	T.S. Eliot	*'Tradition and the Individual Talent'	tradition
c.1920s	Harlem Renaissance; Lost Generation		
1920	D. H. Lawrence	*Women in Love*	
	Wilfred Owen	*Poems*	anthem, pararhyme
1922	T. S. Eliot	*The Waste Land*	epistrophe, loan word, obscurity
	James Joyce	*Ulysses*	bathos, interior monologue, pun
1923	Wallace Stevens	*Harmonium*	anadiplosis
	Jean Toomer	*Cane*	emphasis
	T.S. Eliot	*'The Function of Criticism'	criticism
1925	F. Scott Fitzgerald	*The Great Gatsby*	
1926	W.B. Yeats	*A Vision*	myth
1927	Virginia Woolf	*To the Lighthouse*	interior monologue
1928	William Butler Yeats	*The Tower*	falling rhythm
	Bertolt Brecht	*Die Dreigroschenoper (The Threepenny Opera)*	alienation effect, opera
	W.H Auden	'The Unknown Citizen'	forced rhyme
	Robert Frost	*West-Running Brook*	tercet
	D.H. Lawrence	*Lady Chatterley's Lover*	censorship
1929	William Faulkner	*The Sound and the Fury*	
	Ernest Hemingway	*Farewell to Arms*	

	Virginia Woolf	*A Room of One's Own*	
1930s	Socialist Realism		
1931	Virginia Woolf	*The Waves*	
	John Steinbeck	*Of Mice and Men*	
	J.R.R. Tolkien	*The Hobbit*	
1932	Aldous Huxley	*Brave New World*	
1934	F. Scott Fitzgerald	*Tender is the Night*	Lost Generation
1937	David Jones	*In Parenthesis*	prose, war poets
	Zora Neale Hurston	*Their Eyes Were Watching God*	
1938	Louis MacNeice	*The Earth Compels*	ellipsis
1939	James Joyce	*Finnegan's Wake*	pun, portmanteau word, readerly/writerly
	Thornton Wilder	*Our Town*	
1940	W.H. Auden	*Another Time*	psychoanalytic criticism
1941	Noël Coward	*Bltihe Spirit*	drawing room play
1942	Robert Frost	*A Witness Tree*	dimeter
1943	Bertolt Brecht	*Die gute Mensch von Sezuan (The Good Person of Szechwan)*	alienation effect
	Keith Douglas	*Selected Poems*	war poets
1944	T.S. Eliot	*Four Quartets*	
1945	George Orwell	*Animal Farm*	allegory, beast fable
	Saul Bellow	*The Adventures of Augie March*	picaresque novel
	Elizabeth Bowen	*The Demon Lover and Other Stories*	short story

1946-PRESENT (POSTWAR, POSTMODERN)

1946	Dylan Thomas	*Deaths and Entrances*	syllabic verse
	Elizabeth Bishop	*North and South*	anaphora
1947	Tennessee Williams	*A Streetcar named Desire*	
	*Cleanth Brooks	**The Well-Wrought Urn*	paradox
1949	Eugène Ionesco	*The Bald Soprano*	theatre of the absurd
	George Orwell	*Nineteen Eighty-Four*	dystopia
	Arthur Miller	*Death of a Salesman*	antihero, domestic tragedy
	C.S. Lewis	*The Lion, The Witch, and The Wardrobe*	
c.1950s	Angry Young Men; Beat Generation; Black Mountain Poets; The Movement		
1950	C.S. Forester	*Mr Midshipman Hornblower*	historical novel
1951	J.D. Salinger	*The Catcher in the Rye*	*Bildungsroman*
	Patricia Highsmith	*The Talented Mr Ripley*	crime fiction
1952	Ernest Hemingway	*The Old Man in the Sea*	
	Ralph Ellison	*Invisible Man*	
1953	Arthur Miller	*The Crucible*	history play
1954	Kingsley Amis	*Lucky Jim*	campus novel
	William Golding	*Lord of the Flies*	
	J.R.R. Tolkien	*Fellowship of the Ring/Two Towers*	fantasy
	*Benjamin Britten	**Turn of the Screw*	opera

1955	Samuel Beckett	*Waiting for Godot*	theatre of the absurd
	Vladimir Nabakov	*Lolita*	
	William Gaddis	*The Recognitions*	
1956	Allen Ginsburg	*Howl and Other Poems*	Beat Generation, hypallage
	Saul Bellow	*Seize the Day*	*carpe diem*
	John Osborne	*Look Back in Anger*	Angry Young Men, kitchen sink drama
	Robert Conquest (ed.)	*New Lines*	Movement, the
1957	Harold Pinter	*The Birthday Party*	
	Samuel Beckett	*Endgame*	tableau
	Jack Kerouac	*On the Road*	Beat Generation
1958	Iris Murdoch	*The Bell*	
	Chinua Achebe	*Things Fall Apart*	
	Alan Sillitoe	*Saturday Night, Sunday Morning*	kitchen sink drama
1959	William Burroughs	*Naked Lunch*	Beat Generation
	C.P.Snow	**The Two Cultures and the Scientific Revolution*	humanities
	Samuel Beckett	*Krapp's Last Tape*	monodrama
	(film)	*Ben-Hur*	epic
1960	Harper Lee	*To Kill a Mockingbird*	unreliable narrator
	Harold Pinter	*The Caretaker*	
	Anne Sexton	*To Bedlam and Part Way Back*	confessional literature

1961	V.S. Naipaul	*A House for Mr Biswas*	
	Joseph Heller	*Catch-22*	catch-22 situation
1962	Edward Albee	*Who's Afraid of Virginia Woolf*	
	Anthony Burgess	*A Clockwork Orange*	slang
	Gabriel Garcia Marquez	*A Hundred Years of Solitude*	
	Doris Lessing	*The Golden Notebook*	
	*Thomas Kuhn	**The Structure of Scientific Revolutions*	paradigm
1963	Sylvia Plath	*The Bell Jar*	*roman à clef*
1964	J.R.R. Tolkien	**Tree and Leaf*	faery
1965	Sylvia Plath	*Ariel*	confessional literature
1966	Jean Rhys	*Wide Sargasso Sea*	
	Ngugi Wa Thiong'o	*A Grain of Wheat*	
	*Michel Foucault	* *Les Mots et les Choses (The Order of Things)*	episteme, discourse, new historicism
	*Susan Sontag	**Against Interpretation*	essay
1967	Tom Stoppard	*Rosencrantz and Guildenstern are Dead*	
	Vladimir Nabokov	*Speak, Memory*	*sic*
1968	Marianne Moore	*Collected Poems*	anacoluthon
1969	John Berryman	*The Dream Songs*	asyndeton, confessional literature

	B.S. Johnson	*The Unfortunates*	surrealism
1971	Geoffrey Hill	*Mercian Hymns*	prose poem
1973	Thomas Pynchon	*Gravity's Rainbow*	
	Peter Shaffer	*Equus*	Apollonian/Dionysian
1974	Richard Adams	*Watership Down*	allegory
1976	Ted Hughes	*Season Songs*	enjambement, title
	*Jacques Derrida (trans. Gayatri Spivak)	**Of Grammatology*	deconstruction, postcolonial criticism
1977	Philip Larkin	*The Less Deceived*	aubade, dramatic monologue
	Roald Dahl	*The Wonderful Story of Henry Sugar and Six More*	Chinese box
1978	Maya Angelou	*And Still I Rise*	parallelism
1980	*Stephen Greenblatt	**Renaissance Self-Fashioning*	new historicism, self-fashioning
1981	Salman Rushdie	*Midnight's Children*	
1982	Alice Walker	*The Color Purple*	dialect, epistolary, womanist
	Caryl Churchill	*Top Girls*	problem play
	*Elaine Showalter	**A Literature of Their Own*	gynocriticism
1983	*Gillian Beer	**Darwin's Plots*	literary Darwinism
1984	J.G. Ballard	*Empire of the Sun*	
	Martin Amis	*Money*	*mise en abyme*
	William Gibson	*Neuromancer*	cyberfiction
1985	Charles Tomlinson	*Collected Poems*	line
	Douglas Dunn	*Elegies*	elegy
1987	Toni Morrison	*Beloved*	viewpoint

	Alan Bennett	*Talking Heads*	monodrama
1989	Kazuo Ishiguro	*Remains of the Day*	
1990	Derek Walcott	*Omeros*	consonance
	(sitcom)	**Seinfeld*	comedy of manners
1991	Bret Easton Ellis	*American Psycho*	protagonist
	Iain Sinclair	*Downriver*	psychogeography
	Christopher Logue	*Kings*	translation
1994	A.S. Byatt	*Possession*	
	(film)	**Pulp Fiction*	pulp fiction
	(film)	**Forrest Gump*	tenor
1996	Paul Muldoon	*New Selected Poems*	vernacular
	*John Kerrigan	**Revenge Tragedy*	revenge tragedy
	Alice Munro	*Selected Stories*	short story
	David Foster Wallace	*Infinite Jest*	hysterical realism
	*Mark Turner	**The Literary Mind*	parable
1997	(film)	**The Full Monty*	kitchen sink drama
	J.K. Rowling	*Harry Potter and the Philosopher's Stone*	children's literature
	Don DeLillo	*Underworld*	postmodernism
1999	Carol Ann Duffy	*The World's Wife*	dramatic monologue
2000	Kevin Crossley Holland	*The Seeing Stone*	medievalism
2002	Ian McEwan	*Atonement*	adaptation
	*The Streets	**Original Pirate Material*	rap
2003	Margaret Attwood	*Oryx and Crake*	dystopia

2005	Samuel Menashe	*New and Selected Poems*	rhyme
	J.H. Prynne	*Poems*	obscurity
	*John Carey	**What Good Are the Arts?*	arts
2006	Linton Kwesi Johnson	*Selected Poems*	creole
	Thomas Pynchon	*Against the Day*	hysterical realism
2007	(film)	**Atonement*	adaptation
2008	*John Mullan	**Anonymity*	anonymous
	(film)	**Synecdoche, New York*	synecdoche
2009	*Elaine Showalter	**A Jury of her Peers*	gynocriticism
	*Karen Chase	**Victorians and Old Age*	monograph

List of Print and Electronic Resources

Here are some recommended books and resources intended for those wondering how to follow up the topics introduced in this *Anthem Dictionary*. Most items mentioned should be freely available in public libraries, bookstores or online. Those marked with an asterisk (*) are specialist resources that are less accessible but are suitable for higher study and the more ambitious general reader: they are a bit more expensive to buy, and mostly held in university libraries or by subscription. The list doesn't mention school/student editions because those texts are likely to do the job for those taking particular exams, and be less suitable for everyone else. The web links were all correct at time of going to press; they may change, but were chosen because they deserve to stay in demand.

PRINT

REFERENCE/CRITICISM

The Poetry Handbook, John Lennard (Oxford, 2006)

Explains components of poetry in depth, with an emphasis on close reading. *The Drama Handbook* by John Lennard and Mary Luckhurst (Oxford, 2002) does the same for drama: it is an introduction to reading and watching plays, packed with information on conventions, staging, and theatre history.

Beginning Theory, Peter Barry, 3rd edn (Manchester University Press, 2009)

A thoughtful and thought-provoking introduction for students new to the world of literary theory. 'Stop and think' sections are particularly good at making you stop and think.

York Notes (Longman)

Targeted for exam-takers, and they cover a lot of ground quickly. They are good for introducing you to a work and suggesting areas for further exploration; however, it's a big mistake to think they offer the 'answers' to literary works. They shouldn't substitute for independent thinking and personal judgments about what's important in a work. Online equivalent like SparkNotes and Enotes are often good for jogging your memory, but not much more.

Very Short Introductions (Oxford)

Pocket-sized studies of big ideas if you want quick orientation in a topic (e.g. *Tragedy* by Adrian Poole; *Literary Theory* by Jonathan Culler).

Cambridge Companions

Collections of introductory essays on the lives, works and themes of authors and genres. Excellent for getting a broad outline on a subject, though it isn't exhaustive. Also available online (by library/university subscription).

**New Princeton Encylopedia of Poetry and Poetics*, ed. by Alex Preminger and others, 3rd edn (Princeton, 1993)

The most in-depth guide to world poetry available in English.

*New Critical Idiom (Routledge; Series editor: John Drakakis)

Clearly worded, distinctive explanations of key critical concepts: e.g. *Genre* by John Frow, *Realism* by Pam Morris. A good place to go for more detail on major terms in this dictionary.

*New Accents Series (Routledge; Series editor: Terence Hawkes)

Punchy and well-respected guides to critical standpoints.

Brewer's Concise Dictionary of Phrase & Fable

First published in 1870 and updated many times since, Ebenezer Cobham Brewer's dictionary remains a trove of information for mythological, literary, religious and historical facts. Great for leafing through.

PRIMARY TEXTS

In general, it's important to be aware of what text an edition is based on, and whether it has been adapted, abridged or translated from an original. **Penguin Classics** and **Oxford World's Classics** provide the most respected popular editions of classic works, though the texts are sometimes modernised. Other series like **Longman Annotated English Poets** and the **Riverside** editions of Chaucer, Shakespeare and Milton offer authoritative texts, as do **Norton Critical Editions**. Trusting online texts is risky, unless you know exactly where the text has come from (most Victorian editions, for example, are unreliable). The notes, introductions, timelines and other useful APPARATUS vary greatly between editions.

Another useful print resource for discovering new material is the ANTHOLOGY. **Norton Anthologies** offer big surveys of literary periods, and these books are often used for university teaching. The **New Oxford Poetry Anthologies** contain careful selections of famous and neglected works that are a great window into a historical period. Two other well respected poetry anthologies worth mentioning are ***The Rattle Bag*** and ***The School Bag***, edited by Seamus Heaney and Ted Hughes.

ELECTRONIC

GENERAL REFERENCE RESOURCES AND TEXTS

Representative Poetry Online

http://rpo.library.utoronto.ca/display/
Historical survey of poetry with timeline, criticism and bibliography.

Literary Resources on the Net

http://andromeda.rutgers.edu/~jlynch/Lit/

A good starting-point for basic online research if you're not sure where to look (though it needs updating). Lots of stuff here, arranged by period and author.

Project Gutenberg

http://www.gutenberg.org/wiki/Main_Page

Complete texts for free download to your PC or e-reader, with everything from Saint Augustine to Jane Austen.

The Online Books Page

http://digital.library.upenn.edu/books/

Search by author, title or subject for books freely available online.

Silva Rhetoricae

http://humanities.byu.edu/rhetoric/Silva.htm

Contains all the rhetorical terms contained in this book, and more besides. The most useful guide in print is Richard Lanham, *A Handlist of Rhetorical Terms*, 2nd edn.

Converse

http://aspirations.english.cam.ac.uk/converse/home.acds

A host of resources and games to encourage students aged 11-19 to take an interest in English. See also the Virtual Classroom (http://www.english.cam.ac.uk/vclass/).

PERIOD/GENRE SPECIFIC

The Victorian Web

http://www.victorianweb.org/authors/index.html

Thorough introduction to Victorian authors, with biographies, themes and imagery discussed.

Postcolonial and Postimperial Literature: An Overview

http://www.postcolonialweb.org/
Excellent for history, theory and contexts of postcolonial literature.

Luminarium

http://www.luminarium.org/
A range of primary and secondary texts on major writers from medieval to Restoration periods, along with basic critical material.

The English Renaissance in Context

http://dewey.library.upenn.edu/sceti/furness/eric/index.cfm
An interactive guide to contexts and book production in the Renaissance with tutorials (including some on individual Shakespeare plays) and digitised texts.

Academy of American Poets

http://www.poets.org/
A wide array of texts and secondary material on American poetry. American Poems may also be useful: http://www.americanpoems.com/.

Contemporary Writers

http://www.contemporarywriters.com/
Information on major Commonwealth writers.

SPECIALIST

Intute

http://www.intute.ac.uk/artsandhumanities/english/
Web resources for English Studies reviewed by specialists.

* Literature Online (Lion)

http://lion.chadwyck.co.uk/ (http://lion.chadwyck.com/)

Around 350 000 works of literature in English and, just as handily, full texts from journals and reference resources.

* Early English Books Online (EEBO)

http://eebo.chadwyck.com/home/

Digital facsimiles available for download of almost every book published in Britain from 1475–1700. Eighteenth Century Collections Online (ECCO) is the eighteenth-century equivalent.

TEAMS Middle English Texts Series

http://www.lib.rochester.edu/camelot/teams/tmsmenu.htm

A wide array of medieval texts available.

WorldCat

http://www.worldcat.org/

A mega-catalogue of items in libraries worldwide.

MHRA Style Guide

http://www.mhra.org.uk/Publications/Books/StyleGuide/index.html

A standard scholarly reference work that answers all those small questions about spelling, punctuation, quotations, references and other such details. It is primarily intended for British writers, and other style guides (e.g. MLA or Oxford) won't necessarily agree. Useful nonetheless, and it's free to download.

*JSTOR

http://www.jstor.org/

Huge database of scholarly articles.

* Oxford English Dictionary (*OED*)

http://www.oed.com/

The most authoritative English dictionary, the *OED* also charts the evolution of the English language. Also available as a 20-volume print edition. Learning resources for all levels too.

* Oxford Dictionary of National Biography (*DNB*)

http://www.oxforddnb.com/

The *DNB* contains over 56 000 entries on influential Britons, with every major and minor literary figure. A major scholarly enterprise and a trove of information. Learning resources as well.

www.ingramcontent.com/pod-product-compliance
Lightning Source LLC
LaVergne TN
LVHW050919080826
845145LV00001B/136

9781843318712